Law and Imagination in Troubled Times

This collection focuses on how troubled times impact upon the law, the body politic, and the complex interrelationship among them. It centres on how they engage in a dialogue with the imagination and literature, thus triggering an emergent (but thus far underdeveloped) field concerning the 'legal imagination'.

Legal change necessitates a close examination of the historical, cultural, social, and economic variables that promote and affect such change. This requires us to attend to the variety of non-legal variables that percolate throughout the legal system. The collection probes 'the transatlantic constitution' and focuses attention on imagination in a common law context that seems to foster imagination as a cultural capability.

The book is divided into four parts. The first part begins with a set of insights into the historical development of legal education in England and concludes with a reflection on the historical transition of England from an absolute monarchy to a republic. The second part of the volume examines the role that imagination plays in the functioning of the courts. The third part focuses on patterns of thought in legal scholarship and detects how legal imagination contributes to the process of producing new legal categories and terminology. The fourth part focuses on patterns of thought in legal scholarship and looks to the impact of the imagination on legal thinking in the future.

The work provides stimulating reading for those working in the areas of legal philosophy, legal history and law and humanities and law and language.

Richard Mullender is Professor in Law and Legal Theory at Newcastle University Law School (the UK).

Matteo Nicolini is Associate Professor of Public Comparative Law at the Department of Law of the University of Verona (Italy) and Visiting Lecturer at Newcastle University Law School (the UK).

Thomas D.C. Bennett is a Lecturer in Law at City, University of London (the UK).

Emilia Mickiewicz is Lecturer in Law at Newcastle University Law School and the SLS jurisprudence stream convenor (the UK).

Law, Language and Communication

This series encourages innovative and integrated perspectives within and across the boundaries of law, language and communication, with particular emphasis on issues of communication in specialized socio-legal and professional contexts. It seeks to bring together a range of diverse yet cumulative research traditions in order to identify and encourage interdisciplinary research.

The series welcomes proposals – both edited collections as well as single-authored monographs – emphasizing critical approaches to law, language and communication, identifying and discussing issues, proposing solutions to problems, offering analyses in areas such as legal construction, interpretation, translation and de-codification.

Series Editors
Anne Wagner, *Université du Littoral Côte d'Opale*, France and Vijay Kumar Bhatia, formerly of *City University of Hong Kong*

Titles in the series

Legal Persuasion
A Rhetorical Approach to the Science
Linda L. Berger and Kathryn M. Stanchi

International Arbitration Discourse and Practices in Asia
Edited by Vijay K Bhatia, Maurizio Gotti, Azirah Hashim, Philip Koh and Sundra Rajoo

Phraseology in Legal and Institutional Settings
A Corpus-based Interdisciplinary Perspective
Edited by Stanislaw Gozdz Roszkowski and Gianluca Pontrandolfo

Fiction and the Languages of Law
Understanding Contemporary Legal Discourse
Karen Petroski

Law and Imagination in Troubled Times
A Legal and Literary Discourse
Edited by Richard Mullender, Matteo Nicolini, Thomas D.C. Bennett and Emilia Mickiewicz

Social Media in Legal Practice
Edited by Vijay Bhatia and Girolamo Tessuto

For more information about this series, please visit: www.routledge.com/Law-Language-and-Communication/book-series/LAWLANGCOMM

Law and Imagination in Troubled Times
A Legal and Literary Discourse

Edited by
Richard Mullender, Matteo Nicolini,
Thomas D.C. Bennett and
Emilia Mickiewicz

LONDON AND NEW YORK

First published 2020
by Routledge
2 Park Square, Milton Park, Abingdon, Oxon OX14 4RN

and by Routledge
52 Vanderbilt Avenue, New York, NY 10017

Routledge is an imprint of the Taylor & Francis Group, an informa business

© 2020 selection and editorial matter, Richard Mullender, Matteo Nicolini, Thomas D.C. Bennett and Emilia Mickiewicz; individual chapters, the contributors

The rights of Richard Mullender, Matteo Nicolini, Thomas D.C. Bennett and Emilia Mickiewicz to be identified as the authors of the editorial material, and of the authors for their individual chapters, has been asserted in accordance with sections 77 and 78 of the Copyright, Designs and Patents Act 1988.

All rights reserved. No part of this book may be reprinted or reproduced or utilised in any form or by any electronic, mechanical, or other means, now known or hereafter invented, including photocopying and recording, or in any information storage or retrieval system, without permission in writing from the publishers.

Trademark notice: Product or corporate names may be trademarks or registered trademarks, and are used only for identification and explanation without intent to infringe.

British Library Cataloguing-in-Publication Data
A catalogue record for this book is available from the British Library

Library of Congress Cataloging-in-Publication Data
A catalog record has been requested for this book

ISBN: 978-0-367-34411-5 (hbk)
ISBN: 978-0-367-49344-8 (pbk)
ISBN: 978-0-429-32564-9 (ebk)

Typeset in Galliard
by Taylor & Francis Books

Contents

List of figures		vii
List of contributors		viii

1 Legal imagination in troubled times: An introduction   1
THOMAS D.C. BENNETT, EMILIA MICKIEWICZ, MATTEO NICOLINI AND
RICHARD MULLENDER

PART ONE
Imagination, law, and history: framing the future   15

2 The progress of legal education in England   17
SIR JOHN BAKER

3 The dragon in the cave: *Fleta* as a legal imagining of early English
common law   34
JOHN CASEY GOOCH

4 The apotheosis of King Charles I   53
IAN WARD

PART TWO
The courts and the legal imagination   73

5 Pathologies of imagination and legitimacy of judicial decision-making   75
EMILIA MICKIEWICZ

6 Law and belief: The reality of judicial interpretation   93
SCOTT FRALEY

7 Legal imagination or an extra-legal hoax: On storytelling, friends of
the court, and crossing legal boundaries in the US Supreme Court   109
ALEKSANDRA WAWRZYSZCZUK

vi *Contents*

PART THREE
Thought, stylistics, and discourse 131

8 The French Revolution and the programmatic imagination: Hilary
   Mantel on law, politics, and misery 133
   RICHARD MULLENDER

9 Internal coherence and the possibility of judicial integrity 157
   PATRICK O'CALLAGHAN

10 Legal humanism: 'Stylistic imagination' and the making of legal
   traditions 173
   CRISTINA COSTANTINI

PART FOUR
The future of the legal imagination 193

11 Depicting the end of the American frontier: Some thoughts on Larry
   McMurtry's *Lonesome Dove* series 195
   GIACOMO DELLEDONNE

12 A Coleridgean dystopia: Formalism and the optics of judgment 206
   THOMAS D.C. BENNETT AND OLIVIA REILLY

13 Against the failure of the legal imagination: Literary narratives, Brexit,
   and the fate of the Anglo-British constitution 239
   MATTEO NICOLINI

   Index 260

Figure

12.1 Reason, Imagination, Understanding and Fancy   209

Contributors

Sir John Baker, Q.C., F.B.A., is Downing Professor Emeritus of the Laws of England.

Thomas D.C. Bennett is a Lecturer in Law at City, University of London (the UK).

Cristina Costantini is Associate Professor of Private Comparative Law at the Law Department of the University of Perugia (Italy).

Giacomo Delledonne is Postdoctoral Researcher in Comparative Constitutional Law at the Institute for Law, Politics and Development of Scuola superiore Sant'Anna, Pisa (Italy).

R. Scott Fraley is Senior Counsel with the distinguished law firm of Chamberlin-McHaney in Austin, Texas (the USA).

John Casey Gooch is currently Associate Dean for Graduate Studies and Associate Professor of Rhetoric and Literature at The School of Arts and Humanities, The University of Texas at Dallas (the USA).

Emilia Mickiewicz is Lecturer in Law at Newcastle University Law School and the SLS jurisprudence stream convenor (the UK).

Richard Mullender is Professor in Law and Legal Theory at the Newcastle University Law School (the UK).

Matteo Nicolini is Associate Professor of Public Comparative Law at the Department of Law of the University of Verona (Italy) and Visiting Lecturer at the Newcastle University Law School (the UK).

Patrick O'Callaghan is College Lecturer in Law at University College Cork (Ireland).

Olivia Reilly teaches English Literature for the Montag Centre for Overseas Study, Stanford University in Oxford. She completed her D.Phil. on Samuel Taylor Coleridge at the University of Oxford in 2015.

Ian Ward is Professor of Law at the Newcastle University Law School.

Aleksandra Wawrzyszczuk is currently affiliated with the University of East London.

1 Legal imagination in troubled times

An introduction

Thomas D.C. Bennett, Emilia Mickiewicz, Matteo Nicolini and Richard Mullender

Imagination is a cultural competence, a faculty of mind, a capacity for comprehension, synthesis, and creativity.[1] There is no doubt that imagination in general, and legal imagination in particular, is of the utmost importance to legal scholars. It helps them to recognise legally significant patterns and to respond to them in ways that fit the legal system within which they operate. But it is also useful when it comes to reshaping legal norms in response to novel circumstances. It is something, we argue, that every lawyer, judge, and legal scholar who thinks seriously about their practice should strive to acquire.

But doing this is difficult. There is no obvious procedure to attain it; nor do we have developed specific methodologies or 'reflexive courses on law' that permit students to develop such a critical approach to the law.[2]

In times of crisis, uncertainty, and political turmoil, the need for (and the creative potential of) imagination in law becomes most prominent. Established rules and procedures can quickly become impotent or produce results that are unfair and arbitrary. To mitigate these sorry states of affairs, lawyers seek to connect the novel situation with the body of knowledge and experience they already possess, synthesising and reworking them in order to fashion more suitable norms and practices.

In times of trouble, lawyers are asked to develop their own 'vision' of the future. Influenced, as they are, by the authority of social media, lawyers have also felt compelled to create their own hashtag: '#Beimaginative.'[3] Well, they *may* even be required to do so. However, this may be thought too programmatic, or exceedingly provocative and, to some extent, dangerous. Take, for example, Carl Schmitt. He offered imaginative, although highly contentious, solutions to the constitutional impasse of the Weimar Republic. He proposed pointing to the head

---

1 JB White, *The Legal Imagination* (The University of Chicago Press 1973) xiii.
2 Indeed, 'Framing law as an active and intellectual activity rather than an exercise of reproduction triggers and maintains the student's curiosity': T Blekker, 'Epilogue: an overview, reflections and a student's perspective' in B van Klink and U de Vries (eds), *Academic Learning in Law. Theoretical Positions, Teaching Experiments and Learning Experiences* (Edward Elgar 2016) 313.
3 On how social media create what may be termed 'digital law', see M Nicolini, 'From hard-copy to digital law via "illustrated courtrooms": visualising the history of legal English' (2017) 11 *Pólemos* 241–45.

2 *Bennett, Mickiewicz, Nicolini, & Mullender*

of state as the ultimate guardian of the constitution. Furthermore, he demarcated the 'safe politico-legal space' along the 'struggle between friends and foes.'[4]

Although the idea of an interrelationship between law and imagination does feature in some contemporary jurisprudential writing, it remains a matter that is under-explored. The American scholar James Boyd White introduced the notion of 'legal imagination' into the lexicon of legal scholarship with the publication of his influential book, *The Legal Imagination*.[5] Boyd White's contribution was primarily intended to cross the disciplinary divide and examine the law (and its language) through the prism of literature. *The Legal Imagination* encouraged lawyers to broaden their perspective, mobilising them to complement legal education with the close reading of legal texts, provisions, and documents whereby the real world could be assessed against a stimulating and empowering – because critical, reflective, and imaginative – literary background.

It seems to us, however, that Boyd White's predicament was an academic exercise whereby lawyers could raise their game by paying more attention to literary practices. The exercise was more committed to squeezing significance out of texts and probing their potential than is the case in the field of law. When reading Boyd White, however, we understand that there is also further room for future research. Legal exploration should point to the interaction between the law and the real world – which, for lawyers, counts as *legal reality*. Indeed, its full understanding entails a full understanding of the underlying principles of the context within which the law operates.

Without such an understanding, it may occur that some of the dazzling intuitions of the legal imagination point up limits on what is practically achievable. As Richard Mullender puts it in his essay on Hilary Mantel's *A Place of Greater Safety*,[6] these limits prevent us from grasping the relationship between the under-determinate ends that animate the characters of the novel – that is, the leaders of the French Revolution – and pessimistic political anthropology. On the contrary, the possession of the understanding of the real world makes lawyers' imagination productive, and productive imagination is a way of knitting the various insights together.[7] Although often programmatic, legal imagination may also be cautionary and constrictively conservative. It is then apparent that, here, 'conservatism' should not be taken to mean hidebound. As it has 'to reflect an underlying reality of human nature and of structure of society,' the legal imagination may mark the difference. Indeed, it is the dividing line between utopianism and realistic utopianism.[8]

---

4 See C Schmitt, *The Concept of the Political* (1923 first ed; University of Chicago Press, expanded ed 2007). See WE Scheuerman, 'States of emergency' in J Meierhenrich and O Simons (eds), *The Oxford Handbook of Carl Schmitt* (OUP 2017). Quotations are from R Mullender, 'There is no such thing as a safe space' (2019) 82(3) *MLR* 549, 550.

5 B White (n 1). See also id., *The Legal Imagination* (abridged ed, University of Chicago Press 1985).

6 H Mantel, *A Place of Greater Safety* (Fourth Estate 1992) 147. See R Mullender, 'The French Revolution and the programmatic imagination: Hilary Mantel on law, politics, and misery' at 133.

7 E Mickiewicz, 'Pathologies of imagination and legitimacy of judicial decision making' at 75.

8 H Kissinger, *World Order* (Allen Lane 2014) 74.

Demarcating the new boundaries of the legal imagination

The legal imagination has attracted the interest of academic scholars since Boyd White published *The Legal Imagination*. Another seminal text is Alan Watson's *Failures of the Legal Imagination*.[9] Most recent contributions include Maximilian dal Mar's *Artefacts of Legal Inquiry* and another work by this author and Amalia Amaya: *Virtue, Emotion and Imagination in Law and Legal Reasoning*.[10] Other relevant books deal with the topic; but their scope is limited and mainly related to specific areas of law.[11]

So, there are important (sometimes programmatic; sometimes cautionary) things to be learned – and the insights these, and other such, contributions offer gain practical significance in troubled times. Indeed, 'the way we do things round here' (in the sense of the current politico-legal-cum-cultural settlement) comes under strain – and there is an urgent need for composed creativity.

So far, however, the thrust of the debate has been well-meaning, albeit platitudinous ('be imaginative', 'take up a new perspective', 'think outside the box', 'push the envelope'). To this extent, the collection claims to have a way of moving beyond platitudes. Not only does it suggest legal scholars go above and beyond the traditional cross-disciplinary fields of research, such as law and humanities, but its scope is also broader and – we dare argue – ambitious, as it aims to fill a gap in current legal studies on the topic under scrutiny. As its editors, we set the legal imagination in troubled times. And such an intuition has proved to be *the right intuition*.

Troubled times and contexts of this sort inescapably put productive pressure on us. In such circumstances, lawyers recognise that fresh insight is needed *now*. But there is a need to maintain order while seeking to pursue justice. So, there is time pressure – along with order-pressure and justice-pressure. Therefore, we needed to make responses. We needed to improvise, and, in so doing, we linked legal imagination and improvisation. In troubled times, lawyers also look for normative roads to reflection and action. In order to acquire a deeper understanding of what imagination is and how to use it in realistically decent ways, we also resolved to link it to interdisciplinarity. As it acts as a bridge linking 'reality to an imagined alternative,'[12] interdisciplinary research might encourage us to take steps that are beyond our limited capacities.[13] As Thomas Bennett and Olivia Reilly argue in

---

9 A Watson, *Failures of the Legal Imagination* (University of Pennsylvania Press 1988).

10 M dal Mar, *Artefacts of Legal Inquiry* (Hart 2020); M dal Mar and A Amaya *Virtue, Emotion and Imagination in Law and Legal Reasoning* (Hart 2020).

11 For example, I Ward, *Shakespeare and the Legal Imagination* (Butterworths 1999) delves into law and humanities and focuses on the Tudor constitution. R Janda, R Jukier, and D Jutras (eds), *The Unbounded Level of the Mind: Rod Macdonald's Legal Imagination* (McGill-Queen's University Press 2015) collects a number of essays in honour of Rod Macdonald – and the essays come from sundry areas of law. Finally, J Purdy's *The Meaning of Property: Freedom, Community, and the Legal Imagination* (Yale UP 2011) explores why property is value to society.

12 Watson (n 10) 36.

13 See C Costantini, 'Legal humanism: "stylistic imagination" and the making of legal traditions' at 173.

4 Bennett, Mickiewicz, Nicolini, & Mullender

their essay, 'Just as creation is not an act of singleness or uniformity but contains vast diversity within a complex order, so ... imaginative unity depends on coherent, progressive interconnection' of the different ambits involved in our interdisciplinary research.[14]

When we resolved to link the legal imagination to 'our troubled times', we had not realised how far-reaching its relevance would be to scholars and students working in the fields of legal theory/jurisprudence, sociology, politics, and literature and those studying the workings of the imagination (for instance, in psychology).

Indeed, the idea of collecting a set of essays on this topic originated during the 2018 Annual Conference of the Society of Legal Scholars (held 2–6 September at Queen Mary University, London, UK). During the conference, which was itself titled 'Law in Troubled Times', each of the editors delivered papers addressing the legal imagination. These papers concerned discrete issues relating to the invocation of, and also to the failure of, legal imagination, including: a resurgent legal formalism (mechanical jurisprudence), a lack of politico-legal invention, and authoritarian shifts in politico-democratic societies.

The discussion that ensued attracted the interest of scholars from other disciplines, including literature and literary criticism, rhetoric, and theoretical jurisprudence, which gave rise to the collection at hand. It centres on the interrelationship between law, the imagination, and literature, which places it at the apex of an established field of scholarship (the 'law and literature' movement) and an emergent (but thus far underdeveloped) field concerning the 'legal imagination'. And yet, more could be done with this intriguing, emerging field of research. While bridging legal reality to its imagined alternative, we understood that the legal imagination perfectly matches the idea of imagination as a 'cultural competence'. This also corresponds to the deep-rooted Anglo-American practice of the common law, according to which the law involves an unceasing exercise of imagination.

As already mentioned, there is a burgeoning field of study concerned with the interrelationship between law and imagination, and this collection will make a stimulating and ambitious contribution to the scholarship in that field. There is a well-established field of scholarship concerning 'law and literature', and this collection will be of great interest to those working in that ambit of research. However, the collection moves debate in this flourishing field *beyond* the relationship between law and literature, to consider the interrelationship between legal education, legal imagination, legal change, and broader, and highly disruptive, socio-political pressures. With interdisciplinary study becoming ever more common among academics, and with the changes in UK legal education opening up opportunities for interdisciplinary study among undergraduates, the approach taken in this collection will give it broad appeal. We also understand, however, that 'interdisciplinarity' is often thrown around in a platitudinous way. And this collection shows that, although it is *hard*, it also possible to be usefully interdisciplinary.

---

14 See TDC Bennett and O Reilly, 'A Coleridgean dystopia: formalism and the optics of judgment' at 206.

Legal imagination in troubled times 5

'This stage is turbulent and troublesome,' Ian Ward reminds us.[15] The law is frequently challenged by external (non-legal) factors. These, which can include political, social, and economic matters, undermine the conventional forms of legal education and challenge our understanding of existing legal tools, rules, mechanisms, and terminology. Further reflection is thus required, and lawyers, legal theorists, and rhetoricians are called to explore – to 'reimagine' – how to renew existing legal frameworks and reinvigorate their relevance in the light of broader political and cultural change. An example includes the recent attempts of the Court of Justice of the European Union to address the constitutional crisis in the member states, which exhibit symptoms of democratic backsliding.[16] It is then the duty of legal scholars to bring this politico-legal turmoil back to the fore. The revival, however, is not just a matter of applying the 'subversive potential of comparative legal thinking';[17] it also poses a problem of a new scholarly awareness.

Exploring our 'troubled times': disarticulations, sectionalities, and the legal imagination

Today, the tensions emerging at the institutional interface between the state (as a governing entity) and the body politic over which it exercises authority are substantial.

First, sectionalism may cause tensions and contrasts between the constitutive parts of the body politic. Examples include the impact of the financial crisis that has gripped much of the world since 2008, the effects of which are still being keenly felt.[18] Second, ongoing financial volatility threatens to undermine proposals for novel, innovative structures and weakens the ability of political actors to manage the interweaving complexities that stem from the need for social entitlements, governmental change, and respect for the democratic framework. And powerful contributions in the 'law and imagination' field tend to assume economic buoyancy,[19] as if only economic globalisation could promise an 'impeding radiant future' to humanity.[20] Third, terrorism and extremism are menacing liberal democracy from the outside, threatening its commitment to tolerance and pluralism – the very presuppositions upon which both constitutional democracy and

---

15 I Ward, 'The apotheosis of James I' at 53. Trevor Royle, *Civil War: The Wars of Three Kingdoms* (Abacus 2005) 500–01 refers the quotation to Charles's I Chaplain, William Juxon, minutes before the King's execution in 1649.

16 See Case C-619/18 *Commission v Poland* [2019] ECR ECLI:EU:C:2019:325.

17 GP Fletcher, 'Law as a subversive discipline' (1998) 4 *AJCL* 683, 684.

18 See JE Stiglitz, *The Price of Inequality: How Today's Divided Society Endangers Our Future* (Allen Lane 2013); K Pistor, *The Code of Capital. How the Law Creates Wealth and Inequality* (Princeton UP 2019); G Standing, *Plunder of the Commons: A Manifesto for Sharing Public Wealth* (Allen Lane 2019); JE Stiglitz, *People, Power, and Profits: Progressive Capitalism for an Age of Discontent* (W. W. Norton 2019).

19 See, for example, RM Unger's *What Should Legal Analysis Become?* (Verso 1996) and *False Necessity: Anti-necessitarian Social Theory in the Service of Radical Democracy: From Politics, a Work in Constructive Social Theory* (Verso 2004).

20 M Xifaras, 'The *Global Turn* in Legal Theory' (2016) 29 *Can Journ Law & Jurispr* 216.

global governance are based. Fourth, democracy faces internal – but no less existential – threats from the return of extremist parties to the political mainstream.[21] The tensions are now more acute than during the fiscal crisis of the welfare state in the 1970s, when democracy did not appear to be challenged, as it now is, by populism. Also, the more general turn towards 'populism' threatens to carry us in directions that may tell a story of the undisciplined use of imagination. Populists encourage the view that, 'If you can dream it, you can do it'. They ignore the advice Henry Kissinger offers in his reading of Metternich: 'the belief that whatever was imaginable was also achievable was an illusion.'[22]

The collection probes the role imagination plays in law during troubled times – both in contemporary such times and historically. It focuses on how imagination helps us to identify and understand how troubled times can impact upon both the law and the body politic, and upon the complex interrelationship between the two. This entails reflection on how legal change actually occurs. A full understanding of legal change, it becomes clear, requires us to attend to the smorgasbord of non-legal variables that promote and affect such change that percolates throughout the legal system. They include (but are most certainly not exhausted by) the disposition of the individual;[23] political anthropology;[24] ideology and the background as practical forces relevant to law's operations;[25] and British society's pragmatism as a form of constitutional imagination.[26]

These assumptions are particularly apparent when it comes to examining how the UK and the USA are confronting the current state of flux. Anxiety about how to cope with the post-Brexit scenario percolates through the Anglo-British constitution, as well as its territorial sectionalities. Furthermore, there is a wide perception that the liberal, inclusive attitude that has always characterised the US constitutional narrative is now threatened by the disarticulation of its body politic. Disarticulation is indeed the outcome of sectionalism, which the *Oxford English Dictionary* defines as the 'confinement of interest to a narrow sphere, narrowness of outlook, undue accentuation of minor local, political, or social distinctions.'[27] Let us think of secession of the Confederacy: this triggered a disarticulation, to which Lincoln and the saga of the U.S. frontier opposed their productive responses.[28] Lincoln was prompted (in this crucible) to recognise that the Union was the 'last best hope' of his compatriots (north and south of the Mason–Dixon line).

---

21 See S Levitsky and D Ziblatt, *How Democracies Die: What History Reveals about Our Future* (Penguin 2019).

22 Ibid.

23 See P O'Callaghan, 'Internal coherence and the possibility of judicial integrity' at 157.

24 See Mullender, 'The French Revolution' (n 6).

25 See Mickiewicz (n 7).

26 See Nicolini, 'Against the failure of the legal imagination. Literary narratives, Brexit and the fate of the Anglo-British constitution' at 239.

27 See 'sectionalism' (*OED Online*, Oxford University Press 2019). <www.oed.com/view/Entry/53546> accessed 16 December 2019.

28 See G Delledonne, 'Depicting the end of the American frontier: some thoughts on ·Larry McMurtry's *Lonesome Dove* Series' at 195.

His efforts led to the 14th Amendment and, after a struggle that had been protracted for a century, to *Brown v Board of Education*.[29]

To these sectionalities we might add both Brexit and the Trump presidency as sources of practical pressure.[30] This anxiety is also apparent in continental Europe: Luuk van Middelaar, for example, notes that 'Brexit and Trump' has become something of a term of art in the European Council.[31] Anglo-America appears to be set to pivot away from – and quite possibly damage – a larger form of Western life that, until the day before yesterday, appeared to be its natural home.

The practical pressure triggered by the disarticulations under scrutiny can also become productive through what we term the 'disciplined use of imagination.' This kind of productive imagination does not point to an unfeasible imagined alternative. On the contrary, it finds 'expression in the effort to identify contingencies (most obviously, internal and external threats) that may disrupt the order's operation.'[32] It therefore explores 'sectionalities' from an interdisciplinary standpoint in which we see, inter alia, a commitment to close reading (that is, to the legacy of Boyd White's literary practice) to probe sources of concern to those embedded in legal and political interpretive communities – and to do so in ways that involve the exercise of imagination as a cultural competence.

The collection probes 'the transatlantic constitution'[33] because it focuses attention on imagination in a common law context that seems to foster imagination as a cultural capability.[34] This can be partly owing to the inherently open-textured nature of the common law. Those entrusted with the task of interpreting and reshaping the common law must remain imaginatively vigilant at all times.[35]

It is therefore not surprising that 'transatlantic' legal scholars demonstrate continuous commitment to rejuvenation and innovation in their approach(es) to legal studies. This has led to an explosion of intense, cross-disciplinary research activity that informs much of the present collection. Conceiving of, designing, and deploying novel scholarly method(s) is, of course, a highly imaginative activity in itself. Thus, as legal educators, we frequently find ourselves exercising the very virtue with which our analyses in this collection are concerned. To that extent, the collection represents not only a body of practically relevant, pertinent, analytical work, but also a working example of the impact of imagination on legal scholarship

---

29 *Brown v Board of Education of Topeka*, 347 U.S. 483 (1954).
30 See Levitsky and Ziblatt (n 19) 176–203.
31 L van Middelaar, 'Brexit as the European Union's "Machiavellian moment"' (2018) 55 *CMLR* 3.
32 R Mullender, 'Transmuting the politico-legal lump: Brexit and Britain's constitutional order' (2018) 39 *Cardozo Law Review* 1020–21.
33 See MS Bilder (ed), *The Transatlantic Constitution: Colonial Legal Culture and the Empire* (Harvard UP 2004).
34 As Karl Llewellyn would put it. See K Llewellyn, 'McDougal and Lasswell plan for legal education' (1943) 43 *Colum L Rev* 465, 476. See, in this collection, A Wawrzyszczuk, 'Legal imagination or an extra-legal hoax: on storytelling, friends of the court, and crossing legal boundaries in the US Supreme Court' at 109. S Fraley, 'Law and belief: the reality of judicial interpretation' at 93.
35 HLA Hart, *The Concept of Law* (Clarendon Law Series 1997).

8 *Bennett, Mickiewicz, Nicolini, & Mullender*

itself. This means that not only is there still room left for writing the multi-disciplinary 'constitutive story'[36] of the imagination, but that it also is the duty of legal scholars to participate in such an assessment. And this, we think, reflects the productive pressure we have put on ourselves and each other when writing this book.

Patterns of legal imagination: the book's structure

The first part of the volume ('Imagination, law, and history: framing the future'), begins with an important set of insights into the historical development of legal education in England. Sir John Baker contends that the struggle for legal educa-tion was an unceasing act of legal reimagination, and that legal education and legal imagination have always been intertwined in the course of English legal history. In the fourteenth century, lectures ('readings') were given at the four Inns of Court. These were illustrated with imaginary examples or cases that could be made the subject of disputations. In addition, students took part in practical exercises called 'moots' in which they framed pleadings orally in French. The system broke down in the 1640s, and for over a century there was no formal education in the common law. As John Baker highlights, however, the collapse – that is, in our terms, the effect of those 'troubled times' historians define as 'civil war' – 'was not greeted with the alarm which it would have deserved had the system not already become obsolescent.' Reinvention was 'governed by precedent, as if it were part of the common law itself, and carried on by the impetus of tradition alone.' 'For over a century there was no formal education in the common law.'[37]

William Blackstone was the first lawyer to offer university lectures in English law in 1753, at Oxford, and Cambridge followed suit later in the century. Oxbridge thus encouraged critical reflection on law, but it was London University that pio-neered degrees in English law, and, in the 1820s, Andrew Amos introduced a combination of lectures, classes, and examinations that has remained the norm ever since. Several public investigations into legal education, beginning in 1846, established a general agreement that it was best divided into an academic and vocational stage. At both stages the age-old system of lectures, disputations based on imaginary cases, and the study of real cases in books has remained central.

Sir John Baker's contribution is followed by John Casey Gooch's examination of *Fleta* – a medieval treaty on the common law. A true exercise in legal imagina-tion, it was composed during the reign of Edward I as an effort to assert and solidify royal authority. Gooch insightfully compares *Fleta* with the prior works of Bracton and de Glanvill to demonstrate that these early texts were all products of social interaction, collectively contributing to the emergence of what Stock termed a 'textual community.' In allowing written word and social practice to interact to create a unique interpretive space, we dare say that *Fleta* anticipates some

36 RM Smith, *Stories of Peoplehood: The Politics and Morals of Political Membership* (CUP 2003) 72.
37 Sir John Baker, 'The progress of legal education in England', at 17.

subsequent paradigms, such as Stanley Fish's interpretive communities. The chapter asserts that the law is a product of intricate historical and social processes and it cannot be understood in a vacuum. Rather, law, as an intellectual pursuit, depends upon a number of intertwined interdisciplinary connections and methodologies such as rhetorical and textual analysis.

The first part concludes with Ian Ward's reflection on the historical transition of England from an absolute monarchy to a republic. Ward explores the troubled events of this period through a prism of the canvases on the theme of divine kingship by Peter Paul Rubens. The paintings, of which *The Apotheosis of James I* is most famous, were commissioned by Charles Stuart. He most likely looked at them while awaiting his own execution in the Banqueting Chamber at Whitehall Palace on the morning of 30 January 1649. The event is necessarily ironic: a divinely chosen prince about to be executed by his former subjects. This, according to Ward, has a profound consequence, both constitutional and aesthetic. It is an extraordinary constitutional moment, which marks a transition to a new order. But the shaping of this order requires considerable imaginative effort, which the chapter seeks to capture.

The second part of the volume ('The courts and the legal imagination') examines the role that imagination plays in the functioning of the courts. In the opening chapter, Emilia Mickiewicz investigates the legitimacy of the recent interventions of the Court of Justice of the European Union in the ongoing rule of law crisis in Poland. Drawing on Paul Ricoeur's distinction between constitutive and pathological imagination, Mickiewicz devises an account of legitimate judicial decision-making. On her analysis, judges go about their business on a 'pathological' basis when they render decisions that advance a substantive agenda (such as European integration) without critical reflection of the sort that would prompt them to consider other practically significant considerations (e.g., the distinctiveness and/or urgency of contextual considerations, such as Poland's determination to honour its own distinctive form of life). But, here, acute difficulties arise when judges harbour the suspicion that the contextual impulses to which they might be attentive are morally retrograde. However, judges cannot give these complexities adequate (or, indeed, any) attention if their approach to their work is pathological in Ricoeur's sense. She argues that some aspects of the CJEU's attempts creatively to address the rule of law crisis in Poland are characterised by a blind commitment to the rule of law ideal and disregard for the existing distribution of power under the Treaty of the European Union, as well as the established orthodoxy on the relationship between the Treaty and the Charter. She concludes that, paradoxically, this can lead to undermining, rather than preserving, the rule of law in the long run.

In the following chapter, R. Scott Fraley picks up on the same theme, arguing that the operations of imagination prompt judges to adopt the modes of interpretation that best suit the political causes they seek to advance. He illustrates the point with reference to the US Supreme Court decisions in *Obergfell* and *Hobby Lobby*. Drawing on the work of the late Supreme Court justice Antonin Scalia and his co-writer Bryan A Garner, Fraley argues that, 'theories of legal interpretation

10 *Bennett, Mickiewicz, Nicolini, & Mullender*

have been discussed interminably, and often so obscurely as to leave even the most intelligent readers – or perhaps especially the most intelligent readers – befuddled.'[38] The decades of legal theoretical efforts to advance a clear framework for interpreting the law necessarily failed because of a simple truth: no single literary or legal theory of interpretation will suffice in every situation. No single, correct approach to interpretation works for each text, each statute, each constitutional conundrum. In Fraley's view, what is needed is the application of legal imagination to envision and apply that theory or technique that most aptly solves the problem at hand. In some situations, that approach will be literalism; in another, it may be drafter intent. The case, language at issue, and the factual circumstances will dictate the proper approach.

The final chapter in the second part of the book also focuses on the US Supreme Court. Aleksandra Wawrzyszczuk points up the limitations of appeals to volatile emotions, unchecked facts, and narrative on a literary model as means by which to prevail at trial. She notes that these strategies often come into collision with legal arguments and hard truths that strip them of effectiveness. Wawrzyszczuk forges a link between this point and the fact that the Supreme Court has a context in which advocates and judges give voice to matters of urgent social concern. She notes that storytelling in the Supreme Court has ranged from protests inspired by literary fiction to justices using creative writing devices to probe the murky outer limits of the law. She also focuses her broad-ranging analysis by reference to *amicus briefs* – collections of stories based on the personal experience of individuals typically submitted in support of a case. In recent years, a particular type of amicus brief has been used with increasing frequency. This type, known as a *voices brief*, incorporates first-person accounts of individuals impacted by the legal issues at stake. Despite being formally filed, voices briefs cannot be factually challenged and are not subject to cross-examination. Although they are merely stories told in support of one of the parties, they have generated intense theoretical controversy. Pragmatists have shown little enthusiasm for them – and formalists consider them to be damaging. However, they have won positive responses from legal realists and critical legal scholars. Alongside these analyses, Wawrzyszczuk sets her own response to voices briefs. She identifies them as exercises in literary fiction and concludes that they have the potential to mislead the audiences to whom they are addressed.

The third part of the collection ('Thought, stylistics, and discourse') focuses on patterns of thought in legal scholarship. The first chapter in this part relates the idea of a modern social imaginary (an implicit map of social space) to law and politics in the modern world. To this end, Richard Mullender explores Hilary Mantel's novel, *A Place of Greater Safety* (a fictionalised account of the French Revolution) by reference to the analysis in Charles Taylor's *Modern*

---

38 A Scalia and BA Garner. *Reading Law* (Thompson/West 2013) 15, citing Learned Hand, 'Proceedings in commemoration of fifty years of federal judicial service,' 264 F.2d (1959) ('[M]any sages … have spoken on [statutory construction], and I do not know that it has gotten us very much further').

Social Imaginaries. In Mantel's novel, Georges-Jacques Danton, Maximilien Robespierre, and their fellow revolutionaries wrestle with the question of how to give expression, by legal and political means, to a modern social imaginary. Their respective (and unavailing) efforts to answer this question are fraught with difficulty, for modern social imaginaries are under-determinate (amenable to a range of defensible readings). Mullender argues that Mantel's novel is a practically significant source of insight not just on the French Revolution, but on politico-legal life in the modern world over the last two centuries. This is not just because *A Place of Greater Safety* brings into focus the difficulties in giving expression to under-determinate practical impulses. Mantel's novel also places a large question mark over the optimistic political anthropology at work in bodies of law that have drawn inspiration from the agenda the French revolutionaries sought to advance.

Modes of legal discourse are considered in the second essay in this part of the book, which argues that monologism has distinct advantages over dialogism in certain contexts. Drawing on the work of the philosopher Lynne McFall and Albert Camus's novel *The Fall*, Patrick O'Callaghan seeks to offer an account of integrity that is relevant to judges. Using a schema developed by McFall, O'Callaghan argues that judges must ensure coherence of principle in the interpretation of law and coherence between principle and action in the application of the law. He identifies achieving 'internal coherence' or ensuring coherence between principle and motivation as a further condition of judicial integrity. O'Callaghan argues that, in striving for coherence, judges will need to reflect on their particular 'role-distinct obligations' in our political system as well as on mistakes that they have made in their official function. But *The Fall* demonstrates that judges will need go deeper still in their reflections if they are to achieve internal coherence. The central protagonist in *The Fall* is a former lawyer who maintains that one must become a 'professional penitent' if one is to be a judge. Put differently, he thinks that one must engage in deep introspection, paying close attention to one's personal failings, both past and present, before one has the right to judge others. Camus's protagonist implies that this approach to judging is the exception rather than the rule, but this chapter conjectures that the sort of introspection he describes is common. O'Callaghan concludes that it is likely to be of fundamental importance to most judges if they are to bear the burden of judgement and 'live with themselves.' In his view, this sort of reflection cultivates wisdom about the meaning of justice and fairness, and this explains, in large part, why we tend to trust our judges to do what is right.

The third essay in this part of the book dwells on the construction of legal traditions and the stylistic features that underpin such processes of construction. Cristina Costantini offers an anticonventional understanding of legal traditions, reconceived as palimpsests or, ontologically and memorially, as complex bodies of emplotted texts. Moving from a reassessment of the idea of 'stylistic imagination', the chapter is devoted to clarifying the relevance of the compositional tones of legal texts in performing social constructions and aspirational projections. Costantini attaches particular importance to the analysis of the signatorial strategies

12   *Bennett, Mickiewicz, Nicolini, & Mullender*

that affect legal discourse. Her aim in doing this is to propose a semantic construction of the transpositional borrowings of concepts and ideas from different domains to the juridical sphere.

The fourth and final part of the collection ('The future of the legal imagination') examines the impact imagination may have on legal thinking in the future. In Chapter 11, Giacomo Delledonne engages with the novels of Larry McMurtry. Delledonne looks into how the end of the American frontier and the transition towards a different cultural, political, and legal scenario are hinted at in McMurtry's *Lonesome Dove* series. One of its main achievements, in Delledonne's view, is to depict a web of complex interactions on both sides of the US–Mexican border, with the legacy of 'European' and 'Eastern' culture and institutions being deeply shaped by this entirely different setting. Hence, the cultural collisions about which Delledonne writes tell a story of incessant flux to which lawyers must strive to be responsive.

In Chapter 12, Thomas Bennett and Olivia Reilly draw on the work of the poet and philosopher Samuel Taylor Coleridge in order to ground a critique of a resurgent formalism evident in a particular practice of judging. The practice with which they are concerned is the production of 'unitary' judgments (multi-member judicial panels producing single, joint, or agreed judgments, rather than individual ones), which has taken on a renewed prominence in the UK Supreme Court during the last decade. Coleridge's accounts of the 'Imagination' and the 'Fancy' illuminate the formalism present in this practice and the dangers to which this formalism gives rise. The Fancy is a faculty of mind that achieves a very limited, formal level of thought through a death-like fixity and simplification. The Imagination, by contrast, enables us to comprehend the often complex and messy realities of the objects of our attention. The unitary judgment practice, which pursues a particular, formal kind of legal clarity – of the same *genus* as that upon which the Fancy fixates – is shown to mask significant legal, political, and social controversies within cases in which it is employed. This, the authors argue, impoverishes our jurisprudence. Moreover, this impoverishment can be addressed by returning to prominence a more imaginative form of judging – one that sees individual judges on multi-member panels producing their own, individual judgments. In this way, the Imagination's preferred type of clarity can be achieved: a maximalist form of clarity that prioritises transparency, rather than the reductionist form associated with the Fancy.

The collection concludes with Matteo Nicolini's account in Chapter 12 of the ways in which legal imagination can assist us in the transition towards a different cultural, political, and legal paradigm. In this chapter, he focuses on the challenges that lie ahead for the United Kingdom following Brexit. Nicolini contends that the sense of anxiety percolating through the Anglo-British constitution is triggered by a profound lack of legal imagination, and that such a lack is also a consequence of legal positivism. He proposes to resort to the British manufacturing tradition in order to sidestep such lack of imagination. Here, he identifies a twofold interaction between imagination and legislative process, which can usefully inform a transition into a new legal reality. Nicolini argues that anxiety can be sidestepped,

Legal imagination in troubled times   13

if only we consider that both legal imagination and legislative action were conceived as a means for recovering public and shared values within British society. In his view, not only does the law organise society, but it also secures predictability by reforms – complementing legal imagination by giving the latter a rational form. To this extent, Britain has always been able to manage complexity by what Nicolini terms 'acts of constitutional creativity' deeply rooted in British legal culture. The history of Britain has always been a history of reimagination whereby the UK has developed a 'complex' constitutional system.

As is apparent, the book's structure reveals the determinations underpinning the collection. Furthermore, it unfolds our ambitious, albeit limited in range and scope, intellectual project; we encourage lawyers to develop further reflection on how to make use of imagination in disciplined ways. As this is, to say the least, tricky, we dare uphold that all the collected essays have a kind of 'exploratory quality'. By bringing problems into focus, we urge lawyers to explore unprecedented jurisdictions of the legal reality.

But, in so doing, we also point to the *paths* that might avoid the failures of the imagination and, at the same time, counter the danger of indiscipline that is unavoidably triggered by the troubled times we are currently experiencing.

Part One

Imagination, law, and history: framing the future

2 The progress of legal education in England

Sir John Baker

DOWNING PROFESSOR EMERITUS OF THE LAWS OF ENGLAND,
UNIVERSITY OF CAMBRIDGE

The story of English legal education begins and ends with the universities, though for around 500 years the law faculties played no part in the formation of secular lawyers. There was a law school at Oxford by the 1190s, and some *quaestiones disputatae* from that period have survived. Cambridge followed soon afterwards. Although both taught Roman civil law and canon law, it was canon law that drew the students. At Cambridge, the earliest statutes (dating from the 1240s) mention only students of canon law (*decretistae*); a doctor of civil law is mentioned in the 1250s.[1] There had also been a school of civil law in London, perhaps attached to St Paul's Cathedral, though all we know of it is that it was closed down on the king's orders in 1234.[2]

But there is no need to dwell on these law schools, for two reasons. First, their curriculum and methods of education were not significantly different from those used across Christendom, beginning perhaps in Bologna. Although there was a distinct English literature on local constitutions and procedure, the system as a whole was cosmopolitan. Second, and related to that, the universities took no notice of English law. The secular common law was just local custom and had no place in a university, to which students might come from all over Europe. The law faculties were therefore schools not of English law but of universal jurisprudence. Most of their law graduates did not have much to do with the law either. They went into the Church, and only a small proportion of the few who stayed the course long enough to take the doctorate went into practice as advocates. University-trained advocates could practise only in the Church courts and the Court of Admiralty, because they had learned little or nothing at university about English law.

The break with the Roman curia in the 1530s did not greatly alter this position, although the canon law faculties were closed and effectively merged with civil law. Oxford and Cambridge continued to teach Roman law, including some of the ecclesiastical law needed for practice in the Church courts. An Oxford D.C.L. or

---

1 For this paragraph see JH Baker, *Monuments of Endlesse Labours: English Canonists and their Work 1200–1900* (Hambledon P. for the Ecclesiastical Law Society 1998) 1–5, and the works cited there.
2 See J Baker, *Collected Papers on English Legal History* (Cambridge UP 2013) I, 271–73.

18   *Sir John Baker*

Cambridge LL.D. remained the only acceptable qualification for an advocate or judge in the Canterbury Court of Arches until Victorian times.

But here we may leave aside the universities until the eighteenth century.

Practitioners of the law of England needed a different kind of education. It is possible that some, perhaps many, had spent a little time at university. We have virtually no records of undergraduates from which we might check. But they would not have stayed long enough to read Law, which was a postgraduate discipline. The study of Law did not begin until around the age of 18, and so the years after grammar school were spent studying the liberal arts – principally grammar, logic, rhetoric, and mathematics. There was no law in the Arts course until the nineteenth century, and there was no point staying on to read Law if the intention was to practise the law of the land. Indeed, the law student probably did not even trouble to graduate as a Bachelor of Arts.

What the English lawyer needed to know was not to be found at Cambridge or Oxford. He needed to know the jurisdiction and procedure of the king's courts at Westminster – and perhaps, as a preliminary, the workings of the lesser manorial courts that could be found in every village. He also needed to be inducted into the complex mysteries of land law. No doubt neither of these subjects began by being complicated. But by the mid thirteenth century they had become elaborate and technical. A distinct lay profession had come into being soon after 1200, consisting of pleaders (who appeared in court as advocates) and attorneys (who were analogous to proctors in the Church courts and dealt with the routine of litigation and everyday affairs).[3]

The apprentices of the bench and their Inns

By the 1250s, the lay profession had its own law school. As it was not much later in origin than the university law schools, it is not surprising that in some ways the two systems resembled each other. They used both lectures and disputations as the methods of instruction, and their higher graduates were distinguished by long robes and hoods. Of this early law school, unfortunately, we know very little.[4] Unlike the universities, there were no endowments from benefactors and no

---

3 For the early history of the profession, see P Brand, *The Origins of the English Legal Profession* (Blackwell 1992); JH Baker, *The Order of Serjeants at Law* (5 Selden Soc. Supplem. Series 1984); 'The legal profession' in *Collected Papers* (n 1) I, 19–139.

4 For what follows see also J Baker, 'Legal education' (9 papers) in *Collected Papers* (n 1) I, 255–410; *Readings and Moots in the Inns of Court*, II: Moots (105 Selden Soc 1989) [hereafter *Moots*]; *Readers and Readings in the Inns of Court and Chancery* (13 Selden Soc Supplem Series, 2001); 'The education of lawyers' (1483–1558), in *Oxford History of the Laws of England*, VI (Oxford UP 2003) 445–72; 'The exercises of learning' in *The Inns of Chancery 1340–1640* (19 Selden Soc Supplem Series, 2017) 75–87; P Brand, 'Courtroom and schoolroom: the education of English lawyers prior to 1400' (1987) 60 *Bulletin of the Institute of Historical Research* [hereafter BIHR] 147–65; 'Legal education in England before the Inns of Court,' in JA Bush and A Wijffels (eds), *Learning the Law: Teaching and the Transmission of Law in England, 1150–1900* (The Hambledon Press 1999) 51–84.

The progress of legal education in England   19

statutes, and so there was nothing to record in writing. There do not seem even to have been distinct premises. The students were called 'apprentices of the Bench,' the Bench (or Common Bench) being the principal court in Westminster Hall, and it is not improbable that the Bench was in a physical as well as a metaphysical sense their university. There is mention in 1287 of an Irish student 'residing in the Bench *causa addiscendi*,'[5] and in 1323 there is a maintenance agreement to support a young man for one year at Oxford 'and the next four years at our lord the king's court at the Common Bench, wherever the said bench shall be in England, among the apprentices.'[6]

These apprentices watched the court in action, from an enclosure called 'the crib,'[7] and presumably someone would explain to them what was happening. Indeed, sometimes the chief justice himself did so.[8] But the students also attended lectures and exercises. We know of this because some of the lecture notes survive. They masquerade in the manuscripts as treatises, but, as Plucknett wrote of one of them, they positively reek of chalk and duster and ink.[9]

Most of the lectures were on procedure, but there were also elementary lectures on land law. The interactive exercises were concentrated on pleading – that is, the oral process whereby an issue was framed for trial[10] – and enabled students to learn how to become advocates. As most of the litigation for which they were training concerned landed property, they would also find that the pleading exercises tested their knowledge of the principles of land law. In what precise location these exercises were conducted is not recorded, but that may well be because it was the court itself, vacant after the mid-day dinner. The courts at Westminster did not sit in the afternoon.

By 1292, there were such large numbers of apprentices attending the court that an official attempt was made to reduce them, but it came to nothing.[11] The

---

5 *Moots* (n 4) xxvi n. 72.

6 Manchester University John Rylands Library, Leigh of Lyme Muniments, Box M6/16; MJ Bennett, 'Provincial gentlefolk and legal education in the reign of Edward II' (1984) 57 BIHR 203–8. Cf. an agreement of 1364 to support a student for 7 years in the company of the men of law going to the king's court ('gentz de lei alantz a la court nostre seignour le roy'): *Moots* (n 4) xxvi.

7 FW Maitland, 29 Selden Soc. xvi; GJ Turner, 22 Selden Soc. xli (published after vol. 29); Baker, *Collected Papers* (n 1) I, 310.

8 This is evident from the law reports. See *Anon.* (1312) YB Hil. 5 Edw. II (31 Selden Soc.), 90, *per* Bereford CJ ('Et jeo die un chose pur les jeones qe sont environ ...'); *Anon.* (1316) Mich. 10 Edw. II (52 Selden Soc), 96, *per* Bereford CJ ('jeo di pur les juvenes qe cy sunt pur laprise ...'); *Eyre of Northamptonshire 1329–30* (97 Selden Soc.), 478, *per* Scrope CJ ('Jeo die pur vous apprentiz').

9 TFT Plucknett, *Early English Legal Literature* (Cambridge UP 1958) 90, referring to the family of texts known as *Casus Placitorum*.

10 Pleading was equivalent to the system of *exceptiones* and *replicationes* in Roman law, leading to a *litiscontestatio* (which English lawyers called an 'issue'). In modern lay usage, 'pleading' has the entirely different sense of imploring or cajoling. In law, however, a plea was not an argument or a rhetorical mode of address but a formulaic assertion of facts.

11 Baker, *Collected Papers* (n 1) I, 112–13, 148–50.

20   *Sir John Baker*

growing throng obviously could not sleep in the court, and so they all needed lodgings. That is what the maintenance grants paid for. Some might live alone, but it was more economical to share costs, and there were probably informal communities around Westminster in the early 1300s.[12] In 1326, we learn of a battle in London between the northern and southern apprentices of the Bench, which suggests that they congregated in 'nations' as in other universities.[13]

In about 1340, more permanent housing was found in premises called 'inns' (*hospicia*), which from the beginning were not merely lodging-houses but had some of the characteristics of academical colleges. The immediate cause was the return of the legal profession *en masse* from York, to which it had been exiled for several years while the courts sat in York Castle. The incoming hordes of students and practitioners needed to find shared accommodation in a hurry.[14] But it can be no accident that this was the very period when colleges were beginning to proliferate at the universities, taking over the discipline and much of the teaching from the central *studium*.[15] In the case of the lawyers' inns, any trace of a central *studium* or university disappeared completely, and from the 1340s until the present day the education and qualification of barristers has been the exclusive prerogative of the four principal inns. Two of these inns were located in the New Temple, an area on the north bank of the River Thames (between London and Westminster) which had been given to the Knights Hospitaller of St John of Jerusalem when the Templars were dissolved. The knights no longer required it themselves, but their two halls provided a convenient focus for two communities, known as the Inner Temple and Middle Temple.[16] A third, Gray's Inn, was the former townhouse of the Lords Grey of Wilton. The fourth, Lincoln's Inn, was probably known as Strange's Inn until Lord Strange resumed occupation in about 1417, when the society moved to its present site and had to change its name.[17]

12 Note the petition to Parliament of the people of Westminster in 1337, after the courts had moved to York, that they had lost their principal means of support from lettings: *Moots* (n 4) xxvii.

13 *Calendar of Coroners' Rolls of the City of London 1300–1378* (RR Sharpe ed, 1913) 157, n 30; *Chronicles of the Reigns of Edward I and Edward II* (W. Stubbs ed, Rolls Series, 1882), 313; Baker, *Collected Papers* (n 1) I, 152.

14 Ibid. 153–57.

15 E.g. at Cambridge (which had only one thirteenth-century college) King's Hall (1317, dissolved 1540), Michaelhouse (1324, dissolved 1540), Clare College (1326), Pembroke Hall (1347), Gonville Hall (1348), Trinity Hall (1350), and Corpus Christi College (1352). The King's Hall was founded to educate Chancery clerks, Trinity Hall to provide canon lawyers for the Norwich diocese (and many of them became judges in the Rota at Avignon); Gonville Hall was refounded in 1353 partly to encourage the study of Law.

16 For the division of the Temple, and the mysterious Outer Temple see Baker, *Collected Papers* (n 1) I, 173–84.

17 The society moved to the Bishop of Chichester's inn in Chancery Lane. Strange's Inn had once been the *hospicium* of Henry de Lacy (d. 1311), Earl of Lincoln, and the lawyers reverted to the old name. See J Baker, 'The origin and early character of Lincoln's Inn' in *A Lincoln's Inn Commonplace Book* (GS Brown ed, 2016) 36–49.

The progress of legal education in England   21

These four were known by the early fifteenth century as the *hospicia hominum curiae*, the inns of the men of court, a description that was soon shortened to 'Inns of Court.' There were also about ten lesser inns, known as 'Inns of Chancery,' which in educational terms were intermediate between school (or university) and the Inns of Court. Some of them were associated with Chancery clerks, and during the fifteenth century they all came under the supervision of the chancellor of England.[18] The whole collection of colleges, scattered between the City of London and the king's courts at Westminster, housed a far larger community than the university law faculties; indeed, it was not much smaller than the entire university of Cambridge. In Tudor times, it was unofficially called the Third University of England.[19] A large part of the gentry attended it, with varying degrees of commitment to legal study.

The preparation of a law student was supposed to begin at one of the Inns of Chancery, which he would join around the age of 18 before proceeding to an inn of court (if he proved suited for it and could afford the living expenses) around the age of 21. The lesser inns may have taken over some of the teaching from the earlier law school, giving elementary lectures on land law and on the formulae (known as original writs) by which actions were commenced. They were especially well placed to teach the learning of writs, as it was the Chancery clerks who drafted them, and many collections of precedents of writs contain notes of observations that were probably made at lectures.[20] Some of the inns conducted an exercise called 'the reading of the writ,' though it is not clear whether this was a lecture on a writ or a recitation of the formula, so that the students would eventually know the wording by heart; perhaps it was both. This teaching is the origin of a book called the *Natura Brevium*, an early edition of which (1494) was printed at the instance of Strand Inn, one of the Inns of Chancery. The Harvard Law School has a copy of the 1537 edition, covered in annotations, which belonged to successive principals of Clement's Inn.[21]

The lectures on land law probably account for another student book, called the *Old Tenures*. They seem to have petered out around the fifteenth century, perhaps because it was thought sufficient to read the book. The students also learned how to recite the pleading *formulae* in French, using precedent books called *Narrationes*, and this enabled them to take part in elementary pleading exercises called moots. Reports of such moots from Lyons Inn in the 1490s show the participants using each other's names as parties to the actions. Some guidance must have been needed, but there is no evidence that it was ever formalised by the appointment of tutors. Each generation somehow passed the expertise on to the next. This was a residential law school, and part of every day was spent listening to one's seniors performing. It is not too much to suppose that another part of every day was spent asking questions about what on earth was going on.

18 Baker, *The Inns of Chancery 1340–1640* (19 Selden Soc Supplem Series, 2017).
19 See Baker, *Collected Papers* (n 1) I, 143 fn 1.
20 *Moots* (n 4) xxxii.
21 *Moots* (n 4) xxxii.

22 *Sir John Baker*

The basic grounding in writs, pleadings, and the principles of land law equipped a student to proceed to the more demanding intellectual environment of the Inns of Court. Not all did so. Probably most did not. Many became attorneys rather than advocates, and indeed the attorneys governed the Inns of Chancery in exchange for keeping the rooms from which they practised. Many of those who did go to the Inns of Court were not suited to the study and were not intending to study. They were enjoying their youth in the metropolis, finding out about life and making contacts. The swashbuckling tradition recalled wistfully by Shakespeare's aged Justice Shallow certainly began before Shallow's fictional youth in the fourteenth century. As Professor Thorne quipped, borrowing from C. P. Snow, the students liked their life – but no one else did.[22] Even within the inns, the serious students had cause to complain of the noise made by 'them that be no learners.'[23]

Readings and moots

We are only concerned, of course, with the learners, the serious students. Their curriculum comes into focus in the fifteenth century, chiefly from the Black Books of Lincoln's Inn, a precious series of administrative records beginning in 1422. As far as we can tell, however, all four inns had much the same routine, with their own technical vocabulary, resting on custom rather than statute.[24] There were two principal forms of exercise. First, there was the lecture. In the inns, lectures were called 'readings.' As in the universities, a *lectura* involved reading out an authoritative text and then providing a commentary or gloss on it, usually taking each word or phrase at a time. As there was no text of the common law, the readings had to be upon the statutes, beginning with Magna Carta. However, as the statutes presupposed a body of unwritten law, it was usual for a lecturer to include some common law in his commentary. The earliest datable lectures on statutes are from the 1420s, but in Cambridge University Library there are two copies of a set of *Quaestiones de statutis*, starting with Magna Carta, and giving the names of the speakers, from which it may be deduced that they were distilled from lectures of a similar kind given in the 1340s.[25] Readings were given in the Lent and Summer vacations, which were known as the 'learning vacations.' It may seem odd to have attended lectures in the vacations, but in term time the students were expected to

22 Baker, *Collected Papers* (n 1) I, 275.
23 'State of the fellowship of the Middle Temple' (*c.* 1539), printed in W. Dugdale, *Origines Juridiciales* (3rd edn, 1680) 195.
24 The Inns of Chancery were given statutes in the fifteenth century, and they included some disciplinary regulations about the performance of exercises, but they were more concerned with daily life than with academic matters and did not set out what exactly the exercises were.
25 The texts are in French, as are all texts of readings, even in the seventeenth century. But this was the English lawyer's shorthand. It is impossible to be sure at what point the lectures came to be given in English. See Baker, 'The three languages of the common law' in *Collected Papers* (n1) II, 515–36; *Manual of Law French* (2nd edn, Routledge 1990) Introduction.

The progress of legal education in England 23

attend Westminster Hall and watch the courts in action. It was an all-the-year-round university, including even compulsory Christmas festivities, at which the old English traditions of carols, revels, lords of misrule, boars' heads, and holly were preserved. The lectures continued for at least a month, even if only a few sentences in a statute were glossed. The reason for the slow pace is that the readers illustrated their interpretations with strings of factual examples, or 'cases,' and any of these could be taken up by the audience and made the subject of a disputation. Here was the closest analogy with the academical exercise, which consisted of a factual case (*casus*), the legal question which it raised (*quaestio*), the arguments for and against (*disputatio*), and an authoritative ruling (*determinatio* or *solutio*). The title of the *Quaestiones de statutis* from the 1340s betrays this academical parallel. As the readings were attended by senior members of the inn, and even judges, the associated disputations were an important way of learning the common law.

The other form of exercise was the moot. There used to be some confusion over the original nature of moots, because nowadays a moot is a mock legal argument before an appellate tribunal. It was once thought that late-medieval moots were the disputations at readings, which were certainly closer to the moots of today. But this has turned out to be wrong. It can be shown that a moot, in its original sense, was a pleading exercise based on a given set of complex facts. There are manuscript moot-books containing the cases that were assigned for the purpose, some of which appear to date from the mid fourteenth century. The participants had to choose the right writ and draw up pleadings that would raise the questions in the problem. This was all done orally, as it had been in the royal courts in the days when the earliest moot-books were composed.[26] The hall of the inn was deemed for the purpose to be a real court – not any court, but specifically the Common Bench,[27] the former home of the apprentices – and was arranged with a bar and a bench. The mooters performed at the Bar, and the senior members sat on the bench to make rulings when needed. There was no question of producing a final judgment, as in a modern moot, but that was equally true of a real case at the time, as the final determination belonged to the jury. The law came into play interstitially, and in a moot every legal aspect of the case had to be considered in framing the pleas. The cases were so involved that one moot could take up an entire vacation and involve most of the students in residence.

The old readings had been passed on over the generations, tried and tested in disputation, creating what has been called 'a core of inherited learning.' But in the sixteenth century readers were given a free choice of subject, often taking a recent statute, and some readers were inevitably better at this than others. The readings therefore became variable in quality. Sir Edward Coke complained that they had become more like riddles than lectures, aimed at finding subtle evasions.[28] Coke's own reading of 1592 was not a masterpiece of legal exposition, though that of his rival Francis Bacon in 1600 (on the same subject) was considered a masterpiece.

26 The indications of a fourteenth-century origin are considered in 105 SS xxix–xlv.
27 *Moots* (n 4) xlviii n. 223, and 50.
28 E Coke, *Institutes of the Laws of England*, vol I (1628) fo. 280.

24   *Sir John Baker*

Moots retained their original form and, in so far as they concentrated on writs and forms of pleading that were no longer in use, must have seemed increasingly archaic, though some attempts were made to bring the cases up to date. There was no need for an examination in our sense, because performing adequately was a sufficient indication of expertise. And in this respect, too, the legal university was paralleled in the academical world. A degree was not originally a distinction conferred at a ceremony following a written examination but was taken by performance in a disputation or (in the case of a master or doctor) by giving lectures; the graduate took the step, the *gradus*, himself.

The inns developed an analogous graduation system in connection with moots. When a student performed to the requisite standard in a moot, by arguing at the Bar of his inn, he became a master of the Bar, or barrister.[29] When he had been a barrister long enough, and continued with the exercises, he was elected to read; and as soon as he had lectured he became a master of the bench, or bencher, so called because he could then sit on the bench at moots. To this day, graduation as a barrister is a qualification for practice as an advocate in the superior courts, but it now depends on written examinations. Promotion from barrister to bencher is no longer seen as a graduation; the benchers have become the elected governing bodies of the Inns of Court, responsible for educating barristers and calling them to the Bar.

The old system of readings and moots continued in the Inns of Court and Chancery until the English Civil War in the 1640s, which, for a few years, seriously depleted the resident membership to the point where the exercises had to be curtailed. The collapse was not greeted with the alarm that it would have deserved had the system not already become obsolescent. It was governed by precedent, as if it were part of the common law itself, and carried on by the impetus of tradition alone. As in the universities, there were no paid lectureships. There were no funds for that purpose. Everyone wishing to proceed to the bench had to take their turn as a law teacher. It might have been better if someone with suitable inclinations and talent had been engaged to lecture on the principles of the common law, but that would have required some financial inducement, and no funds were forthcoming. The one attempt to modernise, by taking more recent statutes as texts for the lectures, had only led to confusion.

Although there was an attempt to revive the old system after the Restoration of the Monarchy in 1660, no one seems to have given any thought to changing it. Lawyers were not in a mood for change. It was a time for putting things back as they were. But the lectures now fell to be given, by seniority, by men who thought they had escaped the duty in the 1640s. The performances were perfunctory, often just one or two lectures, accompanied by an expensive dinner to persuade the audience to come. Many of those whose turn came just refused and were fined. This

---

29 In the sixteenth century the benchers achieved control by requiring permission to perform the effective moot. This was known as 'call to the Bar.' When moots disappeared, call to the Bar became a graduation ceremony rather than a permission to graduate. Something similar happened in the universities.

The progress of legal education in England 25

seemingly gross dereliction of duty suited everyone. The fines probably cost the readers less than the dinners. And it did not take the Inns of Court long to realise that the fines were much more useful to them than the lectures. So, readers went on being elected and fined for not reading, and the principal form of education in the common law stopped for 200 years. The Inns of Chancery ceased to function as educational institutions at the same time. Mooting limped on in what became an increasingly formalistic ritual, based on the pleading exercises of the fourteenth century. In 1778 the Inner Temple finally put an end to the last vestiges of the old exercise, still apparently performed in law French, in return for a fine. Not before time, one might say. But nothing was put in its place. The students were, in effect, fined for giving up the last remains of a formal education in law.

Of course, England still produced lawyers after the 1640s, and many of them were of a high intellectual calibre. Two of them, Sir Matthew Hale and Sir Jeffrey Gilbert, wrote the most lucid accounts of the common law in their time. Both of them, rather ungenerously, forbade publication, and so lawyers had to acquire their learning without their guidance and without formal instruction from the Inns of Court.[30] Publishers provided shelves full of reference books, including a growing body of reported cases, in which students could immerse themselves, and there were still wooden galleries at Westminster where they could sit and take notes. But some interchange with others was needed. We hear of informal gatherings in coffee houses, where cases were discussed, and moots arranged. The institution known as pupillage became more formalised and, in the mid eighteenth century, it took on the form that it has retained ever since. A student intended for the Bar would attach himself to a practising barrister and, in return for a fee of 100 guineas, would be allowed free access to his master's papers and precedent books and would follow him into court and take notes.[31] Some senior barristers had numerous pupils, who formed their own select clubs and discussion groups. The best form of pupillage, according to contemporary opinion, was not with a dazzling courtroom advocate but with a good draughtsman. This was because it was still a vital first stage in a barrister's education to understand the intricacies of pleading, now a written art rather than an oral one, and for Chancery barristers to master the arcane science of conveyancing. Much of the pupil's time was therefore spent copying precedents and drafting documents, which a good pupil-master might perhaps find time to correct. One or two pupil-masters went so far as to provide lectures, and some of the lectures on conveyancing were so successful that numerous manuscript copies went into circulation. Attorneys and solicitors were trained in a similar way, by being 'articled' for 5 years as clerks to established practitioners,[32] often serving part of their articles in London – to acquaint them with the practice of the central courts – as well as in their own locality.

30 For the remainder of this paragraph see Baker, *Collected Papers* (n 1) I, 281–88.
31 The pupillage fee was still 100 guineas (£105) per annum when the writer was called to the Bar in 1966, but it has since been abolished.
32 The 'articles of agreement' were a contract with a practising solicitor to serve as his clerk. Service as an articled clerk, prior to admission as a solicitor, was compulsory after 1730.

26   Sir John Baker

Law teaching revived: Blackstone and Amos

Although consciences were occasionally stirred in the Inns of Court by the failure to fill the educational void, there was a general disinclination to spend their resources on students. Between 1758 and 1769, Gray's Inn went so far as to pay a barrister £60 a year to give lectures, though bizarrely they stopped when he became a bencher. The experiment was not repeated. But this is where the story moves back to the universities. In 1753 a barrister called William Blackstone, bursar of All Souls College, Oxford, who had also taken the doctorate of Civil Law, started to lecture at Oxford on English law in the hopes of obtaining a new chair that was under consideration. He had really wanted to be Regius Professor of Civil Law, but in 1753 the Crown appointment had been given on political grounds to someone now long forgotten. Blackstone's venture was very successful, and in 1758 the new chair was finally established, endowed from the profits of a legal reference book (Viner's *Abridgment*).[33] Remarkable as it may seem, his 1753 lectures were the first attempt ever made to present English law to an audience as a rational structure, to explain in outline all its parts and show how they fitted into the whole. No doubt Blackstone's training in Roman law had provided him with a model, and that is evident in the arrangement of the syllabus, but the content was purely English. The reason why the innovation was a success is, no doubt, to be found in the expansive nature of Blackstone's project. The lectures were designed not solely for intending lawyers, but to improve the education of 'such other gentlemen as were desirous of some general acquaintance with the constitution and legal polity of their native country.'[34] They were not included in the Law curriculum but were 'private' lectures aimed at Oxford students who would typically become country parsons and squires, serving perhaps in due course as county magistrates and managing family estates. They were therefore free of technicality and were a far cry from the phase-by-phrase glossing of texts, let alone the alphabetical scheme of the book that had endowed his chair. The object was to reduce the laws of England to a plan 'which the *student* might afterwards pursue to any degree of minuteness, and at the same time be so contracted that the *gentleman* might with tolerable application contemplate and understand the whole.'[35] It was, he said in his inaugural lecture,

> an undeniable position, that a competent knowledge of the laws of that society in which we live is the proper accomplishment of every gentleman and scholar: an highly useful, I had almost said essential, part of liberal and polite education.[36]

33 See DJ Ibbetson, 'Charles Viner and his Chair: legal education in eighteenth century Oxford' in *Learning the Law* (n. 4) 315–28. The impetus evidently came from Viner (whose first will was made in 1752) rather than Blackstone.

34 W Blackstone, preface to *An Analysis of the Laws of England* (Oxford 1762 edn) sig A2v (modernised).

35 Ibid. (emphasis added). Blackstone went on to acknowledge his debt to Sir Matthew Hale's *Analysis of the Law*.

36 W Blackstone, 'Discourse on the Study of the Law,' prefixed to *An Analysis of the Laws of England* (Oxford, 1762 edn) sig. B2.

The progress of legal education in England 27

True as that no doubt was, Blackstone had the more practical motivation of wishing to increase his lecture fees. In reality, the future law student gained even more from this kind of outline than the accomplished gentleman.[37] It would not induct them very far into the mysteries of practice, but it would enable them to undertake pupillage with a reasonable understanding of basic principles. Blackstone thus set legal education on a new course, and incidentally altered the style and quality of English law books for ever.

Blackstone's lectures were delivered in a manner that did not appeal to all his hearers, and – although he had aimed them at the whole university – relatively few paid the 6 guineas for the privilege of listening. But, when they were published, as *Commentaries on the Laws of England* (1765–68), they proved to be a best-seller. They were such a success, indeed, that oral legal instruction was driven back into obscurity.[38] It was enough to buy the book. In the 1780s Cambridge followed the Vinerian experiment with the Downing Professorship of the Laws of England, finally rescued from 50 years of Chancery litigation in 1800. But Cambridge was at first no more successful than post-Commentarian Oxford. Few if any of the early Downing professors made a significant mark on scholarship. Their position was admittedly eccentric. As at Oxford, the lectures were extracurricular and aimed at undergraduates, few of whom (it turned out) could be bothered to take the 10-minute walk to Downing College. They did not lead to a degree, and so there was no college teaching to back them up. Law degrees were still for postgraduates, and the only kind of law that counted in the Law Faculty was that of ancient Rome. The student sensible enough to take an interest in law, for his general education, might just as well read Blackstone.

When London University was founded in 1826, in what is now University College London, new possibilities were opened up for legal education.[39] The University was not far from the centre of the English legal world, and the new Law Faculty deliberately set out to attract law students, even to the extent of holding classes in the evenings. Two professors were appointed, one of English Law and one of Jurisprudence. The latter was John Austin, whose interest in universal legal theory resulted in lectures so abstract and convoluted that they were beyond his audiences. His inaugural lecture was given, appropriately but unwisely, on the difficulty of giving an introductory lecture on jurisprudence. It was delivered with much nervous hesitation, but the audience grasped the point about difficulty, and few came back. After 4 years of struggling with the lectures, and with neurotic illness, Austin resigned. On the other hand, the professor of English Law, Andrew Amos (a practising barrister), was extremely successful. He went to the other extreme. There was hardly a syllabus at all. He meandered from topic to

---

37 In his will (ibid. 317), the founder of the chair (Charles Viner) lamented that when law students attended the courts at Westminster they were apt to 'trifle away their time in hearing what they understand nothing of, and thereupon perhaps divert their thoughts from the law to their pleasures.'

38 Blackstone's successors, though respectable, did not add significantly to his achievement for over a century.

39 For what follows see Baker, *Collected Papers* (n 1) I, 290–307.

28 *Sir John Baker*

topic, taking his lead from the issues of the day and discussing cases in which he was engaged. He used visual aids, organised 'legal conversations' or tutorials, invited eminent guest speakers to talk on their specialities, encouraged the students to debate, and arranged voluntary examinations.

As in Blackstone's case, Amos's successors were mediocre. Even Amos himself, on becoming Downing Professor in 1850, found that his methods could not be transplanted successfully to Cambridge. But he, more than Blackstone, had invented modern legal education as it has obtained in England. As a combination of lecture, discussion, and exercise, it was an unconscious reincarnation of the earliest form of legal education, rediscovered for use in a different legal world. Looking back, we might think it inevitable that this was the way forward. Nevertheless, it met with numerous obstacles. For one thing, students were not easily convinced of its utility, and, if students were not attracted, there was no income for the professor. At Oxford and Cambridge, students planning to go to the Bar continued to read Mathematics and Classics, as in the past, if only because those subjects were the route to the fellowships that – if they distinguished themselves – would support them through pupillage. (Amos himself had been a first-class mathematician at Cambridge.) In London, they had to be persuaded not to go straight into pupillage or articled clerkships. The inaugural lectures of London professors were usually aimed at persuading the audience that law was not merely a vocational subject but a science, and that it was necessary to learn the science before turning to practice. One of them, in 1833, urged potential students to fight against nature and the pleasure-seeking habits of the age, or they would suffer remorse later from their neglected opportunities. Of the 200 who attended his first lecture, only five came to the second, and none to the third. Another professor, in 1846, advocated submission to the 'drudgery' of lectures in order to avoid the 'pain and difficulty, and shame, and humiliation' of trying to acquire the same knowledge later in life.[40] Surprising though it may seem to those older and wiser, many young people were willing to take the risk of skipping the drudgery.

A greater challenge even than indolence came from the vocational courses set up piecemeal in the same period by the solicitors' Law Society. The Law Society charged articled clerks as much as 100 guineas for 12 lectures, and yet the attendance is said to have exceeded 200. Most of the students willingly took the voluntary examinations, which required them to sit down at 10 o'clock in the morning and stay till tea-time, answering as many of the 75 questions as they could manage. The pass standard was low, and success was said to be no more than 'a guarantee against absolute incompetency.' They were focused on practice rather than theory.

Reform of English legal education

By the 1840s there was considerable concern about the state of legal education. The *Law Times* drew attention to the flourishing Harvard Law School and the Russian

---

40 *Collected Papers* (n 1) I, 297, 298.

The progress of legal education in England 29

Imperial Law School at St Petersburg, lamenting that England had no law school at all worthy of the name. John Campbell (a future Lord Chancellor) asked,

> Is it not strange that we should have degenerated from the wisdom of our ancestors in the age of the Tudors? – that the Inns of Court should have discharged their duty in the reign of Henry VII and should neglect it in the reign of Queen Victoria?

The law reformer Lord Brougham joined in, and in 1846 the House of Commons appointed a Select Committee on Legal Education. The Inns of Court, thoroughly alarmed by this, rushed through reforms the same year under which four lectureships would be created.

The Select Committee reported a few months later. They concluded that a law student was left almost solely to his own individual exertions. Although they acknowledged that something had been done at University College London, their praise was in the past tense. The course they recommended was to separate the academic and the practical stages of legal education. The universities should be persuaded to make legal history and jurisprudence part of the Arts course, and the Inns of Court should operate as a kind of law university (in which the four inns would be constituent colleges) to provide more advanced instruction for intending barristers. The latter suggestion was in line with what the inns had already hurriedly decided, and it came to fruition in 1847, though without fusing the inns into a formal university. Within a few years both Oxford and Cambridge responded to the former suggestion by introducing jurisprudence into the BA syllabus, combined at first with other humane subjects, and in the 1860s it became possible to take a BA in Law.[41]

The notion that there should be two stages in legal education has been accepted ever since and was confirmed by the Ormrod Committee on Legal Education in 1971, though the further step was never taken in England of requiring a law degree before entering the profession. A degree in law remains to this day an optional extra, though it is one that many students choose.

Some Victorian reformers were not content with the 1846–47 reforms, and in 1854 there was a Royal Commission to investigate the study of law in the Inns of Court. The principal political concern was to know whether the revenues of the inns, chiefly from chamber rents, were being properly applied by institutions that were arguably educational charities. The more defensive concern of the inns was to find a way of satisfying the commissioners without giving up any of their privileges. To a large extent they succeeded in doing so. The resulting compromise did not go much further than 1846, and again the idea of a great imperial law school including the Inns of Court was shelved. London University twice proposed reviving the idea, but the inns and the Law Society were suspicious of any outside

---

41 The first degree in Law at these universities is still a BA. Other universities, following the lead of London, call it an LLB. At the older universities the bachelor's degree in Law (LLB, now LLM, at Cambridge, BCL at Oxford) remains a postgraduate degree, though no longer in Roman law.

30 *Sir John Baker*

interference, and nothing happened. In modern times, however, the inns have become increasingly aware of their educational responsibilities and now spend more than £5 million a year on scholarships and awards.

Academic and vocational legal education in modern times

The two professional bodies have kept control of the educational requirements for their professions, and that is as it must be. The main issue in the twentieth century was how far they could also dictate what university law schools teach. The universities adhere to Blackstone's principle that the study of Law is 'a liberal and polite education,' an important branch of the Humanities worthy of study even by those who do not intend to earn a living from legal practice. The professions, on the other hand, were afraid lest the formative stage in a lawyer's education be handed over to philosophers in ivory towers whose esoteric interests were irrelevant to practice.

That was not a real risk in the period before the expansion of universities in the 1980s, since the majority of law teachers then were members of the Bar, and very few of them had Ph.D. degrees. Over the last 30–40 years that has changed, so that nearly all law teachers – and they have become a vastly more numerous profession[42] – have engaged in doctoral research, rather than professional training, before appointment.

But the fears have not materialised, because a sensible settlement was reached. The profession would define what it regarded as the 'core subjects,' or 'foundational subjects,' required of anyone wishing to proceed to a vocational course. There are currently seven: Constitutional and Administrative Law, Criminal Law, Contract, Tort, Property Law, Equity and Trusts, and European Union Law. Anyone who passes all seven is deemed to have a qualifying law degree for professional purposes. A university could, in theory, choose not to teach any of them, but then its graduates would be at a disadvantage should they wish to practise law. On the other hand, there was no objection to the universities offering whatever additional courses they wished. In practice, most of the optional courses have also proved to be purely legal, but the better universities offer a range of non-doctrinal subjects. For instance, Cambridge has well-attended classes in Roman Law (compulsory for most law students), English Legal History (not compulsory), Criminology, and Jurisprudence.

It has occasionally been proposed in recent times that universities should take on the vocational training as well, since the Law Society and the Inns of Court no longer employ law teachers themselves.[43] Only a few ordinary universities have taken

---

42 This is partly because the number of universities has increased. There are now around 90 offering law degrees in England, compared with fewer than 20 in 1960. But older law faculties have also increased substantially in size over the same period. At present there are more than 18,000 UK students (60 per cent of them women) reading for a law degree, besides many more from overseas. Under half of them enter practice.

43 The Inns of Court School of Law functioned under the aegis of the inns until 1977, when it was taken over by City University. The writer lectured on legal history in Lincoln's Inn hall in the 1970s. The halls of the inns are now used only for special lectures and events.

The progress of legal education in England 31

on this role,[44] though a number of specialist law schools have been created to teach for the professional examinations, and in recent years some of these have been granted university status.[45] These law schools also offer courses leading to the Common Professional Examination, and a Graduate Diploma in Law (GDL), for those who do not possess a qualifying degree.[46] The GDL is awarded after only 1 year of full-time study, compared with the 3 years normally required for a law degree (LLB), and usually means that the recipient has studied no more than the core subjects.

The system in operation today in academic law schools is an amalgam of the methods from the past that have been outlined in this paper.[47] Lectures are still given, and in an age of statute these are veering back towards the medieval practice of glossing statutory texts, explaining their context and how they are interpreted by the judges. The common law is also expounded in lectures, aided by textbooks. Both legislation and the unwritten common law are studied with the aid of reported decisions in real cases, and the main function of textbooks is to guide the reader towards finding and understanding the case law on the subject in hand.[48] Attempts to introduce interactive lectures, on the Harvard Law School model, have not proved suited to the reticent temperament of the English.

Instead, most English universities have small-group teaching. In Cambridge the groups are called supervision classes; in Oxford, tutorials. Depending on the university, there might be one or two students in a class, or six, or perhaps as many as twelve. These classes typically work from problem sheets, which contain imaginary sets of facts in problematic cases related to the topic being studied. The students are expected to be able to present arguments on both sides and come to a conclusion. It does not matter whether the conclusion is 'right.' The purpose is to identify the legal questions and to marshal the relevant arguments and authorities. Their function,

---

44 There are vocational law courses at Cardiff University, which has been a university since Victorian times, and at four former polytechnics (in Bristol, Manchester, Newcastle, and Nottingham) that now have university status.

45 The College of Law (1962), which had its origin in the old firm of Gibson & Weldon, specialised in preparing candidates for the Law Society's examinations; it became a private university in 2012, called the University of Law Ltd, and claims to be the country's largest law school. City University (1966), which took over the Inns of Court School of Law in 1977, became a constituent part of London University in 2016; its law department is now known as City Law School (though it is not in the City of London). BPP University Ltd became a private university in 2013 and teaches a number of professional courses, including law, in several university towns.

46 The Law Society (with considerable opposition from the profession) has announced that it is going to replace this system with a new Solicitors Qualifying Examination, based on a modified syllabus, in 2020.

47 For some discussions of the structure of legal education in the recent past see R Abel, *The Legal Profession in England and Wales* (Wiley-Blackwell 1988) 261–81; Andrew Poon and Julian Webb, 'Legal education and training in England and Wales: back to the future?' (2008) 58 *Journal of Legal Education* 79–118.

48 English case law and legislation are now available online, and that is probably how most younger people gain access to it for most purposes. But it is still more convenient to read law reports in physical form when pursuing trails of authority from one book to another and back again.

32   Sir John Baker

therefore, is the same as that of the late-medieval readers' cases in the Inns of Court. The principal differences are that they are conducted in a less formal setting and with a smaller group, and also that the students will be asked to answer some of the questions in writing so that they can be marked by supervisors or tutors.

This element of individual attention was missing from the medieval system, because there were no professional teachers, though it has the disadvantage of making education more costly. In addition to ordinary lectures and classes, the better law schools also provide extracurricular education, such as talks from eminent visitors, judges, and practitioners, and moots.

Mooting represents another continuity from earlier times and resembles (even more closely than tutorials) the formal exercises at readings. Although arguing in moots is not a formal requirement for graduation, either in the universities or the Inns of Court, it is a valuable way of learning how to manage conflicting legal principles. Student counsel have to think not only of what their ideal solution to a problem might be, in the way that a judge might, but must try to foresee all the arguments that their opponents might deploy and make sure they can deal with them.

This gives a deeper insight into problem cases than mere essay writing, and if the moot is conducted before fellow students there is also the incentive of not wishing to appear stupid in public. A moot court was incorporated in the new Law Faculty building at Cambridge, and there are numerous mooting competitions in which students may take part, both in the universities and in the Inns of Court. Participation is not essential, but it counts as one of the qualifying activities in which Bar students must engage – the others include advocacy exercises, mock trials, ethics discussions, and mediation training. When it comes to securing a place in chambers, which is highly competitive, prowess in mooting may be an important factor in an applicant's favour. It is also desirable for solicitors, even if they do not have rights of audience in court, to be able to present legal arguments or summarise positions clearly.

Both branches of the legal profession require, in addition to examinations, a year or two of on-the-job training. In the case of barristers, this is the old pupillage system, though nowadays pupils are paid by the barristers under whom they study rather than the other way round. Pupillage is undertaken after call to the Bar, and the minimum period is 12 months, though in the 'second six' the pupil may undertake some work for clients. In the case of solicitors, what used to be called articled clerkship has, since 1990, been called 'traineeship,'[49] and the trainees are paid a salary;[50] the usual period is now 2 years, served before admission.

In all these respects, English legal education is a product of long experience and evolution. The formal division between an academic stage and a vocational stage

---

49 This title, too, is soon to be abolished and replaced by the less succinct 'two years of qualifying work experience.'

50 At the time of writing the recommended minimum trainee salary in London is £22,121, but the larger firms actually pay around £40,000. The recommended minimum pupillage award in London is £18,436, but the best sets of chambers pay £65,000–70,000. Trainee lawyers are therefore now paid more than university law lecturers.

has enabled the typical better student to learn law in a 3-year course at the hands of professional law teachers, who these days will have been appointed by virtue of their proven research capabilities, and then to learn the practice (and some of the more technical branches of law) at the hands of those closer to that world. The principal point of contention is whether it is right that lawyers should be allowed to practise without having undertaken the academic stage at a university. It is not allowed in most other countries. Although it is undoubtedly beneficial to have practitioners with degrees in other subjects, bringing broader perspectives, it is also detrimental to have practitioners who have studied law only to pass examinations in basic doctrine.

However, given the cost of university education, it would no longer be a realistic option in England to insist on two degrees (as in the United States). Perhaps in reality it does not matter too much. Many practitioners today are so specialised that they do not need to know much outside their own area, which is unlikely to have been taught in detail at any university. In the case of City solicitors, everything will be learned in-house. Where wider learning is needed, and an ability to think sideways, as in the upper reaches of the Chancery Bar or the Commercial Bar, a first-class degree in Law from a good university has in practice become de rigueur. The pragmatic solution, as in earlier centuries, has thus been to leave things as they are and let the market sort them out.

3 The dragon in the cave

Fleta as a legal imagining of early English common law

John Casey Gooch

THE UNIVERSITY OF TEXAS AT DALLAS, USA

Legal imaginings manifest as legal texts, written inscriptions that become, for example, collections of statutes, legal codes, or legislation. By the end of the thirteenth century in England, a number of legal texts emerged, and such texts were intended to aid lawyers, judges, and magistrates of the English legal community in administering, yet also imagining, the law. An example of such a text is *Fleta, Seu Commentarius Juris Anglicani* (henceforth *Fleta*), a collection of statutes inscribed during the last decade of the thirteenth century.[1]

Fleta was produced in the context of a socially and politically tenuous and troubled medieval society, and it became part of a wider network of legal texts sharing a common discourse and language. These texts, as well as their shared discourse and legal language, resulted from legal imaginings of their authors who were responding to the legal exigencies of their day and, at the same time, were trying to help their fellow jurists understand their legal world.

Such imaginings formed the basis for English common law; therefore, treatises, such as *Fleta*, and their impact are worthy of reconsideration. As a thirteen-century compendium of statutes, *Fleta* shared a discourse and language in common with other such written texts (e.g., *Bracton, Britton*) that came about in an attempt to ensure justice in troubled times. Indeed, *Fleta* relates an imagining and reimagining of the laws governing freemen, bondmen, criminal institutes (such as homicide, murder, robbery, and theft), and civil proceedings (among them, novel disseisin) to guide jurists in embracing and asserting legal imagination.

Fleta was written between 1290 and 1300, that is, during the reign of King Edward I (1272–1307). The author, most likely in the employ of the Crown, wrote this treatise during a period of Edward's legislative reforms, which granted greater power to land barons over their property and tenants. To this extent, *Fleta*'s extensive treatment of such issues suggested a more complex lord–tenant

---

1 John Selden gave the treatise the following title in his *Ad Fletam Dissertatio* written in 1644: J Selden (ed) *Fleta Seu Commentarius Juris Anglicani Sic Nuncupatus Sub Edwardo Rege Primo, Seu Circa Annos Abhince CCCXL, AB Anonymo Conscriptus, Atque E Codice Veteri, Autore Ipso Aliquantulum Recentiori, Nunc Primum Typis Editus* (London: Typis M.F. Prostant Apud Guil. Lee, & Dan. Pakeman 1647).

The dragon in the cave   35

relationship than had existed in previous centuries.[2] As the author of *Fleta* was writing very much in the context of those reforms, we may assume, as many historians have, that his identity was that of a lawyer named Matthew the Exchequer, who served under King Edward I.[3] Therefore, it becomes a plausible assertion that he responded to legislative reforms and legal developments so that jurists would know the proper courses of action under statutory law while also stimulating the legal imaginings of other members of the legal profession.

Edward I was known as 'The English Justinian'; contrary to Justinian, he did not seek, as Michael Prestwich notes, to codify law. Rather, his legislative reforms became a permanent part of the English legal landscape and helped firmly establish his position in legal history.[4] Two of his most significant reforms were the Westminster statutes, Westminster I of 1275 and Westminster II of 1285, which addressed the issue of novel disseisin, or land dispossession.[5] Westminster I, for example, made it possible for heirs of parties in a property dispute to claim ownership of land.[6] The legislation also mandated for the first time that, if disseisin resulted from robbery or violence, then the plaintiff would recover all he had lost, and the defendant would likely face a fine or imprisonment.[7]

The Statute of Westminster II extended the scope of an action that enabled plaintiffs in disseisin, or land possession, cases to recover costs as well as damages.[8] It also expanded the scope of novel disseisin in other ways, such as making the law applicable to woodlands where rights to collecting fruits and nuts were concerned.[9] Prestwich contends that Edward remained determined to introduce stiffer penalties, especially related to novel disseisin, and stiffer penalties for royal officials who abused the law. His intents lie not in undermining or destroying principles of novel disseisin, but in promoting the principles of effectiveness and efficiency in executing the law. As evidence for this claim, Prestwich cites that 84 per cent of

---

2 See TFT Plucknett, *A Concise History of the Common Law* (Liberty Fund 1956) regarding legislative reforms and baronial power in England during the late 1200s and early 1300s. See also J Biancalana, 'The writs of dower and Chapter 49 of Westminster I' (1990) 49 *CLJ* 91–116.

3 See GO Sayles, 'Introduction' in GO Sayles (ed), *Fleta: Volume IV, Book V and Book VI* (Selden Society 1984). Sayles challenged the idea that Matthew the Exchequer wrote *Fleta* while incarcerated in Fleet Prison. Sayles argued that the author would not have wanted his work associated with an imprisonment.

4 For a fuller account of the Westminster I and Westminster II reforms, see M Prestwich, 'Chapter 10: The statutes and the law' in M Prestwich (ed), *Edward I* (Yale UP 1997).

5 Respectively, Statute of Westminster of 1275 (3 Edw. I c 5) and Statute of Westminster of 1285 (13 Edw 1 c 1).

6 Prestwich (n 4) 271. He also notes that Edward's legislative reforms were almost innumerable.

7 Ibid.

8 Ibid. The Statute of Gloucester of 1278 (6 Edw I) first established that plaintiffs could recover both costs and damages. Westminster II built upon the Gloucester statute and went further in expanding the scope of novel disseisin.

9 Prestwich (n 4) 272.

36 *John Casey Gooch*

approximately 500 cases appearing before Justice Ralph Hengham between 1271 and 1289 were resolved with judgment on the first day.[10]

A considerable portion of *Fleta* captures legal imagining as it still provides a compendium of statutes the exigencies for which lie in legislative reforms such as Westminster I and II. *Fleta*, however, also became important in the legal imagination of the late thirteenth and early fourteenth centuries. It represented – and still represents – one of several legal texts that contributed to the further development of English common law during this time. Notably, 'The English Justinian,' in addition to being known for his legislative reforms, 'granted a full reissuance' of the Magna Carta based upon its 1225 charter.[11] The 1297 version of Magna Carta included some subtle changes, but, essentially, it reflected a recitation of the 1225 charter.[12] The year 1300 marks the final reissuance of Charter, which was 'once again distributed to counties and cathedrals of England under the king's great seal.'[13] The charter was confirmed over 40 times in the next 200 years; those confirmations, however, manifested as promises to uphold the terms of the charter and not as the material distribution of copies.[14]

Odd as it may seem, the writing and publication of *Fleta* and the final reissuance of Magna Carta occurred in approximately the same decade (i.e., 1290–1300).[15] Edward never personally supported the 1297 Charter, and its royal confirmation now receives treatment as an Act of Parliament. In 1305, Edward, like his grandfather, John, before him, obtained papal dispensation from his oath to observe the 1297 version. Probably, the Magna Carta and *Fleta* coinciding with one another may not mean much and may only represent (legal) coincidence. The two textual events, however, do suggest something about the history and evolution of common law as well as the legal imaginings of the time.

Its author organised *Fleta* into six books comprising multiple chapters.[16] Each chapter begins with 'Of' (or 'De,' in Latin); for example, the opening chapter of Book I is titled 'Of persons' ('De personis'), and the final chapter of Book VI is called 'Of prescription [by lapse] of time' ('De tempore prescripto'). Although no theme necessarily ties all the books of any one volume together, the last three books in the series (Books IV, V, and VI) focus more on civil and transactional matters, with more emphasis given to warranties and exceptions, whereas the first

---

10 For more on these topics, see Prestwich (n 4) 272.
11 N Vincent, *Magna Carta: A Very Short Introduction* (OUP 2012) 87.
12 Ibid.
13 Vincent (n 12) 88.
14 Ibid.
15 Sir John Baker, *The Reinvention of Magna Carta, 1216–1616* (CUP 2017) 8–12.
16 Book I contains 45 chapters, and Book II 88 chapters. Book III, however, only contains 18 chapters, and 31 chapters make up Book IV. The author arranged Book V into 40 chapters and Book VI into 54 chapters. No evidence points to precisely why the author chose to include, for example, only 18 chapters in Book III while offering up 88 chapters in Book II. This variation was mostly arbitrary, or so it would seem, as no unified themes function as organizing principles for any one book. References come from GO Sayles and HG Richardson (eds), *Fleta* with a translation (three volumes, Selden Society 1955–1984).

three books give more attention to criminal and procedural matters. Book I has the most to say about criminality and crime ('Of criminal actions': Chapter 16), murder and homicide ('Of homicide': Chapter 23; 'Of murder': Chapter 29), and theft ('Of theft': Chapter 36). That distinction, however, remains imperfect as all the books take up procedural matters.[17]

Imagining of royal authority in the Prologue

The three-page Prologue in Volume II serves largely to reimagine – that is, to assert and solidify – the authority of the king. That authority becomes critical to the legal imagining in *Fleta*, as all the law contained within the volumes rests on the king as an absolute legal authority, with that authority coming from God. *Fleta*'s author, however, goes to great lengths to emphasise the sovereignty of the Crown. In a lengthy opening statement, for example, the author declares:

> Kingly power should be equipped, not only with arms against the rebellious and the nations that rise up against the king and his realm but also with laws for the meet governance of his peaceful subjects and peoples, to the end that, the pride of the unbridled and untamed being shattered by the right hand of power and justice being administered with the rod of equity to the humble and meek, he may at once be ever victorious over his enemies and without ceasing show himself impartial in his dealings with his subjects.[18]

This opening statement speaks to the king's authority, both domestically and in foreign affairs. The author's reference to 'the rebellious and the nations that rise up against the king' suggests a need to maintain order in the kingdom, both at home and abroad.

The author then heaps praise upon King Edward I by extolling 'how finely, how actively, how skilfully, in time of hostilities our most worthy King Edward has waged armed war against the malice of his enemies there is none to doubt.'[19] He goes on to lift King Edward to an even more exalted position, claiming that, 'for now his praise has gone forth to all the world and his mighty works to every border thereof, and marvellously [*sic*] have his words resounded far and wide to the ends of the earth.'[20]

The Prologue continues with even more such embellishment, with the author asking a series of rhetorical questions. He asks,

> what man is there could praise him to the full measure of his due, whose famous deeds from youth up should be commended in everlasting memorials

---

17 E.g., procedures jurors must follow in 'Of the verdict of the jurors,' Chapter 9 of Book IV.
18 GO Sayles and HG Richardson, 'Prologue,' in Richardson and Sayles (eds) (n 16) 1. The passage reflects Sayles and Richardson's translation of the Latin text.
19 Ibid.
20 Ibid.

38 *John Casey Gooch*

and whose noble acts, as his age increased, should be set down with pen in books, nay, graven on the rocks with chisel, as a testimony for those to come?[21]

The author, however, does not stop there; he continues expressing his platitudes regarding King Edward, referring to the 'rich abundance of his graces,' and his 'comeliness, beyond the sons of men, is the desire of nations, whose outflowing bounty draws like a loadstone.' The author renews this flattery of King Edward by telling the audience that 'tongues falter, mouths fail, lips tremble, and the eloquence of a Tully is stilled.' He then shifts to the imperative mood with a call to action. He orders his audience to

> arise therefore, ye young men bold and valorous; unfurl your flags, sound your trumpets, and make merry for such a king, who in his youth manfully assumed the shield and, unweakened and vigorous maturity, has fought for his right.[22]

The Prologue, therefore, is dedicated to celebrating Edward I while serving to establish that all judicial authority ultimately comes from the Crown.[23] In short, the emphasis makes sense in that the author wishes to establish the king as the authority and source of law. As Ernst Kantorowicz describes it, 'Edward I, quite unexpectedly, appears like another paradisian Adam, a cosmic ruler' or a 'messianic prince.'[24]

Praise for Edward I aside, the author's statements also point to something else about the time that *Fleta* was written. The words suggest that challenges – possibly numerous challenges – to King Edward's authority had taken place. The emphasis on kingly authority in these passages suggests a need for stability; however, one must consider the exigency – that is, the need for subjects to respect the authority of the Crown because of inherent instability within the kingdom. A stable authority in law is necessary precisely because of a need for legal imagination in a troubled time lacking political and social stability.

It would be remiss, however, for one not to acknowledge which books of authority influenced the author in his writing of the Prologue. Although its assertion of royal authority remains unquestionable, the author plagiarised, to use contemporary terminology, the opening from *De legibus Angliae* by Ranulf de Glanvill, who, himself, had paraphrased from Justinian's *Institutes*.[25] Furthermore, Kantorowicz's study of the *Fleta* Prologue reveals that the *Eulogy* for Frederick II 'served *Fleta* for the embellishment' found in the opening.[26] Kantorowicz

---

21 Ibid.
22 The quotations are all from Sayles and Richardson, 'Prologue' (n 18) 1–2.
23 Plucknett (n 2) 81.
24 E Kantorowicz, 'The "Prologue" to *Fleta* and the School of Petrus de Vinea' (1957) 32 *Speculum: A Journal of Mediaeval Studies* 232.
25 Kantorowicz (n 24) 231. See also RV Turner, 'Who was the author of Glanvill? Reflections on the Education of Henry II's Common Lawyers' (1990) 8 *Law and History Review* 97–123.
26 Kantorowicz (n 24) 233.

describes the *Eulogy* as a 'panegyric oration' or 'panegyric,' but, in all likelihood, no one recited or spoke the *Eulogy* aloud. Rather, the *Eulogy* represented a 'written encomium,' or a text written to praise someone.[27] Kantorowicz finds it curious that the *Fleta* author had access to this oration, as the *Eulogy* author would have only released it as part of an epistolary or rhetorical collection (i.e. 'letter books') – named after Vinea or some other well-known dictator – and not as a separate piece.[28] Kantorowicz concludes that this panegyric was actually part of the Vinea collections, to which he assumes the *Fleta* author had access. Kantorowicz explains that the Vinea collections 'were composed in the late thirteenth century – perhaps in Paris, perhaps at the [Frederick's] Curia [in Palermo], perhaps at both places.'[29] Kantorowicz implies that copies of these collections were readily available in England, and he suggests that the *Fleta* author probably owned one or more of these 'letter books.'

One can also draw other parallels between the *Fleta* Prologue and publications associated with Frederick II. In 1231, Frederick II himself published the *Liber Augustalis*, also known as *The Constitutions of Melfi*, in an attempt to establish his authority in the Kingdom of Sicily and to bring about the end to a power struggle between the Sicilian aristocracy and Markward of Anweiler, a 'ministerialis' claiming 'to carry out the last will of the Emperor Henry VI,' Frederick's father.[30] A 'Prooemium' and three books comprise the *Constitutions of Melfi*.[31] Its Prooemium functions similarly to *Fleta*'s Prologue in that it establishes God as the basis for royal power, and that power will instill social and political stability in the kingdom. *The Constitutions* says that God created the 'princes of nations' who could correct the 'license of crimes,' and that 'these judges of life and death for mankind might decide, as executors in some way of Divine Providence, how each man should have fortune, estate, and status.'[32] Like the Prologue, the Prooemium, as an opening to *The Constitutions*, positions the emperor (or king) as the giver of law and as the one who must be seen as the ultimate legal authority. Frederick, like Edward, draws from God the authority to make law.

27 Kantorowicz (n 24) 236. For Aristotle's explanation of the three different kinds of rhetoric, which include forensic or judicial, deliberative, and epideictic See also Aristotle, *The Rhetoric and Poetics of Aristotle* (WR Roberts tr, EPJ Corbett ed, Random House 1984) 4–5.
28 Kantorowicz (n 24) 236.
29 Ibid.
30 JM Powell, 'Introduction,' in *The Liber Augustalis or Constitutions of Melfi Promulgated by the Emperor Frederick II for the Kingdom of Sicily in 1231* (JM Powell tr, Syracuse University Press 1971) xiv. A 'ministerialis' was an agent of the emperor who had been placed in a position of power.
31 Book I addresses public law; Book II focuses upon procedural law in civil and criminal cases, and Book III explains feudal and private law as well as stipulating the punishment of crimes. See Powell (n 30) xix.
32 'Prooemium,' in *The Liber Augustalis or Constitutions of Melfi Promulgated by the Emperor Frederick II for the Kingdom of Sicily in 1231* (JM Powell tr, Syracuse University Press, 1971) 4.

40 *John Casey Gooch*

'Either free or bond': an imagining of the legal statuses of royal subjects

The author of *Fleta* devotes a significant portion of the first book to imagining the categories and statuses of different citizens. The opening paragraph of Book I indicates that 'all men are either free or bond.'[33] The writer defines freedom as the 'natural power of every man to do what he please, unless it is forbidden by law or by force.'[34] He goes on to say that freedom can also be defined as the 'purging away of bondage,' as freemen and bondmen are 'clean contrary one to the other.'[35] His making this distinction suggests that a significant number of people were born into bondage or became villeins sometime in their lives.[36] Circumstances created this need to define and distinguish freemen from bondmen. The definition serves purposes of clarification, but it also establishes categories of both citizenry and property.

The chapter stipulates that one can also refer to bondmen as *mancipia*, as 'they are taken by the hand of their enemies.'[37] Both of these terms, *mancipia* and *servi*, imply property designations and suggest something about another person's ownership. The writer elaborates the distinction between freedmen and bondmen by indicating that, if a child is born to a bondman and freewoman, then the child is considered bond. The writer, however, does not address whether or not a child born to a freeman and bondwoman is, in turn, 'free,' given that the paternal, not maternal, relation determines the free or bond status of the child.[38]

Men, the writer explains, become 'bond by capture.'[39] The wording of the text suggests warfare as a given for the time, and the author states, 'Wars, for example, break out and captures are their consequence.'[40] The text reflects careful consideration of how a person can become 'bond' as opposed to 'free,' only then to offer a conclusion that no distinction in status exists for bondmen. The writer explains that, in addition to a person becoming bond as a result of capture, the royal court can decree that he become bond. He, however, also notes that a bondman can choose to become a monk or clerk, noting that he can obtain freeman status by choosing religious or monastic life.[41] The writer then stipulates that, should a man choose to leave that life, then 'he should be restored to his lord as a bondsman.'[42] Such precise laws governing bondmen suggest that some exigency

---

33 'Chapter 1: of persons,' in Richardson and Sayles (eds) (n 16) II.1 13.
34 'Chapter 2: of freedom,' in Richardson and Sayles (eds) (n 16) II.1 13.
35 Ibid.
36 See JH Baker, *An Introduction to English Legal History* (4th edn, OUP 2011) 468–472. A 'villein' provided services to a feudal lord in exchange for holding and occupying land.
37 'Chapter 3: of bondage' in Richardson and Sayles (eds) (n 16) II.1 13.
38 Ibid 13–14. A child born out of wedlock represents an exception. In such cases, the child took the status of the mother.
39 Ibid 14.
40 Ibid.
41 Ibid.
42 Ibid.

The dragon in the cave   41

existed that created a need for a legal statute. In other words, imagining specific definitions of 'bondmen' and 'freemen' implies that, in many cases, it had become difficult to distinguish between the two.

Confronting a troubled society: imagining penalties for violent crimes

Book I represents the only book of *Fleta* that addresses crime and criminality directly or deals with crime or criminality in an explicit way. Twenty-two chapters of Book I, twenty-one of which appear in succession, offer treatment of the issue. One of the first chapters to do so, 'Of the crime of lèse-majesté,' presents in some detail how courts must contend with the crime of treason, and it spells out, in some considerable detail, the procedure and punishment of persons found guilty of any action against the Crown. *Fleta* outlines punishment for any man found guilty of treason by decreeing that he 'shall suffer the extreme penalty, with an intensification of bodily pain' (torture).[43] The writer continues by specifying that he will suffer 'the loss of all his goods and the perpetual disherison of his heirs, and hardly indeed shall his heirs be permitted to live.'[44] The writer reimagines these penalties in order to confront oftentimes troubled English society trying to cope with violent crime; furthermore, the passages capture the king's need to confront those problems.

The chapters become even more compelling upon closer examination of the distinctions the writer of *Fleta* chose in his reimagining of English law. The writer, for example, imagines –and therefore draws – a distinction between 'murder' and 'homicide,' with one chapter titled 'Of murder' (Chapter 30) and one chapter titled 'Of homicide' (Chapter 23). Both chapters begin with a definition of each concept. Homicide is defined as 'the slaying of man by man with evil intent, and there may be bodily slaying by deed or by word.'[45] The 'Of homicide' chapter explains the act as one with intent but done in the moment; in other words, the accused intended to kill but he (or she, in some cases) did not plan the attack, and so the killing as 'homicide' was not premeditated. The 'Of murder' chapter, on the other hand, clearly defines murder as 'the secret slaying of men, committed wickedly by men's hands.' The act, moreover, 'is done to the knowledge and in the sight of none except the slayer and his accomplices and maintainers alone, so that the hue and cry will not straightway be raised.'[46] Here, the writer differentiates the act of murder from the act of homicide with the words 'secret slaying committed wickedly' and by defining murder as a premeditated act. The accused planned to kill his victim and did so with a plan and necessarily with his accomplices.

---

43 'Chapter 21: of the crime of lèse-majesté,' in Richardson and Sayles (eds) (n 16) II.1 56.
44 Ibid.
45 'Chapter 23: of homicide,' in Richardson and Sayles (eds) (n 16) II.1 60.
46 'Chapter 30: of murder,' in Richardson and Sayles (eds) (n 16) II.1 78.

42 *John Casey Gooch*

The author also qualifies that a person can commit a homicide, or 'bodily slaying,' by 'deed or by word,' meaning that he can commit the act himself or order someone else to do the killing. He then states provisions for self-defence in matters of homicide by stating that, if the accused goes before a justice and jury, and they find that 'he did the deed by mischance or while defending himself, then let him be sent back to the gaol [prison].'[47] He goes on to note that 'when the king is certified of the truth of the matter, he will deal graciously with him saving the right of any other person.'[48] 'Deal graciously' means the king can grant a pardon; the author points to the authority of the king in this matter (and in all matters), and his words imply that he trusts the king implicitly to take the most just action in matters of self-defence or homicide committed 'by mischance.'

When it comes to murder, *Fleta* emphasises the premeditated act of murder in differentiating it from homicide, but the writer makes an exception regarding 'murder' as a label for the killing. After he describes murder as 'the secret slaying of men, committed wickedly by men's hands,' the writer indicates that 'it is called murder because the slain man is reputed a *foreigner* [emphasis added] unless englishry [*anglescheria*] be presented in regard to him.'[49] This passage (and the 'Of murder' chapter, generally) describes the late medieval practice of the murder fine, which remained in place for two and half centuries – or possibly longer – and had become integral to both the administration of English criminal law and the collection of royal revenue. Frederick Hamil explains murder fine as a theory that the local community was obligated to carry out certain communal duties and could be fined for not fulfilling obligations.[50] A county or township, for example, could be held liable for robberies taking place within its borders unless it could produce those criminally responsible.[51] The king saw the administration of such justice as a source of revenue, and the Crown could assess fines 'more for the sake of the exchequer than the preservation of the king's peace.'[52] Similarly, the king held counties or townships responsible for those persons murdered in their respective areas, and, if proof of 'englishry' existed, then the township, for instance, could avoid the murder fine, or murdrum. The community, however, could only avoid the murder fine if its 'twelve best men' swore an oath that the slain person was English.[53]

Like the 'Of homicide' and 'Of murder' chapters, the chapters 'Of theft' (Chapter 36) and 'Of robbery' (Chapter 37) also reflect imaginings of legal

---

47 'Chapter 23: of homicide' 61.
48 Ibid.
49 'Chapter 30: of murder,' in Richardson and Sayles (eds) (n 16) II.1 78.
50 FC Hamil, 'Presentment of englishry and the murder fine' (1937) 12 *Speculum* 285. For more recent study on the origin of the murder fine, see BR O'Brien, 'From Mordor to Murdrum: the preconquest origin and Norman revival of the murder fine' (1996) 71 *Speculum* 321–357.
51 It is the so-called 'frankpledge:' see J Hudson, *The Formation of the English Common Law* (2nd edn, Abingdon 2018) 53–58.
52 Hamil (n 50) 285.
53 Hamil (n 50) 289.

The dragon in the cave   43

categories to address persistent crime problems. The writer opens the 'Of theft' chapter with an explicit definition that 'theft is the fraudulent appropriation of the property of another, with the intention of stealing, against the owner's will.'[54] He then distinguishes between two different kinds, stating 'there is manifest theft and secret theft.'[55] Manifest theft takes place when the perpetrator is 'arrested seised of stolen property, hand-having and back-bearing, and has been pursued by him to whom the property belonged, who is called the sacrobar.'[56]

In a lengthy exegesis, the writer describes manifest theft as both a civil and criminal matter. If the accused cannot 'deny the theft, in the presence of the coroner,' then 'he shall be condemned to death, unless he can warrant the goods.'[57] Here, the accused can be found guilty if he cannot justify his right to those goods. The criminality of his actions becomes clear, and, as the writer has stated, he receives the death sentence. The accused, however, has recourse according to this chapter. He can 'warrant the goods,' meaning he can vouch for the warranty of those goods, or he must prove his right to possess them. The writer discusses manifest theft at length and acknowledges the various gradations of such criminality while once again offering his exceptions and qualifications. Much of this discussion focuses on warrant and warranty, which pertained to proof of the transfer and exchange of goods. He explains that clerks, for instance, must sometimes justify that they had indeed given a warranty to the accused for the alleged stolen goods. The writer points out, though, that cases of fraud did exist, and that a clerk engaging in fraudulent behaviour 'shall be required to defend himself as principal, and the clerk shall be committed to gaol [prison] for his knavery and put to ransom.'[58]

The 'On theft' chapter not only qualifies actions the court should take against unscrupulous clerks issuing false warranties, but one of its paragraphs addresses how the law should treat the wives of accused thieves. The writer states clearly that a thief's wife 'will not be held responsible for her husband's delict,' and the penalty should only affect the one who committed the act.[59] The following sentence then, in a somewhat paradoxical turn, indicates a wife 'should neither accuse her husband nor assent to his felony,' but 'she is required to hinder him so far as she is able.'[60] The writer does *not* stipulate a penalty for the 'accusing' or 'assenting,' and, furthermore, he proposes no punishment for failing to 'hinder him so far as she is able.' Hinder would imply her a priori knowledge of his crime, and the statute makes a wife, in some way, culpable or responsible for her husband's actions.

54 'Chapter 36: of theft,' in Richardson and Sayles (eds) (n 16) II.1 90.
55 Ibid.
56 Ibid.
57 Ibid. 'Coroner' refers to a type of law enforcement official with quasi-judicial authority.
58 'Chapter 36: of theft' in Richardson and Sayles (eds) (n 16) II.1 92.
59 Ibid.
60 Ibid.

44   *John Casey Gooch*

The writer does go on to articulate conditions for liability for husbands and wives who are partners in crime. He simply says that the wife 'will be held jointly liable with her husband,' and that 'partners in crime' should also be 'partners in penalty,' assuming the stolen property is located 'under the wife's lock and key.'[61] He also states, however, that, should the stolen property 'perchance be found in her hand,' then 'she alone will be held liable,' regardless of whether or not her husband actually committed the crime.[62] In other words, if the stolen property is located anywhere on her body or on her person, then she will face charges and penalties. This paragraph points to the lower status of women, and even necessarily makes the wife liable for her husband's crime. It makes wives responsible not only for their own behaviour, but also for their husband's behaviour. These statutes treat women with fewer rights in that they can essentially be accused of their husbands' wrongdoings and suffer penalties for those wrongdoings. Such statutes illustrate that a woman experienced difficulty asserting her personhood apart from her husband, thereby exemplifying her lack of power under this particular law.

The author then presents two new categorical distinctions that distinguish two different kinds of theft; that is, theft can be 'of a great thing and of a small.'[63] He explains that a thief taking something small means that the accused took the item using stealth, and that it was worth 'twelve pennyworth or under,' but, for such offenses, 'no one will be condemned to death.'[64] The writer decrees that the perpetrator of secret theft should only serve for a limited time in the pillory, or stocks, but he should not suffer any punishment more severe.[65] The writer, however, indicates that, if the value of the stolen item be more than 'twelve pennyworth,' then the thief would be put to death for the 'theft of the chattels,' or property.[66] The chapter 'Of robbery' (Chapter 37) follows 'Of theft' in succession; as with manifest and secret theft, however, it does not explicitly define the distinction between robbery and theft. Based on the author's description, though, one can assume that robbery implies that a perpetrator took property by force, not surreptitiously or by stealth. The writer exemplifies robbery as someone 'coming with his force [and] wickedly and feloniously and against the king's peace took from him in robbery a hundred shillings, a three-pence and a horse of such-and-such price.'[67]

In these chapters, the writer adopts a procedural attitude that is typical in common-law legal literature: it focuses on the procedure by which one can bring appeal against an accused perpetrator of a crime as opposed to more precise explanations of categorical distinctions. Both of these chapters, moreover, illustrate a

---

61 Ibid.
62 Ibid. See also JL Herskowitz, 'Tort liability between husband and wife: the interspousal immunity doctrine' (1966) 21 *University of Miami Law Review* 423–456.
63 'Chapter 36: of theft,' in Richardson and Sayles (eds) (n 16) II.1 92.
64 Ibid.
65 Ibid. The writer uses the example of the thief surreptitiously cutting the straps of a purse and then stealing the purse.
66 'Chapter 36: of theft,' in Richardson and Sayles (eds) (n 16) II.1 92.
67 'Chapter 37: of robbery,' in Richardson and Sayles (eds) (n 16) II.195.

The dragon in the cave   45

growing concern over private property and, more to the point, the protection of individual private property. The writer struggles with the concept of ownership and how one can establish ownership in the event of a theft or robbery. Repeatedly, in both chapters, *Fleta* specifies death as punishment for anyone found guilty of these crimes. The death penalty represents a deterrent, but it also functions as evidence of a society in which potentially large numbers of people were stealing to survive, as well as exemplifying efforts of a central governmental authority seeking to exercise greater control over criminality.[68] 'Of robbery' and 'Of theft' suggest the author's efforts to imagine his legal world and legal distinctions comprising it.

Litigating possessory interests: imagining of novel disseisin

Fleta pays considerable attention to the possessory assizes. An extensive treatment of landholding comes as no surprise, especially given that ownership of land and property served, without question, the upper echelons of English feudal society. The person, in this case, became a tenant, and, assuming he fulfilled services to the lord, an heir would likely succeed him.[69]

It would make sense that, by the late thirteenth century, the practice had grown and necessitated a reimagining so that the courts could appropriately address illegal seizures of land. The author of *Fleta* provides in-depth discussion on disseisin and the procedure for issuing assizes to dispossess landowners whom someone had claimed had no legal right to the land. At the beginning of Book IV, Chapter 1 ('Of real actions'), he stipulates that disseisin 'is done in many ways, and it does not matter whether it is done to the owner when he is present or to an agent or to his household when he is absent.'[70] This paragraph goes even further, with *Fleta* qualifying that, 'not only is a man disseised when he is in any way ejected forcibly, wrongfully and without judgement from his seisin of his tenement,' but he can also be removed from the land while he travels.[71] If someone else enters into possession, as the *Fleta* puts it, an individual can repel him 'forcibly, either by himself alone or taking his men with him.'[72] The chapter continues to identify all the ways in which some individual or group can dispossess someone occupying the land; despite this, *Fleta* makes no judgement about the legality or illegality of disseisin. The writer, rather, establishes all the conditions under which disseisin can take place.

---

68 Several references in Book I of *Fleta* establish jurisdictional rules indicating where certain matters should be referred in the kingdom. In 'Chapter 36: of theft,' in Richardson and Sayles (eds) (n 16) II.1 93, the writer explains that every sheriff in the kingdom 'defers to a command from the justices of Newgate in London.' The passage cites Newgate as a kind of centralised legal authority when it is unclear where an accused perpetrator should be tried.

69 J Hudson, 'Maitland and Anglo-Norman law,' in J Hudson (ed), *The History of English Law: Centenary Essays on 'Pollock and Maitland'* (OUP 1996), 42–4.

70 'Chapter 1: of real actions,' in Richardson and Sayles (eds) (n 16) III.3 46.

71 Ibid.

72 Ibid.

46 *John Casey Gooch*

Chapter 2 of Book IV (notably titled 'Chapter 2: Of the remedy for dispossession') does establish remedies for dispossession so that the dispossessed tenant is granted some recourse should he find himself without possession of his land. *Fleta* gives rules for 'lawfully' disseising the disseisor by stating that those

> who intend to eject disseisors should make such provision for expelling them immediately while the wrongdoing is fresh so that they do not allow the wrong of disseisin to grow cold by their sufferance, indifference, negligence, weakness, apathy or failure to provide aid.[73]

Should a tenant risk the 'wrong of disseisin to grow cold,' then he might also lose possession of 'both kinds,' natural and civil, 'while the disseisor begins to acquire both and thus cannot lawfully be ejected without a judgment of the court.'[74] *Fleta* carefully puts forth timeframes and constraints for the original tenant to act, with the author deliberately accounting for all possibilities and conditions.

Placing these kinds of time constraint indicates legal prescription by creating time limits. Legal prescription relates to the role that time plays in establishing (and de-establishing) certain rights, as well as the parameter or constraint (e.g., time constraint) normally inherent within a statute. 'Chapter 5: Of the writ of novel disseisin' continues putting forth these kinds of parameter, and it outlines the procedure by which jurists will issue an assize and how the sheriff, for example, will go about delivering it. The chapter also explains the roles of the courts, the bailiffs, and the serjeants (*sic*) of the king, as well as those who bring the complaint and wish to dispossess the tenant of his property. The author also notes that the writ of novel disseisin must have a time limit and does not extend beyond that limit.[75] *Fleta* upholds the argument by stating that, 'time is a means of getting rid of an obligation and an action because time runs against the slothful and those who are scornful of their right.'[76] The plaintiff, therefore, may lose 'his right of action and his seisin by his negligence,' and the person holding the land would engender an exception against that plaintiff.[77]

In his more recent work on novel disseisin, Joshua Tate addresses the influence of the *ius commune*, or the blending of Roman and canon law, on disseisin law, and he argues that this influence may have been greater than other historians once thought. Tate's analysis indicates that Roman jurists carefully distinguished between ownership, or the title of land, and possession, the actual enjoyment of it.[78] He investigates whether or not this distinction also appears in early English

---

73 'Chapter 2: of the remedy for dispossession,' in Richardson and Sayles (eds) (n 16) IV 50.
74 Ibid.
75 'Chapter 5: of the writ of novel disseisin,' in Richardson and Sayles (eds) (n 16) V 58.
76 Ibid.
77 Ibid.
78 JC Tate, 'Ownership and possession in the early common law' (2006) 48 *American Journal of Legal History* 281.

The dragon in the cave   47

common law, hypothesising that, if present, it might signify that 'Roman ideas had some bearing on the development of the English system.'[79]

Ultimately, Tate concludes that right and seisin in English common law 'were not interchangeable with Roman ownership and possession.'[80] Whether or not Roman canon law 'influenced' common law, Tate posits, depends upon how one defines 'influence.' He argues that, if one defines influence as appropriating the 'specific tools of another legal system,' then that kind of influence most likely did not take place in English common law.[81] The other definition of influence, however, has implications for the current study. Influence occurred, Tate notes, if one defines it as 'drawing on a concept from one system and building a new framework that departed in significant ways from the original system.'[82] The *Fleta* author's imagining of legality coincided with other imaginings of law found in other similar texts, such as *Bracton* and *Britton*, with all of those texts contributing to imagining the legal world of late thirteenth-century England.

Fleta in the thirteenth-century legal imagination

Fleta existed in a milieu with other late thirteenth-century legal and statutory texts, such as *Hengham Magna* and *Fet Asaver*, both of which are closely related to each other. The key to understanding the relationship between these two texts, as Thomas McSweeney has surmised, lies with Henry de Bracton's *De Legibus*.[83] He argues that the relationship between Bracton's work, *Hengham Magna*, and *Fet Asaver* 'opens up exciting possibilities for the study of the legal-literary culture of the justices and clerks of the royal courts.'[84] McSweeney sees *Fet Asaver*, in particular, as a treatise that broke with *Bracton* in ushering in a new legal literature and offering a novel line of legal thought that broke with Romanist tradition and, more precisely, Justinian's *Digest*.[85] In summarising TFT Plucknett's work, he relates that *Fet Asaver* 'represented the sensibilities of the new professional pleaders, the serjeants, laymen who had little use for learned tomes that attempted to explain English law in terms of the two learned laws,' thereby suggesting a shift away from Bracton's treatise, which was written for justices with training in Roman and canon law.[86]

Hengham Magna represents one of two treatises traditionally 'attributed to Ralph de Hengham (*c.* 1235–1311):' originally a clerk to justices, he then became a justice himself, serving as Chief Justice of the King's Bench and the Common

---

79 Tate (n 78) 282.
80 Tate (n 78) 313.
81 Ibid.
82 Ibid.
83 TJ McSweeney, 'Creating a literature for the king's courts in the later thirteenth century: *Hengham Magna, Fet Asaver*, and *Bracton*,' (2016) 37 *The Journal of Legal History* 42.
84 Ibid.
85 McSweeney (n 83) 67.
86 McSweeney (n 83) 67.

48 *John Casey Gooch*

Bench.[87] (The other treatise traditionally attributed to Hengham is another late thirteenth-century treatise known as *Hengham Parva.*)[88] *Fet Asaver*, however, 'appears in over eighty manuscripts of the late thirteenth and early fourteenth centuries,' and, similar to *Hengham Magna*, 'it was copied into many of the small-format miscellanies that we often call statute books.'[89] According to McSweeney, however, *Fet Asaver* differs from *Hengham Magna* in that 'it is written in French, the language spoken in the court, and makes no claim to being a civilian *summa*,' or a text written with the intent to make it accessible to a wider audience.[90]

Like *Fleta*, *Hengham Magna* became a procedural text reflecting an author's imaginings of several issues, including complaints and answers, as well as delaying tactics a litigant could use in court. Most of the treatise 'takes its reader through all the twists and turns of bringing an action by writ of right, from acquiring the writ onward.'[91] A 'writ of right' pertains to a common law writ for restoring property to its owner if another party held that property. McSweeney explains that *Hengham Magna* offered up twelve different variants of the writ of right most likely taken from the register of writs.[92] *Hengham Magna*'s treatment of the writ of right for restoring lands to owners necessarily paralleled the treatment of seisin and novel disseisin in *Fleta*, particularly related to how the treatises expressed the procedures for issuing a writ and under what circumstances an owner could possess or repossess land.

McSweeney's concluding remarks on *Hengham Magna* and *Fet Asaver* provide something valuable when one considers legal imagination as it pertains to *Fleta*. Assuming that two different clerks wrote the two treatises under consideration in his study, we may infer that: (1) these books 'were being written within a small circle of people who were part of the judicial establishment and that those people had close ties to each other';[93] (2) these clerks seemingly had access to each other's writings.[94] McSweeney notes that solitary authors did not perform the 'textual production of the royal courts,' but that clerks and justices 'in dialogue with each other' produced these texts. He also emphasises the relationship between these texts as a critical factor in understanding their development.[95] Under these kinds of assumption, it becomes less difficult to argue that the author of *Fleta* was also connected to other clerks and members of the royal court preparing statutory treatises between 1250 and 1300.

Fleta also shares a common discourse – as well as common concerns over troubled times – with *Britton* – that is, another treatise written at approximately the same time and one that Edward I, himself, likely commissioned. According to

87 McSweeney (n 83) 43.
88 Ibid.
89 McSweeney (n 83) 52.
90 Ibid.
91 McSweeney (n 83) 48.
92 Ibid.
93 McSweeney (n 83) 68.
94 Ibid.
95 McSweeney (n 83) 68.

Plucknett, *Britton* 'is a rather different book' in that it was authored in French, not Latin, and reflects the form of a code, not simply a collection of statutes.[96] Plucknett raises the possibility that Edward I had 'entertained the idea' of codifying English law based upon the fact that he had done something similar with the Statute of Wales in 1284.[97] Furthermore, *Britton* had 'enjoyed a great popularity for many centuries,' whereas *Fleta*, as a legal treatise, was less successful; the likely reason for this lack of success probably lies in the notion that, over time, common lawyers read Latin with less ease and, therefore, turned to the more familiar French of *Britton*.[98] *Britton* also shares with *Fleta* the question of its authorship. The name itself lacks clarity, although many have taken it to suggest John le Breton, the Bishop of Hereford, as its author. Plucknett disagrees with this assertion, arguing that most scholars have agreed that no real evidence exists to support John le Breton as the author of *Britton*.[99]

Upon cursory examination, *Britton*'s organisational pattern is very comparable to *Fleta*'s structure. It opens with an introduction and is organised according to chapters, with each chapter titled in a similar way to *Fleta*. Every chapter begins with 'de' ('of' in English), which is followed by a brief descriptor of the chapter's content (e.g., 'Of coroners,' 'Of rape' or 'Of homicides'). The treatise is much shorter than *Fleta*, containing only twenty-five chapters including the introduction; its first chapter is titled 'Of coroners,' and its concluding chapter is titled 'Of appeals of mayhems.'[100] Both *Britton* and *Fleta* explain specific laws and then the procedure that justices must follow in the event someone violates the law surrounding homicide, murder, rape, larceny, and so on. Like *Fleta*, *Britton* makes definitional distinctions between crimes such as 'homicide' and 'murder,' but it mostly establishes the laws governing crimes without explicitly addressing civil matters, namely seisin, disseisin, and writ of right. Nevertheless, *Britton* represents another text that helped establish legal procedure in late thirteenth-century England.

Fleta's later influence on legal imagining

A question remains, however, as to whether or not *Fleta* retains any historical significance and impact on legal imagination after 1300. Generally, the statutes from *Fleta* were applied in future centuries and ostensibly still inform present-day English (and likely US) law. More precisely, though, *Fleta*'s author articulated themes, particularly in the introduction, that resonated with key historical figures in, for example, the seventeenth century.

---

96 Plucknett (n 2) 265.
97 Ibid. The Statute of Wales established the constitutional basis for Wales from 1284 until 1536.
98 Plucknett (n 2) 266.
99 Ibid.
100 See *Britton. Containing the antient pleas of the crown, translated; and illustrated with references, notes, and antient records* (R Kelham tr, H Woodfall and W. Straham, Law-Printers to the King's most excellent Majesty 1762). Reprinted by Eighteenth-Century Collections Online Print Editions, 2010.

50   *John Casey Gooch*

A case for this resonation is that of Thomas Hobbes and his keen interest in the ideas from *Fleta* as those ideas pertained to the monarch's sovereign power and the inalienability of that sovereignty, which represent dominant themes of Hobbes's *Leviathan*. Kinch Hoekstra explains that Hobbes's *The Elements of Law*, which was published in 1640, a few years before *Leviathan*, gives his first treatment of the rights of sovereignty and the inalienability of such rights.[101]

In *The Elements of Law*, Hobbes argued 'that the sovereign must retain the legislative power and the power to ensure the laws are observed,' and that 'appointing and limiting magistrates and ministers' would become, according to Hobbes, 'an inseparable part of the same sovereignty, to which the sum of all judicature and execution hath already been annexed.'[102] For Hobbes, the sovereign power 'must have impunity,' but it cannot possess impunity if it delegates any of the essential powers; these rights of sovereignty, moreover, 'are necessarily absolute' and 'cannot be limited or separated.'[103] Hoekstra cites Hobbes description of the sovereign monarch's rights as the power to make laws and levy taxes as well as to make peace and war, command the militia, and prohibit the making of other laws.[104] Hobbes steadfastly maintained these rights as indivisible, and the sovereign monarch must always retain them, otherwise he will be 'thereby divers times thrust out of their possession.'[105]

Hoekstra notes that Hobbes, in *Leviathan*, withheld information about his sources, but he was explicit about engaging the works of Edward Coke and John Selden, particularly as those sources addressed the issue of the monarch's inalienable sovereign rights. Hoekstra ponders the possibility that, 'if Hobbes underscored the inalienability of sovereign rights at this time, he may have been provoked by a lawyerly treatment of the topic.'[106] He then raises the possibility of John Selden's well-known dissertation on *Fleta* as an 'impetus' for this treatment of sovereign rights.[107] Hoekstra briefly relates the story of Hobbes's exclusive friendship with Selden, and Hobbes himself, in *Leviathan*, refers to Selden's dissertation on *Fleta* as a 'most excellent Treatise.'[108] His praise for Selden's work leads Hoekstra to believe that 'Selden may have been on Hobbes's mind particularly when he was writing about the inalienability of sovereign powers.'[109] Hobbes, through Selden's dissertation, became especially attracted to *Fleta*'s treatment of the inalienable rights and privileges of the king

---

101 K Hoekstra, '"Leviathan" in its intellectual context' (2015) 74 *Journal of the History of Ideas* 243.
102 T Hobbes, *The Elements of Law Natural and Politic* as quoted in Hoekstra (n 111) 243.
103 Hoekstra (n 101) 243.
104 Hoekstra (n 101) 244.
105 Hobbes, *Elements*, quoted in Hoekstra (n 101) 244.
106 Hoekstra (n 101) 247.
107 Hoekstra (n 101) 248.
108 Hobbes, quoted in Hoekstra (n 101) 248.
109 Ibid.

that could not be divided or minimised, and, thus, the king could not diminish his own authority.[110]

Selden, however, had taken issue with *Fleta* – as well as with Bracton and others – over its treatment of the *lex regia*, a Roman legal concept pertaining to the people turning over power to the emperor.[111] Selden perceived a 'distortion of the *lex regia*' in *Fleta*, and he argued that *Fleta* had departed 'from reliable and authoritative sources available' that described how power was transferred from the people to the ruler.[112] The people, therefore, were 'wholly stripped of rule.'[113]

According to Hoekstra, Selden said that the *Fleta* author, for instance, framed his 'interpretation to fit the English situation and the power of Parliament, not wanting to incur the people's displeasure or diminish the power of their lawyerly caste.'[114] Hoekstra indicates that Selden argued for the proper interpretation of *lex regia* as the Roman people giving up sovereignty to their rulers, but, after making this argument, Selden dismantled the notion that Roman law was relevant or had authority in England.[115] He then claims it possible that Hobbes wanted to avoid 'the danger, the clutter, and the indeterminacy of the legal historical argument by postulating a kind of theoretical principle without the ambiguity of the *lex regia*' and with an even greater 'nullifying power' than *Fleta* had given it.[116]

The one time, according to Hoekstra, that Hobbes quoted from *Fleta*, 'he did so precisely to assert sovereign inalienability.'[117] Hoekstra's footnote indicates that Hobbes explicitly cited *Fleta* in *A Dialogue Between a Philosopher and a Student, of the Common Laws of England*.[118] Hobbes noted, 'Again you'll find in *Fleta* that Liberties [*sic*] though granted by the King, if they tend to the hinderance of Justice, or subversion of the Regal Power, were not to be used, nor allowed.'[119] Essentially, Hobbes chose to ignore Selden's analysis of *Fleta* in favour of his own interpretation of the text as related to monarchical sovereignty. *Fleta*'s expression of sovereign authority served Hobbes's agenda, and the concept manifested in *Leviathan*, one of the most significant treatises on western political theory.

The legal imagining reflected in *Fleta* shared imaginings with other related thirteenth-century common-law treatises. *Fet Asaver, Hengham Magna*, and *Britton* parallel *Fleta* in both structure and language, suggesting a common discourse of law in the 1200s. Furthermore, all these treatises borrowed from authors of other previously written texts, such as those of Henry de Bracton, Ranulf de Glanvill, and Justinian. *Fleta*, as a compendium of statutes, suggested something

---

110 Ibid. See also TFT Plucknett, *Early English Legal Literature* (UP 1958) for additional discussion of the king's authority and inalienable rights and privileges of the king.
111 Hoekstra (n 101) 249.
112 Ibid.
113 Ibid.
114 Ibid.
115 Ibid.
116 Hoekstra (n 101) 249.
117 Ibid.
118 T Hobbes, *A Dialogue Between a Philosopher and a Student, of the Common Laws of England* (A Cromartie ed, Clarendon Press 2005).
119 Hobbes, *A Dialogue* (n 118) 37.

52   *John Casey Gooch*

about procedures to which the legal community should adhere, but, at the same time, it captured a particular imagining of English common law. That imagining extended its influence beyond the thirteenth century by quite likely inspiring the work of Thomas Hobbes and a political philosophy that affected western civilisation for years after the Enlightenment.

American Supreme Court justice and twentieth-century legal philosopher Oliver Wendell Holmes once said about the practice and study of law:

> The rational study of law is still to a large extent the study of history. History must be a part of the study, because without it we cannot know the precise scope of rules which it is our business to know. It is a part of the rational study, because it is the first step toward an enlightened scepticism [*sic*], that is, towards a deliberate reconsideration of the worth of those rules. When you get the dragon out of his cave on to the plain and in the daylight, you can count his teeth and claws, and see just what his strength is. But to get him out is only the first step. The next is either to kill him, or to tame him and make him a useful animal.[120]

Holmes criticised the overemphasis on history in law and thought that law, in his day, had become essentially a study of history. He argued that lawyers, judges, and law students should embrace the law as its own discipline with intrinsic value. In doing so, the legal profession needed to unleash the 'dragon' and then, ideally, 'tame' him, thereby making 'him a useful animal.'

Holmes's analogy of the law as a deadly, mythological beast that breathes fire captures how he *imagined* the study and practice of law, although it failed to consider that the legal history of any society is very much part of that dragon in the cave. *Fleta* contributes to understanding the 'dragon' that was English medieval common law and the impact of a particular imagining of it.

---

120 OW Holmes, Jr, *The Path of the Law* (first published 1897; American Classics Library 2012) 8.

4 The apotheosis of King Charles I

Ian Ward

NEWCASTLE UNIVERSITY

We will start at the Banqueting House on Whitehall. Half a millennium ago, Whitehall Palace was the primary royal residence in the city of London. A fire in 1619 destroyed much of the existing wooden Tudor construction. An excuse to build something new and flashy. King James commissioned the very fashionable Inigo Jones to design something in the Palladian style. Which he did for £15,600. Finished in 1622. Though a bit of decorating remained. James died in 1625. It was left to his son Charles to finish the job. Most obviously, something for the ceiling in the main hall on the upper floor. Someone suggested Peter Paul Rubens, presently in London. A good choice, though hardly cheap. At some point in 1629, Rubens accepted the commission and returned to Antwerp.

Six years later, over came a set of nine canvasses. Brilliant colours, but the wrong size, a Flemish inch not being the same as an English. A year spent sorting out, and then up they went. A grateful King Charles sent over a large gold chain and completed the scheduled payments. It had cost a further £3,000 in all. But it was splendid, and Charles rarely worried much about cost, especially when it came to buying art.[1] As to Rubens's masterpiece, the three central canvasses were dedicated to the memory of his father, entitled in turn, *The Wise Rule of James I, The Apotheosis of James I*, and *The Union of Crowns*. Some ironies approach.

The Banqueting House was just not just for banquets. A principle court room, it was also used for formal receptions, masques, and other dramatic performances. And as a waiting room for kings about to be executed. Which brings us to 30 January 1649, the last day in the life of King Charles I. Shortly before breakfast Charles had been awakened by Colonel Hacker, in command of the guard at St James Palace, and escorted through the park to the Banqueting House. Up the stairs to his former bedroom, where he was offered a glass of port and some bread. And then into the hall. Everything was ready. A raised scaffold had been erected

---

1 He was, at the time, bidding for the famed Gonzaga art collection, lots of Titian and Raphael, plus Mantegna's vast *Triumph of Caesar*. Charles was a particular fan of Mantegna. He got it, of course, for £20,000. Charles generally did, and generally paid too much, because any seller knew that the King of England would spend whatever it took. Charles was not the only fan of Mantegna. When the royal collection was sold off in 1649, Cromwell kept the *Triumph of Caesar*. A famed republic general. The rest went. The former royal plumber was paid off with one of the Titians.

54 Ian Ward

outside, where a hooded executioner awaited. Along with a couple of personal chaplains, an expectant crowd, and a troop of grim-faced New Model cavalry, there to make sure that everyone behaved.

But everything was not, in fact, quite ready. So, Charles was invited to take a seat, and some more port. And wait. And then wait a bit more, and then a bit more still. A polite man, he apparently made little complaint. We can only assume that he glanced around, and probably upwards. And maybe smiled, perhaps in appreciation of his own good taste, but perhaps also in appreciation of the finer ironies of the moment. After all, it was his dad who had, in large part, got him into the mess. Putting silly ideas about the 'divine right' of kings into his head and then going on and on about a 'union' of crowns. If Charles had not decided to try to force the Prayer Book on his Scottish subjects in 1637, he would not have ended up losing the so-called Bishop's Wars, or very probably the English civil wars that followed.

But why the wait? All had been going fine until it occurred to someone that executing King Charles I would not, in fact, bring the monarchy to an end. It would simply mean that his son would become King Charles II in his stead. The person of the monarch may die, but the office does not. And no-one had thought to abolish the monarchy. Or much else, in truth. Which is why no-one had thought to abolish the House of Lords either, or the Church. It was assumed, in essence, that the Republic would be instantiated by default. Fortunately, the House of Commons was quorate, and so an Act could be rushed through declaring it unlawful to proclaim a successor. A practical expedient, if hardly comprehensive. But that is the nature of revolutions. Not always that well thought through.

Finally, at some point around 2pm, they were ready to proceed. Charles stepped on to the scaffold. Draped in black. Unsure as to how he might react, iron staples had been driven into the wooden floor. If need be Charles could be restrained. But there was no need. Charles Stuart was ready for his martyrdom. Chilly, snowflakes gently falling. Not wanting to be thought fearful, Charles had taken the precaution of a second shirt, to stop him shivering. Time for a few last words. Scaffold speeches were part of the custom. The surrounding New Model troopers had been instructed to clap to drown out his voice. But William Juxon heard.

As the King's chaplain, Juxon was there to provide reassurance and consolation. Later that night he refined his draft of their final conversation and sent it to the publisher John Rushworth. A few days later it was on the streets. 'There is but one stage more,' Juxon had told his king as he knelt, 'This stage is turbulent and troublesome. It is a short one. But you may consider it, it will soon carry you a very great way. It will carry you from earth to heaven, and there you shall find your great joy the prize. You haste to a crown of glory.' To which Charles had replied, 'I go from a corruptible to an incorruptible crown, where no disturbance can be.'[2] Or so we are told. A short, but brilliant, closing speech on what had been the most trying, and dramatic, of days.

2 T Royle, *Civil War: The Wars of Three Kingdoms* (Abacus 2005) 500–01.

The apotheosis of King Charles I   55

Chat over, Charles had taken off his cloak, and his Order of the Garter, and asked Juxon to ensure that his hair was tucked into his white cap, probably in the hope that it might help the executioner to avoid the kind of hideously botched decapitation that had been inflicted upon his grandma, Mary Queen of Scots. He then laid down his head and spread his arms, as in a crucifixion, to signal that he was ready. No-one ever discovered the identity of the executioner. The official hangman, Richard Brandon, declined to serve. Royalist propagandists would later venture that it might even have been Cromwell himself, or maybe the hated puritan divine, Hugh Peter. Or a woman, some surmised, wearing, it seems, a very improbable beard. If so, she got lucky. It was a clinical piece of butchery. One blow – and the head was cleanly severed. At, a later post-mortem supposed, the second vertebrae.

The formal proceedings were over. They had started barely a month earlier, with the passage of the trial ordinance on 6 January 1649. Though it might be supposed that the preparation had begun with Colonel Pride's purge of Parliament on 6 December 1648. The trial had commenced on 20 January and concluded on 25 January 1649. Longer than hoped. But Charles had proved to be a recalcitrant witness, and the trial had wandered off script repeatedly. But if the trial, like the execution, had ended up being a bit more of a hassle than expected, it was nothing compared with what was to follow. Decapitating the king was the easy bit. Next came the appeal. Untrammelled by legal formality, it would last for centuries, embroiling generation after generation of poets and historians.

We, though, are concerned only with the very start of this process. And with three particular texts. The first, entitled *Eikon Basilike*, or *The King's Book*, was already at the printers by the time Charles stepped on to his scaffold. The second, entitled *Eikonoclastes*, was written in confutation and appeared 8 months later. The third, which came a year later, was different again. Recently appraised as the 'greatest political poem' in the English language, *An Horation Ode Upon Cromwell's Return from Ireland* was the work of a hitherto 'cavalier' poet named Andrew Marvell.[3] Each was about the events of 30 January 1649. But each was very different. Because making sense of the King's execution was difficult. And it was going to take an awful lot of imagination.

The King's Book

Royalist presses had started templating 'King Charles the Martyr' long before the axe fell on the afternoon of the 30 January 1649. *A True Relation of the King's Speech to the Lady Elizabeth and the Duke of Gloucester, the day before his death* was circulating by the day after. An 'abundance of tears' from the Lady Elizabeth, and some fighting talk from the young Duke, promising to be 'torn in pieces' before he agreed to become king, ahead of his exiled brothers Charles and James.[4] Rushworth's account of the scaffold speeches was pending. *A Handerkerchief for*

3 N Smith, *Andrew Marvell: The Chameleon* (Yale UP 2012) 80.
4 *Eikon Basilike: or, the King's Book* (E Almack ed, De la More 1904) 296–97.

56   *Ian Ward*

Loyal Mourners, attributed to the later Dean of Worcester, Thomas Walmstry, was likewise available by 2 February.[5] A literary complement to the familiar custom. And an opportunity, indeed, for those unable to attend on 30 January to still feel part of the experience.

The most renowned of the regicide hagiographies was though, without doubt, the *Eikon Basilike: The Portraiture of His Sacred Majesty in His Solitudes and Sufferings*.[6] Or the *King's Book*, as it became more popularly known. Precisely when the *Eikon* hit the streets remains uncertain. Some have supposed that it was circulating later on 30 January, possibly even in the hours before the execution.[7] First editions were printed and distributed by Richard Royston, of 'Ivie Lane.' Royston had form, having been charged with printing 'scandalous' books in 1645 and duly sent to the Fleet prison. He would be again, a few months later in 1649; on this occasion bound over 'not to print or sell any unlicensed or scandalous books and pamphlets.' Royston later claimed to have received the manuscript of the *Eikon* on 23 December, having been alerted to its existence as early as October. It seems probable that any version circulating on 30 January was an advance copy, to be followed by the revised copy, sold on the streets by hawkers. Royston later confirmed that this second issue, which sold out in a couple of days, ran to 2,000 copies. A third issue was then distributed, most probably to trusted booksellers. George Thomason annotated a copy of this third issue for his collection, dated 9 February.

Authorship remains a matter of some controversy. At the Restoration, the newly appointed Bishop of Exeter, John Gauden, was quick to assert a claim, suggesting that he had begun drafting the work as early as summer 1647. Clarendon leant some credence.[8] So too Dr Walker, in his *True Account of the Authour of a Book, entitled Eikon Basilike*, published in 1692. The quality of prose has led some to suspect the involvement of another Restoration bishop, Jeremy Taylor. A protégé of Archbishop Laud and chaplain in ordinary to the King, Taylor is known to have been in London in Autumn 1648, though the extent to which he attended the King remains a matter of conjecture.[9]

5 Warmstry was a moderate Anglican royalist with an apparently wide range of interests. An essay on church decoration in 1641 was followed by a defence of Christmas in 1648. Ten years later he published perhaps his most renowned work, a conversion narrative entitled *The Baptized Turk*.

6 In early prints, the title was given in the classical Greek, probably as an attempt to throw off the censors, for a day or two at least.

7 Thus, it has been suggested, 'literally' taking the 'place of the king.' See ES Wheeler, '*Eikon Basilike* and the rhetoric of self-representation' in TN Corns (ed), *The Royal Image: Representations of Charles I* (OUP 1999) 122.

8 Somewhat begrudgingly. Gauden was never satisfied. No sooner was he appointed to Exeter than he was agitating for a wealthier bishopric, not so far away. Hoping for Winchester, in the end he got Worcester. Clarendon, like many, found the whingeing prelate thoroughly annoying. But he did concede that he was probably lead author of the *Eikon*.

9 As is the rumour that he received the king's watch and some jewellery in appreciation of his services. Taylor was renowned for his devotional writings, most famously perhaps *Holy Living and Holy Dying*, originally published as two essays in 1650 and 1651. Later admirers would include John Wesley and Samuel Taylor Coleridge.

The apotheosis of King Charles I 57

This leaves us to conjecture the extent of Charles's involvement. The later Bishop of Winchester, Peter Mews, suggested that the king had already begun dictating some 'reflections' to his secretary Sir Edward Nicholas as early as summer 1645. Mews suggested that early drafts were seized with the King's Cabinet at the battle of Naseby.[10] Another of the King's personal chaplains, Dr Gorge, attested the same, and that Charles was especially perturbed at the loss of his manuscript. It became commonplace to suppose that Charles had wiled away his spare hours at Carisbrooke recovering a draft. Colonel Hammond, the governor of the castle, later confirmed that it was 'writ when he was my prisoner.' William Levet, a groom of the bedchamber, likewise confirmed that the text was 'Writ with his Majesty's own hand' while in captivity on the Isle of Wight.[11] The testaments came later of course.[12] Back in spring 1649, the inference was plain. The *Eikon* articulated the personal reflections of its martyred king, the word 'personal' being everything.

This perception was reinforced by the famous frontispiece to the first edition, an engraving by William Marshall, inspired almost certainly by Titian's *Saint Catherine of Alexandria*.[13] The king is seen kneeling in prayer, an earthly crown at his feet, clutching a crown of thorns, his eyes fixed reverently on the heavenly crown which awaits.[14] Other versions of the *Eikon* would incorporate different images.[15] But it is Marshall's engraving that inscribed itself on the memory of royalist England. Thereafter follow twenty-eight chapters, from the 'calling' of the king's 'last Parliament' in 1641 through to successive captivities at Holdenby and Carisbrooke. The final two chapters comprise a long letter to his son, Prince Charles, on how best to govern his kingdom, and some suitably maudlin 'meditations' written in anticipation of his 'violent, sodaine and barbarous death.'[16] Above all,

10 The 'Cabinet' contained the King's private correspondence. Its capture during the battle, among the baggage train, was a huge propaganda coup for Parliament, revealing the king's ongoing negotiations for military support from the continent and, worse still, the Irish.
11 Almack, *Eikon* (n 4) xi.
12 Substantially later in Levet's case, given in 1690.
13 A painting with which Charles would have been undoubtedly familiar. It has been suggested that the Royal Collection included a copy, if not the original, which would have been sold off with the rest of the collection in the early years of the Republic. A copy was acquired by the Court of Monterrey at some point around 1653; provenance uncertain. Another Titian, on a similar theme, *Virgin and Child with Saints Catherine of Alexandria and John the Baptist*, was sold for £200 in 1650. Titian was an especial favourite of both Charles and Henrietta Maria. The latter had herself painted in the pose of St Catherine by Van Dyke in 1639.
14 For commentaries on the imagery, see R Helgerson, 'Milton reads the King's Book: print, reference and the making of a bourgeois idol' (1987) 29 *Criticism* 9–11, and also SN Zwicker, *Lines of Authority: Politics and English Literary Culture 1649–1689* (Cornell UP, 1993) 41–42.
15 There was never any 'authorised' version as such, though most texts remained fairly consistent in their writing. See Wheeler (n 7) 123–24.
16 Almack, *Eikon* (n 4) 267.

58 *Ian Ward*

he advises the prince, be 'settled in your Religion,' avoid 'exasperating any factions,' and guard against the 'pretensions' of Reformation.[17] Well, indeed.

Each chapter follows the pattern. A moment is recalled, a 'misery' or a 'misfortune,' a betrayal perhaps, then a prayer offered in atonement. The inference is patent. Charles Stuart has been chosen by Him to atone for the sins of 'his people.' 'Impute not me with the blood of my subjects,' Charles prays, as he reflects on those who lost their lives in the 'unhappy war,' but 'wash me with that precious blood which hath been shed for me by my great peacemaker, Jesus Christ.'[18] This is not just a simple defence of the divine right of kings, though it is certainly that. For, 'yet hath He graven such characters of divine authority and sacred power upon king as none may without sin seek to blot out.'[19] It is a personal divinity, a sacrifice necessary for the redemption of a 'chosen' people momentarily led astray. Charles as the Christ. A 'parricide so heinous, so horrible, that it cannot be paralleled by all the murthers that ever were committed since the world began, but onely in the murther of Christ.' The martyred king was 'Thy Priest, Thy sacrifice.'[20] A couple of years later, the rabidly royalist Owen Feltham would make the same explicit, in his *Epitaph to the Eternal Memory of Charles I*: 'Here Charles the First and Christ the Second lies.'[21]

The *Eikon* was not, then, written merely to explain what Charles Stuart had done, still less defend it. It was written to sanctify his person. And it worked. Gauden would later claim that 'In a word, it was an army, and did vanquish more than any sword could.'[22] Gauden had reason to oversell himself. But it is also clear that the authorities, back in early 1649, had reason to worry. A first print run of the *Eikon* was reputedly sold out in 2 days; a third within 10. And it kept selling; thirty-five editions in circulation by the end of the year. And growing. An edition published by William Dugard, in March, added some further accounts of the King's final days, plus four handy prayers that had been 'Delivered to Doctor Juxton, Bishop of London, immediately before His Death.' Not just a testament, but a devotional manual for bereft royalists.[23]

---

17 Ibid 245–56, 252–53.
18 *Eikon* (n 4) 189. See also *Eikon Basilike* (PA Knachel ed, Folger 1905) 123.
19 Knachel, *Eikon* (n 18) 92, 179.
20 Almack (n 4) 113, 276, and Knachel, *Eikon* (n 18) 147.
21 In L Cable, 'Milton's iconoclastic truth,' in D Loewenstein and JG Turner (eds), *Politics, Poetics and Hermeneutics in Milton's Prose* (CUP 1990) 135.
22 CV Wedgwood, *A King Condemned: The Trial and Execution of Charles I* (Tauris 2011) 206–07, and Knachel, *Eikon* (n 18) xi, xxvi–xxx.
23 Including the famous 'Pamela prayer,' which Milton would later denounce for reason of plagiarism, and which has since fascinated conspiracy theorists. Milton accused Charles, or whoever had edited the *Eikon*, of plagiarising the prayer from Sir Philip Sidney's *Arcadia*. Or, the counter-argument goes, he and Bradshaw conspired to forge spurious editions of the *Eikon*, to include the prayer, just so they could then denounce the plagiarism. See MY Hughes, 'New evidence on the charge that Milton forged the Pamela prayer in the *Eikon Basilike*' (1952) 3 *Review of English Studies* 130–40.

The apotheosis of King Charles I   59

And so it would continue throughout the 1650s. Getting bigger all the time, ever more saintly, ever more lachrymose. And selling and selling. In time, there would be editions in Dutch, Danish, French, German, and Latin. Even a version put to music, another to verse.[24] Needless to say, it did better still at the Restoration. Royston produced a new edition in 1681, with a fresh poem attributed to Charles entitled 'Majesty in Misery.' In time, the *Eikon* and its various poetic and devotional accretions would become the centrepiece of a grand folio edition of *The Works of King Charles the Martyr*, published in 1687.

Casting down imaginations

Back in early spring 1649, however, it was clear that the authorities had a problem. Evidence of a lack of planning was everywhere. No-one had even thought to prevent access to the king's burial site at Windsor, nor pass any kind of ordinance prohibiting the display of the king's portrait on private property. As for the *Eikon* and the various other works of hagiography now rolling off the royalist presses, a few possibilities; none especially convincing. A bit of bullying perhaps. Royston was summoned to a personal audience with Cromwell and told to print a letter admitting that the *Eikon* was not really the work of the martyred King.[25] They could chase around the streets harrying hawkers and raiding shops. And reinforce ordinances prohibiting the printing and distribution of 'unlicensed, scandalous and seditious books.' A fresh ordinance was passed in September 1649, prohibiting 'spreaders of false and seditions news, lyes and rumours,' with fines of £10 for the author, £5 for the printer, 40 shillings for the bookseller, and a fine of 20 shillings for any found in possession, with powers for magistrates to 'grant warrants for searching of Packs and Packets.' But bullying and harrying could only do so much.

An alternative was argument. To play the hagiographers at their own game. It would not be easy though. An official *Declaration of the Parliament of England* appeared a few weeks after the execution. It played heavily on the theme of a trust broken and sought to dispute the notion that an 'anointed' monarch was somehow rendered immune from the law. All rather pedantic. So too a justificatory account of the trial, published by the chief prosecutor, John Cook. Neither likely to baffle royalist elegists. Jurisprudential disputation was not going to bring the *Eikon* of the martyred king crashing to the ground. Scriptural disputation might though: recasting the crucifixion of the martyred Charles as a foretelling of the apocalypse. A revised Leveller text entitled *More Light Shining in Buckinghamshire*, which appeared in the March, worked the theme, reminded its readers that kings were 'the horns of the beast.'[26] So too John Owen's *The Shaking and*

---

24 The musical version, the *Psalterium Carolinum*, was composed by John Wilson, former member of the King's Musicke, and based on the versified meditations put together by Thomas Stanley.

25 Royston apparently refused and was imprisoned for his impertinence.

26 LB McKnight, 'Crucifixion or apocalypse? Reconfiguring the *Eikon Basilike*' in DB Hamilton and R Stier (eds) *Religion, Literature and Politics in Post-Reformation England 1640–1688* (Cambridge UP, 1996) 147.

60   Ian Ward

Translating of Heaven and Earth, the printed version of a sermon given to the Commons on 19 April. Chapter 11 of the Book of Revelations proved a predictably popular recourse: 'The kingdoms of this world have become the kingdoms of our Lord, and of his Christ' (11:15). Useful, unless of course Charles was Christ. In which case Parliament started to look like the 'ravaging' Beast.

More substantive rebuttals followed. A first, entitled *Eikon Alethine*, appeared at the end of August, promising its readers an alternative 'portraiture' of the events of the previous winter 'wherein the false colours are washed off.' The 'King's Book,' it surmised, was not in fact written by Charles at all, but by a 'presumptuous priest,' in tones of 'effeminate Rhetorick.'[27] Then, a few weeks later, came another, more substantive still. It was entitled *Eikonoclastes*. No uncertainty here regarding authorship. It was written by the new Secretary of State for Foreign Tongues, in effect the Republic's Foreign Secretary. And chief propagandist. An office that required a variety of skill sets, along with a willingness to be publicly associated with the new regime; to include impeccable godliness, fluent Latin, and a proven record of writing good prose. All of which narrowed the field. But there was one stand-out candidate.

John Milton had already cut his teeth as a polemicist, writing a number of fiercely anti-Laudian tracts back in 1641 and 1642.[28] The most famous was probably *Of Reformation*. Each moved around the same animating theme: the defence of the 'Word' against those who would have it silenced or corrupted; the 'fierce encounter,' as he termed it, 'of truth and falsehood.'[29] A couple of years later, in 1644, he would publish *Areopagitica*, a still-renowned defence of liberty of conscience and expression. Same again, from a different perspective.[30] So, the right man, for a very difficult brief. *Eikonoclastes* was in fact the second of two essays that Milton published in the months that followed the regicide, both to the same purpose. To persuade those still coming to terms with the execution of Charles Stuart that there was a 'safer interest in the common friendship of England, than in the ruins of one ejected Family.'[31] The first, entitled *The Tenure of Kings and Magistrates*, was out in the February. A painstaking defence of the new Republic, with a necessary justification for the regicide inscribed, the tone was constructive, if defensive.

Eikonoclastes was very different. Written on the attack, a piece of literary iconoclasm intended to destroy the incipient image of the martyred king. We will start at the beginning, with Milton alluding to the events of the previous January:

---

27 The title, in translation, meant 'truthful image'. For a commentary, see Wheeler (n 7) 127.
28 Critical opinion divides, not so much on their merit, as their tone and expressions. Essays of 'blind passion' and 'hysterical spite,' according to H Trevor-Roper, *Catholics, Anglicans and Puritans* (Secker and Warburg 1987) 253.
29 J Milton, *The Complete Prose Works of John Milton* (MY Hugues ed, 8 vols, Yale UP 1962) 1.796, 3.493.
30 *Areopagitica* was actually stimulated by Presbyterian demands to tighten regulation of the presses.
31 Milton (n 29) 3.493.

The apotheosis of King Charles I   61

And he who at the Barr stood excepting against the form and manner of his Judicature, and complain'd that he was not heard; neither he nor his Friends shall have that cause now to find fault; being met and debated with in this op'n and monumental Court of his own erecting; and not onely heard uttering his whole mind at large, but answer'd.[32]

A prescient metaphor, presaging a painstaking counter-narrative of the events depicted in the 'King's Book.' There was room for aspersion of course, not least in regard to the authenticity of the *Eikon Basilike*. And some familiar arguments about the justification for removing unwanted kings. And a very long list of precedents: Ahab, Nimrod, Herod, Nero, Caligula, and plenty more. The message was plain enough, proved by scripture. Kings had been deposed before, rightly and with God's blessing. Especially when the tyranny had become something more. Kings who pretended to divinity committed an 'abomination.'[33]

Thus, the prosaic violence.[34] Charles Stuart was not just misguided or badly counselled. He was a bloodthirsty, papist zealot, a 'Tyrant' whose 'deepest policy' had 'bin ever to counterfeit Religion.' The reader is reminded of Charles's fraught embassy to Spain, along with the Duke of Buckingham, in 1623, in the hope of securing marriage to the Infanta; a shameful 'madding.' And then there is the princess he did eventually marry, Henrietta Maria. Rather than convert his wife to Protestantism, Charles preferred to make his subjects 'half way Papists.'[35] But perhaps worst of all, Charles seemed to like the Irish, 'ever friendly,' and ever pleading with them to send over an army.[36] This was the 'Popish Plot' writ large, raising memories of the Armada and the Powder Plot, so many other incidents of Roman malignancy.[37] And Charles Stuart was personally responsible, not just for starting a hellish war against 'his faithfull subjects,' but for perpetuating it.[38] There could be no quarter.

But neither was it just a matter of casting aspersions, or doggedly challenging each of the king's 'meditations'. There was something much greater at stake. A battle for the 'truth,' or, more pertinently, who got to write it.[39] The lawyer and diarist Bulstroke Whitelock would later suppose that the civil war had begun as a 'paper combat.'[40] The ferment of print and political opinion. *Eikonoclastes* was itself a testament to the difficulties of regulating either. If Milton was to confound

---

32 Milton (n 29) 3.341.
33 See here D Loewenstein, 'Casting down imaginations: Milton as iconoclast' (1989) 31 *Criticism* 1989, 258–59 and Helgerson (n 14) 15–16.
34 See JS Bennet, 'God, Satan and King Charles: Milton's royal portraits' (1977) 92 *PMLA* 441–42.
35 Milton (n 29) 3.422.
36 Milton (n 29) 3.473.
37 Milton had written up the 'Popish Plot' before, most notably perhaps in his essay *On Reformation*. See here S Achinstein, 'Milton and King Charles' in TN Corns (ed) *The Royal Image: Representations of Charles I* (OUP 1999) 142, 145–49.
38 Milton (n 29) 3.595.
39 See here Achinstein (n 37) 154–55.
40 Royle (n 2) 180.

62   *Ian Ward*

the 'King's Book,' he would have to write a better, more convincing, 'truth,' nurtured by the 'Christian conscience of libertie.' Such a truth would lay bare, for all to see, the 'papistical' politics of counterfeit and 'suttle dissimulation.'[41]

Easy enough in some cases. The 'knowing Christian' was satiated by the simple 'truth' of the Word. But what of the unknowing, the 'blaspheming Cavaliers,' and the 'inconstant, irrational, and image-doting rabble'?[42] All those who craved the 'quaint emblems' and 'devices' of 'Romish guilded Portrature.' All those too easily seduced by 'some Twelfth-nights entertainment.'[43] All those who passed their Sundays dancing 'Jiggs' and cavorting about 'May-poles.'[44] A decade earlier Milton had trusted the 'capacity of the plain artisan' to come to the right decision. Not anymore.[45] But what to do? A dilemma indeed. How to counter the collected delusions of 'fansie' and 'imagination' without resorting to the same.[46]

To which the answer was, in fact, to do exactly the same, but more cunningly. To make a 'fansie' out of simplicity. Plenty of scriptural reinterpretation of course. All the familiar deposed tyrants. But not, interestingly, the same recourse to the Book of Revelations. Only, at the very end, a quiet reminder that kings who join 'their armies with the Beast' will 'perish with him.' Instead, Milton revisits a different theology, and a different history; that of the English Reformation.[47] Ground already covered in his earlier anti-Laudian tracts. Charles as a particular tyrant, whose particular tyranny had to be presented for all to read. A tale of popery and perversion, of a treacherous King and his craven prelate who conspired to subvert the English church, to place it under the 'servile yoak of Liturgie,' and to distract its congregation with 'fantastik dresses' and 'gaudy Copes,' and 'painted Windows, Miters, Rochets, Altars.'[48] No need to invoke the poetics of revelatory theology.[49] A couple of decades of history was enough to condemn Charles Stuart.

In his 1641 essay *Of Reformation*, Milton had cited 2 Corinthians 10:5, a popular text among puritan window-smashers, for 'Casting down imaginations, and every high thing that exalteth itself against the knowledge of God.' The 'spirituall words of holy censure,' to be applied just as readily against kings who exalt themselves. *Eikonoclastes* revisited the same history, to the same purpose. Justification by purification. Charles Stuart, the papist dissimulator, had been

41 Milton (n 29) 3.348–49, 376, 469.
42 Milton (n 29) 3.343, 601.
43 It is difficult to be sure if the inference is directed more precisely towards Shakespeare and his *Twelfth Night*. Elsewhere, Milton insinuates disparagingly that Shakespeare was the author of the king's language; the 'Closet Companion of these his solitudes.' For a discussion here see Zwicker (n 14) 54.
44 Milton (n 29) 3.358, 498. For a commentary, see Zwicker (n 14) 48–51.
45 See Trevor-Roper (n 28) 255, 268–69.
46 Milton (n 29) 3.343, 406, 498–9. For a discussion of this dilemma, see Zwicker (n 14) 39–40, 45–6 and Wheeler (n 7) 128–9.
47 On the engagement between Milton and the 'King's Book' being a matter of competing histories, see Wheeler (n 7) 129–30.
48 Milton (n 29) 3.505, 558.
49 See here McKnight (n 26) 152–53.

The apotheosis of King Charles I   63

despatched as a 'speciall mark of favour.'[50] But it was not simply a matter of reinvesting a congregation. It was also a matter of reinvesting a constitution. In despatching their tyrant-king the English had also rid themselves of his 'grinding' prerogative courts. The 'ancient' constitution was restored, its laws 'so ingrav'd in the hearts of our Ancestors, and by them so constantly enjoy'd and claim'd, as it needed not enrouling.'[51] The union of church and constitution was indissoluble. The pith of the English Reformation.

Eikonoclastes was long and painstaking, each chapter rebutting an equivalent chapter in the 'King's Book.' Milton argued closely. But he also argued coldly. Meanwhile, the royalist presses ran ever hotter. All running the Christology theme. *King Charles, His Imitation of Christ, Or the Parallel Lives of Our Saviour and King's Sufferings drawn through forty-six texts of Scripture* did well. George Thomason acquired a copy in early December. So too, *The Life and Death of King Charles the Martyr Parall'd with our Saviour*. A closer rebuttal to *Eikonoclastes* had appeared within weeks, entitled *The Princely Pelican: Royall Resolves Extracted from His Majestie's Divine Meditations, with satisfying reasons that his Sacred Person was the only author of them*. In effect a sequel to the *Eikon*, written in familiar tones. Lots of meditations, lots of prayer. 'As for princely policy; I hold none better than sincere piety,' and so on, and on.[52] The voice beyond the grave again. Shortly after came a text entitled *Defensio Regia pro Carolo I*, written by a French scholar named Claudius Salmasius. More ghostly incantations. Rebutting it would be Milton's next commission. In 1651, he would publish a rebuttal to Salmasius, entitled *Pro Defensio*. And then, in 1654, a *Defensio Secunda*. And so it would go on. The spirit of Charles Stuart would not be easily exorcised.

We might revisit some statistics before we move on. The *Eikon Basilike* went through thirty-five editions in a year. *Eikonoclastes* managed just three, all subsidized. Not cunning enough, it seems; or maybe too cunning?[53] The reason matters less than the fact.

A comely head

Time for our third text, which takes us away from the heat of the London presses and up to the comparative tranquillity of Nun Appleton in Yorkshire, the country estate of Sir Thomas, Lord Fairfax. Still the 'Captain-General' of the Parliamentarian army, Sir Thomas was, however, in semi-retirement, having rather conspicuously declined to serve as a nominated commissioner in the trial of the King. A refusal rendered even more conspicuous by the recoded antics of his wife,

---

50 Milton (n 29) 3.348.
51 Milton (n 29) 3.401–402.
52 In K Sharpe, *Remapping England: The Culture of Seventeenth Century Politics* (CUP 2000) 195.
53 According to one commentator, a 'dismal defeat.' Milton 'simply never had a chance.' See B Boehrer, 'Elementary structures of kingship: Milton, regicide and family' (1987) 23 *Milton Studies* 99, 105.

64 *Ian Ward*

Lady Anne, who had attended the first day of the trial to berate the assembled.[54] Later in the autumn, Sir Thomas would resign his commission, a necessary consequence of refusing to subscribe to the Oath of Engagement that Parliament decided to impose on the country. Royalist presses put it about that he was 'melancholy mad.'

Life in republican England was certainly proving to be something of a challenge for a number of Parliamentarians. Sir Henry Vane surmised that his colleagues 'were now in a far worse state than ever yet they had been.'[55] Sir Henry decided to battle on. Not Sir Thomas. In his resignation letter to Speaker Lenthall, Fairfax alluded to 'debilities both in body and mind.' Time for a rest, some gardening and some poetry.[56]

And more time with his daughter, Mary. Who, coming up to the age of 12, was in need of a tutor. Fairfax invited Andrew Marvell. Marvell would spend just over a year up at Nun Appleton, declining Latin verbs with Mary and pricking roses with Sir Thomas. And writing some of the most beautiful pastoral poetry in the English canon. Most notably perhaps *Upon Appleton House*, completed in summer 1651. Pastoral, but also political. *Appleton Moor* closes with a pointed allusion. The garden was neat enough. Outside though, a 'rude heap together hurl'd; / All negligently overthrown, / Gulfes, Deserts, Precipices, Stone' (772–74).[57] England was a mess. Still. Travelling up to Nun Appleton a year earlier, Marvell had been putting the final touches to another poem, entitled *An Horation Ode Upon Cromwell's Return from Ireland*. Premised on the same, unarguable, fact. Rebuilding a constitution on a 'bleeding head' was proving more difficult than had perhaps been imagined. It 'Did fright the architects to run' (69–70).

As the title suggests, the immediate pretext for the *Ode* was Cromwell's campaign in Ireland, which had commenced in late summer 1649. A venture purposed to defeat the Earl of Ormonde, who had finally raised an army, and give the New Model something useful to do. Cromwell had crossed the Irish Sea, duly scattered Ormonde's army, and then embarked on a vicious campaign designed, not just to secure a string of port towns along the coast, but to cow a people. Most notorious were alleged massacres at Drogheda and Wexford.[58] Reporting

---

54 When the name of Sir Thomas was read out as a nominated commissioner, a voice rang out from the gallery. He had 'more wit' than to be there. It was later put about that it was a couple of 'whores.' Bulstrode Whitelock knew who it was though. The commander of the guard, Colonel Axtell, offered to have a trooper fire into the gallery. But was persuaded to send some up instead. Of course, by the time they got there, the hecklers were long gone.

55 In B Worden, 'The politics of Marvell's *Horatian Ode*' (1984) 27 *Historical Journal* 527.

56 In Worden (n 55), 527.

57 All quotations from Marvell's poems are taken from *Andrew Marvell* (Frank Kermode and Keith Walker eds, OUP 1990).

58 It is not known precisely how many were slaughtered, though Hugh Peter was able to provide Parliament with the oddly precise figure of 3,352 at Drogheda. Something around 2,500 is commonly estimated for Wexford. Plus thousands more captured and transported into slavery.

back to Parliament, Cromwell provided a simple, and familiar, reason. It was the 'righteous judgement of God, on these barbarous wretches.' Leaving his son-in-law, Henry Ireton, to mop up around the Pale of Dublin, Cromwell then set sail back to England in May 1650.

To a rapturous welcome. Landing at Bristol, the returning hero was met with a triple cannonade on the dockside. After which he made a stately progress through the Thames Valley to Windsor, where he was met with more 'vollies of shot,' and assorted delegations from Parliament and the Council of State. A two-day pause, and then a carefully staged 'passage' into London, the streets lined with a guard of honour, which ended at Hyde Park Corner with another cannonade of 'great guns.'[59] Spectacular by all accounts; though not, it seems, as spectacular as the parade accorded after the victory at the battle of Worcester a year later. The new Republic needed a bit of flash, the 'chosen people' some reassurance. Cromwell provided it, time and again. A hero indeed. Well worthy of *An Horation Ode*.

A genre that was suitably republican and virtuous, but which still required some selective reading. Milton preferred Horace too, littering his writing with lots of similarly heroic republican generals, a counterpoint to all the variously insane imperial tyrants who stagger drunkenly though the pages of *Eikonoclastes*. But it was not just the virtuous Horace who provided lyrical inspiration. There was a greater providence. That which had been witnessed at Marston Moor and Naseby, and Drogheda and Wexford. And which, a year before, had gestured Cromwell toward the fateful decision to put Charles Stuart on trial. The providence which, as Milton famously affirmed, had made Cromwell 'God's Englishman.'

Marvell opened his *Ode* in like tone: ''Tis Madness to resist or blame / The force of angry Heaven's flame' (25–26). Drawn from 'his private gardens, where / He lived reserved and austere' (29–30). Imbued with all the requisite republican virtues. Not least fidelity. A devoted servant to his country:

> How good he is, how just,
> And fit for highest trust.
> Nor yet grown stiffer with command,
> But still in the Republic's hand:
> How fit he is to sway
> That can so well obey.
>
> (79–84)

> Victorious, he returns, and
> to the Commons' feet presents
> A Kingdom for his first year's rents:
> And what he may, forbears

---

59 S Kelsey, *Inventing a Republic: The Political Culture of the English Commonwealth 1649–1653* (Manchester UP 1997) 72–73.

66   *Ian Ward*

His Fame, to make it theirs:
And has his sword and spoils ungirt,
To lay them at the Public's skirt.
(87–90)

At that very moment, as Marvell is pouring over his scansion, Cromwell is assuming his position as the new Commander-in-Chief, in place of Fairfax. And preparing to invade 'the Pict.' A miraculous victory at Dunbar will shortly follow. And yet the ambiguities lurk. A 'Caesar' on the outside, perhaps; but a Machiavellian prince on the in?[60] And the spectres.

Which must be raised, and then laid. Back to summer 1648, and then swiftly forward, to January 1649. Charles Stuart at Carisbrooke. From:

thence the royal actor borne
The tragic scaffold might adorn:
While round the armed bands
Did clap their bloody hands.
He nothing common did or mean
Upon that memorable scene:
But with keener eye
The axe's edge did try:
Nor called the gods with vulgar spite
To vindicate his helpless right,
But bowed his comely head
Down as upon a bed.
This was the that memorable hour
Which first assured the forced power.
(53–66)

Moving, conspicuous, consonant. Charles Stuart as actor and martyr. Almost certainly inspired by the passage in Horace's 'Actium' Ode, in which the audience is drawn away from Octavian's brilliance to the tragedy of the defeated Cleopatra. And very probably also by contemporary accounts of another beheading, that of the Earl of Montrose by the Presbyterian Kirk. The Earl, contemporary reports confirmed, had carried himself with a 'comely' dignity.[61]

Whether Marvell's verse betokens more than sympathy must, however, be left to conjecture. Regret perhaps? The theatre consumes the moment; almost. The *Ode* does not touch directly on the legality of the King's trial. But it does cast an aspersion: a 'right' rendered 'helpless' before a 'forced power.' The same point made a few lines earlier:

---

60 See here Worden (n 55) 535–39, noting Clarendon making a still more patent comparison; Cromwell as the embodiment of a Machiavellian prince.
61 Worden (n 55) 543.

The apotheosis of King Charles I 67

Though Justice Against Fate complain,
And plead the ancient Rights in vain:
But those do hold or break
As Men are strong and weak.

(37–40)

A dose of reality. Tears might be shed, but history moves on: 'To ruin the great work of time, / And cast the kingdom old / Into another mould' (34–6). A new state will be constructed, 'A bleeding head where they begun' (69).

A pragmatist then? Perhaps a Hobbesian. A few months later, in early 1651, Thomas Hobbes would publish his *Leviathan*. At the heart of it was a simple truth born of bitter experience: that 'Covenants, without the Sword, are but Words, and of no strength to secure a man at all.'[62] *Leviathan* was written in reconciliation. Not as a gesture to the Republic, but to reconcile conscience-stricken Royalists to the fact that they might have to live in it. More particularly, that they might be able to subscribe to its Oath of Engagement. The same brusque sentiment could be found in Marchamont Nedham's *Case of the Commonwealth of England*: 'The power of the sword is, and ever hath been, the foundation of all titles of government.'[63] If the 1640s had taught Englishmen and women anything it was this. In a contest between 'ancient Rights' of a tiny, posturing prince and 'forced power' of 'angry Heaven's flame,' there was only ever going to be one winner.

Was Marvell trying to do the same as Hobbes and Nedham? Is the *Ode* as much a poem of reconciliation, or resignation? It is tempting, always, to try to read the writer into the writing. Never easy though, especially not with Marvell; by his own admission, 'inclined to keep my thoughts private.'[64] And not just the writer, but also the audience. Has Marvell captured the mind of a shattered generation, trying to reconcile itself to life in a world turned truly 'upside down'? It was, in a sense, his thing. The young Marvell had cut his teeth as a 'cavalier' poet writing fashionable laments.[65] We can, however, only surmise. Marvell moved on. To the quieter contemplations of *Appleton House* and its companion piece, *Upon the Hill and Grove at Bilborough*. Lots of foliage and reminiscing; 'oracles in oak' (*Upon the Hill and Grove at Bilborough*, l.74).

And insinuation. *Appleton House* has long been acclaimed as a defining expression of 'Protestant historiography.' Reaching back to the Reformation to

---

62 T Hobbes, *Leviathan*, (Penguin 1985) 223.

63 Worden (n 95) 533.

64 See Smith (n 3) 6–7, and also Worden (n 55) 525 and also 539, referring more closely to the *Ode*: 'It is not merely that there is ambiguity in the ode. There is layer upon layer of it.'

65 He had cut his teeth during the later 1640s writing cavalier 'laments.' In late 1648, he published an *Elegy Upon the Death of My Lord Francis Villiers*. Villiers had been killed during the Earl of Holland's fated uprising in Kent earlier that summer. A year later, the 19-year-old Lord Hastings had also died. Smallpox this time, so not quite so heroic. But worth an elegy all the same. Which duly appeared in Richard Broome's *Lachrymae Musarum*.

68 *Ian Ward*

emphasise the continuity of English history; despite all present appearances.[66] And the stability lent by families such as the Fairfaxes. But maybe also to chide a little? England needs heroes. Only half a day's ride away, the New Model is in camp at Ripon, preparing to invade Scotland. But Fairfax is pottering about his garden.[67] Why? A principled objection to waging war on the Kirk? Simple weariness perhaps. But it might also, perhaps, be the 'prickling leaf' of 'conscience ... / which shrinks at ev'ry touch' (357–58).

At what though? Perhaps the Engagement Oath, perhaps something more. Later that summer, the anguished Fairfax, a bit of a poet himself, wrote a few lines in his commonplace book: 'Oh Lett that Day from time be blotted quit / ... But if the Power devine permitted this / His Will's the Law and we must acquiesce.'[68] A terrible deed demanded by an irresistible God. As Marvell had intimated in his *Ode*. Something for the pair to chat about, as they wandered around the knot garden on a late summer's evening. Along with early drafts of verses 69 and 70 of *Appleton House*, which describe the falling of the 'tallest oak,' made weak by a 'traitor-worm, within it bred' (551–52, 554). Not just an irresistible God then.

Marvell departed Nun Appleton in late 1652. Cromwell needed a new tutor for his ward William Dutton. William was rumoured to be a prospective suitor to Frances, Cromwell's ninth and youngest daughter. By then it was clearer still that 'angry heaven's flame' was the coming man. Back in London, Marvell wrote *To His Coy Mistress* and met Milton for the first time. In due course, he would become Milton's secretary, working at the heart of government. And write a set of songs for the marriage of another of Cromwell's daughters, Mary. By then he was firmly part of the Cromwellian 'court' too, its unofficial laureate.[69] Ever the 'trimmer,' Marvell had made his peace. A 'prickling' conscience perhaps, but history moves on, leaving the poets to write it up.

A remarkable revolution

And we will too. On to 13 February 1689, to be precise. And an irony, recurrent and irresistible. The nineteenth-century Whig historian Thomas Babington Macaulay can lay the scene. Whitehall is 'filled with gazers.' The 'magnificent Banqueting House, the masterpiece of Inigo, embellished by masterpieces of Rubens, has been prepared for a great ceremony.' A 'large number of Peers' are

---

66 See CA Brand, '"Upon Appleton House" and the decomposition of protestant historiography' (2001) 31 *English Historical Renaissance* 477–510.

67 Designed apparently in 'the just Figure of a Fort' (286). Gardens that looked like little fortified islands had become fashionable in the Elizabethan period and stayed so. And the same was true of poetry that worked the garden-as-fort, or conversely garden-as-sanctuary, theme. For a commentary on Marvell's contribution to the genre, see GD Hamilton, 'Marvell, sacrilege and Protestant historiography: contextualising "Upon Appleton House"' in GD Hamilton and Richard Strier (eds), *Religion, Literature and Politics in Post-Reformation England 1640–1688*, (CUP 1996) 173–77.

68 In Brand (n 66) 483.

69 D Hirst and S Zwicker, 'High summer at Nun Appleton 1651: Andrew Marvell and Lord Fairfax's occasions' (1993) 36 *Historical Journal* 265–66.

assembled on one side, the Commons on the other. The 'Prince and Princess of Orange' take 'their place under the canopy of state.' The reason is about to become apparent. Lord Halifax asks the prospective monarchs to hear a resolution of both Houses. It is the Declaration of Right, and what it does, in effect, is set out the conditions by which William and his wife Mary might be permitted to become king and queen.

Another piece of theatre, of course. Everyone knew that they would agree. It was Halifax who had invited them over in the first place. And William had made a serious effort, gathering an army together and sailing across the Channel, before landing in Torbay, an oddly circuitous journey intended to give his predecessor, King James II, ample time to lose his nerve and run off. James was a man of some military experience and, by all accounts, no little personal courage. It has been surmised that it was memories of his father's demise, along with the fickleness of the army, that turned his head. Not that he had seen his father being executed, of course. But he had read about it. And imagined it.

The reading of the Declaration complete, William confirmed his assent: 'We thankfully accept, what you have offered us.' He would govern by 'the laws of England' and 'constantly recur to the advice of the Houses, and should be disposed to trust their judgment rather than his own.'[70] Words that were, Macaulay tells us, 'instantly answered by huzzas from many thousands of voices.' And:

> Thus was consummated the English Revolution. When we compare it with those revolutions which have, during the last sixty years, overthrown so many ancient governments, we cannot but be struck by its peculiar character.[71]

Macaulay wrote his *History of England*, in which he described these events, in the late 1840s. The 'last sixty years' was calculated to reach back to the French revolution. The message was familiar enough to celebrants of Whig history. The English revolution had been a very 'great' thing indeed. And was now complete, finally, after so many travails and adventures. In that same Banqueting Hall, under that same Rubens ceiling. For Macaulay, at least, an apotheosis of the English constitution.

It is in the nature of Whig history to play with the imagination. And Macaulay was among the most playful. The 'great dramatist,' as Walter Bagehot termed him. Bagehot, a bit of utilitarian and a lot of an ironist, rather admired Macaulay. Even if he did seem to make up much of the history he wrote. In a sense, things were about to change. History was going to get rather more scientific and a lot less fun. Much the same was true of jurisprudence too: more positive, less pleasing. Complementary Benthamite mutations. Milton might have nodded a long-awaited approval. The 'casting down of imaginations,' eventually.

But not finally. Narrative history has endured, nowhere more obviously than in the 'story' of the English constitution. Why? Partly because it is more enticing. But mainly because there is nothing else. As the French writer, Alexis de Tocqueville,

---

70 TB Macaulay, *The History of England* (Penguin 1986) 287–88.
71 Macaulay (n 70) 288.

70   *Ian Ward*

famously confirmed in his *Democracy in America*, published in 1830. In 'England the constitution can change constantly, or rather it does not exist at all.'[72] What he meant, of course, is that the English have no written constitution, or at least no formal document that describes itself in those terms, though the Declaration of Right that was read out to William and Mary on the morning of 13 February 1689 comes among the closest. They do, though, have a constitution. In part enacted. Whig histories dwell lovingly on documents such as the Declaration of Right, as well as Magna Carta, the Petition of Right, the 'great' Reform Act. But also acted; performed and scripted. Magna Carta needs its grumpy barons. The Petition of Right needs its truculent Commons. The Reform Act needs both. And they all need witless kings. But it is not, of course, simply a matter of reimagining famous statutes. Famous trials too, and murderous depositions; none more famous or murderous than that of the spectacularly witless Charles Stuart.

Not always easy, of course, and requiring some imagination. Macaulay tended to approach tangentially. An early essay on Milton, published in 1825, concluded that Charles Stuart was 'a tyrant, a traitor, a murderer and a public enemy.'[73] But that his execution was wrong, not for reason of justice, but because it was detrimental to the national interest. A similarly pragmatic justification was written into his slightly later essay on the historian Henry Hallam. The 'great and glorious' Revolution of 1688 was a wonderful thing. But revolutions, more generally, are not a good idea; still less butchering kings. Charles, though, presented 'an extreme case' that demanded a 'remedy which is in its own nature most violent.'[74] And, although Charles assumes a more marginal place in Macaulay's grander *History* of the 'glorious' revolution, his demise is written similarly. And for the same purpose. There could have been no 1689 without 1649.

A sacrifice demanded by history. And a tone set, for generations of variously Whiggish historians to come. Take, for example, Winston Churchill's monumental *History of the English-Speaking Peoples*. A 'strange destiny had engulfed this King of England.' Charles had 'been in his heyday the convinced opponent of all we now call our Parliamentary liberties.' And yet, in his final moments, had acquired a certain dignity, standing against an army that was about to 'plunge England into a tyranny at once more irresistible and more petty than any seen before or since.' He was 'not a martyr in the sense of one who dies for a spiritual ideal.' Not quite. And neither did he die as a 'defender' of Church and constitution. But he did, in a strange way, die 'for them.'[75]

And for variously Whiggish poets too. Such as Alexander Pope.[76] A century on, Pope recounted an anecdote passed down, apparently, by the Earl of Southampton. The earl

---

72 A de Tocqueville, *Democracy in America* (Fontana 1994) 101.
73 RE Sullivan, *Macaulay: The Tragedy of Power* (Harvard UP 2009) 58.
74 Sullivan (n 73) 71. For a commentary on Macaulay's sometimes rather conflicted view of King Charles and his fate, see B Worden, *Roundhead Reputations: The English Civil Wars and the Passions of Posterity* (Penguin 2002) 228–30.
75 W Churchill, *A History of the English-Speaking Peoples* (Cassell 1974) 2.216–17.
76 A Tory in his politics, and Whig in everything else. On the elision of Whig and Tory responses to the seventeenth-century revolutions, see Worden *Roundhead Reputations* (n 74) 13–17, 170–73, 181–89.

The apotheosis of King Charles I 71

had attended the coffin of the king as it lay in rest in St George's Chapel, Windsor, on the evening of 30 January. And dropped off. To be roused, at some point, by the arrival of a cloaked figure, which stared for some moments at the body of the king, head now stitched back on, and then muttered the words 'cruel necessity.' The earl could not be absolutely certain, but he was pretty sure it was the voice of Oliver Cromwell. Maybe, maybe not. But, either way, far too good a story to be ignored. Poetic licence comes easier to poets of course. Like Pope. And Marvell, who adopts much the same strategic tone, as we have already noted, in his *Horatian Ode*. Though here it is a necessity demanded by an 'angry' God, as well as circumstance and an angry Cromwell.

But it is not, of course, purely about what was described, the theatre of that moment. It was also about how it should be described; about the reach of poetic licence, the place of anecdote and irony, for the moment and its story are never distinguishable. There is only the telling. As Marvell knew, and Milton, and Gauden. The execution of Charles I was an extraordinary moment in English history, not just because of what happened, but because of how it was imagined. And then how it was written. The Republic, which came into being on the afternoon of 30 January 1649, lasted 11 years. The conversation about its invention would endure for centuries.[77] In their joyous parody of English history, *1066 and All That*, WC Sellar and RJ Yeatman famously characterised the civil war period, which culminated in the 'very memorable' execution of the King, as a struggle between those who were 'wrong but romantic' and those who were 'right but repulsive.'[78] Indeed. The fighting of it, and the writing of it.

---

77 For a brilliant account, see Worden, *Roundhead Reputations* (n 74).
78 WC Sellar and RJ Yeatman, *1066 and All That: A Memorable History of England* (Alan Sutton 1993) 78–79.

Part Two

The courts and the legal imagination

5 Pathologies of imagination and legitimacy of judicial decision-making

Emilia Mickiewicz

NEWCASTLE UNIVERSITY LAW SCHOOL[1]

Imagination plays an important role in the application and development of the law. It allows judges and legislators to respond creatively to the issues before them.[2] However, the extent to which a judge is able to exercise his or her imagination compared with a legislator remains contested.[3] It was brought into sharp focus by Jonathan Sumption in the 2019 Reith Lectures.[4] Sumption argued that, whereas judges regularly reshape the existing law in the general areas of judicial deference, the separation of powers doctrine makes judicial intervention in politically sensitive fields highly problematic.[5] Judges who exceed their powers are not only likely to compromise the legitimacy of their decisions but can also undermine confidence in their office.[6] Although Sumption appreciates the complexity of the issue, he leaves it unresolved.

This chapter examines the extent to which the Kantian distinction between productive and reproductive imagination can be used to assess the limits and legitimacy of judicial decision-making.[7] Whereas reproductive imagination plays an important role in promoting continuity in the existing law, productive imagination allows judges to reshape it in creative ways. It is the exercise of productive imagination that typically gives rise to questions of legitimacy. A legitimate decision is defined in this chapter as one that most effectively narrows the gap between the claim advanced by the court and the public's belief in that claim.[8] Drawing on the

---

1 I am particularly grateful for the comments on the draft to Ruth Houghton, Christine Beuermann, Richard Mullender, Ben Farrand, Ian Ward, Matteo Nicolini, Robert Schuetze, Francesco de Cecco, and Josh Jowitt.
2 See: JB White, *The Legal Imagination* (Abridged ed. Chicago: U of Chicago 1985); I Ward, *Shakespeare and the Legal Imagination* (Butterworth 1999); A Watson, *Failures of the Legal Imagination* (2016); S Lee, *Judging Judges* (Faber 1989); M Del Mar, *Artefacts of Legal Inquiry. The Value of Imagination in Adjudication* (Hart 2020).
3 See: *Duport Steels v Sirs* [1980]1 All ER 529.
4 J Sumption, *The Trials of the State. Law and the Decline of Politics* (Profile Books 2019).
5 Ibid. See also: Lady BM Hale, *Law and Politics: A Reply to Reith;* Dame Frances Patterson Memorial Lecture 2019 (8 October 2019).
6 Sumption (n. 3).
7 I Kant, *Critique of Pure Reason*, B151 (New York: St Martin's Press, 1963).
8 M Weber, *The Theory of Economic and Social Organization* (AM Henderson and Talcott Parsons tr, The Free Press of Glencoe 1964) 130.

76 *Emilia Mickiewicz*

hermeneutic philosophy of Paul Ricoeur, this chapter shows that productive imagination operates in either 'constitutive' or 'pathological' ways. It is the former that most effectively fills the legitimacy gap.[9] Whereas constitutive imagination seeks to meaningfully situate its product in the wider context, pathological imagination is characterised by escapist tendencies. They emerge 'when human life pursues the vital illusions, with the help of which it can haphazardly replace the actual world with the imaginary one.'[10] These are typically 'projects of self-realisation, which cannot be fulfilled within the horizon of actuality.'[11]

The argument put forward in this chapter is that judges cannot always escape the pathological tendency for self-deception. This can make their office and their decisions less legitimate. Pathological tendencies can be detected in the recent attempts of the Court of Justice of the European Union (CJEU) to creatively respond to the perceived threats to the rule of law in Poland. In *Associação Sindical dos Juízes Portugueses* and the subsequent ruling in *Commission v Poland*, the CJEU stretched the limits of legitimate adjudication by ignoring the division of powers provided for under the EU Treaty.[12] It also disregarded its own jurisprudence on the relationship between the Treaty and the EU Charter on Fundamental Rights.[13] The Kantian distinction and Ricoeur's insights on constitutive and pathological imagination help to illuminate the extent to which the CJEU could recast its position. As should become apparent, however, the analysis can be applied to various areas of the law.

Productive and reproductive imagination

Kant defines imagination as a faculty of making present what is absent; a capacity for representation. As he puts it, '[i]magination is the faculty of representing in intuition an object that is not itself present.'[14] Depending on what it is that is being represented, Kant distinguishes between productive and reproductive imagination. Whereas reproductive imagination represents something already seen, something already familiar, productive imagination generates things that have never existed. In this sense, imagination makes both present: the past and the future, mobilising in equal measure memory and 'the faculty of divination.'[15]

Yet, imagination cannot be simply reduced to memory or spontaneous projection. The key characteristic of imagination is its capacity to *synthesise* experience

---

9 P Ricoeur, 'Ideology and utopia as cultural imagination' (1976) 7 *Philosophic Exchange* 17.
10 D Nikulin, 'What is productive imagination?' in S Geniusas and D Nikulin (eds), *Productive Imagination: Its History, Meaning and Significance* (Rowman 2018) x.
11 Ibid.
12 Case C-64/16 *Associação Sindical dos Juízes Portugueses* [2018] ECLI:EU:C:2018:117; Case C-619/18 *Commission v Poland* [2019] ECR ECLI:EU:C:2019:325.
13 Article 13(2) TEU; Article 5(2) TEU.
14 Kant (n 6) B151.
15 Kant, *Anthropology from a Pragmatic Point of View* (MJ Gregor tr, Nijhoff 1974) § 28 (italics added).

and understanding. A thing we encountered in the past is not simply recreated in imagination. As Kant discerns in the *Critique of Pure Reason*, 'our recognition of an object as a tree does not derive simply from an impression of the tree in the mind but from schematism's interrelation of an impression with thought.'[16] The product of imagination, 'the schema', is not simply an isolated mental image, but one that meaningfully connects to its surroundings.

Imagination links past experiences, future projections, and demands of the present into a coherent whole. Thanks to its synthesising and associative capacity, imagination plays an important epistemic role making knowledge possible and feeding into other faculties of mind. As Kant puts it: 'Synthesis of the manifold ... is what first gives rise to knowledge. [It] gathers the elements for knowledge, and unites them into a certain content.'[17] He explains that, 'this synthesis is the mere result of the faculty of imagination, a blind but indispensable function of the soul, without which we should have no knowledge whatsoever but of which we are scarcely ever conscious.'[18]

While stressing the somewhat elusive nature of imagination, Kant recognises that imagination is indispensable to the fields that generate knowledge and deepen our perception of reality. Although imagination itself defies structure and schematisation, it structures and organises the world around us. It connects thought with experience. As imagination begins with the empirical world, Kant identifies imagination as a domain of reflective as opposed to determinant judgements.[19] Whereas determinant judgements subsume the particular under a general rule, reflective judgements derive the rule from the particular, bringing forth the 'exemplary validity' of our experience.[20] Imagination brings the manifold and shapeless experience into a coherent whole; it makes particulars communicable and meaningful to us.

As it is a faculty of reflective judgement that defies any prior determination, according to Kant imagination has no place in law. To him, law is a sphere of determinant judgements. It operates in a deductive fashion and is governed by rules and principles.[21] In contrast, Kant reserves imagination, which defies rules and begins with experience, to the sphere of aesthetics. However, others have argued that this view of imagination is too restrictive. For example, Hannah Arendt, in her contested account of 'Kantian political theory, which he never wrote,' argues that reflective judgement and imagination are at the core of

---

16 Kant, *Critique of Pure Reason*, A 103; GH Taylor, 'Ricoeur's philosophy of productive imagination' in Geniusas and Nikulin (n 10) 160.

17 Kant (n 16) A78/B10.

18 Ibid A78/B103.

19 Ibid A78/B104; H Arendt, *Lectures on Kant's Political Philosophy* (University of Chicago Press 1992) 83.

20 Ibid.

21 Some commentators fail to distinguish between Kant's theory of law, which involves the operation of pure reason, and his theory of right, which engages practical reason. Accordingly, they argue that it is a domain of practical reason. See R Maliks, *Kant's Politics in Context* (OUP 2014).

78   Emilia Mickiewicz

political 'common sense,' the 'enlarged mentality.'[22] It is the faculty that allows individuals to put themselves into others' shoes, enabling political coexistence.[23]

Ricoeur makes an even bolder assertion, arguing that imagination permeates all those areas of human practice that exhibit linguistic dimension.[24] Language represents and transforms reality, and this, in Ricoeur's view, is mediated, respectively, by productive and reproductive imagination. Reproductive imagination works by recreating our experience in language, and productive imagination transforms it, synthesising a whole network of references, past connections, and future possibilities. Ricoeur assigns greater ontological significance to productive imagination as it has the power to restructure semantic fields. It operates 'at the moment when a new meaning emerges out of the ruins of literal predication,' giving us a glimpse of a 'new predicative pertinence.'[25] Whereas reproductive imagination takes us back to an existing referent, productive imagination functions by eliminating the reference to some original in external reality.[26] In this sense, words are not simply pictures of reality, but also 'icons', which display the meaning by way of a depiction.[27] They are 'constitutive of semantic fields,'[28] opening to vision the interrelatedness of our experience.

In his analysis, Ricoeur examines the relevance of imagination in social action and culture.[29] Drawing on Karl Mannheim, he identifies two types of social imagination: *ideology* and *utopia*. He connects them to reproductive and productive imagination, respectively. Both types involve an inverted image of the real social practice and are characterised by incongruence with collectively imagined forms and reality. Ricoeur defines ideology 'as the sphere of representations, ideas, and conceptions versus the sphere of actual practice.'[30] This definition reveals the integrative function of ideology. Ideology preserves the existing social practice by concealing the gap between the imagined and actual reality. In contrast, utopia has a disintegrative and revealing function: it breaks and transcends the existing order. As Ricoeur puts it, '[t]he utopian mode may be defined as the imaginary project of another kind of society, of another reality, another world. Imagination is here constitutive in an inventive rather than integrative manner.'[31] Although ideology and utopia exhibit discontinuity with reality, they also constitute it. They operate in constructive and destructive ways as confirmation and contestation of the present situation.[32]

---

22 Arendt (n 19).
23 To this effect, she directs us to Section 40 of aesthetic judgment on *sensus communis* in the first critique.
24 P Ricoeur, 'Imagination in discourse and in action' in G Robinson and JF Rundell (eds), *Rethinking Imagination: Culture and Creativity* (Routledge 1994).
25 Ricœur (n 9) 172–73.
26 Taylor (n 16) 158.
27 P Ricoeur, *The Rule of Metaphor* (Routledge 1975) 204–45.
28 Ibid.
29 Ricoeur (n 24).
30 Ricoeur (n 9) 18.
31 Ibid 24.
32 Ibid 26.

Pathologies of imagination and legitimacy 79

The capacity to confirm or contest the existing reality is what makes imagination central to the functioning of authority. Whereas ideology plays an important legitimising function, utopia helps to break free from an order that no longer serves its purpose and can no longer be justified. As Ricoeur explains, 'the privileged place of ideological thinking occurs in politics; there the questions of legitimation arise.' Ideology's role is to provide authoritative concepts that make a given political vision defensible. In contrast, '[t]he function of utopia is to expose the credibility gap wherein all systems of authority exceed ... both our confidence in them and our belief in their legitimacy.'[33] The question of authority is brought to light at the point of intersection between ideology and utopia. Here, the tension between the two exposes the gap between the claim to power and belief in that power to view. Whereas ideology seeks to conceal the gap offering a conceptual basis or a 'code', which serves to preserve the authorities' claim, utopia reveals that gap showing the shortcomings of the existing order. If the gap becomes too great, the authority breaks down, giving way to a new vision of social reality.

Law and imagination

Ricoeur's analysis of ideology and utopia as cultural imagination and the Kantian distinction between productive and reproductive imagination help to critically engage with the practice of adjudication. In contrast to the Kantian view that imagination is irrelevant to the field of law, this chapter advances a position that imagination is operative in the process of application and extension of the law. Against the Kantian assertion that the law is a domain of deductive a priori judgments, the law is conceived in this chapter as a field derived directly from everyday practice.

This is particularly evident in the case-by-case development of the law. The synthesising function of imagination is fundamental to this process. Here, experience and understanding are fused in the law's responses to the disputes it addresses. Imagination plays a central role in the process of reasoning by analogy, which informs the application and development of the law. Analogy is engaged whenever the existing authorities are applied to the case before the court. This involves identifying material similarities and differences between the examined case and the established authorities. In Ricoeur's view, this exercise is characteristic of metaphorical use of language, which he links to the operation of imagination. In *Imagination in Discourse and Action*, he associates a metaphor with an idea of identifying resemblance.[34] Following Aristotle, he argues that to 'make a good metaphor ... is to perceive the similar.' In law, this would entail a relatively uncontroversial exercise of applying the existing authorities to the facts of the case that, in material respects, resemble one another. However, to Ricoeur, the use of metaphor goes beyond simply spotting similarities and differences and often involves semantic innovation, which engages the productive imagination.

33 Ibid 21.
34 See also L Wittgenstein *Philosophical Investigations* (GEM Anscombe tr, Blackwell 1958).

80 *Emilia Mickiewicz*

Similarly, a careful analysis of analogical reasoning in law reveals that the process can rarely be reduced to mapping past authorities on to the facts of the present case. Postema emphasises that analogising in law is typically carried out on two levels: the base level, which identifies 'credible analogies' and reproduces them in the present case, and the reflective level, which enables innovation when a shift in the wider context justifies it.[35] The reflective level becomes most evident when a cognitive dissonance dictates that the case no longer fits with its surrounding context. The law's deliberation

> is driven, or at least encouraged, to ascend to the reflective level by a sense that the understanding achieved by means of base-level analogical reasoning is problematic in some way. One might come to sense that, although the proposed pattern fits well with its closest neighbour, it is out of phase with the law when one casts a broader eye over it.[36]

The reflective level of analogising encourages the judge to make the law intelligible against the wider background against which it operates, even if it means that he or she will have to depart from the existing authorities.

The engagement of productive imagination at the reflective level, however, is contestable. Although today nobody doubts that the higher appellate courts regularly reflectively reshape the law, the extent to which they can legitimately do so remains limited. One of the most contentious areas of judicial activism is constitutional law. This is because, here, the questions of authority arise, and, typically, they are posed at two levels. One pertains to the legitimacy of the constitutional order itself; another concerns the authority of the courts to address the first question. We can call them, respectively, the questions of constitution and justiciability. From our perspective, it is also the area where the two modes of social imagination, ideology and utopia, potentially clash. This occurs whenever the courts attempt to reinvent the law to advance political goals. We can say that the courts mobilise ideological modes of imagination whenever they seek to preserve political values enshrined in the already existing constitutional order. Conversely, utopia is engaged when attempts are made to depart from that order. Often the courts invoke ideology and utopia simultaneously. This is when the courts seek to creatively expand their own powers in order to preserve an existing social or political vision. We will examine some examples of this later on in the chapter.

Drawing a line between legitimate and illegitimate judicial decision making can be a daunting task. However, Ricoeur's analysis of ideology and utopia as social imagination provides a useful source of guidance. First, Ricoeur stresses that this line is fluid. Although it is tempting to simply conclude that only reproductive acts of imagination in law (i.e. those that simply restate the existing precedent) are

---

35 G Postema, 'A similibus ad similia: analogical thinking in law' in D Edlin (ed), *Common Law Theory* (Cambridge UP 2007) 116.
36 Ibid 132.

legitimate, this is a conclusion that both Kant and Ricoeur would find difficult to accept. This is because every act of reproduction involves a productive element. It occurs owing to the synthesising capacity of imagination. The very act of applying the known to the unknown is already productive.[37]

Conversely, the acts of productive imagination always exhibit a measure of continuity with the past, as they start with what is already given. For example, a centaur is produced out of what already exists: a horse and a man.[38] Similarly, utopia and ideology, with their integrative and disintegrative functions, operate in tandem, they dialectically imply each other. As Ricoeur recognises, '[t]here is no social integration without social subversion.'[39] The most repetitive ideology necessarily puts utopia at a distance, and, vice versa, the most radical utopia cannot be communicated without having at least minimal connection to the established ideology. They remain in a dialectic relationship whereby one 'bears the trace' of the other.[40] This fluid conception of legitimacy provides an attractive alternative to the static and detached theories of adjudication that assert that judicial decision-making outside the clearly defined frames is illegitimate.[41] Although such theories offer clarity, they fail to reflect the actual practice of adjudication and ignore the need for the law to remain flexible in novel circumstances.

Second, although it is difficult unequivocally to determine the boundary between legitimate and illegitimate decision-making, the extreme cases of illegitimate adjudication are more obvious to spot. We can connect such cases with what Ricoeur described as the 'the dark side' or 'pathological' expression of imagination.[42] In the fields of social practice, pathology manifests itself as an ideological or utopian tendency for self-delusion, an escapist flight into fancy.[43] Ricoeur observes that, whereas a healthy ideology 'tries to secure integration between legitimacy claim and belief' by skilfully connecting ideas with actual practice, its pathology is characterised by a complete non-congruence with the existing reality.[44] Similarly, whereas a healthy utopia seeks to 'expose the credibility gap wherein all systems of authority exceed ... both our confidence in them and our belief in their legitimacy,' the pathological modes of utopia compromise this function. Whereas a healthy utopia is concerned with the 'exploration of the possible,' its pathology turns to the 'completely unrealisable.'[45]

Pathologies of imagination often manifest themselves as a blind commitment to a non-existing reality, and the consequences of such commitment could be

---

37 Ricoeur (n 27).
38 Arendt, 79.
39 Ricoeur (n 9) 16–17.
40 JM Balkin, 'Deconstructive practice and legal theory' (1987) 96 *Yale LJ* 752.
41 EJ Weinrib, 'Law as a Kantian idea of reason' (1987) *Columbia Law Review* 472; J Bentham, *An Introduction to the Principles of Morals and Legislation* (Athlone Press 1996).
42 Geniusas and Nikulin (n 10) x.
43 Ibid.
44 Ricoeur (n 9) 16.
45 Ibid 22.

devastating. This point was skilfully pictured by Flaubert in his novels, most notably *Madame Bovary*. The main character, Emma, longs for a more glamorous life, away from her conformist husband and parochial surroundings. She harbours a feeling that something is missing, something that would make her feel alive. She wants to experience what the words 'felicity, passion and rupture' (which she knows from romantic novels) mean exactly.[46] She is consumed with the vision of a glamorous self and she soon loses touch with reality. Unfortunately, the 'reality is just as unbearable as the imaginary is unlivable,' so she eventually makes a tragic decision to take her own life.[47] Similarly, a blind commitment to a political vision or a social practice can paradoxically contribute to its demise. This is because defending it at all costs, and invoking arguments that are impossible to square with reality, could contribute to expanding instead of narrowing the 'credibility gap' between the claim and subjects' belief in that vision.

A disposition for self-delusion of this kind, the conjuring, as it were, is likely to emerge in various areas of human activity, including the law and politics. A passion for political vision can keep one captive, to the point where one not only elevates what is a matter of contestable opinion to eternal truth, but also identifies oneself so closely with that vision that every criticism directed at it is felt like a personal, deeply wounding assault. Defending it is no longer a matter of reason, but one of pride and dignity. This can lead one to be so entangled in that internalised position that one is prepared to sacrifice other valid considerations just to preserve the unity of the cherished view.

Below, some examples of the pathological exercise of imagination are examined in the context of the perceived contemporary crisis of the rule of law in Poland. Although Ricœur's distinction between ideology and utopia reveals that drawing a boundary between legitimate and illegitimate judicial decision-making is necessarily imperfect, on the edges, where the pathological tendencies reveal themselves, it is easier to argue that a given decision lacks legitimacy.

Pathologies of imagination and the constitutional crisis in Poland

Regardless of their political complexion, a vast majority of legal and political commentators today agree that 'liberal democracy has enjoyed much better days.'[48] Authoritarian governance is on the rise, becoming a symptom of 'constitutional rot': a slow, insidious decline of the rule of law.[49] One of the much cited examples in this context is the constitutional crisis in Poland, which ensued from a series of reforms to the judiciary. These included such controversial measures as removal of the ordinary court judges by lowering their retirement age and politicisation of the judicial appointment process by means of restructuring the

---

46 N de Warren 'Imagination of stupidity: Jules de Gaultier, Flaubert and Le Bovarysme' in Geniusas and Nikulin (n 10) 124.
47 Ibid.
48 CR Sunstein, 'It can happen here,' *New York Review of Books*, 28 June 2018.
49 Ibid.

National Judiciary Council. The reforms also included an introduction of an extraordinary chamber to the Supreme Court composed of the judges appointed by the governing party and endowed with the power to review the decisions of the Supreme Court and rule on the validity of elections.[50]

The reforms not only gave rise to a series of protests and relentless opposition domestically, but also prompted the European Commission to initiate for the first time in history the rule of law infringement proceedings under Article 7(1) of the Treaty of European Union (TEU). This provision endows the Commission with the authority to notify the European Council if it believes there is a clear risk of a serious breach by a member state of the rule of law values. If the Council finds such an infringement, it could then impose sanctions on that member state.[51] Despite exerting some political pressure, in the Polish case, the proceedings had little chance of success. The imposition of sanctions under Article 7(3) of TEU requires a unanimous decision of all member states.[52] This was almost certain to be vetoed by Hungary, which was also targeted by the EU for rule of law violations and democratic backsliding.[53] The stakes were high, and the chances of success slim. The alternative route of challenging the reforms before the Court of Justice of the European Union (CJEU) appeared highly controversial as no provision of the TEU expressly endows the CJEU with the power to rule on the independence of the national judiciary of the member states.

However, the CJEU took an opportunity to creatively expand the scope of its competences only 2 months after the infringement proceedings against Poland commenced, in an unrelated dispute of *Associação Sindical dos Juízes Portugueses*.[54] Here, the Portuguese judges sought to challenge domestic austerity measures, which adversely affected their salaries. Although the application of the Portuguese judges was dismissed, the CJEU used the dispute as a vehicle to reshape imaginatively the existing provisions of the TEU.

To attain this objective, the Court had first to depart from similar cases on austerity measures, in which it claimed to 'clearly' have no jurisdiction as there was no evidence that the measures in question were intended to implement EU law.[55] The requirement that the Court can only review measures designed to implement EU law was derived from Article 51(1) of the European Charter of the Fundamental Freedoms.[56] The

---

50 See Venice Commission, Opinion No. 904/2017; Reasoned Proposal Brussels, 20.12.2017 COM (2017) 835; W Sadurski, 'How democracies die', 5–6, 'On democratic backsliding' 15, Matczak 'Poland Constitutional Crisis.'

51 Article 7(3) TEU.

52 7(3) TEU.

53 W Sadurski, *Poland's Constitutional Breakdown* (OUP 2019) 225.

54 *Associação Sindical dos Juízes Portugueses* (n 12) para 29.

55 Case C-264/12, *Sindacato Nacional dos Profissionais de Seguro v Fidelidade Mundial* [2014] ECLI:EU:C:2014:2036 para 19; Case C-128/12, *Sindicato dos Bancários do Norte* [2013] ECLI:EU:C:2013:149. See also C Kilpatrick, 'Are the bailouts immune to EU social challenge because they are not EU law?' (2014) 10 *European Constitutional Law Review* 393. It should be noted that that hearing took place before the decision in Case C-258/14, *Florescu*, i.e. before the change of orientation of the Court on the matter.

56 Article 51(1) TEU. See also Article 47 (TEU).

84   *Emilia Mickiewicz*

provision implies that the Court has no competence to intervene, unless the matter relates to the implementation of Union law. To avoid the difficulty, the Court decided to bypass the charter altogether and instead it grounded the claim on Article 19(1) TEU. This Article states that 'The Member States shall provide remedies sufficient to ensure effective legal protection in the fields covered by Union law.' However, Article 19(1) has never served as an autonomous basis on which to review domestic measures.[57] Even more confusingly, the CJEU found that the scope of Article 19(1) is broader than the scope of Article 51(1). The Court argued that,

> as regards the material scope of the second subparagraph of Article 19(1) TEU, that provision relates to 'the fields covered by Union law', irrespective of whether the member states are implementing Union law, within the meaning of Article 51(1) of the Charter.[58]

The finding that Article 19(1) is broader in scope than Article 51(1) of the Charter constituted another major departure from the previous case law, which (as established in *Åkerberg Fransson*) indicated that the scope of application of the Charter is coextensive with EU law, whenever fundamental rights are engaged.[59] By stating that the material scope of Article 19(1) is wider than that of Article 51 (1) of the Charter, the CJEU arrived at a rather perplexing conclusion that there are some cases that fall under the jurisdiction of the CJEU, as they belong to 'the fields covered by EU law', but they are not at the same time covered by the notion of 'the Member States implementing EU law.'[60] It has thus created what has been described as an 'entirely new sphere' of EU law.[61]

The Court then went on creatively to expand the content of Article 19 TEU. As the plain reading of the Article indicates that the scope of its operation relates to the matters covered by Union law, the CJEU had to find support in other provisions of the TEU to show that the Article is relevant to the operation of the national courts in general. The Court began by invoking Article 2 TEU, which refers to the rule of law as a fundamental value of the Union. It then indicated that the rule of law is given 'concrete expression' in Article 19, which entrusts not only the CJEU, but also national courts and tribunals, with the vital function of judicial review in EU-related matters. As domestic courts might from time to time apply EU law, all domestic judges are now 'European judges.'[62]

---

57 M Krajewski, 'Associação Sindical dos Juízes Portugueses: the Court of Justice and Athena's dilemma' (2018) 3 *European Papers* 402.
58 *Associação Sindical dos Juízes Portugueses* (n 12) para 29.
59 Case C-617/10, *Åklagaren v Hans Åkerberg Fransson* (2012) ECR ECLI:EU: C:2012:340 para 21
60 M Bonelli and M Claes, 'Judicial serendipity: how Portuguese judges came to the rescue of the Polish judiciary' (2018) 14 *European Constitutional Law Review* 630.
61 Ibid.
62 Opinion of AG Saugmandsgaard Øe, *Associação Sindical dos Juízes Portugueses* [2017] ECR ECLI:EU:C:2017:395 para 41.

The Court then suddenly brought back Article 47 of the Charter and claimed that combined with Articles 6 and 13 of ECHR, it imposes an obligation on domestic courts to ensure effective protection of individuals in the fields covered by the EU law. To 'meet the requirements of effective judicial protection,' the courts must, however, be independent, as required by Article 267 TFEU. This was another surprising move, as the case law on Article 267 TFEU indicates that, 'independence is not a requirement imposed by the EU law, but rather a condition, which must be met for the body to be considered a court or a tribunal in the first place.'[63] Yet in this dispute, the CJEU had no hesitation in transforming judicial independence into a universal obligation on all national courts that will potentially apply EU law.

The key to understanding the steps that the Court of Justice took in *Associação Sindical dos Juízes Portugueses* can be found in the constitutional crisis in Poland, which was unfolding in the background.[64] It was very likely that the Court was motivated by a desire to have a say in the current situation in Poland and Hungary where, after the adoption of controversial constitutional and institutional reforms, the independence of the national judiciaries had been called into question.[65] This view is supported by the fact that, shortly after the decision in *Associação Sindical dos Juízes Portugueses*, the Polish judges brought direct challenges to the controversial reforms before the Court of Justice, and, in the resulting *Commission v Poland* case, the CJEU relied heavily on Article 19 (1) TEU to assert its jurisdiction over the matter and support a conclusion that the reforms indeed amounted to violation of the rule of law.[66] In short, the Portuguese case became a vehicle for the Court to indicate its willingness to assess national measures that are likely to undermine the independence of a national judiciary, irrespective of whether the Charter applies.

The CJEU is typically prepared to go beyond the express wording of the acquis, as well as its established case law, if the constitutional foundations of the EU are in danger. The CJEU will, in such circumstances, give effect to a view that it thinks the majority of the member states would have adopted.[67] This position, however, comes at a cost. By ignoring the plain wording of the Treaty and departing from the established orthodoxy on the relationship between the TEU and the Charter,

---

63 Bonelli and Claes (n 60) 633.

64 M Taborowski, 'CJEU opens the door for the Commission to reconsider charges against Poland,' *Verfassungsblog* (13 March 2018) <https://verfassungsblog.de/cjeu-op ens-the-door-for-the-commission-to-reconsider-charges-against-poland/> accessed 9 December 2019; Daniel Sarmiento, 'On constitutional mode,' *Despite Our Differences Blog*, 6 March 2018, <https://despiteourdifferencesblog.wordpress.com/2018/03/ 06/on-constitutional-mode/> accessed 9 December 2019; Michal Ovádek, 'Has the CJEU just reconfigured the EU constitutional order?' *Verfassungsblog*, 28 February 2018, <https://verfassungsblog.de/has-the-cjeu-just-reconfigured-the-eu-constitutiona l-order/> accessed 9 December 2019.

65 Bonelli and Claes (n. 60) 623.

66 Ibid.

67 MP Maduro, *We the Court: The European Court of Justice and the European Economic Constitution* (Hart 1998).

86 *Emilia Mickiewicz*

the CJEU stretched the legitimacy of its decision-making. It demonstrated little regard to the fact that the agreed procedure for dealing with the rule of law infringements under the Treaty is a measure enshrined in Article 7 TEU. Although the procedure proved impotent because of its requirement for unanimity, it was precisely that requirement upon which all member states agreed when the Treaty was adopted. In other words, there has never been a political will to put in place a procedure that would result in what might be perceived as unwarranted intervention in the internal matters of a given member state by the remaining member states.

Although most commentators argue that the EU institutions did not go far enough in addressing democratic backsliding in Poland and Hungary, one can argue that the CJEU intervention paradoxically undermined, instead of protecting, the rule of law.[68] By assuming powers with which it had not been expressly endowed, the Court fed into the populist tendencies it was trying to defeat. The unwarranted expansion of the EU powers has become a prominent argument in the Euro-sceptical movements on the rise across the EU, and the Court just made this point only more credible.[69] Following Brexit, the EU legal order and its sustainability have come under unprecedented strain, and other factors are likely to weaken it further. Norman Davies argued that all political structures are inherently transient, but it is a truth that many choose to ignore.[70] When an end comes, it is often a result of ignoring the warning signs and acting without caution. The CJEU needs its credentials more than ever before, and bold moves without a clear political mandate are likely not only to compromise the legitimacy of the CJEU, but also to undermine the legal order it is committed to defend. The way in which the CJEU acted could be perceived as an act of hegemony, instead of being an expression of the plurality to which the EU institutions are meant to be committed.[71]

Associação Sindical dos Juízes Portugueses and the subsequent rulings on the Polish reforms have not only been characterised by a sense of blindness to the long-term consequences the interventions are likely to produce. The CJEU has also exhibited an exaggerated commitment to the advanced cause: an immediate need to address the threat to the rule of law in Poland. This objective became, in the eyes of the CJEU, the ultimate and exclusive criterion justifying intervention. The sense of urgency was emphasised by the fact that the challenges to the Polish reforms were granted an accelerated hearing owing to 'the seriousness of the situation.'[72] The remedies, too, have been extraordinary, as they involved interim suspension of the measures in question. This left no margin for Poland to find a flexible solution and potentially undermined the principle of mutual trust, antagonising this member state even further.

---

68 N Davies, *Vanished Kingdoms* (Penguin, 2012) 5.
69 I Krastev, *After Europe* (University of Pennsylvania Press 2018); R Mullender, 'After Europe publication review' (2018) *PL* 562–66.
70 D Kochenov and P Bard, *The Last Soldier Standing? Courts vs. Politicians and the Rule of Law Crisis in the New Member States of the EU*, University of Groningen Faculty of Law Research Paper Series No. 5/2019.
71 I Krastev and S Holmes, *The Light that Failed. A Reckoning* (Allen Lane, 2019).
72 *Commission v Poland* (n 12) [2018] ECR ECLI:EU:C:2018:910 Order.

Pathologies of imagination and the constitutional crisis in Poland

Drawing on Ricoeur, we can argue that the sense of immediacy and detachment from context found in the CJEU interventions is a symptom of pathological exercise of imagination. As Ricoeur demonstrated, imagination has 'a constructive and a destructive side, a constitutive and a pathological dimension.'[73] Whereas the constitutive exercise of imagination shows appreciation for the situatedness of the imagined projects, its past conditions and future possibilities, its pathological expression is 'motivated by a necessary obliviousness to the existing conditions' and a totalising tendency for immediate realisation.[74] Pathological imagination shows no interest in careful, considerate implementation of the imagined projects and leaves no space for revisions. Instead, it is driven by 'a logic of all or nothing, which ignores the labour of time' and strives to produce models that are immediately perfect.[75] Conversely, the heathy, constitutive imagination allows for the introduction of variations on the existing conditions. It encourages exploration of possibilities, instead of being bound to an absolute cause or a single way of doing things.

The decision of the CJEU in *Associação Sindical dos Juízes Portugueses* not only abruptly breaks with the established case law but also shows little regard for the existing political constraints, most notably the existing distribution of power under Article 7 TEU. The pathological disregard for that background and a blind commitment to the advanced cause here take on a distinctively political character, inviting the questions of legitimacy that Ricoeur associated with the figures of ideology and utopia. Here, ideology manifests itself as a commitment to the rule of law and utopia in creative ways of departing from the established legal and political framework for the sake of the cherished cause. Whereas a healthy ideology and utopia serve as valuable correctives to one another, here the dialectic between the two exhibits gaps in the Court's undertaking that are simply too wide to square with the material conditions against which it operates. The pathological stretching of ideology and utopia can be identified at several junctions.

The Court's attempt to expand its powers creatively under Article 19 TEU involves a rebutting of the orthodoxy on the relationship between the TEU and the Charter. It amounts to a pathological exercise of utopian imagination. This is because the reasons why the established relationship has, in the CJEU's view, changed are not articulated. Similarly, the unexpected transformation of the national courts into the European judiciary whose independence became a matter for the CJEU, based on previously non-existing duty, is executed on no clearly stated grounds.

The stretching of utopia at justiciability level does not serve to correct and strengthen the rule of law ideology, but can paradoxically undermine it. Whereas a healthy exercise of imagination helps to synthesise experience and understanding, advancing our grasp of the existing reality, the series of rhetorical steps undertaken

---

73 P Ricœur, *Lectures on Ideology and Utopia* (GH Taylor ed, Columbia UP 1986) 1.
74 N Coleman, *Utopias and Architecture* (Routledge 2005) 60.
75 Ricœur (n 9).

88 *Emilia Mickiewicz*

by the Court transforms the relevant legal provisions into unintelligible, detached, and suspect propositions. When mixed with the resultant unwarranted assumption of powers, it expands what Ricoeur called the 'credibility gap' between the claim to authority and belief in that authority.[76] The legitimacy of the Court's decision is compromised by the dubious means adopted to advance it. This in turn feeds into the wider perception of the EU institutions and their credibility.

Judicial independence, legitimacy, and the Court of Justice

In *Associação Sindical dos Juízes Portugueses* and the subsequent cases on the Polish constitutional crisis, the CJEU devised strict criteria that courts must meet to be truly independent, bringing questions of legitimacy into focus. In *Commission v Poland*, the CJEU observed that for a tribunal to be deemed independent its decisions must be such 'that they cannot give rise to reasonable doubts, in the minds of individuals, as to the imperviousness of the judges concerned to external factors and as to their neutrality with respect to the interests before them.'[77] The CJEU added that this applies in the same measure to the external aspect of judicial independence – that is, freedom from external pressure – as well as its internal aspect, which requires that 'an equal distance is maintained from the parties to the proceedings and their respective interests with regard to the subject matter of those proceedings.'[78]

One is left wondering to what extent the CJEU satisfies its own criteria of independence. Could the parties in *Associação Sindical dos Juízes Portugueses* and *Commission v Poland* be certain 'beyond reasonable doubt' that a decision that offers little or no justification for a departure from the express wording of the TEU or its own previous findings is not driven by a partisan commitment to one or another cause? The CJEU's standard *modus operandi* is to provide no detailed justifications for its conclusions.[79] Its institutional design leaves no space for dissenting judgments, greatly limiting its capacity to acknowledge that, while not prevailing on a given occasion, other valid considerations are engaged in most disputes before it. It is the only EU institution that is not routinely scrutinised for compliance with the EU Treaties.[80] One could question whether, in the light of this, the decisions of the CJEU and its operation indeed leave no doubt in the minds of individuals as to 'the imperviousness of the judges' of this court.[81]

The analysis of the CJEU case law on the constitutional crisis in Poland reveals unreserved commitment of the CJEU to the ideal of the rule of law. The CJEU

---

76 See also Weber (n 8).
77 *Commission v Poland* (n 12) para 111.
78 Ibid para 73.
79 See M Dawson, B de Witte and E Muir (eds), *Judicial Activism at the European Court of Justice* (Edward Elgar 2013).
80 Ibid 5. With an exception of Case T-577/14 *Gascogne Sack Deutschland GmbH EU* [2017] ECLI:EU:T:2017:1and Case T-673/15 *Guardian Europe v European Union* [2017] ECLI:EU:T:2017:377.
81 *Commission v Poland* (n 12).

openly recognises its partiality in this respect when it devises an exception to its strict rules on judicial independence. In *Commission v Poland*, the Court declares that judicial independence requires 'objectivity and the absence of any interest in the outcome of the proceedings *apart* from the strict application of the rule of law.'[82] In practice, this exception allows the CJEU to cover its own questionable decisions, as long as it can argue that it did so to advance the rule of law. This would include circumstances such as those in the *Portuguese* case where the Court departed from the express wording of the TEU to create powers for itself which it did not have under the Treaty, in order to protect the rule of law. All this, however, is very difficult to square with the CJEU's own definition of the rule of law. As it established in *Kadi*, '[t]he [Union] is based on the rule of law, inasmuch as neither its member states nor its institutions can avoid review of the conformity of their acts with the basic constitutional charter, the [Treaties].'[83] If the rule of law implies that all the EU institutions must act in conformity with the TEU, is it acceptable for the CJEU to depart from the TEU in order to defend the rule of law?

When devising its exception to judicial independence, the CJEU not only implied an understanding of the 'rule of law' that could hardly be squared with its own jurisprudence, but also one that implies that 'the rule of law' has a fixed, uniform content that always pulls in one direction. However, the rule of law is a complex notion exhibiting commitment to values that are often incommensurable. Its procedural aspect might require that the existing rules ought to be followed, whereas the substantive one can sometimes justify a departure from the existing rules, if it appears right to do so from a moral perspective.[84] In *Commission v Poland*, the procedural aspect of the rule of law would dictate that the CJEU should refrain from interference, as the existing TEU provisions preclude it from doing so, whereas the substantive aspect might pull in another direction. But there is complexity within the substantive aspect too. How best to preserve the rule of law is a question that receives no definitive answer. A hasty move could help to preserve the rule of law on one occasion, but it might compromise it in the long run. The rule of law, with its capacity to accommodate difference and complexity, has too much to offer to be compromised by an absolutist or pathological implementation.

---

82 Ibid para 73.
83 Joined Cases C-402/05 P and C-415/05 P *Kadi and Al Barakaat International Foundation v Council and Commission* [2008] EU:C:2008:461 para 281.
84 See TAO Endicott, 'The impossibility of the rule of law' (1999) 19 *Oxford Journal of Legal Studies* 1–2; P Craig, 'Formal and substantive conceptions of the rule of law: an analytical framework' (1997) *PL* 467; J Waldron, 'The rule of law and the importance of procedure,' *New York University Public Law and Legal Theory Working Papers*, Paper 234 (2010) <http://lsr.nellco.org/nyu~plltwp/234> accessed 9 December 2019.

90 *Emilia Mickiewicz*

Towards a constitutive account of legitimate adjudication

By putting Ricoeur's findings together, we can devise more nuanced criteria of legitimate decision-making than those developed by the CJEU. The distinction between constitutive and pathological imagination implies that a decision or some of its aspects lack legitimacy (i.e. are less likely to effectively bridge the gap between the claim and belief in that claim), if it exhibits a rigid commitment to an abstract ideal that is detached from the relevant context. A commitment to that ideal will lead a judge to conceal the grounds for the decision or fail to admit that no such grounds exist. Such a decision will show little or no regard for the tradition in which the decision is embedded and it will be indifferent to the future consequences that it is likely to produce. Instead, a blind commitment to advancing an immediate concern before the court will dominate the decision-making process.

Implementation of the identified ideal will typically be invested with a sense of urgency, to the exclusion of all other relevant considerations. It will demonstrate preoccupation with 'time as now' and 'neglect of the actual effort … required to get things right.'[85] It will show tendency 'to delineate self-contained schemas of perfection severed from the whole course of the human experience.'[86] It will furthermore show lack of care for the steps to be taken in the direction of achieving the identified goal. Detachment from context will manifest itself as 'the eclipse of praxis, the denial of the logic of action which inevitably ties undesirable evils to preferred means and which forces us to choose between equally desirable but incompatible goals.'[87]

In contrast, a 'healthy' or constitutive exercise of imagination would lead the judge to explain instead of concealing the grounds on which the decision was made. Such a decision would seek to embrace 'action, practice, obstacles and incompatibility,' recognise imperfection, and exhibit 'tolerance for conflict between goals.'[88] Such a decision would furthermore demonstrate sensitivity to competing considerations and seek to accommodate them or explain the reasons as to why one, rather than another, had prevailed on a given occasion. Exercise of the constitutive imagination will lead the judge to recognise legal and political constraints and arrive at a decision that is situated instead of being detached from past and future conditions. It will seek to connect the present action with past accomplishments and future consequences. Whereas pathological decision might be driven by an erratic need for immediate realisation, a constitutive decision would be likely to promote considered implementation of the identified ideal over a longer period of time and will remain open to revisions.

The above account of constitutive adjudication can be applied to the interventions of the CJEU in the constitutional crisis in Poland. It indicates that these decisions would be more legitimate if the CJEU had identified a clearer basis on

---

85 Ricoeur (n 9) 121.
86 Ibid.
87 N Coleman, *Utopias and Architecture* (Routledge 2005) 60.
88 Ibid.

which to proceed or alternatively specified the grounds for the extension of Article 19(1). These decisions would be better justified if the CJEU offered an explanation for departing from the exiting case law on the relationship between the TEU and Charter and for substituting its own competence for the European Council's authority under Article 7 TEU.

Further, the decisions would benefit from recognition that important contravening considerations of division of power were prominent here, and, if the CJEU was of the opinion that these were not strong enough, the grounds on which such a conclusion was reached should be made plain. These decisions would also appear more legitimate if the CJEU was to admit that abstract standards, such as the rule of law, provide no unified criteria for conduct and might dictate various defensible outcomes.

If it was impossible for the CJEU to offer a more robust justification of its position and/or identify an express legal basis that gives it the authority to act on a given matter, it would have strengthened its legitimacy by refraining from the intervention altogether.[89] The EU's constitutional order is based on carefully devised competences, and any conduct of the EU institutions that appears to ignore the existing division of power is highly controversial. Article 13(2) TEU imposes an obligation on EU institutions to act within the limits of the powers expressly attributed to them by the Treaty. This also gives effect to the principle of conferral under Article 5(2) TEU. Judicial 'acts of self-empowerment' continue to present an important aspect of the ongoing constitutional debates surrounding the viability and sustainability of the EU order.[90] If the CJEU demonstrates greater sensitivity towards express statements of constituent authority while exercising its adjudicative functions, it is likely to advance the agreed status of the member states as 'Masters of the Treaties' and help to promote durability of the European legal order in the long run.[91]

Conclusions

Drawing on Ricoeur's insights, we can develop criteria for legitimate judicial decision-making. A legitimate decision is one that effectively narrows the gap between the authority's claim and the public's belief in that claim. Although Ricoeur alerts us that the boundary between legitimate and illegitimate action is not always sharp, judgments that result from pathological, as opposed to constitutive, exercises of imagination are more likely to lack legitimacy. The symptoms of pathological adjudication include, but are not limited to: a blind commitment to the advanced cause to the exclusion of other valid considerations; detachment from context, requirements for immediacy, and absoluteness; rigidity; insensitivity

---

89 AM Bickel, 'The passive virtues' (1961) 75 *Harv L Rev* 40.
90 T Horsley, *The Court of Justice of the European Union as an Institutional Actor* (CUP 2018) 269.
91 Ibid 270. See also KJ Alter, 'Who are the "masters of the treaty"? European governments and the European Court of Justice' (1998) 52 *International Organization* 121.

92 *Emilia Mickiewicz*

to past and future constraints; and a tendency to declare rather than justify. In contrast, a constitutive exercise of imagination is likely to promote adjudication that is: situated; demonstrates sensitivity to past, present, and future constraints; recognises imperfection; leaves space for amendments; recognises complexity; and is committed to explanation and considerate implementation of the advanced cause rather than its immediate implementation.

This chapter examined the extent to which the recent interventions of the CJEU in the Polish constitutional crisis satisfied the above criteria. There are reasons to believe that some aspects of the intervention have been driven by the exercising of pathological imagination. The CJEU demonstrated an unreserved commitment to a rigidly understood rule of law ideal and excluded other relevant considerations, most notably the existing division of power under the TEU. The hasty intervention might have helped to address the immediate concern, but had the potential to undermine the credibility of the intervening institution in the long term, weakening an already fragile EU legal order and the rule of law on which it is founded.

Pathological tendencies detected in the CJEU cases, however, can be identified in decisions of courts and tribunals in various fields of law.[92]

No human practice is immune from heteronomous forces that, from time to time, affect our capacity to make clear judgments. The best one can do is to adopt what Ricoeur called an attitude of 'suspicion' towards one's own findings – that is, a disposition to distinguish between appearances and reality.[93] Although imagination has the negative capacity to lure us into the world of fancy, in its positive guise it brings us back to reality and helps to reshape it in a meaningful fashion. It is here that the synthesising force of imagination finds its most powerful expression.

---

92 For example, we can identify pathological tendencies in *Miller and Cherry* [2019] UKSC 41. This involves Lady Hale's attempt to invoke the principle of 'parliamentary accountability,' which she derives from the Privy Council's decision in *Bobb v Manning* [2006] UKPC 22. Here, she chooses to overlook the fact that the Privy Council decisions are not binding on the UK courts. But we can also find pathological tendencies in the critical responses to Lady Hale's decision. For example, John Finnis argues that the Queen's actions in Parliament are 'Proceedings in Parliament'. In doing so he ignores the modern understanding of parliamentary sovereignty, which presupposes the involvement of both Houses of Parliament. See: J Finnis, 'The unconstitutionality of the Supreme Court's prorogation judgment,' *Policy Exchange*, Judicial Power Project. <https://policyexchange.org.uk/wp-content/up loads/2019/10/The-unconstitutionality-of-the-Supreme-Courts-prorogation-judg ment.pdf> accessed 9 December 2019.

93 P Ricoeur, *Freud and Philosophy. An Essay on Interpretation* (Yale UP 2008) 33–35.

6 Law and belief

The reality of judicial interpretation

Scott Fraley

SENIOR COUNSEL AT CHAMBERLAIN MCHANEY, AUSTIN, TX

In their text *Reading Law*, former U.S. Supreme Court Justice Antonin Scalia (deceased) and Bryan A. Garner note that, 'theories of legal interpretation have been discussed interminably, and often so obscurely as to leave even the most intelligent readers – or perhaps especially the most intelligent readers – befuddled.'[1] Scalia and Garner express a view shared by many legal scholars – namely, that 'theories' have not been helpful in clarifying what exactly it means to interpret the law. To be sure, legal interpretation is in many ways mired in the same tired debates that have taken place for 230 years, without significant progress.

The reason we are stuck in the same tired dialogue about legal interpretation is not that there are not many candidates battling for attention, but that we continue to discuss 'theories of interpretation' at all. For example, although Justice Scalia and Garner complain about theories of interpretation, they of course inevitably promote their own.[2] Instead, we should be talking about theories of adjudication, how real-world cases get decided.[3] This subject in turn, I propose, really turns not on theories of interpretation, but on the inherent beliefs of judges and justices about on what criteria to decide cases, beliefs that exist *independent* of any theory of interpretation.

I will argue in this chapter that, at least in the exemplar cases examined, the Court in effect uses theories of legal interpretation not to reach a result, but to explain a result reached. Such a claim is indeed bold, for, if true, such an approach represents at a minimum a failure of the legal imagination, an inability to achieve intellectual honesty in the application of theory to practice. It turns out, however, that this is nothing more than what we all do in our every choice, for we can never escape or step beyond the bounds of our individual belief systems. I submit that a

---

1 A Scalia and BA Garner, *Reading Law* (Thompson/West 2013) 15, *citing* Learned Hand, 'Proceedings in commemoration of fifty years of federal judicial service' (1959) 264 F.2d (1959) ('[M]any sages ... have spoken on [statutory construction], and I do not know that it has gotten us very much further').

2 Justice Scalia was a leading proponent of textualism, how a reasonable reader would have understood the text when it was written. See G Lawson 'Did Justice Scalia have a theory of legal interpretation?' (2017) 92 *Notre Dame L Rev* 2143–62.

3 Ibid 2155–56.

94   *Scott Fraley*

better use of legal imagination would be to substitute the values of the American public as displayed through social mores of the day, the *ethos* of the land, so to speak, as the Court's guiding principle.[4]

Constitutional theories of interpretation

Constitutional scholar Philip Bobbitt, in his text *Constitutional Fate: Theory of the Constitution*,[5] suggests that prudential arguments – based on the reasonable expectations of the public and prudential wisdom of the court regarding appropriate outcomes – are one of five possible approaches to the interpretation of the Constitution. Others include textualism (the study of the words in the text and their meaning); intentionalism (trying to determine the intentions of those who drafted and ratified the Constitution); precedent (reliance on prior court decisions); and natural law (universal law or God's law). This chapter will examine the U.S. Supreme Court's application of various methods of constitutional interpretation and evaluate the relative consistency or inconsistency with which the Court implements those techniques. The examination of a few sample cases offers clues as to the Court's interpretational approach.

Exemplar Supreme Court cases[6]

One recent example of the Court's use of interpretive theory is *Obergefell v. Hodges*,[7] in which a majority of the Court held that the Fourteenth Amendment requires states to allow gay marriage. Marriage between two persons of the same sex was not a public issue when the Constitution was drafted and ratified. Thus, the Court's decision could not have been based on either the text of the Constitution itself or on the intent of the framers (as Justices Scalia and Roberts insist repeatedly in multiple opinions and books; the 'intentionalism' mentioned in the previous paragraph), but instead had to be concerned with the effect on the populace, the reception of the public, the culture at the time of the decision, and social changes in the interim.[8] The decision reflects an analytical mode somewhat like, but not explicitly mirroring, the literary critical technique of reader-response theory, in which the interpreter considers the reasonable expectations and response of the reading community in interpreting a text.[9] Here, the Court

---

4 See, e.g., JR Dyer, '*Texas v. Johnson*, symbolic speech and flag desecration under the First Amendment' (1991) 25 *NE L Rev* 895.
5 P Bobbitt, *Constitutional Fate: Theory of the Constitution* (OPU 1982) 7, 59–73.
6 I have chosen these cases for the similarity of the subject matter of the cases compared in order to allow a direct juxtaposition of the application of the constitutional theory in question. This chapter obviously is not intended as a comprehensive review of Supreme Court case law, nor could it be, but rather to raise an important question and to start a useful conversation about the Court's use of interpretive theory.
7 135 S. Ct. 2584 (2015).
8 There is the possibility, of course, beyond the scope of this chapter, of the reimagination of the body politic so that the Court's decisions become consistent with the mores of the populace.
9 See S Fish, 'Working on the chain gang: interpretation in the law and literary criticism' (1982) 9 *Critical Inquiry* 201–16.

Law and belief 95

was not examining the strict text of the Constitution, but rather 'taking the pulse of the public,' investigating the public imagination, so to speak, evaluating the fabric of today's society and what is now socially acceptable. Like reader-response theory,[10] the reasonable expectations of the community are at stake.

The problem, however, is that the Court is completely inconsistent in its application of interpretational approaches. This inconsistency in the Court's interpretational approach is particularly evident in two examples from the Roberts Court, *Citizens United v. FEC*, 130 S. Ct. 876 (2010) ('*Citizens United*'), and *District of Columbia v. Heller*, 128 S. Ct. 2783 (2008).

Citizens United v. FEC

Citizens United was a 5–4 decision authored by Justice Anthony Kennedy. The case involved a documentary – *Hillary: The Movie* – written from a critical perspective about Senator and then presidential candidate Hillary Rodham Clinton and released by Citizens United, a conservative non-profit corporation. The FEC argued that the film, released within 30 days before the Democratic primary elections, violated Section 203 of the Bipartisan Campaign Reform Act of 2002 (BCRA) and Section 44(b) of the Federal Election Campaign Act of 1971 (FECA).

The BCRA had banned corporate spending on political elections, including 'electioneering communications' regarding a candidate for federal office made 30 days before a primary. The Court had upheld Section 203 in *McConnell v. FEC*,[11] which cited *Austin v. Michigan Chamber of Commerce*,[12] holding that the federal government has the right to ban political spending by corporations to prevent them from distorting the election process. In *Citizens United*, the Court reversed both *McConnell* and *Austin*, holding that corporations have the First Amendment right to engage in political speech, and voided Sections 203 and 44(b). Justices Roberts, Scalia, Alito, and Thomas joined the majority opinion.

In effect, *Citizens United* recognized corporations as 'persons' on the theory that such business entities are 'associations of persons,' and as such should be entitled to the same rights as the individuals themselves. Criticism of the opinion was immediate and included the likes of President Barack Obama, Senator Russ Feingold, media, activists, and the public.[13] In effect, after *Citizens United*, artificial entities – profit-driven and frequently politically motivated – have electioneering rights as great as or greater than individuals.[14]

It is difficult to characterize *Citizens United* as anything other than a belief-oriented approach to the interpretation of a statute. The result was not only unprecedented, but directly in conflict with statutory language, intent, and prior

10 Ibid.
11 540 US 93 (2003).
12 494 U.S. 652 (1990).
13 AR Ellis, '*Citizens United* and tiered personhood' (2012) 44 *John Marshall L.R.* 717, 718.
14 Ellis (n 13) 726.

96　*Scott Fraley*

case law. The Court did not stop with simply invalidating the relevant portions of the Acts in question, but rather granted broad constitutional rights to corporate entities, when it could have reached a more limited result.[15]

The dissent, by Justice Stevens, noted the risk of corporations distorting the political process and found corporations fundamentally different from natural persons.[16] In effect, corporations can effectively 'buy and sell candidates.'[17] It makes no sense under the originalist approach advocated by Roberts and Scalia – looking to the intent of the founders – to suggest that the drafters and ratifiers of the Constitution equated corporations with people. Instead, the Court majority appears to have selected a method of interpretation to achieve a result consistent with their preexisting beliefs. I suggest that this is the Court's usual method of imagination.

Richard Hasen, writing in the *Michigan Law Review*,[18] notes that the broad language used in *Citizens United* will demand the Court agree that there are *no* limits on campaign financing, including spending by foreign nationals and governments.[19] He points out the marked inconsistencies among the Court's contribution and expenditure rulings.[20] Indeed, Hasen gets to the very heart of the problem: the Court's decisions appear to be politically motivated.[21] He cites the differences among the Court's decisions regarding foreign and domestic contributions. The only limit to the Court's willingness to abandon valid interpretational reasoning for belief-oriented decisions appears to be the limits of public opinion.[22] It is significant, as Hansen points out, that the Court's decisions in these cases have swung from left to right, based primarily on the leanings of the various justices.[23]

District of Columbia v. Heller

A second illustrative case is *District of Columbia v. Heller*, 128 S. Ct. 2783 (2008). *Heller*, also a 5–4 decision, struck down a D.C. regulation that prohibited the possession of a handgun in operable condition. The majority opinion, by Justice Scalia, is notable for its claim to be an 'originalist' interpretation of the Second Amendment. The interpretational theory of original meaning as advanced by Scalia, Roberts, and others claims to find meaning in the intent of the drafters and, more specifically, the meaning that the words and phrases used had when the text

---

15　Ibid 743.
16　Ibid 744–45.
17　Ibid 746.
18　LR Hasen, '*Citizens United* and the illusion of coherence' (2011) 109 *Michigan LR* 581.
19　Hasen (n 18) 583–84.
20　Ibid.
21　Ibid 585.
22　Ibid.
23　Hasen (n 18) 586.

Law and belief 97

was drafted and ratified.[24] It is notable that, at the time of *Heller*, no significant controlling precedent restrained the Court.[25]

As the history of originalism is laid out by Lawrence Solum, it originated in the 1970s with Robert Bork and William Rehnquist. Other originalist scholars followed, including Raoul Berger and Edwin Meese.[26] In 1980, Paul Brest wrote on several criticisms of the originalist approach, including: (1) the difficulty of discerning the intent of a multi-member body or bodies; (2) more specifically, the problem of identifying the intent of the framers versus that of the various ratifying states; (3) the generality or specificity of the framers' intent; (4) the problem of inferring intent from a written document; and (5) the difficulty in applying intent as circumstances change over time.[27]

An example might be instructive. Suppose a city council passes an ordinance forbidding sunbathing in a public park. Of the seven-member council, one member intended to prohibit all sunbathing, one member voted yes for political reasons, one member intended only to prohibit sunbathing while scantily clad, one member simply did not care, one member opposed the ordinance but went along because he owed the chair a favor, and one member intended only to prohibit sunbathing in the nude. The statute was a compromise that satisfied no one on the council. What, then, was the council's intent? It is difficult to know and speculation to guess. This ambiguity is one of the major problems with the originalist approach.

Brest argues that the framers wanted the Constitution to be interpreted based on its language as written, not their supposed underlying intentions. In other words, they meant that their intentions be disregarded.[28] Further, he points out that there are so many versions of 'originalism' that one cannot know which to apply; indeed, they appear to be chosen based on the beliefs of the author.[29] Others, such as Stephen Griffin, argue that originalism is non-normative, and therefore inherently flawed.[30] Indeed, Scalia himself appears to allow departure from originalism based on (1) precedent, (2) justiciability, and (3) historical practice.[31]

The really telling fact of the *Heller* opinion, however, is the fact that Scalia could not consistently apply the theory even in a single opinion professing to adhere to originalist theory. Although he begins with what appears to be a straightforward analysis of the meaning at the time of constitutional adoption of the words 'people,' 'keep,' 'bear,' and 'arms,' Scalia includes supposition,

---

24 Note, however, that Scalia maintains a strict distinction between the original intent of the drafters and the initial meaning of the legal provisions.
25 LB Solum '*District of Columbia v. Heller* and originalism' 103 *Northwestern Univ L Rev* 923, 925.
26 Solum (n 25) 927–28.
27 Ibid 928–29.
28 Ibid 929.
29 Ibid 935.
30 Ibid 937.
31 Ibid 938.

98 *Scott Fraley*

supposed facts not in the record, and assumptions about modern-day Washington D.C. that are wholly unsupported.[32] More tellingly, at the end of his opinion, Scalia resorts to pure *obiter dicta* (opinion on issues that do not arise in the case), writing that, '[N]othing in our opinion should be taken to cast doubt on long-standing prohibitions on the possession of firearms by felons and the mentally ill,' and so on.[33] But these prohibitions date back to only 1968. Likewise, he states that there is no reason the state cannot prohibit gun-free zones in 'sensitive' places such as schools and government buildings,[34] but the term 'sensitive' is neither defined nor analyzed historically. Furthermore, he allows regulation of the commercial sale of guns and concealed carry, again with no historical support.[35]

Nelson Lund characterizes this approach as 'half-hearted originalism.'[36] Lund examines alternatives, which he outlines as (1) living constitutionalism: replacing the written Constitution with the political will of judges; (2) judicial deferentialism: refusing to strike down a statute unless it is clearly inconsistent with the Constitution; (3) living originalism: read vague provisions as warrants for broad principles of justice and convenience; and (4) conscientious originalism: relying on text and history except where they provide no useful guidance.[37] There are a wide variety of other and variant approaches. Rory K. Little argues that Scalia's opinion in *Heller* is so inconsistent and so disingenuous as to more closely resemble constitutionalism than originalism.[38] To put it another way, Scalia chose the result his beliefs warranted, then applied an interpretation to achieve it. Little points out the fallacy in such an approach:

> What the Framers said, envisioned, or meant cannot plausibly continue as the specific and exclusive meaning given to general words and phrases in the Constitution, as we grow farther and farther away from the culture, realities, and understandings that underlay the Framers' words.[39]

Finally, as Geoffrey Stone suggests, Roberts and Samuel Alito, who claim to be strict believers in the rule of precedent, more often abandon it in the name of a desired result.[40] As Stone puts it, '[t]he sad truth is that Roberts and Alito seem to have been driven by nothing more than their own desire to reach results they personally prefer.'[41] Further, he argues,

---

32 Nelson Lund, '*Heller* and Second Amendment precedent' (2009) 56 *UCLA LR* 1335.
33 Lund (n 32) 1356.
34 Ibid 1358.
35 Ibid 1359.
36 Ibid 1368.
37 Ibid 1371–72.
38 RK Little '*Heller* and constitutional interpretation: originalism's last gasp' (2009) 60 *Hastings LJ* 1415, 1418.
39 Little (n 38) 1429.
40 GR Stone, '*Citizens United* and conservative judicial activism' (2012) *U Ill L Rev* 485, 537–39.
41 Stone (n 40) 543.

[t]he crabbed, frightened originalism of Clarence Thomas and Antonin Scalia would have seemed absurd to the Framers ... it not only invites manipulative and result-oriented history, but it also ... denies the true original understanding of the Framers of our Constitution.'[42]

He proposes that the remedy is honest judicial activism (exercising the full authority of the Court to implement changes in the law consistent with evolution in societal values) that embraces the responsibility the framers placed on the judiciary while exercising judgment, restraint, humility, curiosity, wisdom, and courage.[43] At least this approach would have the virtue of intellectual honesty.

Texas v. Johnson

Another example of the Court's inconsistent interpretational methodology is *Texas v. Johnson*, in which the U.S. Supreme Court considered the constitutionality of the conviction of a defendant for publicly burning an American flag. The State of Texas convicted Gregory Lee Johnson of violation of Tex. Penal Code Ann. § 42.09(a)(3) (1989) for desecration of a venerated object by burning an American flag during a public protest of the Reagan administration's nuclear policies and those of several Dallas-based corporations.[44] After a march by demonstrators through Dallas, chanting slogans and staging 'die-ins,' accompanied by minor vandalism, Johnson took a flag on the steps of City Hall, doused it with kerosene, and set fire to it.[45] No one was injured, but several witnesses were 'seriously offended.'[46] The Texas Fifth Court of Appeals upheld the conviction, but the Texas Court of Criminal Appeals reversed,[47] finding a violation of Johnson's First Amendment rights.

Johnson makes an interesting case study of the interpretive issues under examination. In *Johnson*, the Court claims to be relying on precedential interpretation of the commands of the First Amendment to the U.S. Constitution.[48] As we shall see, it is this author's position that, although clothed in language of precedential review, the Court actually is engaged in an interpretive approach known as 'responsive interpretation.' Responsive interpretation is an interpretational method in which the Court evaluates the Constitution in view of society's current concept of morality.[49] As described below, this method of deciding cases evaluates the changing 'social needs and aspirations' of the public.[50] Although this approach

42 Ibid 557.
43 Ibid 558.
44 491 U.S. 397, 399 (1989).
45 Ibid.
46 491 U.S. at 399.
47 755 S.W.2d 92 (1988).
48 'Congress shall make no law ... abridging the freedom of speech.'
49 S Levinson, *Constitutional Faith* (Princeton UP 1988). This issue is a central one for contemporary studies in comparative law. See M Hailbronner, *Traditions and Transformations: The Rise of German Constitutionalism* (OUP 2015) 156–57.
50 See RC Post, 'Theories of constitutional interpretation' (1990). *Faculty Scholarship Series*. Paper 209 23–24.

100　*Scott Fraley*

may seem beneficial in certain cases, it usurps, however, the legislative role of Congress and places the Court in a decision-making mode for which it possesses no effective methodology.

In analyzing the case before the Court, the majority of justices (with William J. Brennan, Jr. authoring the opinion) first considered whether the burning of the flag under the circumstances constituted expressive speech. The Court noted that conduct may be 'sufficiently imbued with elements of communication to fall within the scope of the First and Fourteenth Amendments.'[51] In that context, the Court had previously recognized as speech attaching a peace symbol to a flag and refusing to salute the flag.[52] The Court also agreed that the flag's purpose is expressive: 'to serve as a symbol of our county.'[53] Indeed, the State of Texas conceded, and the Court concurred, that burning the flag under the circumstances was expressive conduct. The act was the culmination of a political protest, and its expressive and overtly political nature was clear.[54]

The next issue was whether the government of Texas was free to restrict that expressive conduct. Although political entities generally have more freedom to restrict expressive conduct than they do the written or spoken word,[55] 'a law directed at the communicative nature of conduct must ... be justified by the substantial showing of need that the First Amendment requires.'[56] On the other hand, where speech and non-speech aspects combine in a single course of conduct, a more lenient standard applies allowing restriction if the government demonstrates 'a sufficiently important governmental interest in regulating the nonspeech element.'[57] This looser *O'Brien* standard only applies, however, if the governmental interest is unrelated to the suppression of free expression.[58]

In this case, the interests offered by the State of Texas to justify the statute were related to the prevention of breaches of the peace and preserving the flag as a symbol of national unity.[59] The majority of the Court found the former interest irrelevant to the case and the latter to be related to the suppression of expression. Thus, the stricter 'substantial need' standard applied. Further, the Court found the restriction to be content-based, *as it depended on the meaning and impact of the message Johnson conveyed.*[60] Thus, a strict-scrutiny standard applied.

The Court relied on the 'bedrock principle' that 'the government may not prohibit expression of an idea simply because society finds the idea itself to be offensive or disagreeable.'[61] Put another way, that 'the government may not

51 *Spence v. Washington*, 418 U.S. 405, 409 (1974).
52 491 U.S. 397, 404.
53 491 U.S. 397, 405.
54 491 U.S. 397, 406.
55 See *United States v. O'Brien*, 391 U.S. 367, 391 (1968).
56 *Community for Creative Non-Violence v. Watt*, 703 F.2d 586, 622–23 (1983).
57 491 U.S. at 407, citing *O'Brien, supra.*
58 Ibid.
59 Ibid.
60 491 U.S. at 412.
61 491 U.S. at 414.

Law and belief 101

prohibit expression simply because it disagrees with its message, is not dependent on the particular mode in which one chooses to express an idea.'[62] On these grounds, the Court affirmed the holding of the Texas Court of Criminal Appeals reversing Johnson's conviction. The Court found that Johnson's expressive act of burning the flag was protected speech, and that the state's alleged reasons for prosecuting Johnson did not survive strict scrutiny under the First Amendment.

Litigating opinions in Johnson

Let us examine in more detail Brennan's opinion in *Johnson*. The ultimate question, according to Brennan, was whether Johnson's conviction was 'consistent with the First Amendment.'[63] The Court accepted the Court of Criminal Appeals' conclusion that, 'Johnson's conduct was symbolic speech protected by the First Amendment,' in that, given the context, those who observed the display would have understood the message Johnson intended to convey.[64]

The State of Texas claimed that two state interests supported the conviction: 'preserving the flag as a symbol of national unity and preventing breaches of the peace.'[65] The Court of Criminal Appeals found neither interest compelling, citing *West Virginia Board of Education v. Barnette*.[66] The latter case held in 1943 that making schoolchildren salute the U.S. flag was an unconstitutional breech of their freedoms of speech and religion.

Brennan began with an analysis of whether Johnson's burning of the flag was expressive conduct under the First Amendment,[67] citing *Spence v. Washington*.[68] The next issue was whether Texas's regulation of that speech was related to free expression under *United States v. O'Brien*.[69] If not, then *O'Brien*'s less-stringent standard for non-communicative conduct applied.[70] If the regulation was related to expression, then *O'Brien* did not control, and a more stringent strict-scrutiny standard applied to the state's action.[71]

Brennan noted that the First Amendment only deals with prohibition of 'speech' but pointed out that the Court has long held that 'speech' is not limited to words. Rather, the Court has interpreted 'speech' to include any conduct that intends to express an idea.[72] The Court then cited several cases in which conduct

---

62 491 U.S. at 416.
63 491 U.S. at 399.
64 Ibid.
65 491 U.S. at 400.
66 319 U.S. 624 (1943).
67 491 U.S. at 403.
68 418 U.S. 405 (1974).
69 391 U.S. 367 (1968).
70 491 U.S. at 404.
71 Ibid.
72 *O'Brien*, 391 U.S. 376.

102 *Scott Fraley*

related to flags has been deemed expressive, such as attaching a peace sign to it or refusing to salute it.[73] Texas conceded that Johnson's conduct was expressive.[74]

Although the Court pointed out that the government has greater power to restrict expressive conduct than speech per se, 'a law *directed* at the communicative nature of the conduct must ... be justified by the substantial showing of need that the First Amendment requires.'[75]

The next question, then, was whether the state's claimed interests were unrelated to the suppression of expression.[76] Brennan's analysis examined two asserted state interests: preventing breaches of the peace and preserving the flag as a symbol of national unity.[77] The Court found the first interest not implicated by the facts, and the second directly related to suppression of expression.[78] Specifically, Brennan noted that Johnson's burning of the flag created no disturbance or breach of the peace. On the second issue, Brennan pointed out that the state's asserted interest went to the very heart of Johnson's expressive conduct. The Court found – *citing no precedent, evidence, or specific authority* – that the state's concern was that conduct such as Johnson's would

> lead other people to believe either that the flag does not stand for nationhood and national unity, but instead reflects other, less positive concepts, or that the concepts reflected in the flag do not exist, that is, that we do not enjoy unity as a Nation.[79]

Thus, the state could only be attempting to suppress the free expression of ideas it found offensive.[80] The Court found, however, that 'it is a bedrock principle underlying the First Amendment [that] the government may not prohibit the expression of an idea simply because society finds the idea itself offensive or disagreeable.'[81] The prior decisions of the Court hold that the government may not prevent the expression of an idea merely because it disagrees with its content.[82]

The *Johnson* opinion, then, on its face appears to be a straightforward interpretation of the word 'speech' in the First Amendment as defined by previous Supreme Court precedent. One could certainly make a cogent argument that Brennan's opinion is exactly such a precedential analysis. The problem comes, however, in the key decision points in the case, points for which there is neither direct evidence, precedent, nor specific Constitutional language on which to rely. Specifically, what did the State of Texas really intend to accomplish by its criminal

73 491 U.S. at 404.
74 491 U.S. at 405.
75 491 U.S. at 407.
76 491 U.S. at 408.
77 Ibid.
78 Ibid.
79 490 U.S. at 411.
80 Ibid.
81 491 U.S. at 415.
82 491 U.S. at 417.

statute, and how was that interest threatened by Johnson's action? In that context, Brennan found that the state's alleged interest in preserving the U.S. flag as a symbol of national unity was related to suppression of expression.

Likewise, the Court determined that Johnson's intent was expressive: to protest the nuclear policies of the Nixon administration and various corporations. On these conclusions the opinion turns.

In effect, Brennan really is engaged in an elaborate guessing game regarding the true, as opposed to stated, intent of the state; about the intention behind Johnson's actions in the context of the moral situation in which Johnson found himself; and about the national meaning of the U.S. flag.

The last issue is highlighted by the dissent authored by Chief Justice Rehnquist and joined by Justices White and O'Connor, as summarized by James R. Dyer in his article '*Texas v. Johnson*: symbolic speech and flag desecration under the First Amendment.'[83] According to Dyer, the dissent did not agree with Brennan that the Texas statute was intended to enforce a particular view of the flag.[84] Rather, to the dissenting justices, the flag 'transcended political ideology' and was largely ceremonial, not a 'trademark of the government.'[85] The flag's inherent meaning was intangible, an 'embodiment of the national ethos.'[86] The respect for the flag is historical, not a function of government command. The dissent also pointed out that all but two states at the time had statutes prohibiting flag-burning, suggesting a national consensus.[87]

Thus, we see a dispute between the justices here, not about the interpretation of words in the Constitution or the meaning of precedent, but rather about what value the American public places on the flag, about a matter of national *ethos*.

What, then, are we to make of the *Johnson* decision's theoretical approach to constitutional interpretation? As noted above, the opinion itself claims to rely on precedential interpretation of the First Amendment. I would argue, on the other hand, that Brennan's opinion is an example of what Yale scholar Robert C. Post refers to as 'responsive interpretation' or interpretation based on ethos.[88] This theory, as stated by Oliver Wendell Holmes, holds that, 'the Constitution is not exhausted in a single creative act of consent, but continues to inhere in the national "being" that the Constitution has "called into life".' This authority is not laid down in precedent or bound up in original intent; rather, it flows from the 'whole experience of nationhood.'[89] In this context, the Constitution is not a fixed text; rather, it represents a 'working Constitution,' the content of which may be characterized as 'extra-documentary.'[90] Another way to put this is that the Constitution becomes a 'living document' whose content adapts to the needs of a

---

83 25 *NE L Rev* 895 (1991).
84 Ibid 916.
85 Ibid.
86 Ibid.
87 Ibid.
88 Post (n 50).
89 Ibid 22–24.
90 Ibid 24.

104 *Scott Fraley*

changing society. This view requires judges to see the Constitution 'as a form of what Phillipe Nonet and Phillip Selznik have called "responsive law," law that submits to "the sovereignty of purpose" by functioning "as a facilitator of response to social needs and aspirations".'[91]

In this case, what we see is a social need for Johnson and his companions to protest policies they believed supported nuclear war, and the State of Texas's need to suppress such conduct as anti-authoritarian and anti-American.

According to Post,[92] responsive interpretation constitutes a broad variety of differing approaches to interpreting the Constitution under a single umbrella. In that context, it is neither liberal nor conservative, but is applied by both left and right. As such, the courts are tasked with determining 'the fundamental character and objectives of the nation.' The obvious question arises in this context as to why the courts – which in the case of federal justices are not democratically elected – should be assigned such responsibility. What qualifies them to carry it out? They have no investigative powers, as a rule, unlike the legislature, which can convene committees, subpoena witnesses, and gather evidence. Indeed, appellate justices would appear to be the least likely candidates to carry the great weight of determining the goals and aspirations of a nation.

In other words, responsive interpretation places the Court in the uncomfortable position of 'speculating' about the current attitudes, morals, judgments, feelings, intentions, and goals of the American populace. Unlike Congress, however, the Court lacks any fact-finding or research mechanism or method that would enable it to make a factual evaluation of these attitudes. It has only the facts in the record before it. In effect, responsive interpretation allows the Court to usurp the rightful role of Congress to represent the desires and will of the populace, engaging the Court in a dangerous arena of speculation.

Further, as Post points out, reader-response theorists such as Hans-Georg Gadamer suggest that 'all interpretation involves a conversation between a reader and a text, and so effects a merger between a text and a reader's own purposes and perspectives.'[93] Put another way, the judges' own biases, prejudices, and points of view are inevitably intertwined with their interpretation of the text of the Constitution in any given scenario. It would thus seem impossible for responsive theory to give rise to an unbiased interpretation independent from the feelings and beliefs of the individual judges making the decision.

This result – that responsive interpretation is, at the end of the day, an avenue for implementation of judges' beliefs – is entirely consistent with the prior work of literary critics such as Steven Knapp and Walter Benn Michaels in the 1980s and Stanley Fish more recently. Knapp and Michaels, in their seminal and controversial essay 'Against theory,' posited that it is impossible to create a theory that is outside its own theoretical framework.[94] In other words, one cannot create an

---

91 Ibid.
92 Post (n 89) 25.
93 Ibid.
94 S Knapp, S and W Benn Michaels, 'Against theory' (1982) Univ of Chicago Press 723–42.

interpretational theory of theory or step out of a theory or interpretation to discuss its truth value. Likewise, it is impossible, according to Knapp and Michaels, to achieve intentionless meaning. Meaning inherently implies intent. The two are inseparable.[95] We always inhabit our assumptions; they are inescapable at every level of thought. We carry them with us whenever we attempt to enter a theoretical framework. If Knapp and Michaels are correct in this conclusion, and I would argue that they are, then any attempt to find the 'meaning' of the Constitution or a precedent in any given situation is tied up with the beliefs of the interpreter regarding both that meaning and the nature of the situation. We see both things going on in *Johnson*.

Stanley Fish supports this view as well. In his book *Is There a Text in This Class?*, Fish explains that when one interpretation prevails over another, 'it is not because the first has been shown to be in accordance with the facts but because it is from the perspective of its assumptions that the facts are now being specified.'[96] In other words, the interpreter chooses to emphasize the facts that support the belief that the interpreter holds.

All this is but to say that, in any system of constitutional interpretation, what we ultimately are dealing with is not a specific theory that is coherent, credible, distinct, logical, and explicable from without. Instead, we are merely faced with a methodology for explicating the belief system of the majority who make the decision. This fact, in and of itself, is not a bad thing; it simply is how the world works. From a theoretical point of view, as Knapp, Michaels, and Fish demonstrate, no other result is possible, other than openly admitting what the Court is doing, which would be politically unpalatable. From the standpoint of the public, the 'charade' of constitutional interpretational theory is a necessary evil.

In any event, other scholars have noted the difficulty of making sense of the *Johnson* opinion. For example, a note by Deborah Tully Eversole in the *Florida State University Law Review* points out that, after *Johnson*, scholars continued to debate whether and how a state might write a flag-burning statute to circumvent the opinion.[97] In addition, the opinion left open the possibility that the government could prosecute dissenters under other circumstances.[98] Indeed, shortly after the *Johnson* opinion, Congress passed a national flag-burning statute, which the Court then struck down, and opponents of such conduct continue to seek a constitutional ban on such protest.[99] Nicholas Barber argues that the *Johnson* court got it right based on the attitudes reflected in the Declaration of Independence and the United States Constitution.[100] This continuing argument reflects the shaky foundation on which the *Johnson* opinion is built.

---

95 Ibid 726–27.
96 S Fish, *Is There a Text in This Class?* (Harvard UP 1980) 340.
97 DT Eversole, '*Texas v. Johnson*' (1989) 17 *Flor State Univ L Rev* 869.
98 Ibid 896.
99 Ibid 891, the Flag Protection Act of 1989.
100 N Barber, 'The constitutionality of flag burning: hate or free speech? An analysis of *Texas v. Johnson*' (2001) *Hinckley J. of Politics* 49–56.

106 *Scott Fraley*

Barnes v. Glen Theatre, Inc.

To further demonstrate the idea that the beliefs of the deciding justices underly their opinions, let us compare *Texas v. Johnson* with another U.S. Supreme Court case involving the First Amendment, *Barnes v. Glen Theatre, Inc.*[101] In *Barnes*, the theatre in question desired to present totally nude dancing, but Indiana statute mandated that the dancers wear 'pasties' and a 'G-string' when dancing.[102] The theatre sued in the Northern District Court of Illinois to enjoin enforcement of the statute, asserting that it violated the First Amendment. The District Court granted the injunction, but the Seventh Circuit reversed and remanded on the First Amendment claim. On remand, the District Court determined that the dancing in question was not 'expressive activity' protected by the First Amendment. The Seventh Circuit, sitting *en banc* (as a court of the whole), held that the performances were expressive activity, and that the statute did infringe on the First Amendment rights of the theatre and its dancers. The U.S. Supreme Court then took up the case.[103]

Chief Justice Rehnquist, writing for the majority, noted that several precedents recognized that nude dancing might involve expressive conduct protected by the First Amendment.[104] As in *Johnson, supra*, Rehnquist began by evaluating whether the less stringent standard under *O'Brien* applied. O'Brien was convicted of publicly burning his draft card in violation of a statute prohibiting such acts. He claimed his act was 'expressive conduct' protected by the First Amendment. The Court determined to apply a four-part test: (1) was the regulation within the constitutional powers of the government? (2) did it further an important or substantial government interest? (3) was the interest unrelated to suppression of free expression? and (4) was the restriction no greater than essential to further that interest?[105]

Applying the *O'Brien* test, the Court found that the Indiana statute was clearly within the constitutional powers of the state. Moreover, it furthered a substantial public interest in limiting public indecency to protect the moral order. In this context, the Court made an interesting and critical intellectual move: *it relied, not on public prohibitions on nude dancing per se* (which clearly are related to suppression of free expression), *but on laws prohibiting public nudity in general* and found, they suggested, 'moral disapproval of people appearing in the nude among strangers in public places.'[106] The Court then relied on the general police power of the state to protect morals and the public order.[107] The Court further found this interest, because it was a broad-based one, to be unrelated to suppression of free expression.[108] The opinion goes to some lengths to make clear that the

---

101 501 U.S. 560 (1991).
102 501 U.S. at 563.
103 501 U.S. at 565.
104 Ibid.
105 391 U.S. 376–377.
106 501 U.S. at 568.
107 501 U.S. at 569.
108 501 U.S. at 570.

Law and belief 107

decision depends not on the erotic content of the dancing, but on the perceived evil of public nudity in general, thereby ignoring completely the inherent message of the dancing itself. Finally, the Court found the restriction no greater than necessary to further the governmental interest.[109]

Concluding remarks

The application in *Johnson* of strict scrutiny to a flag-burning case as compared with the insistence on using the much less stringent *O'Brien* standard for nude dancing reflects, in the author's mind, nothing more than the belief system of the members of the Court supporting the majority opinions. The right to political protest is a long-hallowed right in this country, as *Johnson* points out.[110] The right to publicly dance completely naked is less so. The former is overtly political speech; the latter not at all. The inherent flexibility of the responsive theory of constitutional interpretation comes into play here. That flexibility, even more than with most theories of interpretation, provides a blank slate on which judges may impress their own belief systems under the guise of 'today's societal values' or 'long-held public views.' As Fish points out in his book, in such instances, one cannot appeal to the text (or the evidence) because

> the text as it is variously characterized is a *consequence* of the interpretation for which it is supposedly evidence … Nor can the question be settled by turning to the context … for that too will only be a context for an already assumed interpretation.[111]

Thus, *Johnson* and *Glen Theatre* are exemplars not so much of the responsive/ ethos theory of constitutional interpretation, but of the fact that any approach to constitutional interpretation is, at the end of the day, merely a technical methodology for the expression of judges' beliefs. This truth, if it be one, might suggest a failure of the Court's legal imagination – the inability or unwillingness to engage in the rigor necessary to select and consistently apply a single, specific, honest approach to the interpretation of the Constitution.

Instead, the realization that courts base decisions on the judges' existing belief systems is not a matter for fear and trembling (although I suspect many lawyers and judges would chafe at the idea). We all engage in belief-based choices. We cannot, Fish contends, do otherwise, for we can never step outside our value systems to make choices that are not informed by those beliefs. We are doomed, for good or ill, to live within the bounds of our personal viewpoints. Like it or no, belief is all we have. Judges have different points of view about how best to decide cases. It is all well and good to try to cram those beliefs into scholarly models of legal interpretation, but that effort is doomed to failure. Thus, we would all be

109 501 U.S. 571.
110 See 491 U.S. 413–14.
111 Fish, *Text* (n 97) 340; original emphasis.

better off and save tons of trees and hours of scholar time if we simply recognize that the choices we make, even hugely important legal ones, are informed and controlled by our belief systems.

Instead of the utter failure of legal imagination represented by the Court's inconsistent application of legal interpretation, I propose that a better methodology would be to adopt one and only one theory, that of the public *ethos*, the *public's own legal imagination*, its mores and values as expressed at the time the case is decided through polls, demonstrations, publications, actions, the internet, and other sources of public voice. This theory – this *legal imagination* – surely the Court can apply fairly and consistently, even if disagreements arise regarding what those mores may be. It is past time to restore the public's faith in the legitimacy of the Court and its rulings, and perhaps such an approach would be at least a small step in that direction.

7 Legal imagination or an extra-legal hoax

On storytelling, friends of the court, and crossing legal boundaries in the US Supreme Court

Aleksandra Wawrzyszczuk

UNIVERSITY OF EAST LONDON, UK

Introduction

'With respect but deep sadness, Justices Ginsburg, Breyer, Sotomayor and I dissent.'[1] The closing sentence of Justice Kagan's dissent in a 2019 gerrymandering case strikes as an unusual expression of (usually carefully disguised) judicial emotions in the seemingly sterile normative vacuum of the US Supreme Court.

The Court and academia have grappled with that lack of sterility for decades. Allowing extra-legal considerations into the decision-making process can be seen as either redundant and destructive to judicial legitimacy or the opposite – that is, humane and necessary. Context-restrictive jurisprudence, aligned with the former and embracing a wide range of textualist and formalist principles, portrays judges as professionals who set aside their personal views to deliver a viewpoint-neutral judgment. As it works on a presumption that judges are capable of making impeccably legal choices, such context-restrictive jurisprudence frames judicial mistakes as departures from the statutory canons of interpretation[2] and established legal norms. Context-rich scholarship, on the other hand, defines judgment errors as instances of too literal adherence to the rules to the detriment of fairness.

The context-rich departure goes beyond strictly legal reasons in pursuit of a justiciable outcome. It was famously illuminated by American legal realism,[3] which proclaimed that judges regularly abandon the formalist framework in favour of policies and non-legal considerations. Whereas formalists seek uniquely legal reasons behind judicial decisions, realists observe subjective judgments based on principles of fact-dependent fairness.[4]

---

1 Dissent opinion by Justice Kagan, *Rucho v Common Cause*, No. 18–422, 588 U.S. (2019)
2 While bearing in mind that even those can be read as conflicting. See: KN Llewellyn, *The Common Law Tradition: Deciding Appeals* (Quid Pro 2016).
3 B Leiter, 'American legal realism' in W Edmundson & M Golding (eds), *The Blackwell Guide to Philosophy of Law and Legal Theory* (Blackwell 2003).
4 Ibid.

110 *Aleksandra Wawrzyszczuk*

Unsurprisingly, context-rich scholarship invites and validates stories, narratives, and other extra-legal factors in judicial decision-making. It draws attention to judicial 'internal narratives,' or the 'hidden current' under the seemingly stable surface of a written opinion. Internal narratives, subconsciously shaped by a sum of individual life experiences, are not open to free choice,[5] yet they shape the external narrative (the official interpretation of the law and facts in a case contained in a written judgment) that is consciously determined by a judge and is visible to all.[6]

This chapter contests a thesis posed by a particular strand of context-rich scholarship branded applied legal storytelling (hereinafter ALS). Its proponents profess that the law itself is a sum of internal narratives 'masquerading as neutral rules and principles.'[7] Unlike context-restrictive jurisprudence, ALS associates reason with 'informal and non-algorithmic forms of thought' and utilises factual scenarios to analyse rules and principles.[8] To ALS, conventional rule-based reasoning, which 'generates criteria from the express language ... used in the authoritative enunciation of an existing rule of law,'[9] plays only a supporting role to the prioritised narrative reasoning. Thus, it 'evaluat[es] a litigant's story against cultural narratives and the moral values and themes [they] encode.'[10] In other words, judges are to rely on parties' narratives and select from these competing cultural narratives when interpreting laws. Within these narratives, stories of oppression gain priority, and the emotional value of first-person confessions overtakes context-restrictive reliance on rational arguments.[11] In the world of rules and stories, judicial involvement in policy-making, as Jack Peltason puts it, becomes not 'a matter of choice but of function,'[12] with narratives being placed beside rules at the very heart of the legal system[13] as two constitutive elements of the law.[14]

Admittedly, although over-reliance on stories and narratives is not conducive to good government, their careful recognition may curb the prospect of judges overstepping their authority – at least in a formalist sense. Furthermore, such a recognition may expand the Court's interpretive horizons. In particular, utilising concrete factual scenarios in the form of stories 'provides a method of testing and refining normative principles.'[15] Naturally, appropriate safeguards must be put in

---

5 Shulamit Almog, 'As I Read, I Weep - In Praise of Judicial Narrative' (2001) 26 *Oklahoma City University LR* 471, 474.
6 Ibid.
7 L Edwards, 'Speaking of stories and law' (2016) 13 *JAWLD* 157, 162.
8 D Farber and S Sherry, 'Telling stories out of school' (1992) 45 *Stan LR* 807, 822.
9 L Edwards, 'The convergence of analogical and dialectic imaginations in legal discourse' (1996) 20 *Legal Studies Forum* 8, 10.
10 Ibid.
11 Farber and Sherry (n 8) 808.
12 Jack Peltason, *Federal Courts in the Political Process* (Random House 1955) 3. See further LJ Barker, 'Third parties in litigation: a systemic view of the judicial function' (1967) 29 *The Journal of Politics* 41, 69.
13 Farber and Sherry (n 8) 808.
14 S Paskey, 'The law is made of stories: erasing the false dichotomy between stories and legal rules' (2014) 11 *Legal Comm & Rhetoric: JAWLD* 51, 62.
15 Farber and Sherry (n 8) 808.

place to curb the detrimental effects of an unconstrained narrative flow on the system of adjudication.[16] Those safeguarding tools range from conventions to rigid legal doctrines and procedural rules. Only in the constrained form, embracing certain kinds of narrative in the law is conducive to increased 'accuracy of an argument and contribution to legal reasoning.'[17] That includes storytelling devices that enable a deeper understanding of both rules and a case at hand.

This chapter analyses two such devices available to judges. It begins the analysis with inspecting a judicial hypothetical, a judge-made tool aimed to test the boundaries of a proposed ruling. It then compares it with a voices brief, a kind of non-party submission in the shape of informal narratives in support of a party's case. Although each tool uses extra-legal narratives to assist judges with making their choices, hypotheticals are clearly intended to awaken the legal imagination of the Court, whereas voices briefs go as far as to claim to reduce judicial biases.

The chapter also contends that, although the hypothetical is now inherent in the interpretive process, the usefulness of the latter is grossly overestimated by ALS and should be adequately restrained. Voices briefs risk becoming a seal of approval for extra-legal methods of legal adjudication as they do not serve persuasion on a semantic or rhetorical level; instead, they appeal to emotive, irrational modes of discourse rather than to reason, and do so without a faint pretence of advancing a legal argument. Thus, perhaps unsurprisingly, their proponents profess that judges are simply arbiters of semi-subjective truths with a tendency to tailor their external narratives to fit their personal (and frequently political) attitudes, which a prudent activist group should actively exploit. Hypotheticals demonstrate that the narrative nature of the law can be recognised and explored to perfect the precision of judicial choices without abandoning legal rules underlying and legitimising the legal system.

ALS's mistaken over-reliance on voices briefs as vehicles of attitude change leading to more 'just' results may be a consequence of the erroneous conviction that cases are decided solely based on judicial attitudes being camouflaged under the 'official' judgment. This, in turn, makes judges vulnerable to accusations of partisanship, a risk not present with the use of hypotheticals. As cognitive studies find limited evidence that judges' attitudes can be radically altered by the use of voices briefs over more conventional arguments, voices briefs appear to serve the audience rather than 'justice.' A failure to appreciate the systematic process of conventional legal interpretation may encourage the public to form non-meritorious idea of judicial reputation based on emotions rather than the merits of the case. Voices briefs legitimise emotions in the adjudicative process, validating the volatility of judicial outcomes.

The chapter demonstrates that voices briefs are not only redundant in court proceedings but also outright detrimental to judicial legitimacy. Nonetheless, that by no means equates to an outright rejection of the realist thesis that judges utilise extra-legal tools to assist them with interpreting the law. It simply makes such considerations supplementary to context-restrictive legal principles in which legitimacy is grounded.

16 Almog (n 5) 473.
17 Farber and Sherry (n 8) 822.

112   Aleksandra Wawrzyszczuk

Awakening judicial imagination: judicial hypotheticals

The Supreme Court case of *Bucklew v Precythe*[18] concerned the Eighth Amendment to the US Constitution. Russell Bucklew, the killer of his girlfriend and members of her family, was convicted in 1996 of the killings and lost his final appeal in 2006. After his conviction, the state in which his sentence was to be carried out – Missouri – changed its execution protocol from lethal gas exposure to lethal injection of a combination of drugs. In the Supreme Court, Bucklew challenged the updated method, claiming that the lethal injection would cause complications with his inherent health condition (he suffered from cavernous haemangioma), placing him at risk of unnecessary pain before death. As the US Constitution prevents cruel and unusual punishment, he asked the Court to allow him to be put to death by lethal gas (nitrogen) rather than by injection. During oral argument, the following exchange took place between Justice Breyer and counsel for the respondent state:

JUSTICE BREYER: I thought – I'm trying to get back to my question, which is asking you as a prosecutor, but, look, I guess you would agree that some – X has a rare medical condition that makes the method of execution to him feel exactly like being burned at the stake. Okay? Would – the Constitution would rule that out, wouldn't it?

MR SAUER: The Constitution would rule out burning at the stake, absolutely, Your Honor.

JUSTICE BREYER: And – but, yeah, he doesn't – he has a mental condition of some kind. It makes it exactly the same.

MR SAUER: That is –

JUSTICE BREYER: It feels exactly the same.

MR SAUER: I would have to know more about the hypothetical.

JUSTICE BREYER: Well, that's it. I'm making it up as I go along.[19]

Here, Justice Breyer does not rely on facts. He fabricates a story to challenge the advocate.[20] What in isolation appears to be the basic storyline of a news report or the plot of a paperback thriller becomes, in the context of legal proceedings, an important contribution to the interpretive process. Yet Justice Breyer operates within a prescribed framework of assessment of the scope of the judicial decision. The exchange becomes engrained in the legal debate, despite not fitting a standard formalist frame of interpretation. As law is rooted in language, he uses linguistic tools to his benefit while effectively exercising care in not exceeding his judicial prerogative. His example is purposely radical, as it compares the current set of facts to something obviously unlawful (burning at the stake) in order to grasp the murky boundaries of the rule.

---

18 *Bucklew v Precythe* 587 U.S. (2019).

19 Transcript of oral argument in *Bucklew v Precythe*, p 46; for more examples of hypotheticals see B Prettyman, 'The Supreme Court's use of hypothetical questions at oral argument' (1984) 33 *Cath U LR* 555.

20 For a more general analysis of possible practical reasons for use of hypotheticals and a thorough list of examples, see Prettyman (n 19) 555.

Legal imagination or an extra-legal hoax 113

The exchange illustrates a common interpretive tool used by the judges: a hypothetical. Judicial hypotheticals are not dissimilar to scientific experiments. When an advocate proposes a certain standard or test for deciding a legal issue at stake, the judge identifies a hypothesis. In order to challenge this hypothesis, the judge devises a hypothetical that 'must be different from the new case and somehow easier to decide from a normative viewpoint, but ultimately not rationally distinguishable from the new case.'[21] Such scenarios are designed 'flexibly to facilitate comparisons for purposes of exploring alternatives,'[22] with varying degrees of occurrence probability and complexity. It is a 'systematic methodology for creative, exploratory reasoning' that 'helps the decision-maker explore the space of situations that may and may not be distinguished on a normative and policy basis from the case at hand.'[23] Hypotheticals test the parties' arguments, 'their consistency with relevant legal principles, policies, and past case decisions, application to the case's facts, and sensitivity to changes in the facts.'[24] Through a range of tailored hypotheticals, a judge proposes 'fulcra for arguments that the rule should extend to the case at hand or not,'[25] not only challenging the advocate but also engaging with other justices.[26] In effect, they experiment with the shape of the potential precedent they are about to establish.

In many cases, hypotheticals are the only way the court can tackle complex issues in the moment. In *Bucklew*, justices had no comparable testimony and were required to make an educated prediction as to the potential impact of the execution method on a death row inmate in order to assess whether it would transgress constitutional boundaries. Judges 'use[d] the imagination to supply what life has not yet presented.'[27] Legal storytelling in the shape of a hypothetical does not operate solely as a literary form; it has a normative power to 'declare a particular occurrence as reality,'[28] whether actual or prospective. Notably used by judges regardless of their judicial philosophy, hypotheticals assist the bench with the dual act of grasping a narrative, where 'the interpreter has to grasp the narrative's configuring plot in order to make sense of its constituents, which he must relate to that plot ... [b]ut the plot configuration must itself be extracted from the succession of events.'[29] They tend to explore the very extreme scenarios of 'hard' cases, where the application of the advocated theory would generate a counterintuitive or overtly unjust result, or where the conflict

21 K Ashley, 'Hypothesis formation and testing in legal argument' in *Modeling Legal Argument: Reasoning with Cases and Hypotheticals* (MIT Press 1991) 4.
22 Ibid. 6.
23 Ibid.
24 Ibid.
25 Ibid.
26 Prettyman (n 19) 556.
27 P Gewirtz, 'Jurisprudence of hypotheticals' (1982) 32 *Journal of Legal Education* 120, 120.
28 Almog (n 5) 488.
29 J Brunner, *Acts of Meaning* (HUP 1990) 43.

114 *Aleksandra Wawrzyszczuk*

or uncertainty of intuitions is at its highest.[30] The judges hypothesise about theories put forward by parties' representatives. The fact that a hypothetical is imaginary[31] does not diminish its value[32] as 'narrative can be "real" or "imaginary" without loss of its power as a story.'[33]

When using hypotheticals, judges safely draw from different strands of reasoning without transgressing the limits of their power.[34] Despite their seemingly literary character, hypotheticals are not intended to emotionally manipulate the bench but merely to assist the judges with interpretation. This supports the consistency and predictability of the law, as 'one cannot afford to wait passively for the "right" case to come along before grappling with a potential problem; one must create cases to reason in anticipation.'[35] Proponents of the ALS movement take it one step further to argue that the use of fictitious judicial hypotheticals justifies inclusion of real-life examples from third parties in deliberations.[36] Naturally, if life itself provided the judges with sufficient real-life scenarios, the use of hypotheticals would be limited,[37] but in cases such as *Bucklew* no actual third persons would be available to testify (as no-one executed would survive to tell the tale).

Friends of the Court and their voices

Third parties can participate in the proceedings in formal ways (for example, as intervenors under Rule 24 of the Federal Rules of Civil Procedure) or informal ways, such as by funding litigation or providing amicus briefs.[38] Although the world of litigation funding is largely inaccessible to ordinary citizens,[39] the limitations on amicus curiae have been relatively relaxed. Therefore, amicus briefs

---

30 Gewirtz (n 27) 120.
31 Here, 'imaginary' is used to denote events within the realm of probability – that is, those that might, but need not, occur in the real world. Hypotheticals necessitate the use of curbed judicial imagination as their utility is constrained by the likelihood of their occurrence in real life.
32 We could invoke here an Aristotelian notion of mimesis, capturing 'life in action' and generating what Paul Ricoeur calls a 'metaphor of reality ... that refers to reality not in order to copy it, but in order to give it a new reading' per Brunner (n 29) 46. See also P Ricoeur, 'The narrative function' in *Hermeneutics and the Human Sciences* (CUP 2016) 285–88.
33 Brunner (n 29) 44.
34 Edwards, *Convergence* (n 9).
35 EL Rissland and KD Ashley, 'Hypotheticals as heuristic device' (published in HLT 1986) 166; hypotheticals help ensure that law is moral in a Fullerian sense; see Fuller's desiderata: L Fuller, *Morality of Law* (YUP 1964).
36 L Edwards, 'Telling stories in the Supreme Court: voices briefs and the role of democracy in constitutional deliberation' (2017) 29 *Yale Journal of Law and Feminism* 29.
37 Gewirtz (n 27) 120.
38 See Barker (n 12) 41.
39 See 'Litigation funding: can growth continue?' *Investors Chronicle*, 17 January 2019; https://www.investorschronicle.co.uk/shares/2019/01/17/litigation-finance-can-growth-continue/ accessed 13 July 2019.

(filings made by a non-party who nonetheless has an interest in the proceedings)[40] constitute a popular means of injecting a third-party narrative into a case.[41]

Despite their name, amici curiae are far from non-adversarial or neutral – they tend to nudge the courts in a particular policy direction[42] and rarely support a neutral fact-finding exercise.[43] They are closer to lobbyists than 'friends,'[44] fully engaged in advocacy, frequently with little or no consideration being paid to objective facts or truths.[45] Amici's goals are not short term and focused on an individual case;[46] they file briefs to both 'signal the possible policy significance of the case, as well as the potential political implications of the decision' and 'supplement the arguments made by the litigants.'[47]

Through their inadvertent advocacy, they become a 'link between the Supreme Court and the polity,'[48] with 'amicus participation serv[ing] as a crude barometer of public opinion, particularly in politically-charged cases.'[49] Amici briefs primarily raise awareness of the interests of third parties that will be impacted by the outcome of the case in which they hold no direct stake,[50] be it through reinforcing the arguments made by the parties or (less frequently) introducing new arguments to the debate.[51] By 2019, amicus curiae's role of 'the vindicator of the politically powerless'[52] had been firmly established through a new type of amicus brief: a voices brief,[53] which incorporates first-person accounts of individuals impacted by the legal issues at stake.

In 2016, more than 100 legal professionals submitted stories detailing their personal experiences with abortion in support of the petitioner in *Whole Woman's*

---

40 For a complete analysis of the history of amicus curiae: S Krislov, 'The amicus curiae brief: from friendship to advocacy' (1963) 72 *Yale LJ* 694.
41 Between 1950 and 2000, the number of amici briefs grew 8 times; it maintains no sign of a slowdown. See: AO Larsen and N Devins, 'The amicus machine' (2016) 102 *Va L Rev* 1901, 1902.
42 P Collins, 'Lobbyists before the U.S. Supreme Court: investigating the influence of amicus curiae' (2007) 60 *PRQ* 55, 55.
43 P Collins, 'Friends of the court: examining the influence of amicus curiae participation in US Supreme Court litigation' (2004) 38 *Law & Society Rev* 807, 808.
44 AO Larsen, 'The trouble with amicus facts' (2014) 100 *Virginia LR* 1758, 1767.
45 Ibid. 1757.
46 JM Box-Steffensmeier, DP Christenson, and MP Hitt, 'Quality over quantity: amici influence and judicial decision making' (2013) 107 *The American Political Science Review* 446, 446
47 PJ Wahlbeck, 'The life of the law: judicial politics and legal change' (1997) 59 *The Journal of Politics* 778, 784
48 OS Simmons, 'Picking friends from the crowd: amicus participation as political symbolism' (2009) 42 *Conn L Rev* 185, 191.
49 Ibid. 207.
50 Ibid. 206.
51 JF Spriggs II and PJ Wahlbeck, 'Amicus curiae and the role of information at the Supreme Court' (1997) 50 *PRQ* 365, 368
52 M Lowman, 'The litigating amicus curiae: when does the party begin after the friends leave?' (1992) 41 *American University LR* 1244, 1245.
53 Origins of voices briefs date back to 1986. For a more thorough historical analysis, see Edwards, *Stories* (n 36).

116 *Aleksandra Wawrzyszczuk*

Health v Hellerstedt.[54] The case concerned the constitutionality of Texas's requirements limiting the abortion providers' ability to perform abortions in the state. The following submission was part of the filed voices brief:

> I found out I was pregnant just a few weeks after moving away from home to start college ... My decision to have an abortion was essential to the freedom that allowed me to finish college while working more than one job; to move across the country two weeks after graduation to take my dream job; and to attend law school and ... to continue to pursue my dreams.[55]

Much like in Justice Breyer's hypothetical, the language of the above passage does not resemble that of conventional appellate filings. It represents a personal story without relying on precedent, rules, or evidence in a procedural sense. It does not expressly advocate for any legal principle but rather *tells a story*, which cannot be factually challenged or subject to cross-examination. Whereas amicus briefs allow for social scientific reports, reports from professional associations, and more generalised data, voices briefs are specifically intended to enable individual, highly personal, and informal narratives. Hence, the application of voices briefs is limited primarily to cases that directly impact the personal lives and livelihoods of those affected by their outcome[56] and cases where judges might lack exposure to the amicus's experience.[57] These cases range from abortion and equal marriage rights[58] to prisoners' rights, immigration law, police shootings, and broad 'issues of race, class or power disparity.'[59] Their value is threefold: combating pre-existing cognitive biases, informing the judges of the possible consequences of their judgment in the 'real world,' and enabling the non-parties affected by the law to feel heard, all under the overarching aim to induce democratic involvement with the court.

Voices briefs' intention is to pre-empt and alter judicial attitudes; they attempt to persuade the judge that one view is more justifiable than another, using purely extra-legal means.[60] They aim to fill the real-life 'gap between a Justice's personal experience and the realities of other lives and other perspectives'[61] and, as such, they can 'appear as part of a long-term strategy of persuasion,'[62] effectively contributing to a policy campaign in the court. Unlike general amici briefs, voices briefs do not further merit arguments or rely on normative values; they contribute not with expertise but rather with experience.[63]

54 *Whole Woman's Health v Hellerstedt*, 579 U.S.
55 Brief of McAvoy et al. in *Whole Woman's Health v. Hellerstedt*, 579 U.S.
56 Edwards, *Stories* (n 36) 39.
57 Edwards, *Stories* (n 36).
58 LH Edwards, 'Hearing voices: non-party stories in abortion and gay rights advocacy' (2015) *Mich St LR* 1327.
59 Edwards, *Stories* (n 36) 40.
60 Ibid. 68.
61 Ibid. 37.
62 Ibid.
63 For that reason, they pose issues of relevance and reliability and an increased administrative burden on the Court.

Unfortunately, it proves near impossible to assess the exact impact that amicus briefs generally, or voices briefs particularly, have on judges.[64] Although much of the research on amicus briefs implicitly, if not explicitly, argues that, 'courts often rely on factual information or analytical approaches offered by amici, but not otherwise advanced by the parties to the case,'[65] scholarship on the exact impact of voices briefs as a special category of amici briefs is still vastly underdeveloped.[66]

Although it may not be possible to grasp the actual effect of voices briefs on judicial choices, at least one practical strategy behind filing them is clear. Voices briefs intend to 'expand that judge's realm of identification to include groups not previously a part of the judge's personal world.'[67] In other words, they claim to target cognitive biases of the judges by impacting their internal narratives.[68]

Although judges undeniably experience emotions, particularly in politically charged cases, their internal narratives and personal impressions rarely come through in their written opinions. As context-rich scholars view the text of a judgment as a ruse concealing the *real* reasons behind a judgment, they are willing to embrace the manipulative aspect of storytelling present in voices briefs – that is, the 'power to shape reality by means of the language, to suspend the disbelief of the listeners to the story, to influence and persuade,' in order to incline a judge to view the law through non-legalistic lenses and make value-laden (not rule-based) judgments.[69]

When confronted with the suspicion of a seemingly unfavourable internal narrative that cannot be affected by conscious choice, they seek ways of altering the judges' subconscious to further a party's (and wider community's) interests. To them, voices briefs are means of peeking through the veil of 'presumptions, precedents and conceptions of their [judges'] professional role'[70] in order to alter judicial attitudes. Context-rich theorists' prediction and pre-emption of judicial attitudes comes from their view of legal argumentation being

> dominated by a judge who will ... use his or her moral values and political ideology as the basis for the legal argument, all the while disguising this subjectivity with technical language and other flummery of the law.[71]

If elaborate technical opinions truly were only a disguise for all the very 'real' reasons that judges decide cases, then stories would inadvertently become a focal

---

64 No relevant impact study has been conducted on the issue of voices briefs, and cognitive and political science studies inspecting the impact of amici briefs frequently rely on a single-term sample and are thus unreliable. For a succinct summary of contemporary research, see Edwards, *Stories* (n 37) 41.
65 Spriggs and Wahlbeck (n 52) 365.
66 Edwards, *Stories* (n 36).
67 Ibid. 64
68 Edwards (n 36).
69 Almog (n 5) 488.
70 M Minow, 'Guardianship of Phillip Becker' (1996) 74 *Tex LR* 1257, 1259.
71 J Bickenbach. 'The "artificial reason" of the law' (1990) 12 *Informal Logic* 23, 26.

point of judicial deliberations. Although the Court is unlikely to shift its priorities in that way for reasons set out later in this chapter, it accepts some level of deviation from its 'practical, normative, institutional, and substantively constrained'[72] modus operandi to accommodate the fluid and subjective nature of rich narratives such as voices briefs.

As narratives become ever-present in court proceedings, with multiple actors (parties, attorneys, witnesses, judges) each crafting their own, it becomes clear that, 'in a very literal sense, *no one* can make laws or practice law without telling stories.'[73] Although the existence of rules significantly confines their utility, stories are nonetheless used as tools of persuasion, targeting the motivation for judges' reasoning and attempting to access their internal narratives with new persuasive tactics rooted in cognitive science. Voices briefs are an accurate example of such attempts in practice.

Hearing voices (briefs) – persuasive rhetoric or distracting noise?

It is commonly accepted that personal motivation affects cognition,[74] and judges are prone to motivated reasoning.[75] In a study of the underlying motivations in cognition, Kunda distinguishes at least two types of motivated reasoning.[76] The first type, which is driven by accuracy goals, leads to 'the use of those beliefs and strategies that are considered more appropriate.'[77] The second type, led by directional goals, invokes actions that may likely yield the desired outcome.[78]

Research shows that, when they are motivated by accuracy, as opposed to directional goals, decision-makers tend to focus on 'issue-related reasoning, attend to relevant information more carefully and process it more deeply, using often more complex rules.'[79] Pursuit of accuracy inclines the subjects to choose more complex mental models[80] and show 'less tendency to use ethnic stereotypes in their evaluations of essay quality, and less anchoring when making probability judgments.'[81]

Judges motivated to be accurate may be more likely to access and use those rules and strategies for processing information that is deemed more appropriate,[82] and be less driven by personal biases.[83] Therefore, it seems that judges

---

72 Ibid. 24.
73 Edwards, (n 9) 15 (emphasis added).
74 For a succinct summary of the issue see Z Kunda, 'The case for motivated reasoning' (1990) 108 *Psych Bul* 480.
75 See AM Sood, 'Motivated cognition in legal judgments – an analytic review' (2013) 9 *Ann Rev Law Soc Sci* 307.
76 Kunda (n 74) 480.
77 Kunda (n 74), 482, with footnotes.
78 Ibid.
79 Kunda (n 74) 483.
80 Ibid.
81 Ibid.
82 Kunda (n 74) 484.
83 Ibid.

Legal imagination or an extra-legal hoax 119

should be nudged towards accuracy rather than directional goals. In other words, instead of filing emotionally or politically charged stories, advocates should focus on presenting a strong argument that shows their position to be *objectively* more appropriate.

However, neither parties nor their representatives engage in an impartial truth-finding exercise. They are interested in securing a victory to further their own interest. In order to achieve that, they utilise tools of persuasion to affect judicial attitude, which plays an important role in the process of adjudication in a context-rich theory.[84] An attitude shift from accuracy goals to directional goals might appear particularly tempting to a party arguing for a more progressive stance, whose victory might be subject to a judge exercising strong discretion.

Whereas conventional jurisprudence tends to scrutinise evidence and eliminates unnecessarily inflammatory narratives,[85] Edwards argues that, 'cognitive studies indicate that the best way to minimize inevitable subjectivities' – that is, amend the judicial attitude – 'may be to expand – not contract – the pool of stories.'[86] Edwards's analysis of the persuasive nature of voices briefs relies on cognitive studies completed by Cacciopo and Petty in 1986 and later revisited by Slater and (for legal research purposes) Stanchi. To Edwards, voices briefs emerge as an alternative tool of persuasion to more traditional legal filings as, 'unlike a logically compelling merits argument, anecdotal messages may allow the advocate to counter the effects of negative pre-existing bias.'[87] Context-rich scholars consider voices briefs as an opportunity to alter internal judicial narratives instead of seeking strong arguments to convince a judge to assume a particular external narrative.

Voices briefs and the art of shifting attitudes

Nine Supreme Court justices are subject to close scrutiny, particularly in terms of their internal narratives. It does not come as a surprise that advocates seek new ways to affect judicial attitudes to get the judges to view their arguments more favourably.

Cacioppo and Petty defined a model of attitude change[88] called the elaboration likelihood method, which opened a window into how decision-makers process information and how advocates can adjust their arguments to minimise the effect of unfavourable political or moral attitudes.

---

84 For more information about extra-legal factors determining judicial choices, see PM Collins, 'The consistency of judicial choice' (2008) 70 *The Journal of Politics* 861.
85 RA Posner, 'Legal narratology' (1997) 64 *University of Chicago LR* 737, 645.
86 Edwards (n 36) 74.
87 Ibid. 64.
88 This model is opposed to a model of persuasion, which incorporates it together with factual beliefs. See DJ O'Keefe 'The elaboration likelihood model' in JP Dillard and L Shen (eds), *The SAGE Handbook of Persuasion: Developments in Theory and Practice* (Sage Knowledge 2012) 109.

120   *Aleksandra Wawrzyszczuk*

Elaboration is 'the extent to which a person thinks about the issue-relevant arguments contained in a message.'[89] *High* elaboration indicates a higher likelihood that the interlocutors

> attend to the appeal; attempt to access relevant associations, images, and experiences from memory; scrutinise and elaborate upon the externally provided message arguments in light of the associations available from memory; draw inferences about the merits of the arguments for a recommendation based upon their analyses; and consequently derive an overall evaluation of, or attitude toward, the recommendation.[90]

In legal proceedings, high elaboration is more desirable as it yields central-route processing under which poor argumentation or lack of sound reasoning is likely to lead the subjects to 'employ more mental resources, think more systematically, and allow data to shape inferences.'[91] When elaboration likelihood is high, a judge is more willing to decide an argument on merit rather than on the basis of his or her personal preferences, and is therefore more likely to be persuaded if the arguments presented are of sufficient strength and quality.[92]

In cases of *low* elaboration,

> attitudes may be changed by associating an issue position with various affective cues, or people may attempt to form a reasonable opinion position by making an inference about the likely correctness or desirability of a particular attitude position based on cues such as message discrepancy, one's own behaviour, and the characteristics of the message source.[93]

At lower levels of elaboration, when the individual is not invested in the subject, peripheral route processing is more likely to be triggered.[94] Peripheral routes 'employ fewer resources, rely on simple heuristics, and use top–down, stereotypic inferences'[95] rather than engaging in more thoughtful analysis demanding cognitive resources, making it relatively undesirable in court deliberations (as judges might feel less inclined to engage in merit-focused argumentation).

Higher sensitivity to 'peripheral cues,' or 'extrinsic aspects of the communication situation,'[96] instead of utilising issue-relevant thinking, relies heavily on

89 RE Petty and JT Cacioppo, 'The elaboration likelihood model of persuasion' (1986) 19 *Advances in Experimental Social Psychology* 123, 128.
90 Ibid.
91 J Kuklinski and P Quirk, 'Reconsidering the rational public: cognition, heuristics, and mass opinion' in A Lupia, MD McCubbins, and SL Popkin (eds), *Elements of Reason: Cognition, Choice, and the Bounds of Rationality* (CUP 2000) 17.
92 O'Keefe (n 88) 104.
93 Ibid. 131.
94 Ibid.
95 Kuklinski and Quirk (n 91) 17.
96 O'Keefe (n 88) 104.

Legal imagination or an extra-legal hoax 121

mental shortcuts, such as the communicator's appearance of credibility or personal attitudes towards the communicator, thus leading to less accurate outcomes.[97] Highly desirable central-route processing prioritises quality of an argument over heuristics, including factors commonly affecting the impact of amicus filings such as identity or gravitas.[98] It may also lead to a longer-lasting change of attitude over time than a peripheral route.[99]

In crude terms, judges are likely to experience merely a temporary attitude shift under conditions of peripheral-route processing. Edwards suggests that voices briefs trigger central-route processing by increasing personal engagement with the wider policy stance with which the party aligns.

High elaboration needs more than just stories

The likelihood of high elaboration (and of the desirable central-route processing) increases proportionately to the subjects' motivation and ability.[100] Elaboration motivation improves with the individual's 'need for cognition' – that is, willingness to engage in cognitive analysis[101] – as well as the receiver's prior knowledge.[102] Arguably, 'knowledge' of the subject would primarily refer not to individual narratives contained in the voices briefs, but to a wider spectrum of matters involved in a legal dilemma, including, but not limited to, precedent or the parties' filings. It could relate directly to the question being asked, not to the peripheral arguments that might or might not matter to the legal outcome. Edwards seems to be right: the more background knowledge a judge has about the issue and the more willing they are to engage in analysing the subject, the more likely they might be to engage in elaboration, thus more likely triggering central-route processing.

However, other factors such as personal responsibility and relevance also trigger central-route processing[103] as, when 'the personal consequences of an advocacy increase, it becomes more important for people to form a veridical opinion because the consequences of being incorrect are greater.'[104] Personal relevance is driven by the expectation of the decision-makers that the issue will 'have significant consequences for their own lives.'[105] Although abortion rights might not be 'personally relevant' to a male judge, the consequences of the decision for his

---

97 Ibid. 105.
98 Simmons (n 48).
99 O'Keefe (n 88) 105; please note that the scholarship on factors constituting a 'strong' argument is scarce.
100 The presence of sufficient elaboration ability is not discussed as judges are presumed to possess the cognitive tools to engage in elaboration, i.e. ability, by virtue of their professional role.
101 JT Cacioppo, RE Petty, JA Feinstein, and WBG Jarvis, 'Dispositional differences in cognitive motivation: the life and times of individuals varying in need for cognition' (1996) 119 *Psychological Bulletin* 197, 229.
102 O'Keefe (n 88).
103 Petty and Cacioppo (n 89) 149.
104 Ibid. 148.
105 Ibid. 145.

122 *Aleksandra Wawrzyszczuk*

reputation would be, nonetheless, of great personal relevance. Thus, although voices briefs could contribute to each justice's personal involvement, potentially triggering central-route processing and leading to a more rational outcome, they do not hold a monopoly. With a high need for cognition, a sense of personal responsibility driven by reputational considerations,[106] motivation to deliver the optimal outcome, and outstanding professional ability, Supreme Court justices are already more likely to engage in high elaboration and pay close attention to the merit of the arguments, even without the presence of voices briefs. In fact, as Petty and Cacioppo argue, the presence of a distraction (such as an emotional appeal) in a persuasion setting can interfere with increased elaboration that is driven, for example by cognitive engagement or prior knowledge, turning emotional appeals into a professional gamble.[107] Although Edwards's intention to soften underlying personal biases with voices briefs by triggering central-route processing was noble, it appears that its operation in practice might be more than uncertain.

Non-legal stories' battle for judicial impartiality – preventing the backfire?

Unfortunately, despite increasing the appeal of merit arguments, central-route processing might not detach the judges from their personal belief systems, which subconsciously affect their cognition. Judges under high elaboration[108] might be inclined to 'have a more positive approach to the advocate's arguments if they see the advocated outcome as more desirable.'[109] Edwards takes that risk further:

> Worse yet, the unsuccessful merits argument might even trigger an inoculation effect, in which the reader develops what are essentially antibodies to the argument, making her even more resistant to future merits arguments.[110]

Furthermore:

> If the reader's preexisting values are inconsistent, a strong merits argument actually can be counterproductive. Because it threatens the reader's values, a strong merits argument can arouse resistance and actually move the reader further away – a kind of boomerang effect.[111]

The 'boomerang effect' to which Edwards refers is the so-called 'backfire effect,' demonstrated in a widely cited Nyhan and Reifler study from 2006.[112] The

---

106 Regardless of political affiliations, judges value their reputation as impartial arbiters of the law. (See Posner, *How Judges Think.*)
107 O'Keefe (n 88) 103; Petty and Cacioppo (n 89) 61.
108 O'Keefe (n 88) 105.
109 Ibid.
110 Edwards, *Stories* (n 36) 64.
111 Ibid.
112 B Nyhan and J Reifler, 'When corrections fail: the persistence of political misperceptions' (2010) 32 *Polit Behav* 303.

Legal imagination or an extra-legal hoax 123

'backfire effect' is the strengthening of misconceptions in ideological subgroups in response to counter-arguments intended to address them.[113] Nyhan and Reifler posited that 'humans are goal-directed information processors who tend to evaluate information with a directional attitude[114] bias toward reinforcing their pre-existing views.'[115] If a value-protective judging model is applied, then, when assessing hard cases, the presence of merit arguments incongruent with the justice's attitude might indeed result in the opposite effect; if

> people counterargue unwelcome information vigorously enough, they may end up with 'more attitudinally congruent information in mind than before the debate' which in turn leads them to report opinions that are *more* extreme than they otherwise would have had.[116]

According to the study, individuals 'tend to display bias in evaluating political arguments and evidence, favouring those that reinforce their existing views and disparaging those that contradict their views.'[117] Hence, Edwards suggests that voices briefs can 'prime' a judge for merit-based arguments by successfully shifting their attitudes, thus increasing their impartiality. However, the study did not imply that a change of mind without a shift in pre-existent value preferences was impossible; it simply pointed out that, although 'preference-inconsistent information is likely to be subjected to greater scepticism than preference-consistent information,' confrontation with 'information of sufficient quantity or clarity … should eventually [lead] to a preference-inconsistent conclusion.'[118] In other words, a judge who holds opposing beliefs to a party would still be likely to rule against his personal mindset if faced with a strong merit-based argument. That notion finds support in new research.

The claim that 'direct factual contradictions can actually strengthen ideologically grounded factual beliefs'[119] has been debunked in a subsequent study published by Wood and Porter, which found the backfire effect 'stubbornly difficult to induce, and … thus unlikely to be a characteristic of the public's relationship to factual information.'[120]

Although people are far from 'dispassionate Bayesians,' who 'willingly acquiesce to corrections of their ideological affiliates and to their adversaries alike,'[121] they

---

113 Ibid. 307.
114 Ibid. 311. Citations omitted. Researchers distinguished between factual beliefs (that is, beliefs that can be challenged by empirical evidence) and attitudes (concerning individuals' inherent preferences such as value choices).
115 Ibid. 310. See also Kunda (n 74).
116 Nyhan and Reifler (n 112). Citations omitted.
117 Ibid.
118 Ibid. 316. Citations omitted.
119 Ibid. 329.
120 T Wood and E Porter, 'The elusive backfire effect: mass attitudes' steadfast factual adherence' <https://ssrn.com/abstract=2819073> accessed 31 December 2017.
121 Ibid. 4; Bayes's theorem suggests that people update their beliefs upon exposure to new evidence.

124 *Aleksandra Wawrzyszczuk*

can 'heed the facts' in response to factual information, 'even when doing so forces them to separate from their political attachments.'[122] After all,

> people will come to believe what they want to believe only to the extent that reason permits; [o]ften they will be forced to acknowledge and accept undesirable conclusions, as they appear to when confronted with strong arguments for undesired counterattitudinal positions.[123]

Although the new study might undermine Edwards's argument in favour of voices briefs, it must be borne in mind that both Nylan and Reifler, and Wood and Porter inspected mass public opinion, not specialist work of the type undertaken by individual judges. As such, they underline that individuals who are more sophisticated and willing to expend cognitive effort are more likely to experience the backfire effect (but only if we assert that the effect itself comes from the attempt at constructing counterarguments). The question of whether non-party stories would be sufficient to change an attitude of a professional decision-maker remains open to debate.

Shifting attitudes – much ado about (next to) nothing?

Nonetheless, differences in judicial attitudes, personalities, and characters,[124] which drive ALS's impression of a biased judiciary,[125] do not dominate the discourse owing to the existence of, for example, legal rules, precedent, reputational concerns, and public opinion, which limit their freedom to issue arbitrary, value-laden judgments. ALS appears to be merging the political nature of the law with judicial partisanship.

'In the case of a great judge, one cannot tell the dancer from the dance';[126] the same holds true with ALS, which engages in a type of guessing game, focusing disproportionately on the impression of hidden internal narratives of judges who quickly become partisan villains unless their judgment aligns with a partisan story. However, contrary to their belief that empathy and rhetorical listening form a foundation of the Court's institutional legitimacy, judicial emotions might be a sign of partisanship, exposing the bench to criticism from the demos; 'the idea that one set of rules applies to the sympathetic litigant and another set applies to the unsympathetic litigant is not consistent with the rule of law.'[127]

122 Ibid.
123 Kunda (n 74) 485; cf. Petty and Cacioppo (n 89).
124 Charles Fried, 'Balls and strikes' (2012) 61 *Emory LJ* 641.
125 Ibid. 662.
126 Ibid.
127 AJ Wistrich, JJ Rachlinski, and C Guthrie, 'Heart versus head: do judges follow the law or follow their feelings?' (2015) 93 *Texas LR* 855, 859. Although, as Tamanaha shows, 'When the populace is closely divided on an issue with emotions running hot, any outcome will provoke a backlash in which the losing side charges the court with playing politics because both parties are convinced that the law stands firmly with them.' See B Tamanaha 'The several meanings of "politics" in judicial politics studies: why "ideological influence" is not "partisanship"' (2012) 61 *Emory LJ* 759, 772.

What the ALS ignores is that judges facing political choices tend to employ vast self-restraint and professional responsibility,[128] as non-partisanship is crucial to judicial legitimacy, protected by the life-tenured appointment system.[129] Inarguably, judicial striving for ideological neutrality is by no means 'a pristine form of appellate deliberation ... [based] solely on constitutional and statutory text, judicial precedent, and policy arguments in the form of reliable social science,'[130] with numerous studies showing that factors such as political preferences might impact judicial opinions.[131]

Yet, as 'principles alone cannot do the judging,'[132] engaging with extra-legal sources does not defeat the judicial loyalty to the rule of law; to the contrary, it may enrich the rational debate and ground judicial findings.[133] The inadvertent selection of an external narrative suddenly gains a key role in securing judicial legitimacy as the demos accepts and acknowledges the validity of a judicial decision and reinforces its binding nature, driving the Court's focus on 'ensuring coherence, unity, stability, and orderly law development.'[134] With precedent being an effective method of imposing judicial restraint, the necessity to present 'a public and reasoned explanation of the judicial result'[135] becomes an equally successful deterrent to judicial activism as the desire to maintain certainty of legal outcomes.[136] To paraphrase an extract from Kunda's study:

> Judges do not seem to be at liberty to conclude whatever they want to conclude merely because they want to. Rather ... [judges] motivated to arrive at a particular conclusion attempt to be rational and to construct a justification of their desired conclusion that would persuade a dispassionate observer[137] ... they draw the desired conclusion only if they can muster up the evidence necessary to support it.[138]

It is important to acknowledge that voices briefs are unlikely to become a sole justification for a judicial decision; where

---

128 R Posner, 'Foreword: a political court' (2005) 119 *Harvard LR* 32, 63.
129 Judges are not accountable to other branches of the judiciary, the electorate, or even the president who selected them. See: ibid. 75.
130 Edwards, *Stories* (n 36) 54.
131 Wistrich, Rachlinski, and Guthrie (n 127) 862; see particularly footnote 42; the impact of political views is easily conflated with a more general approach to legal interpretation.
132 WJ Brennan Jr, 'Reason, passion, and the progress of the law' (1988) 10 *Cardozo LR* 3, 4.
133 Ibid. 11. Brian Tamanaha provides a thorough analysis of the dilemma of political judging in Tamanaha (n 127).
134 HP Monaghan, 'On avoiding avoidance, agenda control, and related matters' (2012) 112 *Colum LR* 665, 680.
135 Brennan (n 132) 8.
136 Ibid. 13.
137 Kunda (n 74) 484.
138 Ibid.

126 *Aleksandra Wawrzyszczuk*

objective factors clearly dictate one outcome and make it impossible to justify the opposite result with a straight face, one's desire to maintain a self-image of objectivity will prevail over achieving the desired outcome.[139]

Even Edwards acknowledges that prevalence of emotional decision-making is undesirable: 'this is not to say that constitutional decisions should be made either by polling citizens or by emotional reactions to tearful stories,' but 'neither should they be made in a hermetically sealed environment.'[140] The Court needs a foundation of determinate rules to maintain its legitimacy. Voices briefs, even if impactful, are unlikely to leave the very back of judicial minds.

Voices briefs – making waves out of court

As the likelihood of making a lasting impact on the internal narratives of the judiciary is uncertain at best, ALS assigns an alternative role to voices briefs: they are to continue a tradition of democratic input into the workings of the court.[141] Edwards acknowledges that, although the Court should not become 'a forum for touchy-feely therapy,'[142] it should serve as a model institution for public discourse, with 'rhetorical listening' increasing the public trust in the institution.[143]

Suddenly, the Court not only has to identify the precedent, navigate the socio-political agenda, and assess the parties' arguments, but also conduct a task for which it lacks any competence or even ability: listen to and evaluate the accounts of however many voices a party manages to attract. Its potential for a mistake is high, and the price of such a mistake can be even higher; reliance on voices briefs might undermine judicial legitimacy in the eyes of the public and lead to their mistrust of the judiciary if their pleas are left with no recourse.[144]

As voices briefs attempt to turn the Court into a policy arena, it appears that they are better tailored to resonate with the demos than with the judges themselves. Arguably, as much as they attempt to break through the power hierarchies to tune in to voices of the oppressed,[145] voices briefs are also about politics. Judicial hypotheticals do not bear the same concern, allowing the Court to test the waters without a partisan angle, as 'only judicial stories are directed at entirely eliminating the disbelief of the audience and representing a claim of knowledge.'[146]

---

139 Wistrich, Rachlinski, and Guthrie (n 127) 872.
140 Edwards, *Stories* (n 36) 59.
141 The reference to a 'democratic tradition' presumably refers to a history of filing amici briefs.
142 Edwards, *Stories* (n 36) 69.
143 Ibid. Citations omitted.
144 See A de Tocqueville, *Democracy in America* (Colonial Press 1900) 150.
145 Cf. R Delgado, 'Storytelling for oppositionists and others: a plea for narrative' (1989) 87 *Michigan LR* 2411; RM Cover, 'The Supreme Court, 1982 term – foreword: nomos and narrative' (1983) 97 *Harvard LR* 4.
146 Almog (n 5) 474.

Legal imagination or an extra-legal hoax 127

They lack the personal dimension of voices briefs that are so intimately connected with individual identities. Unlike voices briefs, which tend to focus on limited outcomes for a particular group of individuals who share similar circumstances, hypotheticals induce the judges to 'think about future cases and to formulate general principles that look beyond achieving a favoured result in a single case.'[147] That forward-thinking quality of the hypotheticals visibly supports the certainty and coherence of the legal system, two of the foundations of judicial legitimacy.

Hence, although Edwards's success in using voices briefs to shift attitudes in court might be questionable, there is another outlet where they can truly make a splash: the society at large. It appears that voices briefs are not appealing to the judiciary as much as they appeal to the wider public, benefitting primarily the lobbying groups rather than the parties.

The emotionality and informality of voices briefs stand in direct opposition to the complexity and formality of lengthy legal filings, and not without consequences. Cobb and Kuklinski conducted a study of changes in public opinion in which they distinguished between, on the one hand, easy arguments, which are 'simple and symbolic, making strong assertions without providing support ... [and are] designed to elicit emotional response' and, on the other hand, hard arguments that 'use reasoning or evidence to support claims about the consequences of a proposal ... take some mental work to understand and likely evoke little emotional response.'[148]

The study demonstrated that easy arguments (such as those proposed by rhetorical appeals contained in voices briefs) generally had a more impactful influence than hard ones; 'pure assertion, which can evoke emotion and is easily represented in memory, is what most readily changes opinion.'[149] The voices briefs' emotional value allows them to reach the disinterested public, which likely accepts such 'easy' argument much more willingly than a complex legal or policy analysis offered by parties in formal briefings. Unfortunately, such mental shortcuts pose a risk of creating a difficult conundrum for the public opinion of the judiciary.

Voices briefs go beyond nudging the judges to embrace the easy emotional arguments. They transcend the neutrality of hypotheticals and inadvertently encourage the public to view the court as a body that is making binary value choices, similar to the way in which an uninformed demos might. The briefs can go as far as to pressure the bench into the role of an arbiter of folk truths rather than encouraging impartiality. The demos may interpret the Court's rational decision as readily accepting easy arguments and be quick to judge the outcomes of cases as incorrect or unjust, frequently without diving below the presented narratives. Indeed, 'the preference for easy arguments ... will cause distortion whenever one side in a debate can appeal to easy arguments (even if doing so is largely misleading), while the other side has more to explain.'[150]

147 Gewirtz (n 27) 123.
148 Kuklinski and Quirk (n 91) 32.
149 Ibid.
150 Ibid.

128 *Aleksandra Wawrzyszczuk*

Legitimising an increased reliance on extra-legal arguments and effectively voting on generalised policy stances rather than individual cases promote a distorted image of the Court and might contradict the rule of law by diminishing the value of binding law and procedure. Furthermore, as the Court gets pressured to decide not only in favour or against a party, but primarily for or against an entire social group, voices briefs can quickly become a dirty game intended to force the Supreme Court into active policymaking. 'Vivid information, that is, concrete, sensory, and personally relevant information,' not unlike the stories contained in voices briefs, 'may have a disproportionate impact on beliefs and inference,'[151] turning it into a wonderful tool for persuading the demos and a dangerous blow to judicial reputation and legitimacy.

Gamble not worth the candle?

Not only is voices briefs' potential impact on the judges and their persuasive value in court rather controversial, the briefs present further controversies. An advocate representing a party in the Supreme Court, along with meritorious amicus briefs filers, should be capable of educating the judges as to potential future consequences of a prospective judgment without including anecdotal evidence or unsworn testimonies.

Thus, in reality, voices briefs add little merit beyond what any reasonable advocate and certain types of amici curiae would include in their filings, and any possible gaps would likely be supplemented by judicial hypotheticals. They can, however, create a potential for smuggling new evidentiary facts into appellate proceedings,[152] with no mechanism in place to assure reliability of the information contained in the briefs,[153] as individuals submitting the stories are not subject to cross-examination or making a sworn testimony. 'Evidence is regularly excluded from the jury,'[154] yet voices briefs are allowed to become a part of the proceedings, despite their potential impact on the judges themselves.

However, if, like Delgado,[155] one accepts that there is no single all-encompassing truth about any object, and that it is the general form of a legal narrative rather than its truth value that deserves attention, the issue of reliability bears no significance. That is because the risk of fabrication is relatively low, and there are effective proposals that can limit its impact, including placing more responsibility on the attorneys gathering and filing the stories.[156]

Although Edwards acknowledges that 'the stories related in voices briefs should not be offered simply to prompt a generalised emotional reaction for or against a topic or practice … [but] rather the stories should relate to the particular issue the

---

151 E Loftus and LR Beach, Review: 'Human inference and judgment: is the glass half empty or half full?' (1992) 34 *Stan LR* 939, citing Nisbett and Ross, 190.
152 Edwards, *Stories* (n 36) 79.
153 Ibid. 77.
154 Posner (n 85) 745.
155 Delgado (n 145).
156 Edwards, *Stories* (n 36) 77.

Legal imagination or an extra-legal hoax 129

Court must decide,'[157] she does not specify how to ensure relevance of voices briefs. There is also the issue of administrative overload at the Supreme Court, by now well known to any lawyer or a legal scholar in the field,[158] which most solutions to reliability and relevance issues in Edwards's argument are far from alleviating. Procedural and administrative difficulties surrounding the submission and evaluation of voices briefs have been analysed elsewhere.[159]

The solutions to many of the voices briefs' shortcomings (apart from substituting them with judicial hypotheticals) appear burdensome and difficult to justify proportionately to their potential value to the proceedings. For example, imposing sanctions on the filer or their lawyer for filing briefs that do not meet the required reliability and relevance threshold necessitates a separate process and criteria for assessing those qualities. It engages the Court in yet another decision-making procedure. Would the filers require a procedure through which any refusal or sanction could be challenged? Could they request the Court to provide reasons for rejecting the brief? Edwards suggests 'ignoring the brief' rather than imposing sanctions as an alternative,[160] which could further increase the Court's paperwork without improving the likelihood of the judges taking the voices briefs into account.

Scalia and Garner's summary of amicus briefs in general resonates even louder:

> The amicus brief is an increasingly popular device designed with the hope of giving … other interested parties their say. We say 'with the hope' because judges rarely read all the amicus briefs. They will surely read one filed by the United States, probably one filed by the ACLU in a civil rights case or by the AFL-CIO in a labor-law case, and probably one filed by a lawyer in whose integrity and ability they have special confidence … The rest will likely be screened by law clerks, with only a few (if any) making it to the judge's desk.[161]

Conclusion

There is a place for narratives in court, and this chapter has analysed two storytelling devices used to stimulate judicial imagination: the judge-made hypothetical and the third-party voices brief. Whereas the former enables the judges to successfully test the breadth and depth of their potential judgments, the latter's prospective contribution to the decision-making at the Supreme Court is vastly overestimated.

---

157 Ibid. 79.
158 See DJ Hutchinson and PB Kurland, 'The business of the Supreme Court, O.T. 1982' (1983) 50 *University of Chicago LR* 628 for a summary of issues identified pre-1982; many of the problems, unfortunately, remain the same today.
159 Edwards, *Stories* (n 36).
160 Ibid. from 84.
161 A Scalia and B Garner, *Making Your Case* (Thomson/West 2008) 102.

130 *Aleksandra Wawrzyszczuk*

Even if voices briefs are read by all justices, they are still relatively unlikely to sway the Court without a sufficiently convincing backing in the precedent or even sufficient policies. One might suggest that it would be beneficial to encourage their inclusion if only just to err on the side of caution; there is, after all, a chance that their impact will secure a socially desirable outcome. However, it is argued that voices briefs can result in more trouble than they are worth, as cognitive studies suggest that the voices briefs' impact on judicial attitudes is likely limited.

The analysis posits that judicial experience, commitment to the rule of law, principles and policies, as well as the desire to protect the Court's legitimacy and individual reputations might prompt the judges to engage with merit arguments over heuristics. Between the overly cautious context-restrictive scholarship and the rule-sceptical context-rich theories lies a common ground, where judges are committed to the law while balancing the socio-political values of a pluralist society to maintain the longevity of the legal system.

Under such conditions, hypotheticals and social science data are best placed in the courtroom, and voices briefs would be better placed in Congress, with judicial hypotheticals taking over their role in court. They can lobby for change, thus strengthening the democratic process and judicial legitimacy and reducing the administrative and philosophical burden on the Court. Most importantly, tying up the narratives in Congress would 'make the voices heard,'[162] satisfying the ultimate goal of many ALS scholars, and advancing development of the law in a manner aligned with the legal system's political and social aims.[163]

---

162 Edwards, *Stories* (n 36).
163 J Bickenbach. 'The "artificial reason" of the law' (1990) 12 *Informal Logic* 23, 24.

Part Three

Thought, stylistics, and discourse

8 The French Revolution and the programmatic imagination[1]
Hilary Mantel on law, politics, and misery

Richard Mullender

NEWCASTLE UNIVERSITY, UK

Introduction

In *A Tale of Two Cities*, Charles Dickens presents us with a fictive account of France immediately before and during the Revolution that began to unfold in 1789. Dickens tells us that as France stood on the cusp of this cataclysm it was simultaneously the 'best of times' and the 'worst of times.'[2] As he intones these phrases, he impresses upon us that pre-revolutionary France is a society in which some live well (most obviously, the monarch, Louis XVI, and those around him) while millions struggle to survive. Dickens also conveys a sense that this state of affairs is unsustainable. France stands in a state of gravid arrest – poised between a regime that has a 'superannuated' appearance and an alternative model of human association that has yet to take on even an inchoate appearance.[3]

Hilary Mantel carries us over the same ground as Dickens in her historical novel *A Place of Greater Safety*. As she does so, she focuses on three of the Revolution's most prominent figures, Maximilien Robespierre, George-Jacques Danton, and Camille Desmoulins. Moreover, her narrative is rich in significance relevant to the imagination as a faculty that finds expression in our legal and political institutions and practices. In this essay, we will seek to bring the value of her contribution into focus by introducing the term 'the programmatic imagination.' This term encompasses the human capacity to envision (more or less

---

1 This chapter has grown out of, and benefited from responses to, papers I gave at the Annual Conference of the Society of Legal Scholars in 2018 (Queen Mary University of London), in Newcastle Law School in 2018 (to the Eldon Society), and in City University's Law School (while participating in a symposium on 'Law in Troubled Times' in 2019). I have also benefited from the responses to earlier drafts of this chapter made by Tom Bennett, David Campbell, Martin Loughlin, David McGrogan, Matteo Nicolini, and Ian Ward. Likewise, I have benefited from the responses that Benedict Douglas, William Lucy, Shaun Pattinson, and Kara Woodbury-Smith made to a paper I gave on 'Law and Political Anthropology' in Durham Law School in 2019. Conversations on the French Revolution with Richard Clay and Emilia Mickiewicz and on Hilary Mantel's *A Place of Greater Safety* with Patrick O'Callaghan were also a great source of assistance.
2 C Dickens, *A Tale of Two Cities* (first published 1859, Penguin Books 2003) 5.
3 T Carlyle, *The French Revolution: A History* (first published 1837, Random House 2002) 113.

134   *Richard Mullender*

precisely) social improvements that involve the mobilisation of legal and political resources and that necessitate concerted human action. But it also has to do with a number of practical problems that are likely to arise when people seek to make their plans a reality.

Although the programmatic imagination and the problems that attend its use feature prominently in Mantel's novel (and this response to it), they do not encompass her contribution in its entirety. Rather, they are a hub around which a number of other considerations turn. These considerations include a complex political anthropology that gives us reason to doubt the plausibility of plans for social improvement that tend in a utopian direction. Here, the two phrases from Dickens with which we began have relevance. For Mantel uses the French Revolution between 1789 and 1794 to demonstrate that the 'worst of times' may be the upshot of our efforts to pursue 'the best of times.' By working along these lines, she also gives us a basis on which to argue that she is groping towards what we will call in this essay a theory of egalitarian misery.

To the extent that there are intimations of such a theory at work in *A Place of Greater Safety*, they reveal a strand of anthropological pessimism in her thinking. This pessimism finds expression in the assumption that groups of people are prone to act in ways that undercut plans for social improvement that gain currency among their members. In staking out this position, Mantel also prompts critical reflection on the anthropological optimism on display in modern social imaginaries. But, before dwelling on these matters, we must examine the contents of *A Place of Greater Safety* and the concept of imagination.

Mantel on the French Revolution

'The law-school boys' and the vortex of revolution

Mantel's account of the French Revolution begins in the decades that immediately precede it. The hold on power enjoyed by the absolutist monarch and his *Ancien régime* is far from secure and growing visibly weaker. In her explanation of this state of affairs, Mantel places emphasis on the parlous state of the nation's finances. A succession of more or less assured comptrollers-general of finance take up and leave office (having failed to address France's economic malaise effectively). The presence on the throne of a ponderous monarch, who has little inclination to tackle the financial difficulties that confront him and his compatriots, makes matters worse. But, as the *Ancien régime* moves towards what Mantel calls the 'cataclysm' of revolution, new forces are gaining an ever more prominent place in the life of the nation.[4] For France is becoming 'enfranchised by her intelligence.'[5]

Here, Mantel identifies the eighteenth-century Enlightenment as a political force. Moreover, she makes this force vivid in her three central characters, Danton, Desmoulins, and Robespierre. She devotes close attention to the early lives of this

4 H Mantel, *A Place of Greater Safety* (Fourth Estate 1992) 147.
5 Ibid 159.

The French Revolution 135

trio – and traces their development in the years that run up to the beginning of the Revolution. Danton, Desmoulins, and Robespierre are, as we will see, very different characters. But they each become 'law-school boys' (to use a phrase that Mantel ascribes to another prominent figure in the Revolution, the Marquis de Lafayette).[6] For each of them is the beneficiary of a legal education. Likewise, they each see in law a means to the end of a socially just future. 'Hope' ('the promise of a fairer, cleaner world') is thus a feature of their thinking.[7] More particularly, they make assumptions that the sociologist Pierre Bourdieu associates with the ideal of *noblesse de robe*.[8] *Noblesse* in this form has, on Bourdieu's account, to do with the pursuit of 'the properly political.' This is an ideal that enjoins the state to seek to secure the interests of all its citizens.[9]

Of the three law-school boys, Camille Desmoulins is, in a variety of ways, the least robust. Although eloquent, he is afflicted by a stammer and is prone to exhibit 'the fatal exhaustion of easy prey.'[10] But, at the same time, he possesses what his close friend Robespierre calls 'iron-clad vanity.'[11] This vanity finds expression in and derives, in large part, from his prodigious powers of expression. We see these powers develop while he (in the company of Robespierre) attends France's most prestigious school (the Lycée Louis-le-Grand) and in the pamphlets he writes as the Revolution unfolds. Camille's most well-known and decisive contribution to the Revolution occurs in July 1789. He makes a 'precipitate entry into history' by delivering a speech outside Paris's Café du Foy that effectively incites the storming of the Bastille (a prison and intimidating symbol of the *Ancien régime*).[12] This event drives the process of revolution forward – first in the direction of a constitutional monarchy and, later, a republic.

Desmoulins is (and identifies himself from an early age as being) a republican. While in his teens, he declares that 'we can go beyond Cromwell' and 'set up a republic on the purest Roman model.'[13] As he matures, he weaves strongly egalitarian commitments to the recognition of 'virtue and talent' into his thinking.[14] But simply to attach the label 'republican' to him is to deflect attention from the complexities of his character. Although the ideal of republicanism animates Camille, Robespierre draws attention to an element of perversity in his make-up. Robespierre does this when he observes that, 'the worse things get, the better they get [for Camille].'[15] Although critical of Camille, Robespierre considers him to be

---

6 Ibid 258. (Among other things, Lafayette (along with the Abbé Sieyès and Benjamin Franklin) played a part in drafting the seminal human rights instrument, the Declaration of the Rights of Man and the Citizen, 1789.)

7 Ibid 350.

8 P Bourdieu, *On the State: Lectures at the College de France, 1989–1992* (Polity 2014) 218.

9 Mantel (n 4) 255.

10 Ibid 66.

11 Ibid 778.

12 Ibid 220. See also Carlyle (n 3) 111 (on the Bastille as 'Tyranny's stronghold').

13 Mantel (n 4) 44.

14 Ibid 247.

15 Ibid 27.

136   *Richard Mullender*

his oldest friend. However, Robespierre and those around him (e.g., his increasingly self-assured acolyte Antoine Saint-Just) ultimately conclude that Camille and Danton must stand trial (on, inter alia, the ground of counter-revolutionary conspiracy). They thus set in train a bogus 'legal' process that issues in the deaths of two of the three law-school boys and that stands as an emblem of the Revolution's retreat from *noblesse de robe.*

Mantel finds in Robespierre a single-mindedness quite absent from Camille (whose intellect she describes as 'skittish').[16] While a pupil at Louis-le-Grand, 'American ideas' make Robespierre a critic of the status quo.[17] So too do the Enlightenment and the writings of Jean-Jacques Rousseau (whose republican political philosophy places emphasis on 'the general will' of a united citizenry and is strongly utopian in orientation).[18] When Robespierre, later, enters the legal profession in Arras, he represents the poor – even if this involves working for no fee. At this point in Mantel's narrative, a life of provincial obscurity seems to be his only prospect. However, the King decides, in a desperate bid to retain power, to convene the Estates-General. This consultative body has not met since 1614 and has the tricky task of promoting social harmony in a feudal society. The King's decision to give it new life galvanises Robespierre. He secures a place as a deputy in the Third Estate (whose members represent France's many millions of commoners). Although Robespierre lacks oratorical skill, he conveys the impression that what he says is 'beyond dispute' and gains a reputation as 'the Incorruptible' (a staunch proponent of republican virtue).[19] As the Revolution moves beyond constitutional monarchy, he (along with Danton) becomes one of its prime movers. Ultimately, he becomes the Revolution's most infamous proponent of 'the Terror' (the resort to violence, with exiguous legal constraints, as a means to egalitarian ends). He declares that 'Terror is nothing other than justice, prompt, stern and inflexible.'[20]

While Robespierre embodies the intolerant turn the Revolution takes, Danton (who plays an important role in this unhappy state of affairs) represents what it might have become. Mantel makes this point by presenting Danton as having a disposition quite different from those of her other two central characters. Whereas Camille is 'skittish,' Danton exhibits the focus borne of ambition. Where Robespierre is doctrinaire,

---

16 Ibid 243.

17 Ibid 28.

18 J-J Rousseau, *The Social Contract and Other Later Political Writings* (CUP 1997) 59–60 (bk II, ch 3). Isaiah Berlin brings into clear view not just the utopian orientation of Rousseau's thinking but also the 'monstrous paradox' at work within it. He does this by dwelling on the 'mysterious point of intersection' between 'liberty' (of the individual) and 'control' (on the part of the state) in Rousseau's account of the 'general will.' According to Berlin, it is a point of intersection that makes it possible for Rousseau to find the only basis for (the utopian end of) 'the most untrammelled freedom' in 'the most rigorous and enslaving authority.' See I Berlin, *Freedom and its Betrayal: Six Enemies of Human Liberty* (Pimlico 2003) 38 ('liberty', 'control', and 'mysterious point of intersection'), 40 ('general will'), and 49 ('untrammelled freedom' and 'enslaving authority').

19 Mantel (n 4) 394 and 398.

20 Ibid 491.

The French Revolution   137

Danton is pragmatic. His ambition and pragmatism are apparent in his youth. When a passing stranger tells him that 'law is a weapon,' he resolves to embark on a legal career.[21] He enjoys professional success as he wields the weapon he now possesses. His proficiency in its use enables him to propel himself to the centre of French society. We see him become a King's counsellor and, in the final days of the *Ancien Régime*, turn down a position in a government that, on his analysis, 'won't last a year.'[22] His pragmatic outlook is on display in his assessment of the King's decision to reconvene the Estates-General. Danton recognises that this body is a 'relic' of entrenched hierarchy.[23] However, he argues that 'an old institution can take on a new form' and serve the egalitarian ends that he shares with Camille and Robespierre.[24] Moreover, he (unlike Camille and Robespierre) takes the view that a constitutional monarchy could afford the means to secure these ends. When, however, the King makes plain his lack of commitment to constitutional monarchy, Danton becomes a vociferous republican.

Danton's republican ardour is plain to see when, in 1792, he leads what Mantel refers to as the 'second' revolution.[25] As foreign armies (motivated by a desire to sustain the monarchy) menace France, Danton grasps that the Revolution needs a new and more radical impetus. More particularly, he recognises, in a flash of insight, that '[s]imple words are needed' as a basis on which to unite the nation.[26] Danton finds these words when he dares his compatriots to believe in the possibility of a republican future in which the ideals of 'liberty,' 'equality,' 'fraternity,' and 'democracy' will shape practical life. France moves in the direction he indicates. At this point in her narrative, Mantel tells us that Danton is 'manufactur[ing]' 'actions ... out of speech' and that a new (republican) national myth has, consequently, come into existence.[27] Her point is that Danton has engaged in successful speech-acts – by uttering words (and articulating a vision) that his compatriots have treated as authoritative. As these speech-acts breathe life into republicanism, they strip the monarchy of viability as an institution.[28] But shortly after Danton

21 Ibid 38.
22 Ibid 155.
23 Ibid 74.
24 Ibid.
25 Ibid 431.
26 Ibid 516. The 'simple words' to which Danton refers clearly have the purpose of establishing what John Searle calls 'collective intentionality.' Where collective intentionality exists, it can sustain a shared understanding of social reality (and, as it changes, so too do society's institutional contours). See J Searle, *Making the Social World: The Structure of Human Civilization* (Oxford University Press 2010) chs 1, 2, and 4.
27 Mantel (n 4) 516.
28 To draw on the terminology in JL Austin, *How to Do Things with Words* (first published 1962, Harvard UP 1975) chs 1 and 2 and 25 and 118, the speech-acts in which Danton engages possess perlocutionary force (they motivate people who hear them). They also have a performative character (insofar as they prompt hearers to ascribe authority to a politico-legal structure that ultimately acquires the status of a republic). We might also see Danton's speech-acts as bringing into existence a state of affairs that Rousseau identifies as 'the true foundation of society.' This is because they prompt the formation of an egalitarian collective intentionality 'by which a people ... is [or becomes] a people' or 'association' concerned with pursuing the

138   *Richard Mullender*

demonstrates that '[r]evolution is a great battlefield of semantics,' he takes a step that will issue in many deaths (including his own).[29] He decides to give a 'special tribunal' (*Le Tribunal révolutionnaire*) that had come into existence in 1792 'sweeping powers' to 'uncover [and sanction] all counter-revolutionary enterprises.'[30] Long before he goes to the guillotine, he regrets the way in which pursuit of the ends that animate the Revolution has compromised its commitment to legality (e.g., a prohibition on appeals against the special tribunal's decisions). Moreover, he does so in terms that illustrate the way in which the ideal of *noblesse de robe* continues to inform his thinking. For example, he declares that '[p]erverting justice is a very great evil in itself. It leaves no hope of amendment.'[31]

While Mantel places emphasis on her three central characters, she also pays close attention to the context in which they act. As France teeters on the edge of revolution, this context is 'stifling.'[32] The operations of the *Ancien Régime* are an impediment to the realisation of human potential. But it endures and prompts consideration of the question as to how it sustains itself. Mantel goes some way towards answering this question when she describes lawyers 'shuffling papers across desks' and notes '[t]he constant shuttling of opinions' as political controversies unfold.[33] In each case, we can read her as referring (obliquely) to language (legal and political) that operates as a collection of placeholders. When language operates in this way, it establishes the space within which argument on common concerns can proceed. But, in the context of the *Ancien Régime*, the social consensus that finds expression in language as a placeholder is fragile. This becomes apparent in the Estates-General. When the King reconvenes this body, he assumes that it will sustain the existing order. But the Third Estate offers a startling answer to a question posed by a prominent cleric, the Abbé Sieyès. In response to Sieyès' question, 'What is the Third Estate?', it replies that it is a 'national assembly' (rather than a quiescent component in a feudal order).[34] When the other two estates (composed of the aristocracy and the clergy) concede this point, the centre of gravity in French politico-legal life shifts in a democratic direction.

Developments such as this and the fall of the Bastille convey a sense of the revolutionary 'vortex' (to take a term from Thomas Carlyle) in which the law-school boys find themselves.[35] But so too do an array of other revolutionaries who have a place in Mantel's novel. As these characters interact with one another and the law-school boys, we see regular collisions of will that explain why Mantel

---

'public good.' See Rousseau (n 18) 49 (bk II, ch 5). France formally became a republic on 22 September 1792.

29 Mantel (n 4) 581.
30 Ibid 498, and S Clarke, *The French Revolution & What Went Wrong* (Century 2018) ch 20 iii.
31 Mantel (n 4) 582.
32 Ibid 120.
33 Ibid.
34 Carlyle (n 3) 100 (Sieyès) and 135 ('National Assembly').
35 Ibid 175 and 184.

describes life (even before the Revolution begins) as a 'battlefield.'[36] Three of these characters merit close attention here as they (like Danton, Desmoulins, and Robespierre) conduct themselves in ways that are relevant to our concern with imagination. Madame Roland is a committed republican. Mantel tells us that she experiences 'intemperate joy' when the Bastille falls.[37] She also tells us that Roland resolves to play a part in reshaping French society. However, we learn that Roland is blind to prominent features of the practical scene she surveys. This is because she makes the optimistic assumption that people will act in accordance with the 'disembodied' republican virtues she espouses ('nobility of spirit,' 'brotherhood,' and 'self-sacrifice').[38] Consequently, she fails to confront the fact that people may be ill-equipped to transform France into the republic she sees as an ideal end-state.

Mantel presents a variation on this theme in her account of Antoine Saint-Just. For Saint-Just, like Madame Roland, strives to usher an ideal republic into existence. This fosters in him an intolerant, spiteful attitude towards those who present (or appear to present) an impediment to the pursuit of his plans. Camille Desmoulins (whose thinking tends in a libertarian direction) is one such person. We see Saint-Just encourage Robespierre to put him and those around him (including Danton) on trial. Saint-Just knows that this course of action spells doom for Camille and the others. But the admixture of republican fervour, intolerance, and spite at work within him blinds him to the inadequacy of the grounds on which he is ready to snatch people's lives away from them. Camille's wife, Lucile, is alive to at least some of the defects in his thinking. She observes that 'Saint-Just's main aim seems to be to improve people along the lines of some plan that he has in his head, and which ... he has difficulty articulating.'[39]

Alongside these studies in inflexibility and intolerance, Mantel sets the character of Jacques Pierre Brissot (a former denizen of the Bastille). Mantel tells us that he believes in 'the Brotherhood of Man' and 'good government.'[40] She also impresses on her readers that he is well connected. When she identifies such luminaries as Jeremy Bentham and Tom Paine as members of his network, she makes clear Brissot's determination to join a late eighteenth-century progressive vanguard.[41] Moreover, when she notes that Brissot considers himself to be an adviser to George Washington, and 'the best informed man in France,' she makes apparent tendencies towards self-importance and exaggeration at work within him.[42] Brissot also exhibits, on Mantel's account, a worthiness that verges on absurdity. This becomes apparent when she describes him 'reading, writing, scurrying from place to place, gathering in his thoughts, scattering his good will; proposing a motion, addressing a committee, jotting down a note.'[43] Danton offers a more succinct

36 Mantel (n 4) 5.
37 Ibid 382.
38 Ibid 380.
39 Ibid 571.
40 Ibid 276.
41 Ibid.
42 Ibid 276 and 288.
43 Ibid 637.

140 *Richard Mullender*

and troubling variation on the same theme. He detects in Brissot a 'regrettable busybody tendency' that will find in military force a means by which to mount a revolutionary 'crusade' beyond the borders of France.[44] Here, Brissot's thinking betrays a commitment to 'the imperialism of the universal' (the desire to inscribe on all available space an agenda that he assumes will yield common benefits).[45]

Whereas Mantel places emphasis on her three central characters and an array of other revolutionaries, there are other ways to tell the story of the Revolution and make apparent its significance. This is a point that the historian Simon Schama makes when he contrasts 'lyric engagement' with 'scientific analysis.'[46] The emphasis Mantel places on individuals in *A Place of Greater Safety* makes it very much an exercise in 'lyric engagement'. But, although this is the case, she is plainly alive to structures of the sort that prompt analysis on a scientific model. These structures include institutions – for example, the Estates-General and the National Convention (France's first republican government, in the name of which both Danton and Robespierre exercised powers with the aim of assuring the sovereignty of the French people).[47] Likewise, they include political groupings (e.g., the Jacobins, including Robespierre, Danton, and Desmoulins; and the Girondins, including Brissot and Madame Roland). However, 'structure' is a concept with limited usefulness in the shifting context of the French Revolution. This is a point we with explore below by drawing on the philosopher Alain Badiou and the sociologist Pierre Bourdieu.

'The event' and the state

Alain Badiou identifies the French Revolution as providing an example of what he calls 'the event.'[48] The event is a state of affairs that grows out of an existing situation. But, although this is the case, it marks a rupture with the status quo. This leads Badiou to argue that those who wish to understand any such occurrence must not reduce it to a continuation or development of the status quo. Rather, they should strive to understand it in its own terms. To this end, they should seek to fashion conceptual tools that will be faithful to it as a development that stands outside (or that carries us beyond) the situation from which it emerges. Badiou sees this as a practically urgent matter. This is because the event, on his account, presents us with truths that may make it possible for us to flourish. For this reason, he stakes out a clear normative position on the event. Those who grasp that it may be a repository of truth fall under an obligation to maintain fidelity to it. They discharge this obligation by seeking to articulate the truths that inhere within it.

---

44 Ibid 398 and 403.
45 On 'the imperialism of the universal' see Bourdieu (n 8) 159.
46 S Schama, *Citizens: A Chronicle of the French Revolution* (Viking 1989) 6.
47 C Schmitt, *Dictatorship: From the Origin of the Modern Concept of Sovereignty to Proletarian Class Struggle* (first published 1921, Polity 2014) 130 (on the National Convention's 'authority' and *'toute-puissance* [omnipotence]').
48 A Badiou, *Being and Event* (Continuum 2006) 189–92.

As Badiou indicates, these points have ready applicability to the French Revolution. The Revolution marks a rupture with an existing situation. But, at the same time, it gives expression to an egalitarian philosophy of government that had been gaining currency in France, and Europe more generally, long before the cataclysm of 1789 and the years thereafter. Moreover, as the Revolution unfolds, we see Mantel's central characters and those around them seeking to draw out its significance. Robespierre makes apparent the mental operations this involves when he addresses the question, 'What is the Revolution for?'[49] Likewise, they are on display when he offers the answer that it has to do with 'bring[ing] us to justice and equality, to full humanity.'[50] Here, Mantel presents us with a character who considers himself to be under what his fellow Jacobin Jean-Paul Marat calls 'a duty [of fidelity] to the Revolution.'[51] It is this duty that prompts him to wield power with the aim of establishing a 'Republic of Virtue.'[52]

We can probe this example and others like it (e.g., Brissot's plans for social improvement within and beyond France's borders) by drawing on Pierre Bourdieu's *On the State*. Bourdieu traces the history of the modern state's emergence as an impartial institution in which an at least incipiently egalitarian philosophy of government finds expression. He also picks out the French Revolution as a 'watershed' in this history.[53] For it intensified a process of development (a '*longue durée*') that predated it by centuries.[54] Moreover, Bourdieu says of this process that it presents us with an institutional 'reality' that 'keeps coming into being.'[55] By this he means that the modern state is not an institution that exhibits fixed features. Rather, its features alter as we move through time and explore its potentialities.

These points provide a basis on which to suggest that the state that features in Mantel's novel provides an instance of 'the event' in Badiou's sense. If this point is broadly correct, the characters on whom Mantel focuses her attention sit on the (still unfolding) timeline along which the modern state has been and is continuing to emerge and ramify. On Bourdieu's account, this process begins (in the French context, at least) in the twelfth century and moves, haltingly, in the direction of government on a strongly egalitarian model.[56] In light of this point, we might describe Danton, Desmoulins, Robespierre, and those around them as trying to bring a long-lived process of development to a culmination. This is an activity that involves the exercise of imagination. Before we consider Mantel's contribution on this topic, we must look in some detail at the faculty to which we apply the label 'imagination.'

49 Mantel (n 4) 445.
50 Ibid.
51 Ibid 511. See also ibid 283 (where Marat declares: 'I think of the Revolution for twenty-four hours of the day').
52 Ibid 804.
53 Bourdieu (n 8) 345.
54 Ibid 345.
55 Ibid 337–38.
56 Ibid 46.

142   *Richard Mullender*

Imagination

To possess imagination is to be able to 'create images in the mind's eye.'[57] This inventive capacity is, on one account, 'the very *mark* of intelligence' and has affinities with 'vision': the ability 'to see the invisible.'[58] When vision presents us with an ideal (e.g., a socially just society) or, at least, a desirable state of affairs, we typically experience it as an object towards which we should move. Where this is the case, a vision exerts what we might describe as a normative pull that draws people in its direction (and invests it with 'living power in the imagination').[59]

This is a point that has relevance to concepts to which we have already referred and to which we will devote close attention later – for example, 'liberty,' 'equality,' 'fraternity,' 'democracy,' 'republic,' and 'virtue.' Even in circumstances where the thoughts that move through our minds have a less than definite shape, they may, nonetheless, pull us in their direction. This is a point we can develop by drawing on the analytic philosopher Gilbert Ryle. In an essay entitled 'The Thinking of Thoughts,' Ryle focuses on thinkers who 'want to acquire a grasp of something that is not yet within reach.'[60] He likens them to explorers who seek to move through hitherto undiscovered terrain without a map. Thinkers who go about their business in this way require modesty (attentiveness to the distinctiveness of the objects they scrutinise). They also require creativity (the ability to use language in ways that will pick out the particularities of what they survey and thus provide 'profitably followable pointers').[61]

This creative capacity is on display in the many contexts where imagination manifests itself. We can gain a sense of the practical force it exerts by isolating imagination in a range of distinct forms. Here, we will focus on imagination in its 'legal,' 'sociological,' and 'moral' forms since each of them is relevant to Mantel's account of the French Revolution. 'Legal' imagination is on display in circumstances where a lawyer identifies unrealised possibilities for development in existing law (e.g., the incremental extension of rules and other norms to new sets of circumstances). Imagination in this sense has a conservative aspect. This is because it finds the justification for the development it contemplates in an existing legal framework. The past (existing law) thus exerts a continuing influence over the future.[62] However, it is possible for the legal imagination to tend in a radical (or, indeed, revolutionary) direction. For lawyers may find within existing legal systems,

---

57 S Blackburn, *The Oxford Dictionary of Philosophy* (OUP 1994) 187.

58 J Caputo, *Hermeneutics: Facts and Interpretation in the Age of Information* (Pelican 2018) 251–52 ('the very *mark* of intelligence'), and RM Unger, *False Necessity: Anti-Necessitarian Social Theory in the Service of Democracy* (CUP 1987) 576 (on vision).

59 I McGilchrist, *The Master and His Emissary: The Divided Brain and the Making of the Western World* (Yale UP 2009) 172.

60 G Ryle, *Collected Papers, Volume Two: Collected Essays 1929–1968* (Routledge 2009) 506.

61 Ibid 506–09. Creativity of the sort described in the text carries its possessors in a nominalist direction. This is because it involves the use of language in ways that cling to the 'textures of phenomena.' See T Eagleton, *The Event in Literature* (Yale UP 2012) 8.

62 On influence of this sort as a feature of conservative political philosophy, see A Giddens, *Beyond Left and Right: The Future of Radical Politics* (Polity Press 1994) 45.

or the concept of law, norms or less specific practical impulses (e.g., ideals of justice) that could provide a basis on which to establish an alternative order. This is a topic on which Ronald Dworkin and Roberto Unger have each written. While writing on the common law, Dworkin contemplates the possibility that we may find within it the outlines of a 'purer' legal system.[63] Unger offers a strongly programmatic variation on this theme. He argues that lawyers should cultivate the capacity to engage in 'transformative practice' (by extracting from existing law guidance on how to fashion institutions that serve people's interests more adequately).[64] These two thinkers urge us, in their respective ways, to contemplate movement out of one system and into another. Such movement has a revolutionary character since it involves a break in legal continuity.[65]

Whereas the legal imagination has its life in a legal system that it can either sustain or treat as a point of developmental departure, the sociological imagination's social focus is broader. According to Charles Wright Mills, those who possess the sociological imagination are able to grasp the relationship between personal 'troubles' of milieu and 'issues' of social structure. Personal troubles, as Mills describes them, have to do with the difficulties that individuals encounter and the frustrations they feel in particular contexts. Issues of social structure, by contrast, concern features of a society that, 'while transcending ... local environments,' give rise to and impede the resolution of personal problems.[66] When we view legal and political systems from the standpoint of the sociological imagination, it may become apparent that they are unable to secure the interests of those affected by their operations. Such a discovery may be salutary for the individuals who wield power within such a system (e.g., government ministers and judges). For this reason, we might see the sociological imagination as analogous to the 'splinter of ice in the heart' that enables a novelist to throw light on the deficiencies of human beings.[67] This is because the sociological imagination equips its possessors to attend to realities that people who are invested in a particular system may be unable or unwilling to bring into sharp focus. Moreover, it may foster a 'power of productive apostasy' in those who have hitherto adopted the point of view 'internal' to such a system.[68] They may not merely resolve to 'trash the [existing] script' (legal, political, etc.), but be able to articulate a vision that offers the prospect of a new and better social order.

---

63 R Dworkin, *Law's Empire* (Fontana 1986) 407.
64 Unger (n 58) 395–97.
65 See HWR Wade, *Constitutional Fundamentals* (Stevens 1980) 36 (on 'a break in legal continuity' as an indicator of revolutionary change).
66 C Wright Mills, *The Sociological Imagination* (first published 1959, Penguin Books 1970) 14–15 and 17.
67 C Hitchens, *Love, Poetry and War: Journeys and Essays* (Atlantic Books 2005) 76 (on Graham Greene's notion of a 'splinter of ice in the heart').
68 RM Unger, *What Should Legal Analysis Become?* (Verso 1996) 35 ('productive apostasy'), and HLA Hart, *The Concept of Law* (first published 1961, 3rd edn, Clarendon Press 2012) 57 (law's 'internal' point of view).

144 *Richard Mullender*

Readiness to trash the script is not apparent in Gertrude Himmelfarb's rather conservative account of the 'moral imagination' (which draws heavily on Edmund Burke). Those who exercise the faculty she describes do not assume that they are able to give expression to the insights yielded by a 'conquering empire of light and reason.'[69] Instead, they reflect on the institutions and wider culture that shape their social world and make the assumption that, although they are not perfect, they are not 'destitute of reason' or 'wisdom.'[70] Their aim in doing so is to extract from the culture and institutions they survey morally eligible reasons for action. By working along these lines, they assume it is possible to raise both the culture and the institutions that embody it in their 'own estimation.'[71] Thus, the moral imagination (as it finds expression in Himmelfarb and Burke) involves immanent critique: an appeal to values that inform existing institutions as a basis on which to reform or 'break out' from them.[72]

The various forms of imagination we have considered reveal it to be a large topic. This is a point to which Iain McGilchrist lends support in his account of the human brain's operations. McGilchrist pursues the theme that the bi-hemispheric organ he describes opens up 'two experiential worlds.'[73] He identifies the left hemisphere of the brain as the 'seat' of language and logic.[74] He also identifies it as giving humans the capacity to establish abstract frameworks of thought that make it possible for them to orient themselves in the world.[75] Alongside the obvious practical benefits yielded by the left hemisphere, McGilchrist also sets the fact that it sustains in people a sense of agency.[76] However, he notes that the left hemisphere is prone to a problem of 'stickiness.'[77] By this he means that it is 'remarkably entrapped in its [own] vision' and is ready to 'bootstrap[]' a 'virtual' and far from complete 'world' into existence.[78] Consequently, it encourages people to repose undue confidence in the frameworks that it enables them to establish (with the result that they exhibit tendencies towards inflexibility and 'hubris' and may become 'prisoners of expectation').[79]

McGilchrist identifies the brain's right hemisphere as providing something of a corrective to the problem of stickiness. Here, he makes two points that have relevance to our concerns. The first of these points has to do with what McGilchrist calls 'broad' vigilance.[80] He notes that the right hemisphere engages in what he

---

69 G Himmelfarb, *The Moral Imagination: From Edmund Burke to Lionel Trilling* (Souvenir Press 2006) 11 (making reference to E Burke, *Reflections on the Revolution in France* (first published 1790, Penguin Books 1968) 171).
70 Burke (n 69) 188 ('reason') and 227 ('wisdom').
71 Ibid 171.
72 McGilchrist (n 59) 174 (on the ability to 'break out' imaginatively from existing frameworks of thought).
73 Ibid 132 and Ch 4.
74 Ibid 92 and 228.
75 Ibid 228. See also 27–28 and 197–98.
76 Ibid 228. See also 218–19.
77 Ibid 45.
78 Ibid 49, 93, 162, and 353. See also 229.
79 Ibid 82, 163, and 385.
80 Ibid 27.

The French Revolution   145

describes as 'presencing' operations.[81] By presencing he means the right hemisphere's ability (below the level of conscious appreciation) to monitor the environments through which we move.[82] This ability makes it possible for the right hemisphere to apprehend 'things [while they] are still "present" in their newness as individually existing entities.'[83] Second, McGilchrist argues that the presencing operations he describes regularly result in 'aha! moments.' These moments occur when, for example, we recognise features of our environment that fail to fit with the abstract frameworks we use to make sense of it.[84] We thus find ourselves in possession of an 'anomaly detector' that makes it possible for us to revisit, and reflect critically on, the assumptions that shape our understanding of our environment.[85] More particularly, McGilchrist argues that aha! moments are a spur to imaginative reflection (to which the inflexibility he associates with the left hemisphere is a standing threat).[86]

As we will see in the section below, what McGilchrist has to say on imagination and the brain's operations has relevance to Mantel's novel. So too do the various forms of imagination we have considered.

Imagination in *A Place of Greater Safety*

Imagination in its legal, sociological, and moral forms

The legal imagination, in a highly ambitious form, is on display in Maximilien Robespierre's thinking. He assumes that the skill-set he has acquired in the context of the *Ancien Régime* equips him to play a prominent part in fashioning a legal order that will underwrite the ideals of republicanism. Here, Mantel presents him as animated by an intoxicating vision. This vision is, in a strong sense, revolutionary. For it involves a break in legal continuity with the frameworks that have preceded it (the *Ancien Régime* and the efforts to establish a constitutional monarchy prior to the second revolution of August 1792). But, although Robespierre has this revolutionary cast of mind, there are intimations of the moral imagination (that have their roots in the pre-Revolutionary context) present in his thinking. As we noted earlier, he addresses the question 'What is the Revolution for?' When he finds an answer to this question in 'justice and equality,' he associates these values with a Christian end. This is to bring people to 'full humanity' and 'the kind of society that God intends.'[87]

Alongside these points, on the relevance of the legal and moral imagination to Robespierre, we can set others that concern the sociological imagination. While he

81 Ibid 244.
82 Ibid.
83 Ibid 50, 56, and 93.
84 Ibid 47.
85 Ibid 52 (drawing on VS Ramachandran, *Phantoms in the Brain: Human Nature and the Architecture of the Mind*, HarperCollins 2005).
86 Ibid 40 and 127.
87 Mantel (n 4) 445.

146   Richard Mullender

studies at the Lycée Louis-Le-Grand, he recognises that he enjoys the benefits of 'a reasoning intellectual community.'[88] However, this community exists only 'inside the walls' of the school.[89] There is little prospect of the insights that it yields exerting a benign social influence while the *Ancien Régime* endures. Moreover, he sees, beyond the school walls, a multitude of 'troubles' that owe their existence to the structure held in place by the existing politico-legal framework (e.g., 'beggars [who] sit in roadside filth').[90]

Just as imagination in the three forms we have considered is relevant to Robespierre, so too is McGilchrist's account of the human brain's operations. Robespierre argues for and seeks to establish a republic in which the ideal of virtue (on the ambitious Rousseauian model he embraces) will find expression. Mantel thus presents him as being in the grip of just the sort of abstract framework that, on McGilchrist's account, the left hemisphere of the brain enables us to establish.[91] Moreover, we see in Robespierre's devotion to the framework he seeks to make a social reality (and, likewise, to Rousseau), 'stickiness' of the sort that McGilchrist identifies as a feature of the left hemisphere's operations.[92] Mantel alerts her readers to this feature of his thinking in terms that are highly reminiscent of McGilchrist, for she ascribes to Danton the observation that Robespierre has 'everything he needs inside his head.'[93] Here, Danton directs our attention to the republican vision by reference to which 'the Incorruptible' will seek to justify the deaths of his fellow law-school boys and many others.

As with Robespierre, imagination in its legal, sociological, and moral forms is at work in Danton's thinking. As we noted earlier, he sees the Estates-General as an institution that could serve new (egalitarian) purposes. Here, Mantel presents us with the thinking of a lawyer who grasps that an existing institutional structure may be sufficiently malleable to serve ends that those who put it in place did not contemplate. The ends that Danton has in view are, among other things, meritocratic. He wants to fashion a framework that will make it possible for people such as himself (provincials from modest backgrounds) to compete for positions of prestige and honour. Here, we see the moral imagination, for Danton seeks to give effect to egalitarian practical impulses that had been gaining currency in France in the decades prior to the Revolution.

However, it is when we turn to the sociological imagination that we can draw from Mantel's account of Danton's life and career a particularly powerful insight. We see him playing a prominent part in the creation of a social context that is, at once, oppressive and highly unpredictable (e.g., his decision to confer sweeping powers on the *Tribunal révolutionnaire*). This is the context that prompts commentators to talk of a 'slide' into the Terror.[94] When we talk of 'the Terror,' our

---

88 Ibid 27.
89 Ibid.
90 Ibid.
91 Ibid 446 (where Camille notes the 'small copy of Rousseau's *Social Contract* ... that Robespierre always carried with him').
92 Ibid 400 (where Danton describes Robespierre as having read 'Rousseau by the yard').
93 Ibid 523.
94 C Taylor, *Modern Social Imaginaries* (Duke UP 2004) 134 (on 'the slide into Terror,' or '*dérapage*,' of 1792–1794).

use of the particular article and the capital 'T' draws attention to a social force that has, in its implacability, the character of 'structure' in Charles Wright Mills' sense.[95] As well as making this force apparent, Mantel identifies it as a source of ultimately fatal personal troubles in the life of Danton and many others.

This is an analysis of Danton that we can press further by drawing on McGilchrist. As we noted earlier, McGilchrist identifies the brain's right hemisphere as engaging in what he calls 'presencing' operations.[96] Moreover, he argues that these operations make it possible for people to enjoy the benefits of 'broad' vigilance. He also argues that they may issue in aha! moments that prompt the exercise of imagination. These points throw light on episodes in Danton's life on which Mantel places emphasis. As Danton wins a reputation as a gifted advocate in the dying days of the *Ancien Régime*, he declines a position in government. He recognises that absolutist France is a 'huge poisonous organism limping to its death.'[97] When Louis XVI makes an inept bid to escape from France, Danton is able to see that the case for a constitutional monarchy has lost plausibility. Moreover, he declares that the time has come to 'turn this kingdom into a republic.'[98] He thus positions himself to lead the second revolution of 1792 and grasps that 'simple words' can work to maintain its impetus. But Danton's powers of apprehension are far from perfect. We see him struggling to come to terms with the fact that 'a life in the revolution' could result in his own death.[99] Only when it is too late (at his procedurally unjust trial) does he finally understand that Robespierre and those around him mean to send him to the guillotine. Up to this point, he has assumed that, as a person 'tolerably well known in the Revolution,' he could brush aside the threats his political enemies pose.[100]

Danton and Robespierre each pursue recognisably programmatic aims. Camille Desmoulin's 'skittish' intellect makes him a more difficult character to analyse. However, he tells Danton, in the summer of 1792, that it is possible to exert 'control' over 'events.'[101] He adds that '[w]e must declare the republic.'[102] At this point in her narrative, Mantel identifies Camille as having 'suddenly [seen] the future.'[103] He is, to put

---

95 As an implacable force, we might describe the Terror as giving rise not merely to fear (*peur*) but rather to permanent foreboding (*crainte*) as Montesquieu describes it. See J Shklar, *Montesquieu* (Oxford University Press 1987) 84.

96 See (ns 81–83) and associated text.

97 Mantel (n 4) 27.

98 Ibid 347. At this point in his career as a revolutionary, we might say of Danton that he exhibits 'a sense of timing' that suggests 'political and historical genius' as Isaiah Berlin describes it. For Danton is able to engage in 'the semi-instinctive integration of the unaccountable infinitesimals of which ... social life is composed.' This makes it possible for him to know 'when to leap' in the highly unstable context of revolutionary France. See I Berlin, *The Sense of Reality: Studies in Ideas and Their History* (Chatto & Windus 1996) 33.

99 Mantel (n 4) 467.

100 Ibid 850.

101 Ibid 432 and 435.

102 Ibid 435.

103 Ibid. Although (to draw on Carlyle) Camille exhibits a capacity for 'seeing and ascertaining,' it is Danton who 'dare[s]' and 'decide[s]' and thus becomes 'a fixed pillar' and 'supreme authority' in 'the welter of uncertainty.' See T Carlyle, *On Heroes, Hero-Worship, and the Heroic in History* (first published 1841, Diderot 2017) 154.

148 *Richard Mullender*

the point another way, seized by a vision in which imagination in the three forms we have considered has a place. Law will underpin a republic in which people are free from the troubles that the Revolution and the moral delinquencies of the *Ancien Régime* have brought in train. But we should not let this moment of vision blind us to Camille's inadequacies as a champion of social progress. As the Revolution unfolds, he exercises his rhetorical powers in ways that have sometimes devastating effects on his political opponents. Moreover, he revels in his ability to exert power in this way. Mantel impresses this point on her readers when she describes 'the power of words moving through his bloodstream like a drug.'[104] But, although rhetoric is, for Camille, an intoxicant, he comes to regret the harm he has inflicted on his victims. As the novel drives towards its conclusion, he dwells on the fact that his words have 'killed' people who, at one time, were his 'friends.'[105]

Mantel's account of the context in which she sets Camille and her other central characters merits close examination. This is because it provides support (for reasons we will turn to in the section below) for the conclusion that she makes a distinct contribution on the topic of imagination. Mantel describes France in the years before and during the Revolution in terms that call Thomas Carlyle to mind. In his history of the Revolution, Carlyle describes the *Ancien Régime* as 'a sick moribund System of Society.'[106] As the Estates-General assembles at Versailles in May 1789, 25 million people face the danger of 'starvation.'[107] This is a context in which 'scarcity' sits alongside 'tyranny,' and in which 'fervid' eloquence and pamphleteering drive France in the direction of a revolutionary vortex.[108] This vortex owes its existence not just to the *Ancien Régime*'s deficiencies, but to the ambition of the law-school boys and their fellow revolutionaries. Danton makes the extent of this ambition apparent when he states that 'we are ... trying to alter the nature of things.'[109] But Mantel also alerts her readers to the fact that much of the ambition at work in this vortex has a personal dimension. Danton, for example, seizes the opportunities afforded by the Revolution 'to be somebody.'[110]

As well as being alive to ambition (both political and personal), Mantel places emphasis on factional strife in the midst of the Revolution. The factions on which she focuses (most obviously, the Jacobins and the Girondins) share a commitment to an egalitarian philosophy of government that is underdeterminate and (as such) open to a range of defensible interpretations.[111] Each of these factions has, and is fiercely committed to, its own programme (or, as Mantel puts the point, its 'bright

104 Mantel (n 4) 674. See also 277.
105 Ibid 726.
106 Carlyle (n 3) 125.
107 Ibid 133.
108 Ibid.
109 Mantel (n 4) 393.
110 Ibid 49. See also ibid 406 ('I think perhaps 1792 is my year' (Danton)).
111 On underdeterminacy, see CL Kutz, 'Just Disagreement: Indeterminacy and Rationality in the Rule of Law' (1993) 103 *Yale LJ* 997 1001. See also G.W.F. Hegel, 'On the English Reform Bill', in L. Dickey and H.B. Nisbet, eds, G.W.F. Hegel. *Political Writings* (Cambridge 1999), 265 (on the 'dangerous shape' of the 'abstractions' that found expression in the French Revolution).

The French Revolution   149

new ideas about how the country should be run').[112] Thus the centralising tendencies of the Jacobins come into collision with the liberal enthusiasms of the Girondins. But the strife on which Mantel dwells is not just factional. We see tensions (that are an admixture of the political and the personal) grow up between Jacobinism's most prominent standard-bearers, Robespierre and Danton. These tensions prompt Robespierre (with the strong encouragement of Saint-Just) to send Danton, Desmoulins, and those around them to the guillotine. As Mantel chronicles this conflict and its dénouement, she brings institutional disagreements into focus. Danton (as she describes him) has the appearance of a committed parliamentarian, for he assumes politics to be an ongoing process of change and reversal. On this view, those who suffer political reverses may, after a period in 'opposition,' once again secure the levers of power.[113]

By contrast, Robespierre and Saint-Just assume that their understanding of republican virtue justifies them in applying the guillotine or 'National Razor' to their political rivals.[114] Politics practised on this model presents us not with processes of change and reversal but, rather, with a brutal despotism of virtue, for it involves the hard-edged exclusion of political opponents from life itself. These points lend support to the view that *A Place of Greater Safety* offers us an account of imagination markedly different from the variants we have already considered. Unlike imagination in its 'legal,' 'sociological,' and 'moral' forms, it does not simply hold out the prospect of insights that may yield solutions to practical problems. Rather, it alerts us to dangers that may attend the exercise of our imaginative capacities (and, thus, has a deflationary dimension). In this way, it presents us with a diagnosis of our situation that leaves it looking deeply problematic (even as we make efforts to improve it on an impeccably egalitarian basis).

The programmatic imagination and its discontents

As we noted earlier, imagination may find expression in a vision that we entertain in the mind's eye. When this vision has to do with a group whose members concert their actions with the aim of moving towards a future in which they all enjoy benefits, we can talk of the programmatic imagination. Imagination in this form abounds in *A Place of Greater Safety*. Robespierre's 'Republic of Virtue' provides its most vivid example. But it is also plain to see in the parliamentarianism Mantel ascribes to Danton. Likewise, it is on display in the revolutionary 'crusade' advocated by Brissot and the arguments for constitutional monarchy that enjoyed currency prior to the second revolution. Had Mantel simply stopped with these plans, they would not carry us beyond what we know of imagination in the various forms we have considered. For they are responses (legal, sociological, and moral) to the practical problems generated by the *Ancien Régime*. But Mantel does not rest content with detailing plans of the sort the programmatic imagination encompasses. Rather, she sets these plans in the vortex-like context of which they are

---

112 Mantel (n 4) 39.
113 Ibid 780. Cf. N Hampson, *Danton* (Duckworth 1978), 16–17 (on the 'ambiguous' and 'enigmatic' character of Danton's approach to politics).
114 Mantel (n 4) 870.

150 *Richard Mullender*

constituent parts. This enables her to alert us to three problems that arise with pulverising regularity as the law-school boys and their fellow revolutionaries seek to act on the insights yielded by the programmatic imagination.

Mantel's entry point into the first of these problems is the sketchiness of the plans on which the law-school boys and the revolutionaries more generally are ready to act. Here, she presents us with people who seek to build a future for society out of little more than some normatively appealing slogans (e.g., 'liberty, equality, fraternity') and the underdeterminate egalitarian philosophy that underpins them.[115] More particularly, she makes it apparent that plans of the sort she describes can and do energise people who might have been, but are not, chastened by their sketchiness. This indifference to sketchiness means that we do not see modesty and creative effort of the sort that Ryle's thinker exhibits when he or she strives to present us with 'profitably followable pointers.'[116] Instead, we see the inflexibility and hubris (dogmatic path-dependency) that tend to arise when people assume too readily that they have answers to the problems they seek to address. As we noted earlier, such inflexibility and hubris are features of the left hemisphere 'world' McGilchrist describes.[117]

But, in the context we are considering, two further (and closely related) considerations may play some part in explaining the revolutionaries' commitment to their respective plans. First, they act at a time when the idea of the modern state has ramified along a lengthy timeline and assumed a variety of institutional forms. Second, they find themselves at what they take to be a historical hinge moment (that Badiou explains by reference to 'the event' and Bourdieu characterises as a 'watershed'). However we describe the circumstances in which they act, Mantel's characters grasp that the institution whose operations they seek to modify (the French state) can operate on a strongly egalitarian basis. Moreover, they each make the assumption (clearly, an intoxicatingly exciting assumption) that they have it in their power to move a long-lived process of institutional development in the direction of a moral consummation. But inflexibility and hubris leave them blind to the sketchiness of their plans – and they (as the 'prisoners of [misplaced] expectation') promise those around them a future that they are ill-equipped to deliver.

---

115 Ibid 485.

116 On one account, insights of the sort Ryle describes are the outputs of an imaginative 'workshop' in which there is typically much work still to do. See M Midgley, Foreword, in I Murdoch, *The Sovereignty of Good* (first published 1970, Routledge 2014) xvi. Midgley's remark relates to ibid 17 (where Murdoch reflects on the disposition of one who is 'capable of giving careful and just *attention* to an object which confronts her').

117 Mantel (n 4) 174. Those who inhabit left hemisphere worlds of the sort McGilchrist describes also seem to be prey to 'the perils of Panglossianism,' on which see F Schauer, 'Rights, Constitutions and the Perils of Panglossianism' (2018) 38 *Oxford Journal of Legal Studies* 635, 646 (where Schauer builds on the account of foolish optimism in Voltaire, *Candide* (first published 1759, Yale UP 2005) by arguing that the thinking of those in its grip exhibits, inter alia, a lack of 'modesty' and 'rigour' and a marked tendency 'to see the empirical world through the rose-tinted glasses of [their] own normative desires').

The second problem with the programmatic imagination to which Mantel alerts us has a particularly dramatic aspect in the conflict-ridden context of the French Revolution. She drives home the point that plans that win significant support are also likely to attract resistance from others (even when their aims are broadly similar). She also makes it apparent that the words in which such plans find expression may be a provocation to others and carry (where this is the case) a socially disintegrative charge. The practical effect of this charge manifests itself when others respond negatively to them. We see this when the Jacobins and the Girondins respond in hostile ways to each other's programmes. We also see it when the Jacobins fall into conflict with one another. Here, we might say that an underdeterminate philosophy of government (amenable to a range of readings) will inevitably set the scene for disagreements of this sort.

This reading of revolutionary France is certainly compatible with Mantel's account of the period between 1789 and 1794. However, it does not bring out the richness of her response to the personalities, groups, and events she analyses. She presents us with able, ambitious characters who often bridle when their fellow revolutionaries present them with plans for social improvement that threaten the pursuit of their own schemes. The word 'bridle' seems appropriate in this context as these reactions have an emotional quality that calls to mind the account of 'spiritedness' (or *thymos*) offered by Plato in *The Republic*. According to Plato, people grow spirited when they draw the conclusion that others have failed to give them due recognition or to show them adequate respect.[118] In the context on which Mantel dwells, we can find in the reactions she describes evidence of pride in authorship (or the less elevated desire 'to be somebody') getting out of hand. Brissot, for example, is sure that he was 'born to ... shape governments' and sees, inter alios, Robespierre and Danton as insufficiently appreciative of his plans and abilities.[119] He also sees them as getting in his way (as does his fellow Girondin Madame Roland). But this is precisely how Danton and Robespierre see Brissot and the other Girondins and (in the fulness of time) one another. Consequently, a third problem arises. This is the failure to maintain and foster the social capital (co-operative modes of interaction) necessary to advance a revolutionary agenda effectively.[120] Danton has this problem in mind when he complains that it is impossible to pursue a 'big programme' in 'a country that's falling apart.'[121]

In the light of these points, the readiness on display in Mantel's novel to act on the insights yielded by the programmatic imagination looks like something other than 'the very *mark* of intelligence.'[122] It looks like responsiveness to images in the mind's eye that the revolutionaries in their excited (indeed, hubristic) state fail

---

118 Plato, *The Republic* (2nd edn, Penguin Books 1974) 216–17 (440a–b and 440c–441a). See also F Fukuyama, *Identity: Contemporary Politics and the Struggle for Recognition* (Profile Books 2018), 16–18.

119 Mantel (n 4) 487.

120 D Halpern, *Social Capital* (Polity Press 2005) 2–3.

121 Mantel (n 4) 750. See also ibid 795 ('Unfortunately, everything I say seems to make things worse' (Danton to Robespierre)).

122 Caputo (n 58) and associated text.

152 Richard Mullender

to moderate by reflecting on their adequacy as reasons for action. These points make it possible to describe Mantel as engaging in what Wolfgang Iser has called 'literary anthropology.'[123] For she holds up a 'mirror' that presents us with 'insights into our human equipment' (here imagination and our limited capacity to control the emotions it may stimulate in us).[124] But Mantel's novel is more than an exercise in literary anthropology. We can extract from it a complex political anthropology that leads us (for reasons we will examine in this essay's penultimate section) in the direction of what we might call a theory of egalitarian misery.

Complex political anthropology

A number of prominent legal and political philosophers have forged links, relevant to our concerns, between law and political anthropology (a discipline that focuses on the ways in which groups organise their common life).[125] Ronald Dworkin has argued that people have it in their power to use law in ways that sustain highly co-operative communities in which people bestow equal recognition on one another.[126] The political philosopher Jean-Jacques Rousseau offers a more optimistic variation on this theme. According to Rousseau, people have the capacity to form a general (concerted) will that commits each of them to securing the interests of all on an impartial basis. Here, we find a commitment to community that is utopian in orientation. Both Rousseau and Dworkin make assumptions that are, on the analysis of the jurisprude and sometime Nazi Carl Schmitt, the stuff of misplaced 'anthropological optimism.'[127] On Schmitt's account, people are 'bloodthirsty' and prone to slide towards 'evil' when interacting with one another.[128] He also argues that politics consists of struggles between groups that can turn violent and, ultimately, exterminatory.[129] These points prompt Schmitt to conclude that legal and political institutions can only operate effectively when they reflect the practical impulses at work in homogeneous, rather than plural, collectivities.[130] Schmitt is thus more pessimistic than, say, Thomas Hobbes and

---

123 W Iser, *Prospecting: From Reader Response to Literary Anthropology* (Johns Hopkins UP 1993), ch 13 ('Toward a literary anthropology').

124 Ibid 263 and 264. See also Carlyle (n 3) 38–39 (on 'eleutheromaniac [strongly egalitarian] Philosophedom' and the 'clamour' it fostered in France before and during the Revolution).

125 For a helpful introduction to the development of political anthropology as a distinct field of inquiry, see TC Llewellyn, *Political Anthropology: An Introduction* (2nd edn, Bergin & Garvey 1992) ch 1.

126 R Dworkin, *Law's Empire* (Fontana Press 1986) 195–215.

127 C Schmitt, *The Concept of the Political* (first published 1932, expanded edn, University of Chicago Press 2007) 64.

128 Ibid 94 ('evil') and WE Scheuerman, *Carl Schmitt: The End of Law* (Rowman & Littlefield 1999) 232 ('bloodthirsty').

129 Schmitt (n 127) 26–27 and 29.

130 C Schmitt, *Constitutional Theory* (first published 1928, Duke UP 2008) 138, and C Schmitt, *On the Three Types of Juristic Thought* (first published 1934, Praeger 2004) 47–57.

The French Revolution   153

HLA Hart. For Hobbes and Hart each take the view that, although people are prone to fall into conflict, they can fashion legal and political institutions that treat all people affected by their operations impartially.[131] Of these two thinkers, Hobbes is perhaps the more pessimistic. This is because he describes humankind as the self-assertive, disputatious 'children of pride' (*Filios Superbiae*) who regularly engage in conflicts fuelled by spite.[132]

When we view the programmatic imagination (and the difficulties with which we have associated it) in the light of these analyses, it becomes clear that both optimism and pessimism inflect it. Optimism is plain to see in the assumption that it is possible to establish, for example, a republic of virtue on the model that features in Robespierre's thinking. The same point applies to the assumption, at work in Danton's mind, that processes of change and reversal can unfold in a parliamentary context. But visions of this sort are, as we noted earlier, only part of the complex picture Mantel presents to her readers. Anthropological pessimism also bulks large in her novel. We see it in the factional strife that results in the Jacobins sending the most prominent Girondins (including Brissot and Madame Roland) to the guillotine. Here, the pessimism in *A Place of Greater Safety* has a decidedly Schmittian appearance. This point also applies when Robespierre and his followers mete out the same treatment to their Jacobin rivals.

The admixture of optimism and pessimism on display in Mantel's novel makes it a jarring experience for the reader. This is nowhere more apparent than when she archly poses the question, 'Feeling safe, are we?'[133] With these words she guides her readers towards the deeply pessimistic conclusion that, although people may seek to fashion an enduring and impeccably egalitarian social order, they cannot do so. These points also provide support for the conclusion that a theory of egalitarian misery informs her thinking.

A theory of egalitarian misery

The political anthropology that finds expression in *A Place of Greater Safety* throws light on the troubled times through which the law-school boys live and play prominent parts in creating. But its significance is not simply historical. It has continuing practical relevance. This becomes apparent when we set it alongside 'modern social imaginaries' of the sort that the political philosopher Charles Taylor has described. These imaginaries give the citizens of societies such as France, the UK, and the USA an 'implicit map' of the 'social space' through which they move.[134] Among other things, they acquire a sense of how they 'stand' relative to others.[135] Moreover, ideals (e.g., distributive justice and community)

131 HLA Hart (n 68) 193–200, and T Hobbes, *Leviathan* (first published 1651, CUP 1991) 120.
132 Ibid 221 and T Hobbes, *Behemoth or The Long Parliament* (first published 1681, University of Chicago Press 1990) 120.
133 Mantel (n 4) 247.
134 Taylor (n 94) 25.
135 Ibid 26.

154 *Richard Mullender*

inform their understanding of the spaces they inhabit and share with others.[136] Taylor also identifies security (e.g., freedom from arbitrary interferences and harmful contingencies) as the 'common benefit' to which people attach the highest value in the societies he describes.[137]

Social imaginaries of the sort that feature in Taylor's analysis tell a story of widespread anthropological optimism. The people he describes assume that they and those around them have it in their power to live securely in a highly co-operative social environment. To the extent that people do, in fact, think along the lines Taylor describes, Mantel gives them pause. She does this by presenting her readers with the complex political anthropology we examined earlier. On her account, people are prone to act in ways that undercut the pursuit of large plans for social improvement. In response to this point, we might make the objection that she focuses on a context distant in time from our own and in the throes of a cataclysm. Hence, it is very different from the stable, late-modern societies that are Taylor's immediate concern.

However, there are reasons for thinking that Mantel wants us to take a less optimistic view. The character with the largest ambitions in *A Place of Greater Safety* is unquestionably Maximilien Robespierre. As the Terror grows ever more sanguinary, he asks himself: 'What is our aim?' His answer is predictably programmatic: 'The use of the constitution for the benefit of the people.' But he goes on to ask a further question: 'When will this happen?' His answer is: 'Never.'[138] The word 'Never' does not appear to have come to him in an aha! moment. It has a deliberate, pained ring. This suggests a grudging effort on Robespierre's part to accommodate a thought at odds with the vision that animates him. Such mental torsions are unsurprising in one who, at an earlier point in the novel, had appeared to have 'everything he need[ed] inside his head.'

As Robespierre intones the word 'never,' he presents us with a bleak prospect.[139] And it grows bleaker if we draw the conclusion that our anthropological optimism will prompt us always to press for social improvements while our disputatious nature will inevitably impede their pursuit. If this is the situation in which we find ourselves, misery may be our fate. For we possess imaginative capacities that lay before us the prospect of a bright, egalitarian future. These capacities thus feed a sense of hope (in the form we considered earlier).[140] Hope may, however, fade from our minds when we recognise that we look troublingly like Hobbes's disputatious, spiteful children of pride (who pose an ever-present threat to our ambitions). Our situation may take on an appearance reminiscent of

136 Ibid 24 and 28–29.
137 Ibid 4.
138 Mantel (n 4) 749.
139 Robespierre's 'Never' suggests a descent into utopophobia. On one analysis, utopophobia finds expression in responses to 'moral theories of social justice' that run on the (anthropologically pessimistic) theme: '[B]ut you and I both know that people will *never* do that.' See D Estlund, 'Utopophobia' (2014) 42 *Philosophy & Public Affairs* 113, 114 (emphasis added).
140 See n 7 and associated text.

The French Revolution   155

that in the myth of Sisyphus. Sisyphus strives, endlessly, to push a rock to the top of a mountain while aware that there is no prospect of it remaining there.[141] In light of this point, Thomas Carlyle's observation that the controversy generated by the French Revolution may be rumbling on 'two centuries' later seems prescient.[142] But, whereas Carlyle thought it possible that this controversy may subside, Mantel returns us, insistently, to the question, 'feeling safe, are we?'

Conclusions

Although we have ascribed a theory of egalitarian misery to Mantel, we should also see her as capturing a mood. This mood is misery and it hangs over the events on which she writes like a bank of lowering clouds. These clouds refuse to lift as a succession of comptrollers-general struggle unavailingly to save the *Ancien Régime*. They remain in place as the Revolution unfolds in ways that we have analysed by reference to the legal, sociological, and moral forms of the imagination. When imagination manifests itself in each of these ways, it holds out the prospect of progress (in the form of improvements in our social arrangements). But matters are less cheering when we turn to what we have called 'the programmatic imagination.' This conception of imagination presents us with a deflationary diagnosis of our condition rather than an uplifting spur to action. On our earlier analysis, it embraces large plans for social improvement that assume, in the minds of their proponents, the status of a vision. But it also encompasses three problems that may hinder efforts to make any such plan a reality. McGilchrist brings the first of these problems into sharp focus. It takes the form of tendencies towards inflexibility and hubris on the part of those who seek to implement plans that are the product of the left hemisphere 'world' he describes. These tendencies may, as we have noted, prompt people to pursue plans that, in their sketchiness, are a very poor source of reasons for action. Moreover, they may give rise to a second problem. Whereas sketchy plans or visions may excite their authors, others may find in them not the promise of a better future, but, rather, a provocation (that prompts spirited responses of the sort that Plato describes). Where such responses take an obstructive, hostile form, they give rise to a third problem. This is a failure to generate, or maintain, social capital (in the absence of which it is impossible for a group to concert its actions). In *A Place of Greater Safety*, these problems arise over and over again and throw light on the misery that the law-school boys and their fellow revolutionaries experience.

But misery may be the fate of all those (not just egalitarians) who seek to advance or even sustain a particular course of practical action (e.g., the defenders of the *Ancien Régime*), for the practical problems we have brought into focus (hubristic thinking, hostile responses, and lack of social capital) lie in wait for them. Thus, although we have sought in this essay to bring a theory of egalitarian misery into focus, it may be more accurate to talk more broadly of 'a theory of

141 A Camus, *The Myth of Sisyphus* (first published 1942, Penguin Books 1975) 107.
142 Carlyle (n 3) 113.

156 *Richard Mullender*

misery.' If this way of characterising our concerns is correct, we can find support for it in the complex political anthropology on display in *A Place of Greater Safety*. Both the optimism we found in Dworkin and Rousseau and the pessimism of Schmitt, Hobbes, and Hart throw light on this anthropology. People possess the imaginative capacities that make it possible for them to propose programmes that provide (more or less egalitarian) guides to practical action. But, at the same time, they seem fated to fall into conflict with one another. Moreover, these conflicts may descend into violence and the hard-edged exclusion of those who go down to defeat. When defeat has this obliterating character in a context where the commitment to egalitarianism is strong, it holds particular horrors. We see humankind plunging into 'the worst of times' from a position that held out the hope of 'the best of times.'[143]

Finally, although Mantel's primary focus is on circumstances that lead to this terrible descent, she is at least suggestive on how we might seek to reduce (if not eliminate) the threat it poses. A politico-legal framework that concentrates conflict on underdeterminate language (e.g., 'law,' 'democracy,' 'liberty,' 'equality,' and 'fraternity') may stabilise social life for lengthy periods of time. But, in order for this to happen, there must be sufficient social capital to make terms such as 'law' and 'democracy' authoritative reference points. In the context where the law-school boys acted, there was a dearth of social capital. Consequently, life was a 'battlefield' and law a 'weapon.' If Badiou (on 'the event') and Bourdieu (on the Revolution as a 'watershed') are correct, our circumstances are not discontinuous from those that existed between 1789 and 1794. Terms such as 'liberty,' 'equality,' and 'fraternity' continue to shape our social imaginaries and prompt consideration of the type of society we might realistically hope to establish. If we take seriously the pessimism that inflects Mantel's political anthropology, it may be that we should give up on the ideal of community and content ourselves with a less ambitious model of human association. In such a context, we would make modest assumptions about our capacity to co-operate with one another.[144] These assumptions could find expression in placeholding language that focuses politico-legal disagreement on matters of common concern. In such a context we might hope to maintain and foster social capital – for example, the 'shuffling' of legal papers and the 'shuttling' of political opinions.[145] However, we could not expect, on all occasions, an emphatic 'Yes' in response to the question, 'Feeling safe, are we?'

---

143 See also Dickens (n 2) 289 (describing the revolutionaries' behaviour as 'something, once innocent, given over to devilry').
144 Such a context would have affinities with a *modus vivendi*, on which see J Gray, *Gray's Anatomy: Selected Writings* (Allen Lane 2009) ch 1.
145 See n 33 and associated text.

9 Internal coherence and the possibility of judicial integrity[1]

Patrick O'Callaghan

UNIVERSITY COLLEGE CORK (IRELAND)

Introduction

Even in troubled times, when public confidence in political institutions is low, the judicial profession invariably remains one of the most trusted of all professions.[2] Few doubt that our judges are people of the highest integrity. But what exactly does it mean to say that a judge is a person of integrity? Drawing on the work of the philosopher Lynne McFall and Albert Camus's novel *The Fall*, this chapter seeks to offer an account of integrity that is relevant to those officials who bear the 'burden of judgment.'[3] Using a schema developed by McFall, it will argue that judges must ensure *coherence of principle* in the interpretation of law and *coherence between principle and action* in the application of the law. However, there is a further necessary condition of judicial integrity that is often overlooked: achieving 'internal coherence' or ensuring *coherence between principle and motivation*.

This chapter is chiefly concerned with the notion of 'internal coherence' and argues that most judges will necessarily strive towards achieving such coherence. In so doing, they will need to reflect on their particular 'role-distinct obligations' in our political system as well as on mistakes that they have made in their official

---

1 I presented an earlier version of this paper at the Law and Imagination Workshop, City Law School, London, in June 2019, and a later version at the UCC School of Law Research Colloquium in November 2019. I am especially grateful to Thomas Bennett, Sean Butler, Maria Cahill, Jonathan McCarthy, John Mee, Richard Mullender, Conor O'Mahony, and Mary Tumelty for their helpful comments and critique Please note that for ease of reference in the text, I have placed extracts from Camus's *The Fall* in italics rather than inverted commas.

2 In the UK, opinion polls repeatedly show that the judicial profession is one of the most trusted of all professions. In the 2018 IPSOS MORI Veracity Index, 83% of respondents stated that they would trust judges to tell the truth. In response to the same question, 76% stated that they would trust the police, 62% would trust civil servants, whereas only 19% would trust politicians. See IPSOS MORI, Veracity Index (November 2018) <https://www.ipsos.com/sites/default/files/ct/news/documents/2018-11/veracity_index_2018_v1_161118_public.pdf> accessed 18 November 2019.

3 I borrow this phrase from John Rawls. See J Rawls, *Political Liberalism* (Columbia UP 1993) 54–58.

158 *Patrick O'Callaghan*

function.[4] But, drawing on Camus's *The Fall*, this chapter explores whether judges will need to go deeper still in their reflections if they are to achieve internal coherence.

The central protagonist in *The Fall* is an ex-lawyer who maintains that one must become a 'professional penitent' if one is to be a judge. Put differently, he thinks that one must engage in deep introspection, paying close attention to one's personal failings, both past and present, before one has the right to judge others. Camus's protagonist implies that this approach to judging is the exception rather than the rule, but this chapter conjectures that the sort of introspection he describes is common. In fact, it is likely to be of fundamental importance to most judges if they are to bear the burden of judgment and 'live with themselves.'[5] Moreover, when combined with their experience on the bench, this sort of reflection cultivates wisdom about the meaning of justice and fairness, and this explains, in large part, why we tend to trust our judges to do what is right.

The meaning of judicial integrity

Integrity, as a concept, is difficult to pin down as it may mean different things in different contexts.[6] But the idea of *coherence* would seem to underlie many, if not most, of the ways in which we use the word. When we speak of personal integrity, on a fundamental level, as McFall explains, coherence means 'consistency within one's set of principles or commitments.'[7] More broadly, integrity requires 'coherence between principle and action.'[8] Among other things, this means that we stick to our principles even when challenged or when tempted to abandon them. But 'coherence between principle and motivation' is also a necessary component of integrity.[9] Put differently, integrity requires that we seek to do the right thing for the right reasons.[10] Integrity is offended, for example, when someone appears to be committed to the principles of a particular cause or movement but is actually motivated by self-interest, whether that might be impressing friends or career advancement. McFall applies the label 'internal coherence' to this psychological process and necessary condition of integrity.[11] Building on this analysis, she argues that personal integrity:

4 On 'role distinct obligations' see T Dare, 'Philosophical legal ethics and personal integrity' (2010) 60 *U of TLJ* 1021.
5 The prospect of being able to 'live with oneself' as a lawyer is something that finds frequent expression in public discourse and popular culture. For instance, in Harper Lee's *To Kill a Mockingbird*, Atticus declares: 'before I can live with other folks I've got to live with myself. The one thing that doesn't abide by majority rule is a person's conscience.' See H Lee, *To Kill a Mockingbird* (Harper Collins 1995) 120.
6 For an excellent overview of integrity as a concept, see D Cox, M La Caze & M Levine, 'Integrity' *Stanford Encyclopaedia of Philosophy* (2017) <https://plato.stanford.edu/entries/integrity/> accessed 18 November 2019.
7 Lynne McFall, 'Integrity' (1987) 98 *Ethics* 5, 7.
8 Ibid.
9 Ibid 8.
10 Ibid 7.
11 Ibid 8.

requires that an agent (1) subscribe to some consistent set of principles or commitments and (2), in the face of temptation or challenge, (3) uphold these principles or commitments, (4) for what the agent takes to be the right reasons.[12]

However, we are discerning in the ways we use the word 'integrity.' The principles and commitments to which McFall refers must reach a certain threshold of importance. Crucially, the 'challenge must be to something important,'[13] to a 'higher commitment,' something that goes beyond mere self-interest.[14] She elaborates further:

> When we grant integrity to a person, we need not approve of his or her principles or commitments, but we must at least recognize them as ones a reasonable person might take to be of great importance and ones that a reasonable person might be tempted to sacrifice to some lesser yet still recognizable goods. ... Integrity is a personal virtue granted with social strings attached. By definition, it precludes 'expediency, artificiality, or shallowness of any kind.'[15]

It is instructive to consider the meaning of judicial integrity against this backdrop. Most references to judicial integrity in public and academic discourse seem to concern either the professional integrity of individual judges *or* the role of judges, as a class, in maintaining the integrity of law and the politico-legal system as a whole.[16] A judge is supposed to be a 'person of integrity' in the professional sense in that she must pursue justice 'without fear or favour, affection or ill will.'[17] At the same time, judges have special responsibilities in our political system as custodians of the rule of law, which involves, among other important tasks, ensuring as much consistency and coherence as possible in the interpretation and application of the law. It is tempting to treat professional integrity, at the level of individual judges, and integrity, at the institutional level, as distinct issues, but closer inspection reveals that it is not possible to draw a clear dividing line between the two. Most obviously, if judges are corrupt, then the legal system as a whole will lack integrity.

But even where there is no overt corruption, the integrity of the legal system can suffer from defective decision-making on the part of judges, whether this is

12 Ibid 9.
13 Ibid 10.
14 Ibid.
15 Ibid 11, in part citing *Webster's Third New International Dictionary*.
16 See, for instance, the papers emerging from a symposium entitled 'Professional ethical integrity: cornerstone for rule of law reform around the globe,' published in a special issue of the *Hastings International and Comparative Law Review* (2016) 39 HICLR.
17 This is an extract from the judicial oath taken by appointees to the bench in the UK. The full oath reads: 'I, _____, do swear by Almighty God that I will well and truly serve our Sovereign Lady Queen Elizabeth the Second in the office of _____, and I will do right to all manner of people after the laws and usages of this realm, without fear or favour, affection or ill will.' See Courts and Tribunals Judiciary website (2019) <https://www.judiciary.uk/about-the-judiciary/the-judiciary-the-government-and-the-constitution/oaths/> accessed 18 November 2019.

160   *Patrick O'Callaghan*

the result of lack of competence, laziness, carelessness, or all of the above.[18] When judges do not seek to be the best they can be, as Dworkin would put it, the legal system is more likely to lack integrity.[19] Understood in these terms, there is a very clear link between professional integrity at the individual level and institutional integrity.

In the context of judicial integrity, we might be able to reformulate McFall's words in the following way. Judicial integrity:

> requires that a judge (1) subscribe to a consistent set of ethically and/or legally mandated principles or commitments and, (2) in the face of temptation or challenge, (3) uphold these principles or commitments, (4) for what the judge takes to be the right reasons in the light of her professional obligations and the demands of justice and the rule of law.

This formulation of words, considered against the backdrop of McFall's caveat on 'importance,' captures a range of different understandings of judicial integrity, whether we are referring to the professional integrity of individual judges or the duty of judges to maintain the integrity of law and the politico-legal system as a whole.

Those who are cynical about judicial integrity might argue that judges, as skilled rhetoricians, can easily *show* integrity by performing what is outlined in the first three parts of the definition. But true integrity requires more than a mere outward demonstration of certain behaviour to others; it also requires that the individual achieves internal coherence or coherence between principle and motivation. This is no easy task: achieving internal coherence necessitates deep reflection on the part of the individual and then a suitable response to that reflection. As Dare argues,

> our dominant accounts of integrity … rest upon a common recognition that whether or not a person has integrity turns upon whether or not she or he has engaged in a process of sincere and thorough reflection and displayed a readiness to accept the implications of such reflection.[20]

Some of the literature on integrity in the legal profession touches on this question of internal coherence, but the focus appears to be on solicitors and barristers or 'trial lawyers' rather than judges.[21] Perhaps the classic internal coherence problem

---

18 See in this context the discussion on 'the characteristics that undermine integrity' in *Stanford Encyclopaedia* (n 6) section 6.

19 R Dworkin, *Law's Empire* (Bloomsbury 2003).

20 Dare (n 4) 1027.

21 See, for example, T Dare, *The Counsel of Rogues? A Defence of the Standard Conception of the Lawyer's Role* (Ashgate 2009); S Dolovich, 'Ethical lawyering and the possibility of integrity' (2002) 70 *Fordham L Rev* 1629; D Luban, 'Integrity: its causes and cures' (2003) 72 *Fordham L Rev* 279; RE Loder, 'Integrity and epistemic passion' (2002) 77 *Notre Dame L Rev* 841; FC Zacharias, 'Integrity ethics' (2009) 22 *Geo J Legal Ethics* 541; B Wendel, *Lawyers and Fidelity to Law* (Princeton UP 2010).

for such lawyers is that they may have to 'suspend their values to represent others.'[22] Understood in this way, the lawyer's role-distinct obligations may come into conflict with the conventions of ordinary morality. Although there may be lines that individual lawyers will not cross as a matter of conscience, in other cases, lawyers may be able to move towards achieving internal coherence by reflecting on the importance of their role-distinct obligations for a political system based on the rule of law.[23] So understood, there are sound moral reasons justifying why lawyers may sometimes have to suspend their values to represent others. In this way, as Fuller would put it, lawyers help secure the 'internal morality of law.'[24]

Although judges play a different role in our political system, they will need to reflect in the same way on the distinct obligations of their role in order to work towards achieving internal coherence. An unambiguously worded statute or decisive precedents sometimes lead judges to conclusions that they might not have reached had they been given a free rein to decide the case in whatever way they wished.

In the famous privacy case of *Kaye v Robertson*, all three Court of Appeal judges lamented the lack of privacy protection available for the vulnerable plaintiff.[25] Bingham LJ, for instance, regretted that, 'we cannot give the plaintiff the breadth of protection which I would, for my part, wish.'[26] But where judges are unsatisfied at a personal level with the outcome of a case, they may be able to move towards achieving internal coherence by reflecting on how the constraints associated with their role-distinct obligations help secure the rule of law and ultimately the integrity of law and the politico-legal system as a whole.

Reflecting on the purposes of their role in our political system and being ready to accept the implications of what they find is one step judges must take on the path towards achieving internal coherence. But there are other steps too. Postema argues that, 'integrity is hollow and fraudulent' if we do not make room for a 'self-critical attitude,' which he calls 'regret.'[27] He goes on:

> Integrity calls for responsible coherence of action and principle. This makes it a complex virtue, for it calls for coherence of principle, coherence of action with principle, and appropriate responses to departures from each.[28]

---

22 Loder (n 21) 864.
23 See also Dare (n 4) 27.
24 L Fuller, *The Morality of Law* (Yale UP 1964).
25 [1991] FSR 62.
26 Ibid 70.
27 GJ Postema, 'Integrity: justice in workclothes' (1996–1997) 82 *Iowa L Rev* 821, 828.
28 Ibid.

162   *Patrick O'Callaghan*

Though judges may strive to be like Dworkin's Hercules,[29] they will some-times make mistakes in their official function.[30] Judges may make mistakes in the interpretation of the law (failing to achieve coherence of principle) and in the application of the law (failing to achieve coherence between principle and action). But judges may also fail to achieve coherence between principle and motivation. Even where a judge arrives at the right answer in a hard case, integrity is offended if a judge is chiefly motivated by sympathy for one of the parties or avoiding public criticism, rather than fidelity to justice and the rule of law.

Against this backdrop, as Postema stresses, regret is a profoundly important element in achieving true integrity. Judges must reflect on mistakes they have made in the past and respond appropriately to those departures from coher-ence of principle, coherence between principle and action, and coherence between principle and motivation. The most appropriate response is to acknowledge those mistakes, learn from them, and aim to do better next time.

The argument so far is that judges must reflect on the purposes of their role in the politico-legal system and must maintain a critical reflective attitude about mistakes they have made in their official function if they are to achieve internal coherence. But this author suspects that judges need to go deeper still in their reflections. Judges bear a heavy burden of judgment; they have been appointed by our political system to sit in judgment on the failings of their fellow human beings. The burdensome nature of this responsibility and the unique integrity-related dilemmas to which it gives rise have been recognised since time immemorial. For example, the Talmud, the ancient book of Jewish law, states that, '[w]hen the judge sits in judgment on his fellow-man he should feel as though a sword was pointed at his [own] heart.'[31]

This entry in the Talmud gives expression to a sentiment that would seem to be deeply engrained in us: if one is to sit in judgment on other human beings, then

---

29 R Dworkin, *Taking Rights Seriously* (Harvard UP 1977).

30 The issue of judicial mistakes in the interpretation and application of the law raises all sorts of interesting questions that cannot sensibly be examined within the confines of this short chapter. An especially interesting question is whether appellate judges in hard cases can be wrong. MacCormick outlines two contrasting approaches. The declaratory theory 'pre-supposes that there is some way of achieving a right answer [in hard cases]. This is not because there is in existence some item of law that can be "read off" so to speak, but because appropriate arguments applied to the established body of law can persuasively establish one conclusion on the given problem as more acceptable than any other.' The alternative view is the decisionist theory, which holds that 'what a court decides is right because the court has decided it, and it has not (or not yet) been reversed on appeal. Judges may decide in an unwise or impolite way, but they can't actually make mistakes about the law in problem cases, since there is no anterior truth of the matter about which they could be mistaken.' See N MacCormick, *Rhetoric and the Rule of Law* (Oxford UP 2005) 266. In this author's view, the declaratory theory is more persuasive and informs the analysis in this chapter.

31 H Polano, *The Talmud: Selections from the Contents of that Ancient Book, Its Com-mentaries, Teachings, Poetry and Legends* (Frederick Warne, 1868) 329.

one must first sit in judgment on oneself.[32] Put another way, one suspects that, in order to live with themselves, judges must also be philosophers and examine their lives in the way Socrates recommended.[33]

Understood in these terms, one suspects that most judges will feel compelled to reflect on their own lives and try to come to terms with their personal failings, past and present. This sort of introspection will help judges edge closer to achieving internal coherence, but, when combined with their experience sitting on the bench, it also means that judges are likely to arrive at important insights on what it means to be human – all too human, as Nietzsche famously put it. This process of introspection, then, cultivates *wisdom* about the meaning of justice and fairness, a uniquely important virtue for those who occupy this responsible position.[34] In order to better explain this point, we now turn to Camus's novel, *The Fall*, in which the main character becomes highly sceptical of judicial integrity but comes to the conclusion that one may have the right to judge if one engages in the sort of introspection we have been discussing.

Camus's *The Fall* and the possibility of integrity

The Fall has been described as 'one of the deepest and most beautiful of Camus's works.'[35] Roberts explains how the first critiques of the book found it 'complex, pessimistic and difficult to interpret.'[36] He goes on to note that '[r]esponses over subsequent decades have only added to the sense that this is a multi-layered work, demanding deep reflection on the part of the reader.'[37] This part of the chapter will provide a synopsis of the plot, focussing in particular on those aspects that intersect with our analysis of judicial integrity.

The name of the central character, Jean-Baptiste Clamence (John the Baptist and clemency), hints at some of the core themes of the novel: confession and the possibility of redemption.[38] Clamence is an ex-trial lawyer, now a *judge-penitent*, who has fled his home city of Paris to take up refuge in a shady part of Amsterdam. At the outset he appears to be engaged in a conversation with somebody he has just met, but, towards the end of the book, the reader begins to suspect that Clamence has been talking to himself the whole time.

---

32 Referring to Socrates, Hannah Arendt writes that, 'living together with others begins with living together with oneself. Socrates' teaching meant only he who knows how to live with himself is fit to live with others.' See H Arendt, *The Promise of Politics* (Jerome Kohn ed, Schocken Books 2005) 21.

33 Plato, *The Last Days of Socrates* (H Tarrant and H Tredennick trs, Penguin 2003).

34 For an interesting account of judicial virtues see LB Solum, 'The virtues and vices of a judge: an Aristotelian guide to judicial selection' (1988) 61 *S Cal L Rev* 1735.

35 A Sagi, *Albert Camus and the Philosophy of the Absurd* (Batya Stein tr, Rodopi 2002) 131, cited in P Roberts, 'Bridging literary and philosophical genres: judgement, reflection and education in Camus's *The Fall*' (2008) 40 *Educ Philos Theory* 873, 874.

36 Roberts (n 35) 874.

37 Ibid.

38 H Pulitzer, 'Franz Kafka and Albert Camus: parables for our time' (1960) 14(1) *Chicago Review* 47, 63.

164   Patrick O'Callaghan

He suggests that this is a practice to which lawyers are especially disposed: *Aren't we all the same, continually talking, addressing no one, constantly raising the same questions, even though we know the answers before we start?*[39] His monologue is a confession of sorts, but a confession he is making to himself. Indeed, one gets the impression that this is a confession that he has made hundreds of times before. Clamence appears to be locked in a hellish cycle of self-torment, likening the *concentric canals* of his new home city to the *circles of Hell*, an obvious reference to Dante's *Inferno*.[40]

But things were not always this way. When Clamence worked as a trial lawyer in Paris, he was, on his own account an excellent lawyer, drawn to *good causes* and defending the most vulnerable in society. Although the young Clamence was acutely aware of the power of rhetoric and the benefits associated with playing the part of a successful lawyer,[41] we do not get the sense that he was cynical about law and the pursuit of justice. If anything, there is a sort of naivety in the way he thinks that he was always on the right side in every case. There is no suggestion either that the young Clamence felt he lacked integrity.[42] Though there is more than a hint of narcissism in the way he describes his life in Paris, Clamence intimates that his integrity could not be questioned because he was on *lofty peaks*, a *point above mere ambition*, the *highest summit, where virtue is no longer sustained by anything but itself*.[43] If anything, Clamence seemed to believe that being a lawyer meant it was more likely that he would be a person of integrity.[44]

Clamence continued to *soar*,[45] until a particular evening when, walking alongside the river, he heard some laughter behind him. He turned around but did not find the source of this laughter. There was nothing particularly sinister about it; in fact, *it was good laughter, natural and almost friendly, putting the world to rights*.[46] Later that evening, when Clamence went to the bathroom and looked in the mirror, his *face smiled back* at him in such a way that it appeared that his *smile was double*.[47] Here, Camus appears to be making reference to an idea rooted in Judeo-Christian tradition: 'doubleness of heart,' the belief that, as a consequence of the

---

39 A Camus, *The Fall* (R Buss tr, Penguin 2013) 92.

40 D Alighieri, *The Divine Comedy: Inferno, Purgatorio, Paradiso* (R Kirkpatrick tr, Penguin 2012).

41 Clamence says: *I'm sure you would have admired the precisely judged tone, the precisely judged emotion, the fervour and power of persuasion, and the controlled indignation of my speeches for the defence. … [It took] no effort for me to strike a noble pose.* See Camus (n 38) 12.

42 Stourzh develops a compelling argument that integrity 'is incompatible with naïveté as well as with cynicism.' He explains: 'Without the knowledge of temptation, there is no integrity. The naïve-turned-cynic cannot grasp its meaning of responsible judgment, of a judgment aiming at atonement rather than punishment.' See G Stourzh, 'The unforgiveable sin: an interpretation of "The Fall"' (1961) 15 *Chicago Review* 45, 52.

43 A Camus (n 39) 16.

44 Ibid. Clamence says: *Fortunately, my profession satisfied this call to the heights.*

45 Ibid 19.

46 Ibid 25.

47 Ibid.

Internal coherence and judicial integrity 165

fall of man, there is good and evil within each person.[48] However, the term can also refer to duplicity, which we can define as 'the belying of one's true intentions by deceptive words or action.'[49] Indeed, in the 1797 edition of Samuel Johnson's *Dictionary of the English Language*, duplicity is defined as 'doubleness of heart.'[50]

It is this discovery of his 'doubleness of heart' that turns out to be Clamence's 'fall from the innocence of his naive self-love.'[51] Shortly afterwards, he starts to engage in introspection and make difficult discoveries about himself, his first realisation being that he has always been a duplicitous person. So, for example, though he had spent his time in Paris carrying out good deeds, he was always addressing an audience and was motivated by vanity more than anything else.[52] The more Clamence engages in introspection, the more uncomfortable discoveries he makes about his duplicitous character. In particular, he fastens on his aggressive nature and the way he used other people, particularly women, for his own ends.

But his introspection reveals one *crucial discovery* when recollecting an episode from his past.[53] A few years before he first heard the laugh, Clamence was out for an evening walk in Paris when he passed a woman leaning over the side of a bridge looking into the water. He hesitated for a moment on the bridge but walked on. Clamence reached the end of the bridge and turned towards a quay but then heard the sound of the woman falling into the water. He describes his reaction:

> Trembling ... I told myself that I had to act quickly, but I felt an irresistible weakness flood through my body. I forget what I thought at the moment. 'Too late, too far away ...', or something like that. I kept on listening, not moving. Then, slowly, I walked away though the rain. I reported the incident to no one.[54]

In recollecting this night, Clamence now realises that he had made a terrible mistake, not just in failing to follow his instincts and talk to the woman on the bridge but later too in failing to react to the sound of the body hitting the water. The stranger's fall into the water also led to Clamence's fall to a place where he feels he is beyond redemption.[55] It is at this point too that he becomes cynical about other people and their motivations, but he becomes especially sceptical about those who

---

48 P Brown, 'Late antiquity' in P Ariès and G Duby (eds), *A History of Private Life Volume I: From Pagan Rome to Byzantium* (Harvard UP 1987) 288.

49 Merriam Webster Dictionary (2019) <https://www.merriam-webster.com/dictionary/duplicity> accessed 18 November 2019.

50 S Johnson, *A Dictionary of the English Language* (11th edn, Brown, Ross and Symington 1797).

51 Stourzh (n 42) 46.

52 Clamence says: *I have to admit, with all humility, that I have always been supremely vain. ... Me, me, me: that's the refrain that runs through my precious life and you could hear it in everything I said*. See Camus (n 38) 30.

53 Ibid 43.

54 Ibid 44.

55 Stourzh (n 42) 46.

166   *Patrick O'Callaghan*

want to become judges, for, *the moment that I perceived that there was something to be judged in me, I realized that they had an irresistible urge to judge.*[56]

Clamence had come to a horrible realisation about his past and the nature of his character. In order to keep these feelings at bay, he drank and engaged in debauchery, wanting, in essence, to undermine the reputation he enjoyed. In fact, his whole act, the role he was playing as an upstanding lawyer representing the poor and needy, was *stifling* him.[57] But no matter how hard he tried, he could not escape his past, eventually having to accept that he *was not cured*; he was *trapped* and was now resigned to living in a 'little ease.'[58]

The 'little ease,' as Clamence explains, was the name of a medieval dungeon, the dimensions of which were such that the prisoner did not have enough room to stand up straight, nor did he have enough room to lie down horizontally. Rather, the prisoner had to *live diagonally*. The dungeon served a particular purpose: *[e]very day, through the unchanging pressure cramping his body, the prisoner learned to know his guilt, and learned that innocence is the joyful stretching of one's limbs.*[59] Because all human beings are *strange and miserable creatures*, introspection will reveal all sorts of episodes from our pasts that will *astonish and shock* us.[60] Clamence intimates that we are all fated to end up in a 'little ease,' once we discover our 'doubleness of heart.' Perhaps worst of all, we know what true freedom is because we once experienced it in the naivety of our youth.[61]

In the novel's final chapter, Clamence invites the person to whom he is apparently speaking into his home and opens a cupboard to reveal a painting that has been stolen from a cathedral in Gand. The painting, *The Judges of Integrity*, depicts several judges on horseback on their way to adore the Lamb of God.[62] In the cathedral, the original painting has since been replaced by a replica, and large numbers of tourists continue to come to see what they think is the original, unable to tell the difference between the real and the fake. We will examine the symbolism of this part of the novel in greater detail below.

It is at this point, towards the very end of the novel, that we learn what it means to be a judge-penitent. Since his fall, Clamence is like John the Baptist, a voice crying out in the wilderness, confronting other people and imploring them to examine their pasts and confess. He goes on:

> Since one could not condemn others without at the same time judging oneself, one should heap accusations on one's own head, in order to have the

56 Camus (n 39) 49.
57 Clamence says: *I wanted to break up the mannequin that I presented to the world wherever I went, and lay open to scrutiny what was in its belly.* See Camus (n 38) 58.
58 Ibid 68.
59 Ibid 69.
60 Ibid 88.
61 Ibid 89. In this context, Clamence refers to *the sadness of our common condition and the despair of being unable to escape it.*
62 In most English translations, *les Juges intègres* is translated as 'the just judges.' However, Stourzh (n 42) 51 maintains that the 'judges of integrity' is a better translation.

right to judge others. Since every judge eventually becomes a penitent, one had to take the opposite route and be a professional penitent in order to become a judge.[63]

Only then does someone have the right to judge others: *The more I accuse myself, the more I have the right to judge you.*[64]

True integrity and judicial wisdom

Clamence is highly cynical about the possibility of integrity. As Stourzh puts it, he 'glories in trampling on the idea of integrity. It's a big lie, he says, there is no such thing.'[65] If, by nature, people are double-hearted or duplicitous, then how is integrity even possible?[66] Clamence is especially sceptical of judges and their motivations, but he nonetheless admits that we need judges.[67] Consider in this context the symbolism of the stolen painting, *The Judges of Integrity.* Tourists come to the cathedral thinking they are looking at the original painting, but they are unknowingly looking at a fake. Through the skilful use of rhetoric, judges may give the impression that they are people of integrity, but like the tourists in the cathedral we cannot be sure whether what we are observing is authentic or they are being duplicitous.

To return to our reformulation of McFall's definition for a moment: a judge may *appear* to (1) subscribe to a consistent set of principles and, (2) in the face of temptation or challenge, (3) uphold these principles. But internal coherence (a coherence between principle and motivation) is a necessary condition of integrity. True integrity requires that the judge uphold these principles for what she takes to be the right reasons in the light of her professional obligations and the demands of justice and the rule of law. But whether this is achieved is not something that can be definitively proven from an external perspective; rather, the only person who knows whether a judge has come close to achieving some sort of meaningful internal coherence is the individual judge herself.

What Clamence seems to miss is that true integrity is, in principle, attainable. After all, the original painting exists; it is simply hidden from view.[68] Yet, at the same time, it would be naïve to think that judges routinely achieve the internal coherence necessary for true integrity. The cases that come before our judges are

---

63 Camus (n 39) 86.
64 Ibid 87.
65 Stourzh (n 42) 51.
66 Even in the Judeo-Christian tradition, where doubleness of heart, the potential for good and evil in each person, is acknowledged, a distinction is nonetheless drawn between those who have integrity and those who are duplicitous. Consider, for example, Proverbs 11:3: 'The integrity of the upright guides them, but the unfaithful are destroyed by their duplicity' (New International Version).
67 Camus (n 3) 12.
68 S Horton, 'Camus - The Fall' in *Browsings: The Harper's Blog* (8 August 2009) <https://harpers.org/blog/2009/08/camus-the-fall/>accessed 18 November 2019.

168 *Patrick O'Callaghan*

often messy and complicated affairs. When judges reach their decisions in such cases, it is perhaps more likely than not that they will harbour at least some doubts not only about the legal correctness of their decision, but also about their motivations for deciding the case in the way they did.

Moreover, given the pervasiveness of cognitive dissonance, to which our judges are surely not completely immune, how would we even know if internal coherence has been achieved in any given case?[69] But it does not follow that we should discard the idea of true integrity. This is because it remains an aspiration, one that, like Fuller's eight principles of legality or Dworkin's Hercules or 'right answer thesis,' gives some structure and direction to the judicial endeavour.[70]

A helpful metaphor in this context is Popper's account of a climber trying to reach the summit of a mountain that is covered by a cloud.[71] Popper was fundamentally concerned with the possibility of arriving at 'objective truth' in the natural sciences. Although we may not be able to identify with certainty the criteria of truth, the 'very idea of error – and of fallibility – involves the idea of an objective truth as the standard of which we may fall short.'[72] The climber cannot see the peak of the mountain, thus he is never sure whether he has reached the true summit or a subsidiary peak.[73] But the fact that he cannot see the peak does not affect the 'objective existence' of the summit. As long as the peak is covered by cloud, the climber can never be sure he has reached the top, but it will be possible to establish that he has not reached it: where he comes up against an overhanging wall, for example.

So, though we can never be sure we have found the truth, we can edge towards it by critically reflecting on what we have done wrong and aiming to do better next time.[74] Similarly, for judges, though they may not be sure that they have achieved true integrity in the individual case, they can be satisfied that they are at least striving towards it. As discussed above, this striving involves reflecting deeply on (a) their role-distinct obligations, (b) mistakes made in their official function, and (c) their own failings as human beings.

This chapter contends that judges must reflect on all three matters if they are to work towards achieving meaningful internal coherence. It is probably uncontroversial that judges reflect on (a) and (b). But some readers might question whether judges really need to take themselves to task as human beings in order to be good judges. Indeed, Clamence presents his insight about what it means to be

69 For a similar point about arriving at truth in the natural sciences, see generally K Popper, *Conjectures and Refutations* (Routledge 2002).
70 See Fuller (n 24); Dworkin (n 29). Indeed, it would seem that even prominent postmodernists might accept this sort of argument. Interpreting the work of Jacques Derrida, Caputo argues that, for Derrida, it is the 'promise of *becoming* true' that gives us something to aim for. See JD Caputo, *Truth* (Penguin 2013) 77.
71 Popper (n 69) 306–07.
72 Ibid 311.
73 Ibid 306–07.
74 This argument is inspired by Popper's ideas about falsification; ibid. Consider too, in this context, Samuel Beckett's line from *Worstward Ho* (John Calder 1983) 7: 'Ever tried. Ever failed. No matter. Try again. Fail again. Fail better.'

Internal coherence and judicial integrity 169

a judge-penitent as it if were a unique discovery: *one should heap accusations on one's own head, in order to have the right to judge others.* The implication is that this approach is the exception rather than the rule; that it is only Hercules who would proceed in this way. But this chapter suggests that ordinary judges engage in this sort of introspection as a matter of necessity.

Consider the following hypothetical situation: a judge experimented with Class A drugs when she was in law school many years ago. Now, as a judge, she regularly sees defendants before her who are being prosecuted for possession of drugs. One suspects that this judge will likely have engaged in deep introspection and have tried to come to terms with her past in some way in order to bear the burden of judgment and live with herself.

Nietzsche might have regarded any 'rationalising away' of or 'coming to terms' with the past as an instance of an individual's pride triumphing over uncomfortable truths: '"I did that" says my memory. I couldn't have done that – says my pride, and stands its ground. Finally, memory gives in.'[75] But Stourzh explains that the conventional understanding of pride, associated with hubris, is a by-product of the Reformation.[76] He goes on: '[t]here is also a meaning of pride in the sense of self-respect, informed by moderation, by a sense of proportion.'[77] Ignoring one's past is hubris, but seeking to come to terms with it in a meaningful way is an exercise in self-respect. In this context, Kierkegaard advocated 'remembering poetically' rather than forgetting.[78] The aim here is not to be burdened by a painful past, but remembering that past in such a way that it benefits how we live now.[79] Put differently, coming to terms with the past means learning appropriate lessons from it that help us live better lives today. We might also think of this as a form of wisdom.

Clamence does not seem ready or willing to embark on this particular journey; rather, he wallows in his despair.[80] Yet, there are also signs that Clamence has at least glimpsed the alternative path towards wisdom. If we engage in deep introspection, he says, we might *become mad with grief, or modest.*[81] Clamence has

---

75 F Nietzsche, *Beyond Good and Evil* (RP Horstmann and J Norman eds, J Norman tr, CUP, 2002) 59.
76 Stourzh (n 42) 56.
77 Ibid.
78 S Kierkegaard, *Either/Or: A Fragment of Life* (A Hannay tr, Penguin 1992) 233–34.
79 Ibid.
80 Stourzh (n 42) 53–54 engages in a fascinating discussion about Clamence's despair and his belief that he is beyond redemption. In this way, Stourzh explains that Clamence 'commits the one unpardonable sin, the sin against the Holy Ghost.' Indeed, there are a number of references in the novel to the dove, the symbol of the Holy Spirit, yet Clamence remains unwilling or unable to seek atonement. Though Clamence appears on some level genuinely lost, at the same time one cannot help but feel that narcissism is at the root of his problem. As Pulitzer remarks, Clamence seems to gain some 'intellectual satisfaction' in tormenting himself. See Pulitzer (n 37) 63. For an interesting account of a similar struggle on the part of Soren Kierkegaard, see SD Podmore, 'Kierkegaard as physician of the soul: on self-forgiveness and despair' (2009) 37 *JPT* 174–185.
81 Camus (n 39) 30.

170   *Patrick O'Callaghan*

chosen the first path. Like Dante's Satan in the centre of *Inferno*, Clamence remains frozen in *The Fall*.[82] On that fateful night on the banks of the river Seine, he freezes when the body hits the water and does not react. But afterwards, he continues to remain frozen, *mad with grief*, trapped in his *little ease*. Unlike Clamence, however, this chapter suggests that most of our judges are likely to have chosen the alternative path towards modesty and wisdom.

All of us have made and continue to make mistakes, and we benefit from reflecting on those mistakes, though this is likely to be an uncomfortable experience.[83] 'Moral development,' as Loder puts it, 'emerges from braving the discomforts of self-scrutiny.'[84] This is the path to wisdom, where *anything could happen* as the individual no longer feels trapped in a *little ease*.[85] As Loder succinctly puts it:

> Wisdom is not a culminating state but a perpetual process. ... The person of integrity develops strength, courage, and honesty about missing the mark. Wisdom provides contentment amidst this striving. The person of integrity is humble enough to know her own shortcomings, but caring enough about her moral identity to strive for more.[86]

Clamence's defeatist attitude is in marked contrast to the critical reflective attitude that Loder describes. Again, this is an attitude, one suspects, that most judges necessarily possess. Judges must pay close attention to their own mistakes and learn from them, learning something about themselves but also, more broadly about what it means to be human, all too human, and striving to be better. The end product is practical wisdom, or *phronesis* as Aristotle termed it. Solum explains that, '[t]he practically wise judge has developed excellence in knowing what goals to pursue in the particular case and excellence in choosing the means to accomplish those goals.'[87]

Consider, in this context, the sentencing of offenders, a task in which judges are charged with pursuing a number of different goals (e.g. retribution, deterrence, and rehabilitation) yet must, at the same time, come to a single determination in

---

82 For an engaging new reading of Dante's *Commedia* see V Montemaggi, *Reading Dante's Commedia as Theology: Divinity Realized in Human Encounter* (OUP 2016).

83 It is worth mentioning that there are risks associated with too much introspection, which are highlighted in Kafka's writings. As McGilchrist explains: '[Introspection] will suffer no idea to sink tranquilly to rest but must pursue each one into consciousness, only itself to become an idea, in turn to be pursued by "renewed introspection." The process results in a hall of mirrors effect in which the effort at introspection becomes itself objectified. All spontaneity is lost. Disorganisation and fragmentation follow as excessive self-awareness disrupts the coherence of experience.' See I McGilchrist, *The Master and His Emissary: The Divided Brain and the Making of the Western World* (Yale UP 2012) 396.

84 Loder (n 21) 876.

85 Camus (n 39) 30.

86 Loder (n 21) 858.

87 Solum (n 34) 1753.

Internal coherence and judicial integrity 171

each case as to which particular sentence best serves these goals. Perhaps more than any other area of judicial activity, sentencing is subjected to close public scrutiny. One might think that, if judges lack integrity in the way Clamence imagines, they would seek to sentence offenders in ways that would insulate them from public criticism. Yet, the media are routinely critical of the apparent leniency of the sentences our judges hand down, and public outrage sometimes leads to protests and campaigns to retrain judges or pass new laws to constrain their discretion.

It is worth reflecting on this matter against the backdrop of a part of *The Fall* in which Clamence imagines what hell would look like. A thought occurs to him as he walks through Amsterdam and sees a house of a former slave trader. This house has two statues of slaves outside it, which Clamence points out is a *trade sign*, advertising the fact that *the owner was a slave-trader*.[88] Clamence tries to imagine what the world would look like if everyone advertised themselves in this way:

> [I]f everyone started doing it, I mean advertising his true business, what he really is, then we wouldn't know if we were coming or going! Just imagine visiting cards for: 'Dupont, cowardly philosopher', or 'Christian landlord'; or 'adulterous humanist' – there's no end to it, really. It would be hell! Yes, that's what hell must be like: streets with trade signs and no chance to explain oneself away. You would be pigeon-holed once and for all.[89]

If judges lack integrity in the way Clamence thinks they do, offenders would be sentenced harshly as a rule. There would be no criticism of judges being too lenient. After all, the offenders have committed crimes, sometimes terrible ones. But we do not live in hell; the rule of law requires natural justice or due process, and our judges have not been frozen into inaction and indecision. Rather, they remain very much alive to questions of context and degree.[90]

In approaching the challenging task of sentencing, alongside deliberating on the particular details of the case and any relevant law, the judge must also consider victim impact statements, character and psychological reports concerning the defendant, and arguments about mitigation.[91] The judge must take all of the circumstances into account, weigh them up, and come to a decision that best serves the goals of the criminal justice system. When judges are criticised for their lenient sentences, those few voices in the wilderness who come to the defence of judges

---

88 Camus (n 39) 28.
89 Ibid 30.
90 See also, in this context, Stourzh's remarks (n 42) 52 about Clamence not being able to 'grasp' the 'meaning of responsible judgment.' 'Good judgment,' Stourzh continues, 'is impossible without the unique human – or divine – gift of making distinctions of degree.'
91 See Courts and Tribunals Judiciary website (2019) https://www.judiciary.uk/about-the-judiciary/the-justice-system/jurisdictions/criminal-jurisdiction/ accessed 18 November 2019.

172 *Patrick O'Callaghan*

normally say things such as, 'the judge heard all the evidence' or 'judges are experienced and learned in the law.'

But this chapter contends that we should also accept these decisions as generally right because most judges necessarily strive towards achieving true integrity. Not only does this mean that they have reflected on the purposes of their role in our political system and have analysed past mistakes made in their official function, but it also means that they have paid particular attention to their own failings as human beings. Combined with their experience on the bench coming across everything that humanity has to offer, the good and the bad, judges have necessarily reached important insights about the meaning of justice and fairness. For this reason, if not for any other, we ought to be confident that our judges will arrive at the right decision, at least in the vast majority of cases. As Dworkin famously put it,

> [t]here is no reason to credit any other particular group [in our political system] with better facilities of moral argument; or, if there is, then it is the process of selecting judges, not the techniques of judging that they are asked to use, that must be changed.'[92]

Conclusions

This chapter has argued that our judges necessarily strive towards achieving true integrity. True integrity requires more than coherence of principle and coherence between principle and action; it demands internal coherence or a coherence between principle and motivation. We have discussed three distinct steps that judges must take if they are to work towards achieving internal coherence: reflecting on their role-distinct obligations, mistakes made in their official function, and their personal failings. In each case, judges must respond appropriately to what the reflection reveals.

The third step, reflecting on and coming to terms with personal failings, may seem excessive and unnecessary to some readers. But, if one is to sit in judgment on other human beings, one must first sit in judgment on oneself. Indeed, Ernest Hemingway is supposed to have once said that, '[t]here is nothing noble in being superior to your fellow man; true nobility is being superior to your former self.'[93] Clamence criticises those who strike a noble pose in court. But, if this chapter's conjectures are correct, judges come closer than any other officials to being entitled to strike such a pose.

---

92 Dworkin (n 29) 130.

93 Though this quote is generally attributed to Ernest Hemingway, it is likely that he had borrowed this phrase. In an earlier essay, Sheldon writes: 'Remember there is nothing noble in being superior to some other man. The true nobility is in being superior to your previous self.' See WL Sheldon, 'What to believe: an ethical creed' in *Ethical Addresses* (Press of Innes & Son 1897) 61.

10 Legal humanism

'Stylistic imagination' and the making of legal traditions

Cristina Costantini

UNIVERSITY OF PERUGIA, ITALY

Synaesthetic perception of law and literature through imagination

There are manifold possibilities whereby the man of law encounters the man of letters. They usually cross the bridge that dematerialises the spatial distance between law and literature – that is, two separate estates and portions of the same land, which have been conquered in different times. EM Forster provides us with the following powerful crossing of the bridge in the literary field:

> Margaret greeted her lord with peculiar tenderness on the morrow. Mature as he was, she might yet be able to help him to the building of the rainbow bridge that should connect the prose in us with the passion. Without it we are meaningless fragments, half monks, half beasts, unconnected arches that have never joined into a man. With it love is born, and alights on the highest curve, glowing against the grey, sober against the fire. Happy the man who sees from either aspect the glory of those outspread wings. The roads of his soul lie clear, and he and his friend shall find easy going.[1]

Like literature,

> Law may [also] be viewed as a system of tension or a bridge linking a concept of a reality to an imagined alternative – that is, as a connective between two states of affairs, both of which can be represented in their normative significance only through the devices of narrative. [...] A nomos is a present world constituted by a system of tension between reality and vision.[2]

Furthermore, lawyers, like literary writers, create worlds and impose names; mould shapes and fashion orders; interpret desires and translate aspirations: they are the

---

1 EM Forster, *Howards End* (Edward Arnold 1910) 196.
2 R Cover, 'Nomos and narrative' (1983–84) 97 *Harvard Law Review* 4, 9.

174 *Cristina Costantini*

ministers of a prophetic oracularity.[3] Together with literary writers, lawyers are the keepers of a reservoir of meaning and signification. Both officiate the encounter between experience and prediction, known and unknown, visible and invisible. They are the makers of stories that embody questions of hope and faith.

As the above quotations suggest, EM Forster meets Robert Cover at the crossroad of intellectual intersections and shared projections. Forster's predicament, in particular, recalls Wagner's *Bifrost* – that is, the bridge flaming in three colours between Asgard, the home of the gods, and Midgard, the world of men. The novelist introduces the powerful image of a 'rainbow bridge,' conceived as an inventive device to bring the joy of a metaphysical surplus down into the finitude of the worldly life. In her critical essay dedicated to Forster, her close friend, Virginia Woolf has the merit of lingering over this figure, so to make of it a sort of correlative objective for the author's substantive style.[4] In fact, the most appreciated trait of Forster's writing would be not (or, at least, not only) his exquisite prose combined with an acute sense of comedy and a strong power of creating characters; it is the encrypted message involved in his prose: 'behind the rainbow of wit and sensibility there is a vision which is determined that we shall see.'[5]

The bridge, which Margaret conceives of as an antidote to Henry Wilcox's obtuseness, becomes the synthetic symbol of a wider, literary scope. It allows us to inspect beyond the surface, penetrating the depths of reality; to perceive the solidity of objects through its luminous transparency; to use and depict the paraphernalia of materiality as the veil through which infinity could be seen; synthetically, to connect the actual and singular thing with all the potentialities of its meaning. In Woolf's words: 'Our business is not to build in brick and mortar, but to draw together the seen and unseen.'[6] Ultimately, the human failure that Forster takes pain to combat is the lack of imagination, both penetrative (relevant in epistemological terms) and sympathetic (measuring 'proximity,' that is, the intensity of human relationality).[7]

In a similar perspective, the brilliant jurist Robert Cover has repeatedly affirmed the consubstantiality of law and imagination. The idea of the bridge vigorously returns at the centre of his poetic prose to disclose the unsaid of the law. While inspecting ontological issues (and specifically dealing with the vexed question 'what is law?'), Cover unmasks the social and political struggle that lies at the basis of its various, tentative definitions. The name 'law,' in its bare

---

3 For the vision of common lawyers as the oracles of the law, see P Dawson, *The Oracles of the Law* (University of Michigan Law School 1968). For the representation in ancient times, Sir John Ferne, *The Blazon of Gentrie* (printed by John Windet 1586); W Blackstone, *Commentaries on the Laws of England* (11th edn, printed by A Strahan and W Woodfall 1791).69.

4 V Woolf, 'The Novels of E.M. Forster,' in *Collected Essays*, vol. I (Hogarth Press 1924) 342.

5 Woolf (n 4) 345.

6 Ibid.

7 For a reassessment of the intellectual debate on the concept of imagination, see ETH Brann, *The World of the Imagination. Sum and Substance* (25th edn, Rowman & Littlefield 2017); M Warnock, *Imagination* (University of California Press 1978).

Cover's theory is provocative and critical, bringing to the surface a disturbing uncanniness produced by the radical dichotomy between the social organisation of law as power and the social organisation of law as meaning.[9] In this conceptual framework, the prominent role is assigned to *jurisgenesis*[10] – that is, to the very creation of legal meaning through an essential cultural medium, in a nomic space,[11] in a rhizomatic dimension[12] populated by myths, narratives, and great epics. The complex bulk of materials, which concurs to establish paradigms for 'dedication, acquiescence, contradiction and resistance,'[13] haunts the promises of the positivistic enterprise, condemning it to failure or, at best, to an only imperfect success. The rediscovery of a world of poly-jurality[14] allows Cover to suggest an

---

8 R Cover, 'The folktales of justice: tales of jurisdiction' (1985) 14 *Cap ULRev* 179, 181.

9 Cover, *Nomos* (n 2) 18, where he notes that, 'the uncontrolled character of meaning exercises a destabilizing influence upon power. Precepts must "have meaning," but they necessarily borrow it from materials created by social activity that is not subject to the strictures of provenance that characterise what we call formal lawmaking.'

10 The original concept, deliberately named with the neologism '*jurisgenesis*' (a compound term based on Latin roots), is explained in Cover, *Nomos* (n 2) 11.

11 Properly called *nomos*, that is to say a normative universe, where the rules and principles of justice, the formal institutions of the law, the conventions of a social order represent only a small part of the complex whole. According to the statement that has become notorious, 'no set of legal institutions or prescriptions exist apart from the narratives that locate it and gave it meaning'; Cover, *Nomos* (n 2) 4.

12 This expression derives from the application of Deleuze and Guattari's lexicon to Cover's thought; G Deleuze and F Guattari, *A Thousand Plateaus: Capitalism and Schizophrenia* (B Massumi tr, University of Minnesota Press 1987).

13 Cover, *Nomos* (n 2) 6.

14 The term has entered the contemporary language of legal theory in order to place the emphasis on the multiplicity of norms governing individual and community life. With other synonimical forms, such as 'interlegality' or 'polinormativism,' it better expresses the ideas of complexity and connectivity that are consubstantial with juridical pluralism. In this perspective, even the threshold between law and non-law becomes blurred and porous. For an interesting discussion on the law's historical interaction with other kinds of compelling order, see SP Donlan, 'Comparative? Legal? Histories? Crossing boundaries,' in O Moréteau, A Masferrer, and KÅ Modéer (eds), *Comparative Legal History* (Edward Elgar 2019) 78–95. Another brilliant study on this matter is due to the legal-historical anthropologist Thomas Kuehn, who has introduced the concept of 'patchwork of accommodations' to represent the genealogical ability to 'craft' the principle of law applicable to the concrete case that has characterised the European legal tradition from ancient times onwards. In fact, even in medieval times, the geographical space of Europe was the landscape of multiple, coexisting legal orders: law was polycentric, brought into being by competing centres of power and persuasion; T Kuehn, 'A late medieval conflict of laws: inheritance by illegitimates in *Ius Commune* and *Ius Proprium*' (1997) 15 *Law & Hist Rev* 243, 272.

176   *Cristina Costantini*

imagined view of the law that is not to be conceived as a closed definition, but as a plea to understand the legitimating force of the term.

> Law is a *bridge* in normative space connecting [our understanding of] the 'world- that-is' (including the norms that 'govern' and the gap between those norms and the present behaviour of all actors) with our projections of alternative 'worlds-that-might-be' (including alternative norms that might 'govern' and alternative juxtapositions of imagined actions with those imagined systems of norms). In this theory, law is neither to be wholly identified with the understanding of the present state of affairs nor with the imagined alternatives. It is the bridge – the committed social behavior which constitutes the way a group of people will attempt to get from here to there.[15]

Law comes to be imaginative, liberational, redemptive. A pervasive tension is placed between the constraints of reality and the demands of ethics and it is nurtured by a common interpretative commitment. Law is the transformative and *transferational* medium. As a force that holds and governs the passage from one pole to another, allowing them to remain in their distinctive situatedness, it is also a secular *eschaton*[16] that prevents eschatological, or even utopian, temptations.

In the middle of the common bridge, then, EM Forster meets Robert Cover. Their sense runs into their sensibility; they firmly stare towards the open stage of a new vision. The respectful greeting, shared by the novelist and the lawyer, echoes to us: 'Only connect!'[17]

---

15 Cover, *The Folktales* (n 8) 181. In a corresponding way, in his seminal work, Cover argues that, 'Law may be viewed as a system of tension or a bridge linking a concept of a reality to an imagined alternative – that is, as a connective between two states of affairs, both of which can be represented in their normative significance only through the devices of narrative'; Cover, *Nomos* (n 2) 9. To clarify his thought, Cover borrows Steiner's concept of 'alternity', making of it a constitutive component of his *nomos*, but at the same time warning that nomos is not exhausted by its 'alternity,' insofar as it is neither utopia nor pure vision. 'A nomos, as a world of law, entails the application of human will to an extant state of affairs as well as toward our visions of alternative futures'; ibid. Steiner defines 'alternity' as 'the "other than the case," the counterfactual propositions, images, shapes of will and evasion with which we charge our mental being and by means of which we build the changing, largely fictive milieu for our somatic and our social existence'; G Steiner, *George Steiner: A Reader* (OUP 1984) 402

16 In Cover's opinion, the culminating point of human history, its final and conclusive stage, seems to be immanentised. Law is presented as a messianic force; however, the religious form of Jewish messianism has been transformed into a secular political ideal, into a progressive historical movement towards a world of relational equality and social justice. For this specific understanding of law in Cover's reflection, see S Wizner, 'Repairing the world through law: a reflection on Robert Cover's social activism' (1996) 8 *Cardozo Stud L & Literature* 1.

17 To remember the well-known epigraph of Forster's *Howards End*, which imprints not only Margaret's disposition with respect to Wilcox's mentality, but also, integrally, Forster's moral, political, and social determinations.

'The breaking of the vessels': visions of imagination in the mirror of law[18]

'Never wonder!'

These words resound as a counter-imperative through Charles Dickens's stunning pages of *Hard Times*.[19] They sculpt the first and only commandment of the educational system adopted in Coketown, a city governed by the obsession with facts, means and ends; a town of red bricks, smoking machinery, and tall chimneys that has decreed the perpetual banishment of fancy and imagination.

A severe diet of plain facts[20] forcedly feeds all the children under the supervision of Thomas Gradgrind, the main character of the novel. He is a man of pure rational calculation, square-legged and square-shouldered, with an inflexible, dry voice and an obstinate, if not dictatorial, temper. The atmosphere is grey and monotonous; all appears to be measurable and controlled; reality amounts to a collection of arithmetic figures impressed into a mechanomorphic nature. Yet, the veil of certainty is covering a disturbing perception, that the arrogance of a fierce assertion has pushed beyond the margins of the life on stage.

There is something not declared lurking under the hood of this dense, opaque factuality; there is something invisible that is haunting Coketown people under a sun eternally in eclipse. It is the spectre of fear. Mr Gradgrind humanises himself (in literary and metaphorical terms) when he doubtfully wonders, 'Whether Louisa or Thomas can have been reading anything? Whether, in spite of all precautions, any idle story-book can have got into the house?'[21]

The suspicion comes from misconduct by the young children, caught peeping at the circus by the father. From now on, it is difficult – if not impossible – to save Mr Gradgrind from the emotional bankruptcy of his positivistic philosophy. His stubbornness has been put face to face with anguish that, ultimately, is – as Lacan brilliantly argues – the experience of the presence of the desire of the Other, when it remains unsatisfied or 'unrealisable.'[22] The conventional, practical *ethos* is mined by the potent, even if unexplored, power of imagination. Imagination is, in fact, a living force and it should, therefore, be thwarted and banned.

In the past, even certain lawyers, inspired by the same asphyxiated logic of Gradgrind, have fought against imagination in the declared intent of preserving the purity of law, its intangible technicality. The engagement with a deeper investigation of law's ontology, and a more conscious appreciation of the historical roots of Western legal thought have clarified how the putative corruption of law at

---

18 The title is inspired by Harold Bloom's homonymous work, devoted to exploring the possible models of poetic originality. H Bloom, *The Breaking of the Vessels* (University of Chicago Press 1982).

19 This peremptory imperative is directed by Mr Gradgrind to his daughter Louisa; the same words, for their meaningful relevance, are chosen as the title of Chapter VIII of the novel; C Dickens, *Hard Times* (first published 1854, Penguin 1994) 43.

20 'Fact, fact, fact!' This is the exclamative motto that synthetises Mr Gradgrind's creed. Dickens (n 17) 6.

21 Dickens (n 17) 17.

22 J Lacan, *Ecrits. A Selection* (Sheridan tr, Norton 1977) 311.

178 *Cristina Costantini*

the contact with other forms of knowledge could brought not a pernicious infection, but, quite the contrary, a fruitful illumination. The intersections of routes and courses have been multiplied; the '*ands*' linking the law to a second pole of understanding are exponentially growing; a no longer monolithic view has altered the habitual look of social relations.

An imaginative *hodos* (path, way) has been opened to support unorthodox methods.[23]

At the centre of the rainbow bridge, the force of the law has encountered the force of imagination.

This creative and synergic meeting has been portrayed in various ways and has explored plural horizons of knowability. From one side, law has been perceived as the final outcome of an imaginative construction. From another perspective, it has been considered as a pre-existent and malleable matter on which imagination can be exercised. In yet another vision, it is properly the subject agency of imagination. With respect to each of these viewpoints, imagination can be generative, syncretic, aspirational, even if each of them emphasises one of the possible meanings of the same term 'imagination,' which is in itself ubiquitous and conceptually supported by a long-standing philosophical debate. Common properties are, therefore, inserted in so distant ways of thought and are combined with other, radically different traits, which are assumed to express the specificity of the singular theoretic position.

If one explores the occurrences of the word 'imagination' in legal literature, one may find alternative meanings and uses, depending on the specific understanding that was meant to be privileged. The accent is now on a relationship (in particular, between imagination and perception, or between imagination and truth/falsehood); now on a distinction (such as between imagination and fantasy); now, again, on a precise function (imagination is ontologically poietic). For these reasons, the expression 'legal imagination,' more and more diffused so as to become a recurrent research tag, appears to be differently nuanced and apt to justify and endorse divergent project aims.

According to a first declension, the imaginative potential in the legal field has been expressed by way of representation. A clear example of this peculiar 'imaginative methodology' is offered by legal systemology. One of the main tenets of comparative law, after the primordial yearnings of legal universalism and worldwide irenicism, has been to chart the nomic space creating legal taxonomies, or, more concretely said, to propose a map of the different laws ruling on earth. Commenting this shift in interest, which has suggested a durable line of reflection traduced into an operational practice still applied nowadays, it has been punctually noted that 'the geographer's imagination replaced the philosopher's speculation.' The demarcation of legal families, systems, or traditions and the consequential delineation of nomic relations have served 'as a "guide to the terrain" stepped in to replace cosmopolitan and universalistic conjecture and contemplation.'[24]

---

23 Rediscovering the Greek etymology of the word 'methodology,' that is *meta* ('beside, along') + *hodos* (path), from whence methods as a path of pursuit.

24 G Frankenberg, *Comparative Law as Critique* (Edward Elgar 2016) 48.

On this ground, the aesthetic dimension of law has been qualified making use of the more recent acquisitions on space perception and cognition. The new frontiers of cartographic theory have clearly demonstrated how the activity of mapping is not only epistemological, but also ontological: it is both a way of thinking about the world, offering a framework for knowledge, and a set of assertions about the world itself.[25] Maps imply an ideology and an ethics; enact a conceptual and functional paradigm; silently open to the excess that is not actually captured by marks and lines: they are talkative visualisation of presences and absences.

The critical approach has also unveiled the narrative that lies beyond the apparently neutral description expressed through the charts designed by comparative lawyers. The figure composed, with its internal classifications and partitions, is conceived as a peculiar form of text, made up – as all the others – of processual strategies and tactics. The space inscribed is not just a photographic image of a pre-existent reality, but rather the final product of operations that orient and temporalise it in a polyvalent unity of conflictual programmes or contractual proximities. The map is a synoptic scenario with a syntagmatic nature nurtured by plural syntaxes: it is a complex whole of itineraries, trajectories, traversals.[26]

Therefore, the legal systemology enacted by comparative law gives shapes to nomic morphologies, orderly disposed, and offers the material translation of different forms of imaginations. It is, ultimately, a *nomography*, which renders the space floating in the mobility of the phenomenological gaze.[27] In a more pervasive way, the accent has been placed on the political effects of the spatial allocations, even when the space in question is the nomic one: the individuation of legal units and the measurement of their mutable relationships (influence or subordination; imitation or high reputation) amount to a concrete distribution of power. Therefore, the legal imagination has dialogically faced geopolitical imagination, and both of them have been transformed by their reciprocal, pervasive encounter.[28]

Law has been treated as an object of imaginative representation even in another mode. The legal world, made by ministers, rules, and procedures, has been historically attracted into the pages of literary works. Therefore, it has been transformed into either a distinguished character or an impressive stage of action through the prose of novels and the evocative verses of poems and lyrical hymns.

This inclusion of legal matters in the domain of letters has been usually described as one of the two main branches that articulate the debate on the interdisciplinary approach known as 'law and literature.' In particular, it would be the proper object of inquiry within the so-called 'law in literature' framework.

---

25 M Dodge, R Kitchin, and C Perkins, *Rethinking Maps. New Frontiers in Cartographic Theory* (Routledge 2011) 1.

26 L Marin, *On Representation* (Stanford UP 2001) 208.

27 For the use of this term, see C Costantini, *Nomos e Rappresentazione. Ripensare Metodi e funzioni del diritto comparato* (Mimesis 2017).

28 For the new trends in comparative law methodology, see PG Monateri (ed), *Methods of Comparative Law* (Edward Elgar 2012).

180 *Cristina Costantini*

A deeper investigation distances intellectual perception from the illustration conventionally employed. It is usually asserted that law is merely depicted as it might drop into the plot of the writer with all its virtues and defects, ontologically predetermined, with the equipment of its properties simply collected and exposed. This is a neutralised elucidation of what really happens: literature, as all perfectly know, is not a simple chronicle of facts and events, a repertoire of names and subjects, but a living force of reality's interpretation. The actual power of the crossing method resides in the fact that legal imagination comes to be illuminated by the lamp[29] of literary imagination, which brings new light and projects meaningful shadows.

After this reciprocal meeting, nothing is the same as it was before. Law is emplotted, critically evaluated, even positively reformed. The capture is not a passive reception, but an active work of reconfiguration and requalification. Law is enriched, densified, humanised. In his as-synthetic-as-extraordinary work devoted to Charles Dickens as legal historian, William Holdsworth has vividly explained how literary impressionism restores vibrant atmospheres and vital pictures that are completely lacking in the stereotyped and impersonal account that law gives of itself.[30] The sources of law – according to this view – are not sufficient. They provide a standardised record of what things were actually done, but they are deprived of all that is necessary in order to acquire an honest understanding of the sense of the context, to receive an impression of the contemporary background. As Holdsworth notes, only with the human touches and the shed lights provided by literature and by other non-legal sources one is made able to see the lawyers at work – that is, to enter the carnal side of legal institutions.

Legal imagination has been also invoked to support other considerations that could be developed on a poietic-cognitive level. In this regard, the focus of most of the critical comments is represented both by legal language and by legal reasoning.

First of all, it has been observed how the language of the law lives by the means of a constitutive ambiguity. On the one side, by creating new identities and ontologies, it imposes names and qualities, performs orders, designs patterns, fixes categories. The words used mark reality, producing effects and bounding people. On the other side, the letters of the law compound an institutionalised form of rigid technicality, a bipolar system of communication and of non-communication fashioned by a closed elite as a specific exercise of power and of power over meaning. Since ancient times, the metaphor of the oracles of the law resound across legal traditions. Therefore, legal language appears to be clamped on a vice. As Peter Goodrich has precisely synthesised, one of the major paradoxes of contemporary legal culture consists of the fact that:

---

29 In the sense disclosed in MH Abrams, *The Mirror and the Lamp. Romantic Theory and the Critical Tradition* (OUP 1953).
30 W Holdsworth, *Charles Dickens as a Legal Historian* (Yale UP 1928).

its social practice is founded upon an ideology of consensus and clarity – we are all commanded to know the law – and yet legal practice and legal language are structured in such a way as to prevent the acquisition of such knowledge by any other than highly trained elite of specialists in the various domains of legal study.[31]

There is an artificial reason, as Sir Edward Coke reminded the King, that dictates the words of the law. The natural intelligence, if not educated in a prefixed manner, is incapable of being legally virtuous, even if it belongs to a sovereign entity. It would seem that law aspires to be an internally defined system both of notional meanings and of legal values,[32] a noble and elitist constitution of terms and symbols that makes itself impenetrable to a common access. In response to this separatist exclusionism, imagination inaugurates a politics of resistance, which manifests itself in a double direction.

First, it claims for the prioritisation of the hermeneutic dimension against scientism, so as to create a metaphorical bridge between words and visions apt to put unusual visions into words and to project the words already employed into innovative visions. Second, imagination becomes a potent device for the affirmation of symbolic interactionism that counteracts all forms of 'egological perspectivism' asserting the unavoidable intersubjectivity of the human environment. In this perspective, the lawyer turns out to be a human immersed in human complexities. His gaze falls around and not upon the concreteness of the singularities perceived through all of its formative subtleties; the pseudo-mathematical consideration of premises and consequences, to which acts and behaviours have to be reduced, is abandoned in favour of a penetrant observation of variable elements. Even the man of the law can talk poetically, as Martha Nussbaum invokes.[33] In Nussbaum's poetic inspiration one can find trace of Weisberg's *poethic* admonition, born at the intersection of poetics and ethic imperatives to support his existential Heidegerrian–Kantian vision. 'Poethics – Weisberg asserts – in its attention to legal communication and to the plight of those who are "other" seeks to revitalise the ethical component of Law.'[34]

Law produces a liturgy of inventive ideographs (a concept introduced in semiotic reflection by Michael Calvin McGee),[35] which we can assume as a new kind of legal formant (to enrich Rodolfo Sacco's view[36]) able to structurally

---

31 P Goodrich, *Legal Discourse. Studies in Linguistics, Rhetoric and Legal Analysis* (Macmillan 1987) 7.

32 Ibid 1.

33 M Nussbaum, 'Poets as judges: judicial rhetoric and the literary imagination' (1995) *UChiLRev* 1477–1533; Nussbaum, *Poetic Justice. The Literary Imagination and Public Life* (Boston 1995).

34 R Weisberg, *Poethics and Other Strategies of Law and Literature* (Columbia UP 1992) 46.

35 MC McGee, 'The ideograph: a link between rhetoric and ideology' (1980) 66 *QJSpeech* 1–16.

36 R Sacco, 'Legal formants: a dynamic approach to comparative law (Installment I of II)' (1991) 39 *AJCL* 1–34.

182 *Cristina Costantini*

combine the eloquence of rhetoric with the force of ideology. An authentic humanistic and humanitarian tension claims for an alethic and transformative discovery, so as to bring to the light all the strategical implications of legal discourse, cosmetically camouflaged, and to exhort for a cooperative and vibrant international community.

In a further declension, the role of imagination has been appreciated with respect to the legal reasoning of the courts. Arguing and discussing a case mean to predict, ahead of time, what other skilful colleagues might express in objection or in refutation. Even in this sense, law functions through prophecies and oracles; it exhibits itself through the means of a long-standing anticipation of other counter-moves and counter-responses. Hypothetical reasoning lies at the basis of a universe of alternative plots of facts, motives, quotations, and figures of speech used to persuade or to oppose. Fantasies are able to produce a binding reality by means of the qualified instrument named in legal jargon as *fictio iuris*.[37] Legal fictions ceased to be whimsical entities and become an essential tool for the very functioning of the logical and moral economy of judgment.

Notwithstanding the immense potentiality of legal creativity, the same humanistic imagination admonishes that 'between law and action there always be a space to be filled with decisions which cannot be written in Law.'[38]

Embroidered histories and stylistic projections: the literary making of legal traditions

> The ancient order of arguments by our serjeants and apprentices of law at the bar is altogether altered.[39]

With this peremptory statement, Sir Edward Coke, one of the most influential voices of the Elizabethan age, registered and interpreted the irruption of a significant change in the unceasing flux of English common law. What had been received from the past underwent a mutative reformation that finally encouraged a transfiguration of the pristine appearances of legal discourses. It entailed the *style of legal communication and transmission*, so as to revise the old sense of commonality and, therefore, to model newly constitutive imaginative possibilities.

The historical claim – posed as the epigraph of the paragraph – becomes the inspiring motive for developing contextualised reflections on the subtle link that connects the form to the substantive consistence of law; the style of recording its words to the memory of its origins and evolutions. The methodological purpose, pursued in these pages, is to solicit a *literary aesthetic understanding of legal traditions*. The critical reappraisal of known dichotomies (oral/written law; discovered/decided rules) and the deeper investigation of their symbolic metonymies

37 An interesting perspective is offered in J Kertzer, *Poetic Justice and Legal Fictions* (CUP 2010).
38 Y Simon, *The Tradition of Natural Law. A Philosopher's Reflection* (Fordham UP 1965) 83.
39 Coke, *Reports*, Preface xii.

(mouth/paper; oracles/quotations), suitable to vest a conceptual idea with an ontological concreteness, directly affect the integral perception of nomic morphologies. A careful inquiry reveals that the textualisation of common law and the written canonisation of judicial precedent become, ultimately, systemological devices that allow fault lines to be traced not only between continental and insular law, but also within the same body of Anglo-American law and, even in a narrower perspective, at the heart of the English legal tradition.

All these remarks rest on a specific appreciation of the notion of *style*, already borrowed from other domains and differently applied by legal scholars, depending on their scientific background and on their final goals. The ambiguity of the term, the resistance of which to a definite meaning is constitutive, embedded in its very etymology,[40] makes it a malleable instrument of analysis and argumentation. The pristine polysemy causes and, at the same time, justifies slippage in use and metonymic transfers.

Comparative lawyers have employed the concept of style in two main directions: in a *broader sense*, as a taxonomic tool in order to detect and qualify the differences or the similarities among discrete legal families; and, in a more *circumscribed acceptation*, to describe the techniques for drafting the law and the ways of writing judgments. The first intent seems to be too indeterminate and holistically comprehensive; in fact, it turns the term 'style' into a 'name collector,' under which the observer can group together the historical background of a system and its future development, its distinctive institutions and legal sources, the specific mode of thought in legal matters of its jurists, and its predominant ideology.[41] The second significance is clearly nearer to the usually perceived 'common learning,' even if (as has been noted) an undisputed and pacifically shared explanation of what style is should be excluded.

Notwithstanding their effortless recognisability, the promises associated with such a kind of viewpoint often lack intellectual nimbleness and come to banalise the complexity of the notion of style, reducing its opaque and oxymoronic texture to a deceptive, thin transparency. Therefore, the final outcomes of the research are presented as undeniable results, but more realistically they amount to assertive statements that avoid fundamental questions. Recalling to the mind Susan Sontag's arguments,[42] is it arguable that, as for the arts, there are not styleless works of law? Can it be legitimate to ascribe a feeling of 'antipathy' to a given legal style? How is one to exorcise the haunting fear that style subverts content? How can the

---

40 From the Greek *stylos*, which recalls the verticality of pillar, to the Latin *stilus*, which evokes the shape of the writing instrument. As has been noted, 'retracing the history of the word, we are faced with a polysemy and a series of constantly shifting, metonymic transfers': from the instrument of writing to the activity of writing, to the product of that activity; M Aquilina, *The Event of Style in Literature* (Palgrave Macmillan 2014) 1–2.

41 See how the notion of style developed in K Zweigert and H Kötz, *An Introduction to Comparative Law* (T Weir tr, Clarendon Press 1998).

42 S Sontag 'On style,' in S Sontag (ed), *Against Interpretation* (4th edn, Farrar, Strauss & Giroux 1966) 15–36.

184 *Cristina Costantini*

individual sensibility of law's makers and interpreters be assessed with respect to the collective legal consciousness? To find a new investigative path, it is necessary to de-immunise the image of law from the conventional representations that indulge in an abstractified and objectified dimensionality. The vibrant nature of law, its aesthetic genesis and perceptibility, must be recovered; its enigmatic physiognomy must be interrogated.

In order to answer the above questions, and inspired by an intent so specifically determined, even the idea of style comes to be requalified. Style is here meant as an *act of choice* and as a *modal device*. The first characterisation, which is borrowed from Leonard Meyer,[43] is transposed into the legal domain to underline how the variability of models, patterns, and shapes evidences the possibilities of different options. All the attributes that interact together to compound a legal style are the result of a process of selection (both conscious and innate) among a set of conceivable alternatives and within the constraints posed by the internal rules of a nomic entity, of a nomosphere. In these terms, style is strategic in itself: it is the synthetic expression of compositional choices exercised within the constraints of operational practicability. The second determination is adopted from Giovanni Bottiroli's new insights devoted to rediscovering style in the light of Heidegger's modal ontology.[44] In the same way that thinking authentically about being means to grasp its plural modes, thinking about style aims to thwart the menace of rigidity and monology in sight for the proper appreciation of expressive pluralism. According to this view, style is a dividing force: it translates the scissional capacity of language and thought, even in their legal determinations; it enlightens the ontological articulation of language, the several modes in which language can be said.

Style is, therefore, a relational concept: one style always exists and is defined in connection with at least one other style. The haunting force of a tradition (in particular, for the specific purposes of this work, of a legal tradition) could be identified with the competing movement that reassesses blocks of memories from one pattern style to another. This is an inner source, a crypto-typical dynamic apt to enliven repetition, so as to eventually transform the conclusive aspect of the body of the law and its phenomenological perceptivity. It is also a modelling flow that ties the pages of the law in a living bond of intertextuality.

The anatomy of influence:[45] the textualisation of the English law and its cryptotypic excess

Talking about an *alteration* that occurred in the order of legal reasoning and in the form of its communicative transmission, Sir Edward Coke was intimately

---

43 LB Meyer 'Toward a theory of style,' in B Lang (ed), *The Concept of Style* (Cornell UP 1979) 21–71.

44 G Bottiroli, *Teoria dello stile* (La Nuova Italia 1997); Bottiroli, *La ragione flessibile. Modi d'essere e stili di pensiero* (Bollati Boringhieri 2013).

45 Once again, the title is the re-proposition of the motives and purposes discussed in H Bloom, *The Anatomy of Influence. Literature as a Way of Life* (Yale UP 2011).

Legal humanism 185

acquainted with the presence of a subterranean impulse, able to ripple the calm waters of English law.

What was he referring to? His statement came in the midst of a significant turning point in the ways in which law was declared and reported. The story of the English legal tradition can be reframed and centred around the literary device of legal emplotment, giving specific importance both to the ontology of the support used to carve the words of the law and to the style chosen to register its practical enactment.

Moving from this new line of sight, a cluster of divisions originates. The first partition is placed between an auratic past (the principle of orality was meant as a secular sacrament of the divine ascendancy of English law) and a pre-modern time, when the scriptural canonisation of the voices of law unveiled the modes and techniques of its mundane mastering. Subsequent splittings occur in the manner of linguistic textualisation of the law, producing different genres of legal literature: the *Reports* assumed a form other than the one endorsed by *Records*. And again, the *Reports* changed their logic of composition, dismissing the pristine vest of the *Year books* to become *Named Reports*; eventually, a new radical transformation occurred during the Victorian age before the institutionalisation of a final fashion.

Collectively considered, these shifts are the unequivocal mark of the tensions that underlay the textual reification of what the law was meant to be: the multifarious books of English law faced with representational, ontological, and epistemological issues (and managed through a change of habit),[46] in a continuous process of recognition, assimilation, and renegotiation of the past. The act of rewriting, in new manners and tones, the legal density of the time passed composed the bulk of English common law into a morphology of incremental changes[47] and administered the dialogue between the masters of the law (competing with each other for recognition of a pre-eminent role) and the aspirational tastes and desires of changing audiences. At the same time, it fixed distinctive custodial moments as eminent phases in the sensibility of legal culture[48] and offered the way to distribute the keys of the guardianship of English tradition.

Law Reports originated in a historical paradox, being destined to become the written translation of a law that, by common acceptance, could not be written.

The insular reason of pride and exclusiveness was found in the immemorial antiquity of customary law, that, precisely for this constitutive atemporality, revealed its closer proximity to God's will. The text of this law

> was never originally written, but has ever been preserved in the memory of men, though no man's memory can reach its original thereof.[49]

---

46 A Ben-Yishai, *Common Precedents. The Presentness of the Past in Victorian Law and Fiction* (OUP 2013) 52.
47 Ben-Yishai (n. 45) 13.
48 R Ross, 'The memorial culture of early modern english lawyers: memory as a keyword, shelter, and identity, 1560–1640' (1998) 10 *YaleJL&Human* 229.
49 Davis, *Le Primer Report* (Dublein 1614) at fol. 2b.

186 Cristina Costantini

A unanimous consensus diachronically bound the voices of Fortescue, Coke, Finch, Fulbecke, Davies, and Blackstone, creating a common consciousness as a strong glue for what was already a common law. Tradition preceded scripture, and the sage men of the law were considered *sacerdotes* and *servientes*, oracular ministers deputed to declare a sacred wisdom inherited from an origin out of time.[50] Even the procedure was governed by the principle of orality, and the judges pronounced their decisions at the end of the trial *seriatim*, separately and independently. Every statement was treated not as an opinion, but as an effective judgment; it was impossible to individually qualify a judicial pronouncement as 'dissenting' or 'concurring' a priori, in the moment in which it was declared, it being necessary to postpone this kind of evaluation until all the parted utterances were communicated. The conclusive voice of the Court resulted from a joint reading of the singular expressions.

If one would anatomise the making of English tradition, one could explore the progressive movements, from memory to writing, that ultimately modified the way of acting and thinking, so to create an unprecedented literate mentality.[51] The material supports chosen to textualise rules and remedies, together with the strategies and arts of pleading, envisioned the habits of English common law through the use of different languages. What was precedential became the sedimented selection drawn out from competing narratives apt to vest diverse forms of perceptions of the same facts. In this sense, the stylistic differences that distanced Records from Reports and Reports from Reports impressed a singular mark in the formative moments of the English legal imagination.

From the twelfth century onwards,[52] the bundle of rolls (conventionally known as plea rolls) proposed an apparently neutral record of the bare essentials that lay at the basis of the acts in court.[53] Membranes of parchment, piled on top of each other and numbered, were the tables where the final compositions of the suits had been inscribed. As has been punctually observed, a strong character of anti-narrativity informed the Records. They did not recount a story, but rather issued an order, in the imperative form; synthetically, they functioned as speech-acts, commanding the litigants to do what they were required by law.[54]

---

50 See P Goodrich, *Languages of Law. From Logics of Memory to Nomadic* Masks (Weidenfeld & Nicolson 1990) 117; JGA Pocock, *The Ancient Constitution and the Feudal Law* (Johns Hopkins University 1957).

51 For the use and development of this concept, MT Clanchy, *From Memory to Written Record. England 1066–1307* (3rd edn, Wiley Blackwell 2013).

52 According to John Hamilton Baker, they commenced in 1294, and the innovation seems to be due to Hubert Walter, the same chief justiciar who afterwards introduced enrolment in Chancery. JH Baker 'Records, reports and the origins of case-law in England,' in JH Baker (ed), *Judicial Records, Law Reports, and the Growth of Case Law* (Duncker & Humblot 1989), 15–16.

53 Judicial records (written in Latin until 1732) contain the note of the original writ; the plaintiff's count and the defendant's plea with the following replication and the subsequent pleadings; the process for summoning the jury and the result of the trial; the judgment; any final process; for a description of their content see Baker (n 51), 16–17; Ben Yishai (n 45) 44–46.

54 Ben-Yishai (n 45), 45–46.

The textual fixation of the oral decrees made knowable the formal decision and the relief given, but left tacit the arguments followed by judges in their minds and the referencing authorities, if any there were.

The premises were in place for the formation of a canon of a normative order; at the same time, a cryptotypical force began to operate. During the thirteenth century, an emergent profession demanded a reshaping of legal representation, more suited to the strategical composition of the contending reasons played in courts. Public interest was replaced by an elitist purpose and convinced private men, other than the King's clerks, to begin the first way of law reporting through the composition of the ancient year books. Their anonymity keeps secret the identity of the authors. To the more renowned historians, however, it seemed plausible that they were made by learners for learners, by apprentices for apprentices, even by lawyers for lawyers, in order to deeply understand the very functioning of law in its proper polemical and adversarial administration.

The role of the composers and the specific aim they had in mind moulded the contents of the collections, casting the accounts in dialogic form where the arguments discussed by serjeants superseded the reasons brought by the parties. The greatest preoccupation was to leave a trail of the 'skillful and recondite' game played before the Courts by fierce opponents, who revealed their argumentative virtuosity under the inquisitive and expert eyes of the judges.[55] As Plucknett veraciously notes, '[a]fter such a display, it was an anti-climax to think a decision': the text of the Year Books was indifferent to authorities and final statements; in the economy of learning, what the law could be was less important than how the pleading should be conducted. These were distinguishing features that isolated the Englishness of the former Reports from the common habit of similar creations, drawing a clear mark of separation within the body of the Western legal tradition.

At the same time, they were distanced from the purposes and the form of the plea rolls, making the textual perceptibility of the law complex.[56] The stylistic discrepancy between Records and Reports was masterly captured by William Holdsworth, who juxtaposed the machine intonation of the former with the human inclination of the latter, the impersonal and stereotyped form of words of the first, based on the proper suppression of all dramatic elements, with the living voice of the second, which keenly recount the exciting incidents of the trial and vividly depict the temper of the main characters.[57]

---

55 TFT Plucknett, *Early English Legal Literature* (CUP 1958), 102.

56 For these reasons, as John Hamilton Baker observes, 'neither source by itself furnishes a complete account of what happened. Obviously, for historical purposes, it is desirable to put the two sources together whenever possible, and this policy has been pursued by modern editors of the year books and earlier reports' Baker (n 51) 35.

57 WS Holdsworth, *A History of English Law* (3rd edn, Methuen 1923) II, 545–46. As Holdsworth adds, 'because they do this faithfully, not neglecting that human element which to-day is and to-morrow is not, they supply just that information which is omitted by those who record with mechanical correctness merely the serious business alone. We see not only the things done; we see also the men at work doing them, the way these men did them, and how they came to be done in that particular way. [...] They create for us the personal element, the human atmosphere, which make the things recorded in the impersonal record live again before our eyes' ibid 546.

188 *Cristina Costantini*

In this way, subverting the past trend, narrative became the formal trait that formed a bridge between law and history. But, at the same time, a new point of view, extrinsic to the one of the parties involved in the actual proceeding, was privileged and fixed, so to stimulate the creation of a larger public, beyond the people directly concerned in the individual cases. The personal tastes and the curious inclinations of the individual reporter guided the selection of what had to be preserved; variety of accounts and omission of details came together.

The stylistic story of English law was destined to be transformed: the physical evidence left by the wise men, who were studying and practising law, changed aspect and eventually renovated the way of coalescing past memories. The mutable facets of law reporting registered and expressed the effects caused by the passing of generations on legal practices and traditions.

During the sixteenth and seventeenth centuries, a bulk of innovations irrupted in the domain of the Inns of Court. An evolving propulsion in legal procedure inspired material changes in law's substance and required a new way of textualisation, promoted and favoured, in turn, by a mechanical change in the mode of its conclusive production. These factors interacted together until the ancient Year Books came to shed their skin. In this span of time, we see a progressive shift of interest in common lawyers: from the arguments discussed by their colleagues, needed for the formulation of an issue, towards the final statement upon the already individuated issue. The focus was no longer placed on the debate before the Court, but on the decision of the Court.[58]

As a consequence, even the recognition of legal authority was transferred from the technical steps of argumentative reasoning to the cases that were well decided and frequently reported. A new forensic strategy revealed its potentialities and its attractiveness: the citation of what had already been declared and done went on to win against the general principles discovered by the lawyers' common erudition. The recursive use, even if not abuse, of this device provoked Coke's exasperated comment (previously anticipated) aimed at stigmatizing the excesses in style that had altered the ancient order of argument:

> Then was the citing general, but always true in the particular; and now the citing is particular, and the matter many times mistaken in general. In those days few cases in law were cited, but very pithy and pertinent to the purpose, and those ever pinch most; and now in so long arguments with such a farrago of authorities, it cannot be but there is much refuse, which ever does weaken or lessen the weight of the argument.[59]

In the modern era, the primary concern was to know not how the law was working, but what the law was. The common law seemed inclined to accord an authoritative force to judicial decision in order to consolidate a practice of uniformly binding precedents, even if the definitive establishment of the doctrine of

---

58 Holdsworth, *A History* V, 371–372.
59 E Coke, *Reports* (1614) Preface, pt 10, XXI–XXII.

stare decisis was to be fulfilled at a later time. Nevertheless, the best path to achieve the final style of reporting was embraced, and a demand for accurate published decisions grew stronger and stronger. Reports became nominative and consigned to history the renowned fame or, on the contrary, the ludicrous discredit of their author.

The reputation of the reporter and the quality of his work defined the line that had to be passed to guarantee the continuity between past and present, or the presentness of the past, as the ontological consistency of the law of precedent, together with a sense of commonality. In this regard, Allen has proposed a kind of taxonomy and graduation of modern reports, depending on the prestige and authoritativeness of their creator.[60] Three masterpieces stood out alone, distinguished from the other mass of books: they are Coke's, Plowden's, and Saunders's Reports, the prestige of which was unquestionable.[61] All the remaining Reports are grouped into three classes. The first group of Reports, remembered for their high authority, were followed with great respect, even if they were by no means of even quality. Other Reports were placed on the opposite side and, therefore, were of little value: they were guarded by the members of the Bench with a hint of a satirical smile, or even with a kind of Olympian wrath. Finally, there is the third group: its great number of Reports stood in a midway position and were treated with attention but not necessarily with acquiescence.[62]

The making of the common law tradition was then consigned to the proud battle fought by numerous competitors for attesting the version of the case facts that had to pass to future generations. Over the years, a crowd of Reports gathered to become the narrative form of legal precedent, the repository of the legal and culture identity of common law: the Reports became 'the text of the law that is common to English legal society's perception of itself and its tradition and, indeed, to that of the English people.'[63]

Another important break point occurred in the nineteenth century. The concerned call for certainty and order showed the obscurity and unsystematic nature of the pristine collections more than their vital, productive, even projecting imagination. What had been created and passed on had to be restyled. For these reasons, the form of the texts was submitted to an increasing process of authorisation and institutionalisation.

---

60 CK Allen, *Law in the Making* (7th edn, Clarendon Press 1966) 223–26.

61 The tone used by Allen and his witty notations remain of unsurpassed quality. Coke is presented 'with his enormous superstructure of commentary,' as a '*thesaurus* of English law rather than a mere set of reports'; Saunders was 'the Bullen and Leake of its age and enjoyed successive lusty reincarnations' Allen (n 59) 223.

62 In order to mark a clear line of distinction between the reliable and the unfruitful Reports, Allen makes recourse to a brilliant metaphor: 'These [the one reliable *n/A*] were sheep, with fleeces not as white as snow, but as white as could be expected in the strange pastures through which some of them had strayed. But there was also a class of goats, not to say scapegoats' Allen (n 58) 224.

63 Ben-Yishai (n 45) 51.

190 *Cristina Costantini*

As has been pointed out, this evolution caused a movement from narrativity to anti-narrativity, to be viewed as the constitutive mark of the Victorian Law Reports: they, in fact, replaced the ancient richness of details, comments, and description with a laconic and choppy prose, articulated through abstract and even truncated periods.[64] The new fashion was the formal response to the changed aspirations of the legal profession and to the muted balance reached inside it.

The substance of the law's rainbow bridge

The arguments discussed bring to the fore the centrality of style and stylistic imagination: they both could be considered as useful devices suitable to negotiate different types of constraint, such as theoretical, historical, political, and professional. Despite the conventional vision of an irenic and undisturbed transmission of rules and remedies from a time out of mind towards the present day, the common law tradition had to face tensions, anxieties, and contradictions. If one were to try to assess an anatomy beyond the asperities of the singular crises, one would find that the successful advent of law reporting caused the relocation of legal knowledge from the bodies of judges and lawyers to the pages of written manuscripts and, afterwards, of printed texts: the law, originally embodied in a sapiential and even prophetic mood, underwent an operation of disembodiment and excarnation;[65] similarly and consequently, legal memory moved from instantiation in distinguished persons to installation in several, disseminated books.[66]

At the same time, a potent residue remained to govern cryptotypically the life of English tradition: there was an excess, not kept by folios and sheets, that metaphysically continued to haunt the apparent morphology of the law and, from the outside, returned to vivify legal precedentiality, demanding to be remembered even against the letters shut in material archives. At this time, the anxiety was about the control of access to the invisible, unresolved, and still governing surplus. Later, this earliest manifestation of disquiet was extended from the what of the law over the way the pieces of law that have been captured were to be reported; the urgent issue was to institutionalise the style of the law's imprint, the shape of its footprints, of its secular marks and traces.

In another respect, the permutations of stylistic expressions are the symptomatic evidence of a shift in the balance of powers, whether within the legal profession (between Bench and Bar) or between lawyers and sovereignty, or between sources of law (common law and legislative Acts). On the one side, the increasing relevance of a judge-made common law imposed to fortify the accuracy of the accounts, providing trustworthy, consistent, and timely reports instead of personal notes commended to the leisurely methods and strategic choices of apprentices

---

64 Ben-Yishai (n 45) 23, 51.
65 I have previously developed these concepts of incarnation and excarnation as the two substantive devices of representing law, in C Costantini, *La Legge e il Tempio. Storia comparata della giustizia inglese* (Carocci 2007).
66 Ross (n 48).

and serjeants. On the other, the symbolic charge of the Year Books was violently opposed by Henry VIII at the height of his terror, until he ordered their suppression in 1535.[67]

The books contained the maxims of common law that the King would deprive of force in favour of a potentiated Equity, in those days construed as a lawful arm suited to concretely enacting the pre-eminence of royal prerogatives.

Finally, the anti-narrativity switch that occurred in the course of the nineteenth century was a stylistic reaction against the growing importance acquired by competing formants: the Courts had to manage their new angst by reducing the durable impact of parliamentary activity, so as to confirm a tradition of precedent in the face of a rising force of Statutes and Acts.

Imagination lived and is still alive to suggest answers and possible solutions, appeasing the spasms induced by anguish and anxiety in the rainbow bridge that traduces past and present into a timeless time.

---

67 According to Maitland's words; FW Maitland, *English Law and the Renaissance* (CUP 1901) 77 (note 29). Commenting on Maitland's evocative statement, Plucknett has emphasised the symbolical (not merely professional) force of the Year Books, their intimate connection with the common law, so to conclude 'Their extinction in 1535 therefore seemed to Maitland a dramatic omen that the common law was passing through its darkest hours'; TTF Plucknett, *Studies in English Legal History* (Hambledon Press 1983) 329.

Part Four

The future of the legal imagination

11 Depicting the end of the American frontier

Some thoughts on Larry McMurtry's *Lonesome Dove* series[1]

Giacomo Delledonne

SCUOLA SUPERIORE SANT'ANNA, PISA, ITALY

The constitutional significance of the frontier in the development of the United States

The American frontier experience is a permanent challenge for any attempt to analyse and assess the American 'experiment' comprehensively. Of course, this sounds self-evident to historians: suffice it to mention Frederick Jackson Turner's contribution. His essay on *The Significance of the Frontier in American History*, first published in 1893, has sometimes been labelled as 'probably the best-known work of American historical analysis.'[2] Because of its archetypical nature, the frontier myth has had a far-reaching influence over American culture in the broad sense. More recently, the frontier has also served as a polemical target for revisionist authors and has inspired comparative research.[3] This testifies to the strength of the frontier myth as an interpretive paradigm.

Still, the American frontier is a relevant part not only of the American culture in broad terms, but also of its constitutional imaginary: as one Italian comparative constitutional law scholar has recently argued, the frontier experience 'did generate a specific constitutional tradition, which overlaps with the Founding Fathers' Constitution only to a certain extent.'[4] It is apparent that the frontier experience

---

1 A draft version of this chapter was presented at the workshop Law and Imagination: Legal Change in Troubled Times, which was held at City, University of London on 24 June 2019. I would like to thank Professor Matteo Nicolini as well as all the participants in the workshop.

2 See DM Wrobel, 'The closing gates of democracy: frontier anxiety before the official end of the frontier' (1991) 32 *Am Stud* 49; FJ Turner, *Rereading Frederick Jackson Turner: 'The Significance of the Frontier in American History' and Other Essays*, with a commentary by JM Faragher (Yale University Press 1994).

3 See, e.g., M Lombardi, 'The frontier in Brazilian history: an historiographical essay' (1975) 44 *Pacific Hist Rev* 437.

4 A Buratti, *La frontiera americana. Una interpretazione costituzionale* (ombre corte 2016) 9. See CG Fritz, 'Rethinking the American constitutional tradition: national dimensions in the formation of state constitutions' (1994) 1 *California Sup Ct Hist Soc'y YB* 103; RF Williams, *The Law of American State Constitutions* (OUP 2009) 78–79.

196   *Giacomo Delledonne*

played a pivotal role both in serving as a catalyst for constitutional change and in shaping the constitutional identity of the United States. This role, however, has hardly been exempt from controversy.

The reasons for this attitude are probably to be found in the tepid reception of the idea of constitutional development as a process[5] and, even more importantly, in the embarrassing character of the frontier experience as a mould for the development of the Constitution: indeed, the frontier experience 'ambiguously combines democratic, emancipatory features with imperialistic, aggressive, unilateral attitudes.'[6]

To some extent, ambivalence had been an intrinsic character of this project from the very beginning. After Thomas Jefferson took office in 1801, the frontier project was connected with the rapid growth of the American population. Quite optimistically, the third president highlighted not so much

> the injuries [that the rapid demographic increase] may enable us to do to others in some future day, but ... *the settlement of the extensive country still remaining vacant within our limits* ... the multiplications of men susceptible of happiness, educated in the love of order, habituated to self-government, and valuing its blessings above all price.[7]

Interestingly, Jefferson's statement hinted both at a potential for far-reaching expansion and at the inherent limits of this process. As for its potential, the frontier shaped the dominant feeling – and the 'distinguishing feature of American life'[8] – that the expansion across it was virtually unlimited. This is what Turner called the 'perennial rebirth'[9] of American life – that is, its inherent character that made it so different from European nation-states as well as from the American East Coast. Legal scholars who have looked into Jefferson's constitutional ideas have argued that his view of federalism, officially embraced by the Republican Party, 'held that the Union could expand indefinitely so long as each new state was admitted on an equal footing with the old.'[10]

The limits of westward expansion became more and more visible after the end of the Civil War, until the publication of the results of the federal census of 1890 officially marked the 'end of the frontier.' Only in the final decades of the twentieth century has the uneasy calm preceding the 1890 census formed the subject of

---

5 See EA Young, 'The Constitution outside the Constitution' (2007) 117 YLJ 408.
6 Buratti (n 4) 11.
7 Thomas Jefferson, first annual message (8 December 1801), published in *The Writings of Thomas Jefferson*, vol 8 (HA Washington ed, Riker, Thorne 1854) 6, 9; emphasis added.
8 FJ Turner, 'The significance of the frontier in American history' in *The Frontier in American History* (Henry Holt 1920) 1, 2.
9 Ibid.
10 R Knowles, 'The balance of forces and the empire of liberty: states' rights and the Louisiana Purchase' (2003) *Iowa L Rev* 343, 406.

Depicting the end of the American frontier 197

historiographic research. To the eyes of a few intellectuals, the imminent closing of the frontier was tantamount to the disappearance of an American Eden, by definition distinct from and immune to the typical flaws of European life.[11]

Against the background of the transitional years preceding the official end of the frontier, this chapter will delve into a major example of contemporary Western fiction. The relative stabilisation of frontier life in the final quartile of the nineteenth century and the ensuing anxiety are among the main themes underlying *Lonesome Dove*, the first and most popular novel in the namesake series authored by Larry McMurtry. The purpose of this chapter is to look into how the end of the American frontier and the transition towards a different cultural, political, and legal scenario are hinted at in this very influential novel sequence.

Dissatisfaction and uneasiness in the *Lonesome Dove* series: the legal space as an interpretive paradigm

Larry McMurtry's *Lonesome Dove* series[12] is one of the best examples of twentieth-century Western fiction. One of its main achievements is to depict a web of complex interactions on both sides of the US–Mexican border, with the legacy of 'European' and 'Eastern' culture and institutions being deeply shaped and transformed by this entirely different setting. In this respect, McMurtry's novels reflect a distinctive aspect of frontier life, namely the oscillation between the coexistence and hybridisation of different cultures, on the one hand, and the unilateral imposition of one social, cultural, and legal model, on the other hand.

In order to highlight some of the red threads in *Lonesome Dove* and to make some points about the implications of the end of the frontier, this chapter will resort to the notion of legal space. The concept of legal space, as distinct from legal order, has been coined by Armin von Bogdandy in order to grasp some aspects of European public law starting from its spatial dimension. Interestingly, spatial legal thinking has farther-reaching ambitions than merely pointing at the importance of borders, as it 'expresses the manifold experiences of the thick communication, deep interlocking, and mutual dependency of all involved legal regimes.'[13] Indeed, '[a] legal space is a deliberate alternative to a legal order.' Rather than focusing on top-down processes, the concept of legal space highlights the significance of 'processes of borrowing and peer review.'[14]

---

11 See Wrobel (n 2) 50.
12 The series is composed of four novels: *Lonesome Dove* (Simon & Schuster 1985), *Streets of Laredo* (Simon & Schuster 1993), *Dead Man's Walk* (Simon & Schuster 1995), and *Comanche Moon* (Simon & Schuster 1997). In 1986, *Lonesome Dove* won the Pulitzer Prize for Fiction.
13 Armin von Bogdandy, 'The idea of European public law today' in A von Bogdandy, PM Huber, and S Cassese (eds), *The Administrative State* (OUP 2017) 18.
14 von Bogdandy (n 13) 19.

198 *Giacomo Delledonne*

Of course, the United States in the late nineteenth century has not only common traits with, but also huge differences from, today's European Union.[15] However, European constitutional law scholars have paid great attention to the significance of political spatiality for a proper understanding of the American frontier myth. The intrinsic diversity of frontier life and its (perhaps reluctant) inclusiveness were instrumental in shaping the American spirit around individualistic and democratic values.[16]

For the purposes of this chapter, it is worth mentioning that expansion across the frontier was regulated and shaped by a number of legal instruments, in which very different rationales are recognisable. Suffice it to make reference to the complex programme expounded on in the Northwest Ordinance,[17] as well as to the emergence of a quasi-authoritarian system of territorial governance put in place after the Louisiana Purchase. Leaving this aside, local developments were no less important than top–down governance in defining the legal identity of the frontier. Westward expansion was also influenced by contact with those who lived beyond the frontier, most notably Mexicans – as well as, quite importantly, their system of civil law[18] – and Native Americans. Interestingly, constitutional lawyers have rarely reckoned with the constitutional significance of the frontier experience. In a way, they have not been willing to acknowledge its influence on the constitutional settlement of 1787. When expansion had just begun, federalists' opposition to the Louisiana Purchase, which they supposed to jeopardise the original balance among the states, shows that this process had a strongly destabilising potential.[19]

McMurtry's series is composed of four novels that were published between 1985 and 1997. For the purposes of this analysis, the very first novel in the series, Pulitzer Prize-winning *Lonesome Dove*,[20] will be considered. This author's choice is related not only to the dominant role of this novel in the series, as well as in McMurtry's production, but also to its setting. *Lonesome Dove* is set in the late 1870s, years after the end of the Civil War and the Battle of the Little Bighorn

---

15 Of course, the constitutional development and federalising process of the United States have been highly influential in EU law scholarship. See G Martinico, 'The federal language and the European integration process: the European Communities viewed from the US' (2016) 53 *Politique européenne* 38.

16 See G Scaccia, 'Territory: between state sovereignty and globalisation of the economic space' (2017) 4 *Przegląd Konstytucyjny* 82, 91–92.

17 See DP Duffey, 'The Northwest Ordinance as a constitutional document' (1995) 95 *Columbia Law Review* 929, 953, arguing that, 'the Ordinance reflects a number of political principles that have been important to American political practice: expansionism, imperialism, development, commercialism, risk, and utopianism' and suggesting that '[i]n general, the strand of our constitutional tradition emanating from the Ordinance involves a more substantial role for national government than that which the Constitution formally set out' (ibid 966).

18 The study of mixed jurisdictions is a *locus classicus* of comparative law: see W Tetley, 'Mixed jurisdictions: common law vs. civil law (codified and uncodified)' (2000) 60 *Louisiana Law Review* 677; VV Palmer (ed), *Mixed Jurisdictions Worldwide: The Third Legal Family* (2nd edn, CUP 2012).

19 See Knowles (n 10) 373–76.

20 L McMurtry, *Lonesome Dove* (Simon & Schuster 1985).

Depicting the end of the American frontier 199

(Chapter 93). Events in the novel precede by a few years the official 'end of the frontier,' declared by Census Superintendent Robert P. Porter in 1890.[21] Revolving around the adventures of two retired Texas Rangers who end up escorting a cattle herd from Texas to Montana, the plot is dominated by two distinctive feelings: calm and dissatisfaction. In this vein, the feelings of the main characters mostly reflect the defining attitudes of American life ahead of the end of the frontier. Of course, the description of these feelings is so superbly handled by McMurtry also because he can take advantage of his omniscient, retrospective sight. In this respect, McMurtry's Great American Novel, as it has sometimes been defined,[22] clearly differs from those of novelists, such as James Fenimore Cooper, who were personally involved in the political debates of their time.[23]

Highly representative main characters: two retired Texas rangers

Relative calm is the typical condition of the two leading characters in *Lonesome Dove*, Captain Woodrow Call and Captain Augustus 'Gus' McCrae. After retiring, they have set up the Hat Creek Cattle Company in Lonesome Dove, Texas (Chapter 1). Call, McCrae, and most of the people in Lonesome Dove have mostly been forced to adapt to ordinary life after the end of the Civil War and Indian wars. As Call acknowledges, Lonesome Dove is mostly safe by the time the plot unfolds because the 'business with the Comanches' – a 'long and ugly' affair – is now over (Chapter 2). The death of Chief Kicking Wolf, 10 years before the events in the plot, has marked not only 'the end of the Comanches,' but also 'the end of their real job' (Chapter 16).

The fact that the two leading characters in the novel are two legendary retired Texas Rangers is telling in itself. The history of the Rangers in the Republic and later the State of Texas strongly exemplifies the peculiar character of law enforcement on the American frontier: in its first 50 years, it is marked by the coexistence of a private, loosely regulated initiative and attempts to put it under the control of the state authority. It is also a history of resilience, as the Texas Rangers 'have existed, with a few interruption, for 180 years in one form or another.'[24] First established as a rather informal corps in charge of protecting settlers from Indian raids, the Texas Rangers got official status at the time of the fight for the independence of Texas. After Texas was admitted to the Union, the federal

---

21 See GD Nash, 'The census of 1890 and the closing of the frontier' (1980) 71 *The Pacific Northwest Quarterly* 98.

22 See assessment by M Korda, in J Spong, *A Book on the Making of Lonesome Dove* (University of Texas Press 2012) 40

23 See GJ Becker, 'James Fenimore Cooper and American democracy' (1956) 17 *College English* 325; M Meyers, *The Jacksonian Persuasion: Politics and Belief* (Stanford UP 1960) 57; A Buratti, 'Andrew Jackson e le trasformazioni della Costituzione americana' (2013) 19 *Diritto pubblico* 1051, 1055.

24 See RM Utley, *Lone Star Justice: The First Century of the Texas Rangers* (OUP 2002) x; CH Harris III and LR Sadler, *The Texas Rangers and the Mexican Revolution* (University of New Mexico Press 2004) 15–17.

200 *Giacomo Delledonne*

government refused to muster the Rangers into federal service. In the aftermath of the Civil War, in which some of the Texas Rangers had joined the Confederate camp, they were disbanded.[25] Towards the end of the Reconstruction years, however, the Democratic-controlled Texan state legislature created a Frontier Battalion of Texas Rangers:

> But by the decade of the 1880's, the Frontier Battalion no longer had a frontier to protect. And with the rise to power of the dictator General Porfirio Díaz, the Mexican side of the border was gradually brought under control. The Texas Rangers now became a state police force whose function was to support local lawmen. The Frontier Battalion had become an anachronism. Nevertheless, the organization remained in being until 1901. Ironically, what Indians, outlaws, and Mexicans had failed to do, the legal profession accomplished.[26]

Indeed, in the final quartile of the nineteenth century, the Frontier Battalion all but lost its reason for being:

> [T]he Frontier Battalion should have been disbanded with the death of Major Jones, not because of his death, but because the frontier was gone. Though the organization continued for twenty years longer, it did not operate as a frontier force. No longer could one draw a line from Ranger camp to Ranger camp, a line extending from the Red River south, and say: here is the frontier where the Rangers stand guard between savagery and civilization. Civilization had overtaken the Rangers, encompassed them, and them an interior police force.[27]

Therefore, the individual destinies of two retired Texas Rangers in the 1880s powerfully echo more general uneasiness with the imminent end of the frontier: they have accomplished their mission, an achievement that has somehow deprived them of their function. When assessing the pros and cons of a journey to Montana, Captain McCrae bitterly admits that 'the job wore out' and '[h]e and Call, who had no military rank or standing, weren't welcomed by the Army; with forts all across the north-western frontier the free-roving Rangers found that they were always interfering with the Army, or else being interfered with' (Chapter 7).

Meanwhile, Call and McCrae are still deeply affected by the less ordinary circumstances they had to face in the past. Captain Call, for example, has retained old habits

---

25 As Captain McCrae recalls, '[w]hen the Civil War came, the Governor himself called them in and asked them not to go – with so many men gone they needed at least one reliable troop of Rangers to keep the peace on the border' (Chapter 7).

26 Harris and Sadler (n 23) 17.

27 WP Webb, *The Texas Rangers: A Century of Frontier Defense* (University of Texas Press 1965) 425.

left over from wilder times: checking, looking for sign of one kind or another, honing his instincts, as much as anything. ... Sitting around a fire being sociable, yawning and yarning, might be fine in safe country, but it could cost you an edge in country that wasn't so safe.

(Chapter 2)

However, the leading characters are conscious that much of this has come to an end: 'it was obvious to Call that Lonesome Dove had long since ceased to need guarding' (Chapter 2). In this regard, a pervasive feeling throughout the novel is a sense of dissatisfaction or anxiety related to the imminent end of a crucial phase in the history of the United States: 'If the 1880s are viewed as a calm before the storm of the tumultuous nineties, an examination of frontier anxiety in those years suggests it was an uneasy calm at best.'[28]

The constitutional programme underlying expansion across the frontier had been marked by a massive strive for democratisation: in the first half of the nineteenth century, the clash between the emerging Jacksonian coalition and the advocates of the so-called American system had largely been about the meaning of the expansion towards the West. By the time McCrae and Call think over their past vicissitudes in Lonesome Dove, they find it hard to take stock properly. Have they fought the Native tribes in order to protect 'the bankers' (as well as 'drummers of every description'), as disillusioned McCrae puts it? Or have they contributed to protecting 'women and children' and 'plain settlers' (Chapter 7)? Interestingly, doubts about the actual direction of westward expansion, and its capability to measure up to its early assumptions, had been at the heart of (often fierce) political discussions in the run-up to the Civil War. Two decades after the end of the Civil War, these concerns were being amplified by the emergence of new political structures and cleavages:

The burning issues of race and Union began to be displaced by the crises of industrial capitalism. New movements would emerge from the farms and the cities to challenge the emerging status quo. As the 1870's moved into the 1880's, the air filled with denunciations of big business and its corruption of American government. Like their fathers and grandfathers and great-grandfathers, a new generation would express their populist impulses by founding a new political party, the Populists, as a vehicle for a frontal assault on the status quo.[29]

---

28 Wrobel (n 2) 50.
29 B Ackerman, *We the People*, vol 2 *Transformations* (Belknap Press 1998) 248 (defining the final decades of the nineteenth century and the opening years of the twentieth century as a failed constitutional moment 'with fateful consequences that still reverberate today').

202 *Giacomo Delledonne*

Structural ambivalence: Western life and the rest

Not only is the novel pervaded by these mixed feelings, but the description of the Texan society in *Lonesome Dove* is also ambivalent. Some of the characters are imbued with (and reminiscent of) culture and institutions from the Eastern United States. Talkative Captain McCrae is depicted boasting the fragmentary classical education that he received 'in college, back in Virginia somewhere' (Chapter 2) and has kept an old Latin schoolbook, to which he resorts for rather prosaic purposes. This basic education is then complemented by a genuine talent for telling stories and anecdotes, in line with a typical aspect of frontier culture that had greatly contributed to Abraham Lincoln's political success.[30] In sum, basic classical education is enriched by a well-rooted oral culture.

McCrae and cattle rancher Wilbarger – who pretends, in turn, to have attended Yale College – remotely reflect the fascination of the newly established American republic with classical culture as well as, to some extent, the patrician attitudes of its early political and cultural elites, before the advent of Jacksonian democracy. Significantly, the most prominent representative of state constitutional law scholarship in the United States has argued that the emergence of new constitutional ideas and the patterns of state constitutional change 'blew not only to the West but also back to the East.'[31] 'Eastern' constitutional ideas and models were an obvious component of the legal background of settlers moving across the frontier, but the westward movement also led them to shape new constitutional concepts. Not only did settlers elaborate their own 'autochthonous' constitutional ideas, but they also triggered similar trends in the Eastern states.

For all the accomplished pacification of the frontier, in the eyes of the main characters in the novel, the Rio Grande represents something more than just the border with another nation. In their view, rustling horses at the Hacienda Flores in neighbouring, troubled Mexico is still ordinary business. Youthful Newt Dobbs unconsciously echoes Pascal[32] and is, to say the least, puzzled by the fact that

> such a muddy little river like the Rio Grande should make such a difference in terms of what was lawful and what not. ... [Captain Call] was known for his sternness where horsethieves were concerned, and yet, here they were, running off a whole herd. Evidently if you crossed the river to do it, it stopped being a crime and became a game.
>
> (Chapter 11)

Likewise, Jake Spoon has come back to Lonesome Dove and makes plans for moving to Montana because of his 'hopes of eluding the law' (Chapter 13).

Critics have signalled that McMurtry's literary world, in which irony and relative calm play a significant role, is hardly exempt from violent acts, even extreme

---

30 T Bonazzi, *Lincoln. Un dramma americano* (il Mulino 2016).

31 Williams (n 2) 79.

32 See B Pascal, *Thoughts Preceded by A Sketch of His Life* (E Craig tr, Allen Morrill and Wardwell 1846) 98.

ones.[33] Reference is made to the renegade rapist and slaver Blue Duck, who has repeatedly escaped justice and has been seen by critics as a traditional Western character in McMurtry's novel.[34] Blue Duck, who also appears in other novels in the series, is the son of a Comanche war chief and one of his Mexican captives. In a way, he represents the violent, dark side of the United States–Mexican border. Because of his origin, he belongs neither to a Native tribe nor to the Mexican culture: in this respect, he is a quintessential outcast.[35] The border may well have been porous, but some deeply ingrained pessimism emerges with regard to the possibility of a multicultural society in the West. Meanwhile, the presence of some unconventional characters, such as the Mexican cooks Bolivar ('Bol') and Po Campo, is not without resort to stereotypical characters, mostly the Native ones.[36]

Another point deserves mention. Although much has already been achieved, the leading characters still feel a need for novel challenges. Jake Spoon gives them the opportunity to visit a territory – that is, Montana – where there is still some unfinished business: 'Indian fighting,' but not that much, and huge fortunes to be made thanks to cattle breeding (Chapter 7). In sum, the legal space revolving around Lonesome Dove – understood as an ideal type of frontier life – is porous, diverse, and pervaded by a number of cultural influences and power structures (also including apparently relentless exclusionary dynamics).

Concluding remarks

The purpose of this chapter is not to summarise all the relevant points in McMurtry's novel, let alone in the namesake series. Rather, it has tried to reflect upon it and to consider its plot, characters, and themes as representative of a distinctive way of viewing the final years of the frontier experience and the omens of its end.

Of course, it would also have been possible to make some points on *Lonesome Dove* starting from its context. *Lonesome Dove* can be described as an attempt to revive a declining genre and was written as a result of the failure to transform a film script into a movie.[37] As I have already mentioned, it clearly differs from novels published in the nineteenth century whose authors were involved in the political discussions of their time and took sides or satirised much of the contemporary scene, as Melville did in *The Confidence-Man*. McMurtry, in turn, does not properly take sides: the third-person narrator in *Lonesome Dove* takes a sympathetic interest in multiple viewpoints, which may in fact coexist within the very same character.

---

33 See DL Madsen, 'Discourses of frontier violence and the trauma of national emergence: Larry McMurtry's *Lonesome Dove* quartet' (2009) 39 *Can Rev Am Stud* 185.

34 See M Busby, *Larry McMurtry and the West: An Ambivalent Relationship* (University of North Texas Press 1995) 189.

35 Madsen (n 33).

36 See Busby (n 33) 185.

37 See Busby (n 33) 179.

204 *Giacomo Delledonne*

As one critic has put it, McMurtry's work can aptly be defined as 'a post-modern pastiche of a modern fictional genre (the western) which itself is expressive of a nostalgic desire to return to the conditions of the mid-nineteenth century.'[38] Thanks to this subtle move, the novel is quite successful in making anxiety, even implicit unease, emerge. In this regard, literary imagination is able to supplement some of the shortcomings of legal imagination and to show that a pluralistic, sympathetic viewpoint is necessary in order to fully grasp legal and constitutional transformations.

I have already mentioned that Ackerman identifies a *failed constitutional moment* at the end of the nineteenth century. This is related to the decline of an idea of American exceptionalism revolving around the peculiar features of frontier life, growing disillusionment with political elites, and the rise of populist claims. The West played a major role in this partial shift, as the Midwest had done in the decades preceding the Civil War. Just like the characters in *Lonesome Dove*, the West developed constitutional ideas of its own, based on the historic American tradition, but also on original concepts that were taking shape at the local level.

From the specific standpoint of law, one of the possible interpretive tools for explaining the interaction between the West and the federal government in the final years of the frontier is Article IV of the United States Constitution, most notably its Admissions and Guarantee Clauses (Sections 3 and 4). As the Supreme Court stated in a landmark judgment in *Luther v Borden*, Congress has the power to admit new states into the Union and to decide 'what government is established in the state'[39] and 'whether it is republican or not.'[40]

The republican nature of state governments was somehow taken for granted after the entry into force of the Constitution. In *Minor v Happersett*, the Supreme Court held that

> [a]ll the states had governments when the Constitution was adopted. ... These governments the Constitution did not change. They were accepted precisely as they were, and it is therefore to be presumed that they were such as it was the duty of the states to provide.[41]

But things went differently when territories in the West applied for statehood and admission to the Union, or when the Southern states were re-admitted to it after the end of the American Civil War: indeed, the Guarantee Clause was extensively used and fully implemented: 'only during the period of crisis from 1860 to 1876, it served then as a formidable engine of centralisation.'[42]

---

38 Madsen (n 33).
39 US Supreme Court, *Luther v Borden* (1849) 48 US 1, 42.
40 Ibid. See also TA Smith, 'The rule of law and the states: a new interpretation of the guarantee clause' (1984) 93 *YLJ* 561, 562.
41 US Supreme Court, *Minor v Happersett* (1874) 88 US 162, 175–76.
42 CO Lerche, Jr, 'The guarantee of a republican form of government and the admission of new states' (1949) 11 *J Pol* 578, 578. See also M Nicolini, 'Regional demarcation, territorial alteration, and accommodation of divided societies' (2015) 94 *Revista de Derecho Político*, 53, 69–70.

Depicting the end of the American frontier 205

Decades later, the debate about the admission of Arizona and New Mexico to the Union was the last instance in which the allegiance of a territory to the republican form of government was seriously questioned. President Taft even vetoed the admission of Arizona because its constitution regulated referendum, initiative, and recall of elected officials and even judges, somehow blurring the well-established distinction between republican government and democracy.[43] Be that as it may, the abovementioned influence of Western constitutional ideas and practice on the Eastern states and the willingness of the settlers to experiment with institutional innovations allowed them to attain federal relevance as they were embraced by the populist movement.

In sum, the years that preceded and followed the official end of the frontier were also ones of constitutional turmoil and partial constitutional transformation. Borrowing Ackerman's concepts, they did not result in a fully-fledged constitutional moment. Still, they were marked by complex interactions between different actors and the emergence of novel claims. Likewise, *Lonesome Dove* depicts the subtle anxiety pervading an archetypical frontier village at some point in the 1880s. The quest for novel challenges is a reaction to excessive stillness. Meanwhile, the diverse (but not multicultural) character of frontier life in Lonesome Dove testifies to the original contribution of the West to American life.

43 See Lerche (n 3) 79–80.

12 A Coleridgean dystopia

Formalism and the optics of judgment

Thomas D.C. Bennett and Olivia Reilly

CITY, UNIVERSITY OF LONDON, UK
STANFORD UNIVERSITY IN OXFORD, UK

Introduction

Among the great contributors to the philosophy of imagination is the poet and philosopher Samuel Taylor Coleridge (1772–1834). In this chapter we seek to demonstrate how Coleridge's accounts of the 'Imagination' and its opposite faculty, the 'Fancy,' provide us with the conceptual tools to uncover and engage with a modern legal problem: the increasing prevalence of 'unitary judgments.'

Unitary judgments occur when a multi-member judicial panel – usually an appellate court – produces a single, joint judgment with which all the judges are in agreement. This practice stands in opposition to that of producing multiple judgments – where individual judges on the panel produce their own, separate judgments (which may be concurring or dissenting). We focus on the UK's highest court – the Supreme Court (formerly the House of Lords) – because, since its official formation, replacing the House of Lords in October 2009, it has been a significant institutional proponent of the unitary judgment practice. But the point that we make has wider implications for the practice of appellate judging not just in the UK, but across the common law world (and, in all likelihood, also across the civil law world).

Coleridge enables us to identify the practice of unitary judgments as founded in a strongly formalist mode of thinking. An examination of recent unitary judgments from the Supreme Court suggests that senior judges are going about their business in crude ways that Coleridge would immediately recognise as an expression of the Fancy's only limitedly helpful influence. Coleridge's account of the Fancy facilitates, in this chapter, a critique of the unitary judgment practice and of the formalism that informs it. Dealing in 'fixities and definites,' the Fancy provides stable images and limited concepts, which tend to minimise or erase complexity in search of a simplified clarity. This is an ever-present danger.

The optics of producing unitary judgments seem, at first, to be desirable: unitary judgments give the appearance of certainty, clarity, and authority as the court is perceived to be acting with absolute, unequivocal unanimity and consensus. Judges and lawyers like unitary judgments, which in the 2010s have returned to a level of prominence not seen since the 1980s, because of the certainty they (supposedly) provide. The maintenance of legal certainty, through the achievement of clarity in judgments, is a core aim of legal formalism.[1] But Coleridge's account of the Fancy undermines this impression, revealing it to be deeply misleading. The clarity that the practice appears to give is of a very particular type: a reductionist, simplistic sort of clarity that prioritises the elimination of doubt and ambiguity over the accurate and realistic representation of complex, often messy matters.

By creating a false image of clarity and certainty, the unitary judgment practice misleads by masking matters of disagreement and controversy with a glossy veneer of consensus. This veneer also lends unitary judgments a particular air of authority: they appear to provide a clear, definite, unequivocal statement of law. Moreover, this takes place not only within individual cases, but at an institutional level; the practice reduces the incidence of multiple judgment cases, which in turn reduces the opportunities for multiple judicial perspectives to be brought transparently to bear on matters of controversy. This is of particular significance in the Supreme Court, which only hears appeals on cases in which there is considerable public interest in the substantive point of law under consideration.

A sceptic would ask whether we have cause to believe that the alternative practice of issuing multiple judgments is preferable to that of unitary judgments. Our answer is that Coleridge gives us cause. The Fancy's simplistic clarity 'flatter[s]' what Oliver Wendell Holmes Jr identified as 'that longing for certainty and for repose which is in every human mind,' encouraging us to ignore the illusory, superficial nature of such appeals to certainty.[2] Coleridge seeks to acknowledge and oppose this tendency of the Fancy, by asserting the essential role of the Imagination (or 'completing power').[3] The imagination releases the mind from its passive attraction to fixity to reveal, and to revel in, complexity and plurality. An imaginative approach to the law, then, acknowledges rather than suppresses the *disruptive* nature of the law itself. In the words of Gerald Bruns, 'Legal tradition is … an always highly charged environment of intersecting (bisecting and dissecting) dialogues in which the very idea of law itself is in constant revision,' 'contested, irreducible, resistant to conceptual determination, always in question, open to unforeseen contextualisations.'[4]

The practice of issuing multiple judgments, where members of the court produce their own, individual judgments, is disruptive in character. It encourages

---

1 When we talk of formalism, in this chapter, we broadly refer to a school of legal thinking that insists that law both can and should provide clear answers to legal questions. Although we do not focus our attention on any single formalist scholar in particular, we can exemplify the sorts of matters with which we are concerned through the work of Joseph Raz. The key theme of Raz's account of the judicial obligation is the idea that the central function of law is the provision of authoritative guidance by which the law's addressees may regulate their conduct, and by which courts may judge that conduct. See *The Authority of Law* (OUP 1979) and *Practical Reason and Norms* (Princeton University Press 1990).

2 OW Holmes Jr, 'The path of the law' (1897) 10 (8) *Harv LR* 457, 466.

3 ST Coleridge, *Statesman's Manual* in *Lay Sermons*, (RJ White ed, Princeton University Press 1972) vol 1, 69 (hereafter *LS*).

4 GL Bruns, *Tragic Thoughts at the End of Philosophy: Language, Literature, and Ethical Theory* (Northwestern University Press 1999) 65.

208 *Thomas D.C. Bennett and Olivia Reilly*

dissenting, and also differently reasoned, yet concurring, judgments. It thus encourages the sort of plurality that Coleridge associates with the Imagination. This gives us reason to think that the production of multiple judgments is preferable to the unitary judgment practice.

We proceed as follows. In the first section, we elaborate Coleridge's notions of the Imagination and the Fancy. In the next, we examine the unitary judgment practice in two ways: first, through incidence statistics (giving us a broad overview of the practice), and, second, through a (brief) examination of three unitary judgment cases that highlight the practice's failings. Thereafter, we link the unitary judgment practice explicitly to formalism, using Coleridge's accounts as a framework. Finally, we sketch out how Coleridge's account of the disruptive character of Imagination supports a multiple, rather than unitary, practice of judgment production.

Coleridge on the Imagination and the Fancy

Introducing Coleridge's theory of Imagination and Fancy

In a lecture of 1818, Coleridge declared the Imagination the faculty responsible for the continued development of the human mind and human society, 'the distinguishing characteristic of man as a progressive being.'[5] Imagination guarantees improvement; it is the means by which we move beyond the already known towards the possible. The risks of devaluing the Imagination could scarcely be greater, yet Coleridge was deeply preoccupied by the concern that just such a debasement of the Imagination was taking place.[6] Coleridge's philosophy, politics, and poetry are, as Richard Fogle points out, 'organically one with' his concept of psychology, which identifies 'faculties like reason, understanding, and imagination' as 'fictions' 'necessary' to 'know the mind.'[7] This mental structure that Coleridge deduces becomes the foundation of his wider thinking. As Timothy Michael observes, for Coleridge, 'the structure of the mind itself determines both political organisation and the constitution of political knowledge':[8] '[t]hat, which we find in ourselves, is (gradu mutato) the substance and the life of *all* our knowledge [...] The human mind is the compass, in which the laws and actuations of all outward essences are revealed.'[9] For Coleridge, following Kant, the structure of knowledge was to be found within the mind itself. The Imagination is the cornerstone of his conception of this structure.

---

5 ST Coleridge, *Lectures, 1818–1819 on the History of Philosophy* (JR de J Jackson ed, Princeton University Press 2000) vol 2, 193 (hereafter *LHP*).
6 See J Barrell, *Imagining the King's Death: Figurative Treason, Fantasies of Regicide, 1793–1796* (OUP 2000) 5–46.
7 RH Fogle, *The Idea of Coleridge's Criticism* (University of California Press 1962) vol 1, 7.
8 T Michael, *British Romanticism and the Critique of Political Reason* (Johns Hopkins University Press, 2016) 140.
9 *LS* (n 3) vol 1, 78; original emphasis.

Coleridge's concept of the mind's structure depends on the identification of faculties: the Fancy, Understanding, Imagination, and Reason, in ascending hierarchical order. The Reason provides the 'intellectual or spiritual' pole of the mind's structure, while Understanding and Fancy belong at the phenomenal pole, providing concepts and images available to the senses.[10] The Fancy, which is of particular relevance to our concerns in this chapter, is characterised by 'fixities and definites,' providing 'materials' from the world-as-it-is for the Understanding to form into stable concepts.[11] (We will return to the Fancy in more detail later.) By contrast, the Imagination operates between the Reason's abstract ideas, and the lower faculties operating at the opposite pole: the Fancy and Understanding.

The Imagination opposes the fixity provided by the Fancy. It oscillates 'inexhaustibly re-ebulliant' between the two poles of material and ideal, connecting the mind to the absolute principles of the Reason and to the material actuality of the phenomenal world. It is 'a middle state of mind […] hovering between two images: as soon as it is fixed <on one> it becomes understanding and when it is waving between them attaching itself to neither it is imagination.'[12] The Fancy and Understanding produce images or fixed concepts, 'proper pictures,' or 'the external object.'[13] By contrast, the Imagination depends on a betweenness that eschews fixity to allow an intuition, beyond the limitations of the world as it is, of the possibilities opened by Reason through the Imagination's disruptive influence.

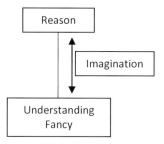

Figure 12.1 Reason, Imagination, Understanding and Fancy

10 D Struwig, 'Coleridge's two-level theory of metaphysical knowledge and the order of the mental powers in the *Logic*' in P Cheyne, *Coleridge and Contemplation* (OUP 2017) 207.
11 ST Coleridge, *Biographia Literaria or Biographical Sketches of My Literary Life and Opinions* (J Engell and WJ Bate eds, Princeton University Press, 1983) vol 1, 305 (hereafter *BL*).
12 ST Coleridge, *Lectures 1808–1819 on Literature* (RA Foakes ed, Routledge 1987) vol 1, 311 (hereafter *LLects*).
13 ST Coleridge, *Table Talk Recorded by Henry Nelson Coleridge and John Taylor Coleridge* (C Woodring ed, Routledge 1990) vol 1, 271.

210 *Thomas D.C. Bennett and Olivia Reilly*

Coleridge's theory of Imagination

Coleridge's most developed discussion of Imagination comes in his 1817 *Biographia Literaria*, where he distinguishes between two aspects of the faculty: primary and secondary. In his writing Coleridge was influenced by German idealist philosophy and the writings of 18th-century theorists of Imagination and Fancy (the Earl of Shaftesbury, among others).[14] He was also deeply preoccupied at the time by the 'the moral and philosophical, no less the social and economic crisis of the "condition of England"' in the aftermath of Waterloo.[15] As Kir Kuiken argues, 'the deduction of imagination' in *Biographia Literaria* can be understood as 'in dialogue' with the political texts that Coleridge was writing, revising, and having published at the time: *The Statesman's Manual* (1816) and *The Friend* (1818).[16] His attempt to provide an extended treatment of the functioning of Imagination is a response to political, as much as to literary, concerns. In these works, he expresses a profound concern about the risks of the rising dominance of a mode of thinking limited to the Fancy, and a limited concept of the mind based on the devaluing of Imagination and Reason. This, he warned, would change the 'status' of fundamental 'principles' and the law, politics, the national character itself would be deformed. In 'the case of Coleridge's theory of the imagination,' as Kuiken argues, the phrase 'political imagination' 'could very well be considered a tautology.'[17]

In Chapter 13 of *Biographia*, Coleridge defines the Primary Imagination as 'the living Power and prime Agent of all human Perception, and as a repetition in the finite mind of the eternal act of creation in the infinite I am.'[18] The Primary Imagination is a creative faculty, connecting the finite mind and the absolute, through what Schelling termed a 'primordial intuition,'[19] a process so essential to the mind's functions that it happens before the intervention of consciousness or the will.[20] Coleridge makes no attempt to limit the Primary Imagination to an

---

14 As James Engell and Walter Jackson Bate point out: 'His concepts are not original in their basic scheme (although no one made exactly the same distinctions or brought together the same terms in doing so), but they are perennially significant because they suggest so much about the relationship between perception, art, and philosophy, and unify these through the idea of the imagination as one kind of power' *BL* (n 11) lxxxv.

15 P Edwards, 'Coleridge on politics and religion: *The Statesman's Manual, Aids to Reflection, On the Constitution of Church and State*' in F Burwick ed, *The Oxford Handbook of Samuel Taylor Coleridge* (OUP 2012) 237.

16 K Kuiken, *Imagined Sovereignties: Toward a New Political Romanticism* (Fordham University Press 2014) 70.

17 Ibid 69.

18 *BL* (n 11) vol 1, 304.

19 FWJ von Schelling, *System of Transcendental Idealism* (Part 6 1800), quoted in N Leask, *The Politics of Imagination in Coleridge's Critical Thought* (Macmillan 1988) 135. Coleridge's debt to Schelling as well as to Kant, Tetens, Fichte, and others, is significant and widely acknowledged. See J Engell and WJ Bate, 'Editor's introduction' in *BL* (n 11), vol 1, cxix–cxxii, and J Engell, '*Biographia Literaria*' in Lucy Newlyn ed, *The Cambridge Companion to Samuel Taylor Coleridge* (CUP 2002) 68.

20 *BL* (n 11) vol 1, 304. See also Leask (n 19) 136.

A Coleridgean dystopia 211

artistic function, asserting instead that it is 'the prime Agent of all human Perception.'[21] The Primary Imagination is, then, the fundamental[22] source of both intellectual and physical awareness.[23]

The Secondary Imagination Coleridge defines as 'an echo of the former, co-existing with the conscious will, yet still [...] identical with the primary in the *kind* of its agency, and differing only in *degree*, and in the *mode* of its operation.'[24] While the 'prime' faculty of the Primary Imagination connects the mind, beyond the reaches of its conscious control, to the unconditional, the Secondary Imagination echoes the process to a different '*degree*,'[25] accessible by consciousness (of which the Primary Imagination is the source) and the will. It is inherently productive and disruptive:

> It dissolves, diffuses, dissipates, in order to re-create; or where this process is rendered impossible, yet still at all events it struggles to idealise and to unify. It is essentially *vital*, even as all objects (*as* objects) are essentially fixed and dead.[26]

The Secondary Imagination is, like the Primary, a 'living power,' characterised by vitality, process, and transformation, and opposed to fixity and objectification. It poses a direct challenge to what Coleridge saw as the reified, deathly fixity of the Fancy, rooted in an empiricist ideology, the consequences of which he considered were to be felt throughout the spheres of social and intellectual life.

The Imagination is a unifying force, the '*modifying*, and *co-adunating* Faculty,' joining or shaping into one.[27] As Perry argues, 'the Imagination promises rich and irreproachable bringings-together, which bestow a powerful affirmative magic not only on the unity it creates but also on the empirical particularity of the elements it takes up.'[28] The unity achieved by the Imagination is, for Coleridge, one that

---

21 *BL*, ibid.
22 'prime, adj (and int) and adv' (*OED Online*, OUP September 2019) <www.oed.com/view/Entry/151295> accessed 12 September 2019.
23 'perception, n' (*OED Online*, OUP September 2019) <www.oed.com/view/Entry/140560> accessed 12 September 2019.
24 *BL* (n 11) vol 1, 304; original emphasis.
25 The question of whether the Primary or Secondary Imagination should be considered to occupy a higher place in Coleridge's hierarchy of faculties is addressed by Jonathan Wordsworth in 'The infinite I AM: Coleridge and the ascent of being' in R Gravil, L Newlyn, and N Roe eds, *Coleridge's Imagination: Essays in Memory of Pete Laver* (CUP 1985).
26 *BL* (n 11) vol 1, 304.
27 ST Coleridge, *The Notebooks of Samuel Taylor Coleridge*, vol 3 (K Coburn ed, Princeton University Press 1973) 4176: 'How excellently the German Einbildungskraft expresses this prime & loftiest Faculty, the power of co-adunation, the faculty that forms the many into one, *in eins Bildung*' (hereafter *CN* vol 3). 'Co-adunation' is defined by the Oxford English Dictionary as 'joining together into one.' See 'coadunation, n' (*OED Online*, OUP September 2019) <www.oed.com/view/Entry/35006> 10 September 2019.
28 S Perry, *Coleridge and the Uses of Division* (OUP 1999) 34.

affirms both unity and plurality; it is 'a faculty devoted at once to unifying *and yet* to particularising.'[29] The Imagination is a process that unites apparently disparate plurality within a subjective experience of 'human feeling,' or what Coleridge terms 'life.' Instead of the lifeless objecthood of the fixed image or words on the page, the Imagination provides unity as a progressive, fluid, subjective awareness: it 'is a kind of life, bringing a vital unity to the senses' meaningless chaos; and so fulfilling the sublime precedent of Genesis [...] causing order to spring forth from confusion.'[30] As such, the Imagination provides a unity that does not reduce plurality into a single uniformity but brings together plurality within an unstable, progressive interconnection, which Coleridge compares to 'life,' 'tone,' and 'spirit.' Just as creation is not an act of singleness or uniformity but contains vast diversity within a complex order, so Coleridgean imaginative unity depends on coherent, progressive interconnection. Profoundly meaningful, it is opposed to chaos, but is 'inexhaustibly re-ebullient,'[31] 'overflowing' with feeling and energy.[32] Imaginative unity promises coherence as well as transformation or the essential balance of 'permanence and progression.'[33]

In *Biographia*, Coleridge presents the unifying energies of the Imagination as characterised by 'tension and resistance'[34] as part of their very nature and as a process that may at times be met with failure. The Secondary Imagination *struggles* 'to idealise and to unify' and encounters occasions where this 'process is rendered impossible.'[35] As Nigel Leask suggests, this resistance can be seen to represent 'the stubborn resistance of established cultural and political forms' to the expansion of norms (which takes place within what we might conceptualise as a normative space) made possible by the Imagination.[36] The process of progress and refinement that the Imagination makes possible is one that can be met with resistance, particularly as it disrupts and opposes stability and certainty in the familiar, the authoritative, the already known. (In this way, the Imagination presents a challenge to, inter alia, legal formalism.) For Coleridge, it is the Imagination that, when responding to 'a space of possibles, a horizon formed by [...] conventions and constraints'[37] or the range of possible interpretations of a

---

29 Ibid; original emphasis.
30 Ibid 130.
31 *BL* (n 11) vol 1, 300.
32 'ebulliency, n' (*OED Online*, OUP December 2019) <www.oed.com/view/Entry/59214> accessed 10 November 2019.
33 Coleridge, *On the Constitution of Church and State* (J Colmer ed, Princeton University Press 1976) 24n.
34 Leask (n 19) 140.
35 *BL* (n 11) vol 1, 304.
36 Leask (n 19) 140. On normative space, see R Mullender, 'Judging and jurisprudence in the USA' (2012) 75(5) *MLR* 914, 921. Benjamin Cardozo talks of judging proceeding in a 'field' in *The Nature of the Judicial Process* (reprinted, Feather Trail Press 2009) 43.
37 M Cohen, *The Sentimental Education of the Novel* (Princeton University Press 1999) 17. See also J Slaughter, *Human Rights, Inc: The World Novel, Narrative Form, and International Law* (Fordham University Press 2007) 10–11: '[L]iterary and cultural

A Coleridgean dystopia 213

piece of positive law (e.g. a statutory provision or a precedent), realises that horizon as 'dynamic,' fluid, capable of change.

Coleridge asserts the value of a kind of thinking (which he terms 'Method') that depends on contemplating 'not *things* only, or for their own sake alone, but likewise and chiefly the *relations* of things, either their relations to each other, or to the observer, or to the state and apprehension of the hearers.'[38] Such an awareness of complex interconnection emerges from the Imagination, which provides a 'pleasurable sense of the Many [...] reduced to unity by the correspondence of all the component parts to each other & the reference of all to one central Point.'[39] From this emerges the possibility of '*progressive transition*'[40] 'as all Method supposes a principle of unity with progression.'[41] This can be contrasted with a concept of language dominated by the Fancy, which acknowledges only a limited, tightly constrained normative space of a sort that appeals to formalists but denies the realist observation of a more transformative, unstable quality (in, for example, legal judgments).

Coleridge developed this notion of unity in multeity, provided by the Imagination, in *Biographia*, where he describes the Imagination as a 'synthetic and magical power' that creates a 'tone, and spirit of unity, that blends, and (as it were) *fuses*, each into each.'[42] Coleridgean unity is provided by a tone or spirit, not by visual fixity or stability. At the same time, the ambiguity in his language implies that the Imagination possesses the power to connect *individuals* 'each into each' in a new 'spirit of unity.'[43] This subjective, affective unity suggests a sympathetic connection, a recognition of an essential unconditional personhood. As Coleridge explains in a notebook, Imagination is 'the power by which one image or feeling is made to modify many others, & by a sort of *fusion to force many into one* ... or it acts by impressing the stamp of humanity, of human feeling, over inanimate Objects.'[44] Whereas, as we shall see, the Fancy operates by fixing and objectifying phenomena, the Imagination infuses them with 'life,' uniting apparently disparate plurality within a progressive, fluid unity.

Crossing from the limited Understanding, bounded by the phenomenal, into the realm of feeling, intellect, and higher intuition is the role of Imagination. It is the source of the unity that spreads over phenomena and releases them from fixity into an organic, progressive, destabilising unity; it is also that which connects us to ourselves and to each other in morality and civic harmony. This kind of unity

forms (like legal forms) do not simply reflect the social world. They in some ways also constitute and regulate it "when they respond to ... [and] resolve [...] the space of possibles"; they help shape how the social order and its subjects are imagined, articulated, and effected.'

38 ST Coleridge, *The Friend* (B Rooke ed, Routledge 1969) vol 1, 451 (hereafter *Friend*); original emphasis.
39 *LLects* (n 12) vol 1, 35.
40 *Friend* (n 38) vol 1, 457; original emphasis.
41 Ibid 476.
42 *BL* (n 11) vol 2, 16; original emphasis.
43 Ibid.
44 *CN* vol 3 (n 27) 3290; original emphasis.

214 *Thomas D.C. Bennett and Olivia Reilly*

Coleridge also saw underlying the community of a nation.[45] Coleridge's commitment is to the plurality and diversity of community, to what Perry terms 'the felt world's discrete, divided-up particulars.'[46] By contrast, the Fancy (to which we now turn) seeks homogeny or singleness, threatening a failure to recognise this sort of pluralism. In law, this core attribute of the Fancy is made manifest by the school of thought known as legal formalism.

Coleridge's theory of the Fancy

Coleridge describes the Fancy as the 'image-forming' power that fixes the plurality of thoughts and images into coherence. Without it, the subject would be unable to achieve 'fixation' in 'distinct perception or conception' – understanding would be impossible.[47] But the Fancy is fundamentally limited by its capacity – its need – to fix and objectify. As such, it is comparable to 'the Gorgon Head, which looked death into every thing.'[48] In creating fixity, it renders thoughts and phenomena stable and deathly, removing the subjective emotion, complex interconnection, and contextual nuance that comprise their 'life.' The Fancy transforms the processes of thought to objectified stability to leave meaning 'essentially fixed and dead' like 'all objects (as objects).'[49]

Coleridge identifies the Fancy as 'the Fetisch & Talisman of all modern Philosophers (the Germans excepted),' 'worshipped on account of its supposed inherent magical powers.'[50] The magic of the Fancy lies in its ability to provide a sense of order and stability to a society beset by instability (such as that which Coleridge himself lived in, for example, a time of profound constitutional change). For the Fancy's magic gives rise to the belief that every mystery can be solved by the Understanding, reduced to its limited scope. The fetish or 'material idol of'[51] empiricist, materialist philosophies, Coleridge identifies the Fancy as producing a 'primitive religion,'[52] whose proponents are metaphorically dazzled into a failure to recognise the limitations of the Fancy's fixed concepts, worshipping the image as the deity itself.[53] The stable notions that the Fancy produces share the 'inherent power'[54] of the image to capture and limit the attention of the viewer, failing to

---

45 *Friend* (n 38) vol 2, 323: 'here, where the powers and interests of men spread without confusion through a common sphere, like the vibrations propagated in the air by a single voice, distinct yet coherent, and all uniting.'

46 Perry (n 28) 4.

47 Ibid.

48 *CN* vol 3 (n 27) 4066.

49 *BL* (n 11) vol 1, 304.

50 'fetish, n' (*OED Online*, OUP September 2019) <www.oed.com/view/Entry/69611> accessed 12 September 2019.

51 WJT Mitchell, *Iconology: Image, Text, Ideology* (University of Chicago Press 1986) 190.

52 Ibid.

53 'idol, n' (*OED Online*, OUP September 2019) <www.oed.com/view/Entry/91087> accessed 12 September 2019.

54 ST Coleridge, *The Collected Letters of Samuel Taylor Coleridge* (EL Griggs ed, OUP, 1956–71) vol 4, 641 (hereafter *CL*).

engage the higher faculties to recognise that the fixed concepts provided by the Fancy are merely tools for the operations of the Imagination and Reason. The key point is this: the materialist concept of meaning that emerges from this reliance on the Fancy reduces the 'idea' to a minimised state. An '*Idea*,' Coleridge reminds us, 'is equidistant in its signification from Sensation, Image, Fact, and Notion' – 'it is the antithesis, not the synonyme, of εἴδωλον' or 'idol.'[55]

The Fancy, though necessary, can only be a *precursor* to the higher faculties of Reason and Imagination, which mediate between the two poles of thought identified earlier (between the fixed and the fluid, the concrete and the abstract, the real and the ideal). To stop at the fixed concepts of the Understanding is to fail to think beyond the confines of the already-known, the 'gross idolatry' of making 'that the goal & end which should only be a means of arriving at it.'[56] Without the Imagination (the 'completing power'),[57] we are limited to forms of thinking governed by the Fancy and the related faculty of Understanding, which 'forms for itself general notions and terms of classification for the purpose of comparing and arranging phenomena,' prizing 'clearness' over 'depth.'[58] Unlike the faculties of Reason and Imagination, the Understanding 'contemplates the unity of things in their *limits* only, and is consequently a knowledge of superficies without substance.[59] It seeks clarity, stability, definition, and classification and achieves these at the expense of nuance and depth, concerning itself with superficial categorisations and connections. The Fancy, thus understood, has clear links with legal formalism – a mode of thinking that prioritises (apparent) clarity and certainty and seeks to expunge often complex and messy realities from the legal realm. This is the resulting danger. As Coleridge warns, a society dominated by such limited thinking as its 'idol' is dazzled by the image of certainty at the expense of genuine knowledge, over-burdened with bureaucracy at the expense of profound thinking, tending to 'exclude the great' and 'magnify the little.'[60]

Having explored Coleridge's theories of the Imagination and the Fancy, we can critique the practice of issuing unitary judgments by linking the formalism that underpins it with the Fancy's emphasis on appearances and clarity as fixity rather than transparency. Before we do so, however, we must first set out the evidence of the increased use of unitary judgments and examine the effects that unitary judgments have. We will do so by focusing on the highest courts of their eras in the UK: the House of Lords and its successor, the Supreme Court.

55 *LS* (n 3) 101.
56 *CN* vol 3 (n 27) 4066.
57 *LS* (n 3) 69.
58 Ibid.
59 Ibid; original emphasis.
60 *Friend* (n 38) vol 1, 47.

Unitary judgments

The statistics

The judicial practice whereby multi-member panels issue single judgments (either written by a single judge and agreed by all, or contributed to by some or all members of the panel) is not a new one. There seems to be no agreed nomenclature for these judgments, with descriptors such as 'single,' 'combined,' 'joint,' and 'composite' being used interchangeably by academics and the judiciary. For clarity, and as an umbrella term encompassing all judgments upon which the entirety of the court's panel is agreed (both in terms of conclusion and reasoning), we will call these 'unitary' judgments. (We will call cases in which multiple judgments are issued 'non-unitary' cases.)

Despite not being a new practice, the issuance of unitary judgments has, in recent years, taken on a new prominence in the UK. Following the creation of the Supreme Court (which replaced the House of Lords as the UK's highest court on 1 October 2009), there has been a clear preference for the issuing of unitary judgments by it. The Court's former president, Lord Neuberger, was a particularly outspoken proponent of unitary judgments,[61] and his successor, Lady Hale, has taken a similar line.[62] Likewise Lord Carnwath, who has sat on the Supreme Court since 2012, spoke out in favour of the House of Lords and the Supreme Court issuing unitary judgments repeatedly during his time at the Court of Appeal.[63] Both Brice Dickson,[64] who has published statistics on the Supreme Court's judgments every year since its

---

61 Lord Neuberger, 'No judgment – no justice' First Annual BAILII Lecture, 20 November 2012; and 'Sausages and the judicial process: the limits of transparency' Annual Conference of the Supreme Court of New South Wales, Sydney, 1 August 2014.

62 'On the first two issues, Lord Hoffmann's view is shared by a majority. The least said by the rest of us who take the same view, therefore, the better. There should be no doubt, and no room for argument, about what has been decided and why. Any perceived inconsistency between what I say and what he says is to be resolved in favour of the latter. Indeed, there would be much to be said for our adopting the practice of other supreme courts in having a single majority opinion to which all have contributed and all can subscribe without further qualification or explanation. There would be less grist to the advocates' and academics' mills, but future litigants might thank us for that' *OBG v Allan* [2007] UKHL 21, [2008] 1 AC 1, [303] (Lady Hale).

63 See, e.g., *Doherty v Birmingham City Council* [2006] EWCA Civ 1739, [2007] HLR 32, [62]; *Grundy v British Airways Plc* [2007] EWCA Civ 1020, [2008] IRLR 74, [45]. See also his extrajudicial writing: R Carnwath, 'Devil we know or new start?' *Counsel*, June 2008, 6.

64 B Dickson, 'Year end' (2008) 158 *NLJ* 170; 'A supreme year?' (2012) 162 *NLJ* 257; 'Supreme confidence' (2013) 163 *NLJ* 170; 'A supreme education' (2014) 164 *NLJ* 17; 'A steady ship' (2015) 165 *NLJ* 26; 'Reigning supreme' (2016) 166 *NLJ* 19; 'Supreme justice' (2017) 167 *NLJ* 20; 'In the line of duty' (2018) 168 *NLJ* 17; 'Supreme justice: a year in review' (2019) 169 *NLJ* 18. NB: each of Dickson's articles gives statistics from the Supreme Court's caseload from the preceding year.

A Coleridgean dystopia   217

formation, and Alan Paterson[65] demonstrate that its issuing of unitary judgments has been commonplace since.[66]

Unitary judgments had been issued consistently by the House of Lords at a rate of less than 20% of its total workload between 2001 and 2009.[67] When the Supreme Court replaced it and had its first full year of casework in 2010, this percentage leapt to 38%.[68] From there, it has increased, hitting a high point of 68% in 2016[69] and remaining well above 60% in 2017 and 2018.[70]

These percentages are high, but not the highest. Paterson's statistics go back to 1981. From these we can see that the percentage of unitary judgments issued by the House of Lords reached its highest point in the last 40 years in 1993, running at 70%.[71] Indeed, the percentage is generally high from the mid-1980s to the early 1990s, averaging around 60%. Nonetheless, given that there was a marked reduction in the percentage of unitary judgments from the mid-1990s through to the late 2000s, where the percentage ultimately reduced to less than a quarter of the heights it had hit in 1993,[72] the return to an average of over 60% in very recent times is clearly significant.

The percentage of unitary judgments in the House of Lords/Supreme Court's case load becomes more significant still when we view it alongside another statistic – the percentage of cases in which one or more judges write a dissenting judgment. In the mid-1980s, when the percentage of unitary judgments was high, the average percentage of cases in which there was dissent was low, at less than 10%.[73] (In other words, even in cases where multiple judgments were issued, dissenting judgments – those that reach a different conclusion to the majority in the case – occurred less than a quarter of the time.) This suggests a broad alignment of views between the judges, because they agree much of the time, and so there is relatively little dissent. It might be taken to indicate the presence of broad consensus on many of the legal issues coming before the court. That said, it must also be acknowledged that the size of the judicial panels involved in those cases is significant. In the 1980s, owing to the lack of space available for judicial hearings in

---

65 A Paterson, '*Final Judgment* revisited' (2015) 21(1) *European Journal of Current Legal Issues* (online). Professor Paterson kindly shared with us some of the raw data upon which he relied in producing the tables that he published in that article. We are grateful to him for this.

66 It is worth noting that Dickson's and Paterson's methodologies for compiling their data appear to have differed slightly, in that they have produced slightly different results. It is also worth noting that, without more detail on their methodologies, it is not possible to determine precisely how each has defined the category of 'single' judgments they are considering. However, the variation in their results is within 1–2 percentage points and is insignificant for our purposes.

67 Paterson (n 65) Figure 1.

68 Ibid.

69 Dickson 2017 (n 64).

70 Dickson, 2018 and 2019 (n 64).

71 Paterson (n 65) Figure 1.

72 Ibid. In 2008, just 13% of the House of Lords' cases featured unitary judgments. The highest percentage between 2002 and 2009 was 18% (in 2005).

73 Paterson, ibid, Figure 5.

the House of Lords, panels generally comprised no more than five judges. (Indeed, in 1981 and 1985, not a single case in the House of Lords was heard by more than five judges.)[74] With smaller panels, the likelihood of consensus-based reasoning is higher because there are, quite simply, fewer voices from which dissent may be drawn. (The new Supreme Court sits in specially designed courtrooms that can accommodate panels of up to 11 justices, and so this problem has fallen away.)

In the first decade of the Supreme Court's existence, however, things differ considerably. The unitary judgment rate is again high, but so is the dissent rate, which reached nearly 40% in 2011 and thereafter averages in the high teens.[75] Moreover, consider that this dissent rate represents the presence of at least one dissenting judgment per case across *all* cases, *including* the unitary judgment cases (in which there obviously is no dissent). Once one removes the unitary judgment cases from the equation (cases in which, by definition, there can be no dissent), the dissent rate among the remaining cases is extraordinarily high. For example, in 2014, dissenting judgments were issued in 15 of the Supreme Court's 68 cases. This amounts to just 22% of all cases that year, but 47% – nearly half – of the non-unitary cases. In 2016, dissenting judgments occurred in 18% of all Supreme Court cases, but a whopping 52% of non-unitary cases. Put simply, dissenting judgments are roughly twice as prevalent in non-unitary Supreme Court cases in the 2010s as they were in the House of Lords in the 1980s.

The presence of this high level of dissent in non-unitary cases paints a muddled picture. For, although the unitary judgment rate suggests, on its face, a high degree of consensus, the dissent rate tells us that there is also a high frequency *and degree* of disagreement. Moreover, as it is clear that the Supreme Court has made a concerted effort to work as more of a team than the House of Lords (one of the factors underlying the increase in the unitary judgment rate), the fact that such a significant dissent rate remains suggests the presence – in around a quarter of all cases and around half of non-unitary cases – of disagreements so serious and fundamental that they could not be ironed out in discussions between the judges.[76] These may well have been matters upon which there was less disagreement between the judges than in non-unitary cases, but the data we have revealed hardly suggest a court operating with a consistently high degree of agreement across the board. Moreover, even where there is agreement between the judges as to the most appropriate conclusion for the case at hand, this does not equate to a lack of controversy. Simply because one panel of judges happens to reach a consensus does not mean that the consensus they reach deals adequately with all of the controversial issues that the case may raise. It simply means that the issues have been minimalized.

---

74 Ibid. In 1981, dissent registered in 4 of the 31 cases heard by the House of Lords (13%). In 1985, dissent featured in just 2 cases out of 24 (8%).
75 Ibid.
76 Ibid section 2.

A Coleridgean dystopia 219

Quantitative data of this sort undeniably form a blunt instrument. But they at least highlight the distinct possibility that, within the unitary judgment cases, matters of acute controversy are being resolved in a manner that cloaks points of disagreement. Paterson characterises this feature of unitary judgments as giving rise to a lamentable lack of transparency.[77] James Lee concurs, noting that:

> [t]he veneer of univocality afforded by single judgments may on occasion be at best disingenuous in so far as it suggests that the court was harmonious when in reality the need to provide a decision has produced the least unsatisfactory solution for all parties to the decision.[78]

In order to demonstrate the credibility of this criticism, we turn now to three examples of cases in which unitary judgments have been issued, and in which these unitary judgments mask matters of acute controversy.

The cases

Unitary judgments encourage the overlooking of tensions between wholly or partly incompatible interests that are in play within a case. They do a job akin to sweeping matters of acute controversy under the carpet. A veneer of clarity covers up unacknowledged turmoil. In this section we will consider three examples.

R v R

In the 1991 case of *R v R*, the House of Lords finally overturned the centuries-old anachronism in English and Welsh law that prevented a man from being found guilty of raping his wife.[79] With Parliament having never gotten around to dealing with this sorry state of affairs, despite numerous legislative opportunities to do so, the House issued a unitary judgment doing so. Undoubtedly, this has considerable appeal: the old law, based on the doctrine of coverture, was demeaning and wholly failed to protect women from sexually violent spouses.[80] It is this appealing sentiment that found expression in a unitary judgment, which was given by Lord Keith (and with which the other Law Lords agreed).

What does not find expression in the judgment, however, is the tension between the normative appeal of doing away with this anachronism and significant

---

77 Ibid.
78 J Lee, 'A defence of concurring speeches' [2009] *Public Law* 305.
79 [1992] 1 AC 599.
80 As William Blackstone put it in *Commentaries on the Laws of England*, vol 1, (1765) (ECCO) 430: 'By marriage, the husband and wife are one person in law; that is, the very being or legal existence of the woman is suspended during the marriage, or at least is incorporated and consolidated into that of the husband: under whose wing, protection, and *cover*, she performs every thing; and is therefore called, in our law-french a *feme-covert*; is said to be *covert-baron*, or under the protection of her husband, her *baron*, or lord; and her condition during her marriage is called her *coverture*.'

220 *Thomas D.C. Bennett and Olivia Reilly*

countervailing concerns about the impact of doing so on the rule of law. Removing the anachronism by legislation would be one thing, because Parliament acts prospectively, and the law's addressees have (at least constructive) notice of the change. But, unlike Parliament, when a court alters the law, it does so retrospectively. This puts the House of Lords in *R v R* on a collision course with an accepted legal convention – namely, that the courts will not retrospectively create new criminal offences.[81] (Today, that element of the rule of law is also enshrined as a human right under Article 7 of the European Convention on Human Rights (ECHR), which has direct applicability in the UK under the Human Rights Act 1998.) The crux of the matter is this: only by retrospectively criminalising the appellant's actions could the House alter the law and protect not only the victim, but also unknown, future victims.

In the common law, there has been a long-running argument about whether the courts ever really create new law or whether they merely recognise existing legal rules that have hitherto gone unrecognised. The latter position, known as the 'declaratory theory' of law, is – as one might imagine – popular with formalists and widely derided by realists. In relatively recent times, leading judicial figures in England and Wales have come out against the declaratory theory, with one prominent jurist declaring it a 'fairy tale' that no-one believes in anymore.[82] But the declaratory theory is precisely what underpins Lord Keith's judgment in *R v R*, as he elaborates a detailed, doctrinal, highly legalistic analysis from which he ultimately concludes that the House is not, in fact, making new law but merely recognising a change in the common law that has already occurred, at some non-specific point in the preceding decades.[83] This is despite the fact that the lower courts were still applying the exemption just months before the House heard the appeal in *R v R*.[84] It is a textbook example of law's 'amazing trick' – its capacity to change dramatically while simultaneously insisting, mantra-like, to onlookers that nothing has changed.[85]

81 Legal commentators have produced a range of different conceptualisations of the rule of law, but a rule against retrospective criminalisation is generally common throughout them. See, e.g., Raz, *The Authority of Law* (n 1); T Bingham, *The Rule of Law* (Penguin 2011).

82 Lord Reid, 'The judge as law maker' (1972) 12 *Journal of the Society of Public Teachers of Law* 22.

83 Although the exemption had arguably been watered down by some decisions, it still clearly persisted. In *R v Steele* (1976) 65 Cr App R 22, the court held that the fact that the spouses were living apart, and that the husband had given an undertaking (which has binding effect, akin to an injunction) not to molest his wife, meant that the wife's consent to intercourse had effectively been withdrawn. Yet in other cases, even in the early 1990s, the marital rape exemption was still enabling husbands to avoid criminal liability for raping their wives. (See *R v Sharples* [1990] *Crim LR* 198; *R v J* (Rape: Marital Exemption) [1991] 1 *All ER* 759.)

84 See *Sharples* and *J*, ibid.

85 S Fish, 'The law wishes to have a formal existence' in *There's No Such Thing as Free Speech* (OUP 1994), 170, borrowing the term 'amazing trick' from H Scheiber, 'Public rights and the rule of law in American legal history' (1984) 72 *California Law Review* 217, 236–7.

The argument between formalists and realists as to whether the declaratory theory is valid or not is clearly of relevance in *R v R*, but that argument finds no expression in the unitary judgment. The judgment simply adopts the declaratory (formalist) position. Likewise, there is clear scope for normative arguments on either side of the retrospective criminalisation debate. That is, even without taking a larger legal-philosophical view on whether a formalist or realist understanding of the adjudicative process should be regarded as reflecting the true state of the common law, there are valid positions that may be taken on either side of the debate as to whether criminalising the appellant's actions in this instance was the 'just' thing to do. But these positions find no expression in the unitary judgment either. What we are left with is a judgment that is highly controversial and that deals with a number of messily interrelated matters, but presents as if it is a simple and straightforward question of law to which there is a single, clear, simple, and straightforward answer. The tensions we have pointed up are glossed over by this veneer of clarity and certainty. To a complex, equivocal question, we are given an apparently simple, univocal answer.

It is surely likely that, if more of the judges had produced judgments, one at least might have flagged up the rule of law concerns that weigh in against the decision to abolish the marital rape exemption, or pointed up the flaws in the declaratory theory of law. Even if the House still decided, on balance, to abolish the exemption – which was undoubtedly the morally appealing thing to do – it could usefully have articulated the values that were in tension with one another, so that the law's addressees might have confidence that this significant change in the law was effected only after due consideration of the impact it would have on those values. As it is, Lord Keith's judgment is so one-sided that it might be thought of more as a piece of rhetoric than a detailed examination and consideration of the relevant legal principles.[86]

Lee v Ashers

In 2017, the case of *Lee v Ashers Baking Company Ltd* reached the Supreme Court.[87] This was a discrimination case that originated in Northern Ireland, which was the only constituent nation of the UK in which same-sex marriage had not, at the time, been legalised. Ashers Bakery offered a bespoke cake-decorating service. Mr Lee was a gay man who ordered from the bakery a cake bearing the words 'Support Gay Marriage.' The owners of the bakery, a married, heterosexual couple – the McArthurs – who identified as practising Christians, refused the order (revoking an initial acceptance of it), on the basis that their religious beliefs did not permit them, in good conscience, to produce a cake bearing this message.

Mr Lee's claim alleged unlawful discrimination on grounds both of his sexual orientation and his political beliefs (the latter being a ground of discrimination

---

86 Indeed, the appearance of law's 'amazing trick' would, to Stanley Fish, indicate that the judgment is squarely rhetorical. See Fish, ibid.

87 [2018] UKSC 49, [2018] 3 WLR 1294.

222   Thomas D.C. Bennett and Olivia Reilly

specifically challengeable in Northern Ireland). The McArthurs responded that, if the law required them to accept his order and produce the cake, it would be forcing them to manifest religious and political beliefs that they did not hold and would, therefore, be incompatible with their rights under Articles 9 (freedom of thought, conscience, and religion) and 10 (freedom of expression) of the ECHR. Mr Lee's claim succeeded in the County Court and the Court of Appeal. Thereafter, the McArthurs appealed to the Supreme Court, which produced a unitary judgment overturning the lower courts and finding in their favour.[88]

The case raises a politically sensitive issue – the tension between the legal rights of LGBTQ+ people to freedom from discrimination and the (formally) equally significant rights of religious adherents to manifest their religious beliefs (which may conflict with the interests of the LGBTQ+ community). The judgment purports to bring clarity to the matter at hand. The lower courts' decisions were overturned on two grounds. First, the lower courts were wrong as a matter of law to conclude that Mr Lee had suffered direct discrimination on the basis of his sexual orientation. Second, although it was arguable that Mr Lee had been discriminated against on the basis of his political beliefs, the legislative provisions protecting those beliefs had to be read compatibly with Articles 9 and 10 of the ECHR. There was insufficient justification to compel the McArthurs to act in a way that would contravene their own religious beliefs, and so the legislative provisions should not be read as requiring them to do so.

On the surface, then, the case appears to give clarity and provide certainty for the law's addressees. But there are legally and contextually relevant matters with which the Supreme Court does not engage that might well – if properly considered – have led to a different conclusion.

First, although the Supreme Court was entirely justified in concluding that no direct discrimination had taken place, it is unclear why, on the facts of the case, it did not find Mr Lee to have been the victim of *indirect* discrimination.[89] It may be the case that the bakery would have refused anyone's order for a pro-same-sex-marriage cake, irrespective of the order-placer's sexual orientation, but it is surely obvious that doing so will disproportionately impact upon members of the LGBTQ+ community. For support for political campaigns aiming to enhance LGBTQ+ rights, although present within the heterosexual community, has a much higher incidence within the LGBTQ+ community. So, *Lee* appears, prima facie, to be a classic instance of indirect discrimination. Yet this possibility does not feature at all in the Supreme Court's judgment.

The second, and perhaps trickier, issue is this. Mr Lee's claim was brought not just against the McArthurs, but against the bakery, Ashers Baking Company Ltd.

---

88 The judgment comprises sections (dealing with different issues) written by two justices: Lady Hale and Lord Mance. All five justices agree with both sections of the combined, unitary judgment.

89 Indirect discrimination occurs when, despite the defendant treating different persons in the same way (thus avoiding direct discrimination), one or more of those persons is disadvantaged because he or she belongs to a class that is disproportionately negatively impacted by the treatment.

A Coleridgean dystopia 223

The company is a separate legal entity from its owners. Its existence shelters its owners and shareholders from personal liability for the company's wrongdoing behind something known, in legal jargon, as the 'veil of incorporation.'[90]

By incorporating as a business, the McArthurs benefit from this veil of incorporation. It protects them from being personally liable for its debts if the company fails, for example, or from liability in damages if the company acts wrongfully. But the flip side of this incorporation is that the company – a body corporate – is its own legal entity, with a legal personality that is very different in character to that of a human. Most obviously, a company has no human rights. At least, it has no human rights in the same sense that humans have human rights. There are certain protections for companies that may arise under the ECHR,[91] but it has no claims in respect of rights that may only accrue to natural – human – persons, such as the right to freedom of thought, conscience, and religion under Article 9.[92] It will have common law rights and some statutory rights. And some of these rights might resemble the things we call 'human rights' in terms of their substance. But

---

90 Incorporating a business as a company has a number of distinct advantages. Quite apart from the various tax benefits it can accrue, the most obvious and best-known advantage is that, in a limited company, the liability of shareholders/directors is 'limited' to a particular sum. In other words, the company may accrue liability, but this liability does not transfer to the shareholders.

91 V Wilcox, *A Company's Right to Damages for Non-Pecuniary Loss* (CUP 2016) ch 3.

92 Wilcox makes clear that, although companies have been granted standing to make some claims under other parts of the ECHR, they have no rights under Article 9 (ibid, 49). See also *Company X v Switzerland* (decision) 27.02.1979, no. 7865/77, in which the European Commission of Human Rights concluded that 'a limited company given the fact that it concerns a profit-making corporate body, can neither enjoy nor rely on the rights referred to in Article 9, paragraph 1, of the Convention.' See further *X and Church of Scientology v Sweden* (decision), 05.05.197, no. 97806/77, § 2. Wilcox contrasts the Strasbourg jurisprudence with a different approach taken in England and Wales in *Exmoor Coast Boat Cruises Ltd v Revenue and Customs Commissioners* [2014] UKFTT 1103 (TC), in which it was suggested that a company could have Article 9 rights in circumstances where it was the 'alter ego' of its human owner, such that the two were in effect indistinct. However, this approach was taken in a tribunal by a county court judge, cited no authority for the proposition outlined, and has only been cited in one subsequent judgment (also of the first-tier tribunal, and by the same judge). Moreover, English and Welsh law generally takes the same stance on the scope of ECHR rights as the Strasbourg court, as it must pay due regard to Strasbourg decisions under s.2 of the Human Rights Act 1998. There is no indication that the Supreme Court in *Lee* was made aware of either the Strasbourg cases or the *Exmoor* decision (suggesting its reasoning on this point may have been made *per incuriam*). Companies may bring claims under Art.10 of the ECHR, and have had Art.10 interests protected in a range of cases – most notably as a defence to defamation and/or privacy claims brought against media corporations by individuals. However, the Art.10 interest in such cases derives not from the inherent dignity of the company (because it is not a human being), but from the public interest in receiving information pertaining to a matter of general public importance. The Art.10 rights of companies, therefore, derive from an intensely human interest – the interest of the broader community in receiving newsworthy information. See *Jameel v Wall St Journal Europe Ltd* [2006] UKHL 44, [2007] 1 AC 359.

the company has these rights not because they are fundamental matters of human dignity, but because various policy matters have combined to convince law-makers (and, in the case of common law rights, judges) that companies should have these rights.[93] Incorporation as a limited company has given the McArthurs certain protections, by removing their humanness from the picture and hiding it behind the veil of incorporation. Yet, by arguing that their Articles 9 and 10 rights would be violated if the law required them to produce a cake bearing a pro-same-sex-marriage message, they are seeking to rely on that humanness once again. If we may be forgiven the pun, they are trying to have their cake and eat it.

This raises an important issue to which, just like the indirect discrimination point, the Supreme Court gives no attention. Put simply, can the veil of incorporation be raised and lowered at will by the company's owners? Unfortunately, at no point in the Supreme Court's judgment (nor, indeed, in the Court of Appeal's) does the court distinguish between the company and the owners; they are treated as one and the same. The question, thus, not only goes unanswered, but unasked.

R (on the application of Miller) v The Prime Minister

The case of *Miller* came before the Supreme Court as a matter of urgency in September 2019.[94] The UK prime minister had sought a prorogation (suspension) of the UK Parliament that would, if lawful, have become the longest such prorogation in more than half a century.[95] The prime minister insisted that prorogation was both entirely normal and a necessary precursor to the government setting out a new legislative agenda. It was relevant that the session of Parliament being brought to an end had itself been unusually long (at just over 2 years). The applicant, Gina Miller, however, was concerned that the prime minister's true motive in proroguing Parliament was that it would enable him to press on with controversial plans in respect of the UK leaving the European Union (the process known as 'Brexit') without the hindrance of parliamentary scrutiny. As such, the applicant sought judicial review of the legality of the prime minister's formal advice on prorogation to the Queen (which is the mechanism by which, under the UK's constitutional arrangements, prorogation is sought).

The case is, constitutionally, the latest in a series of decisions where the courts have had to determine the lawful extent of the government's residual 'prerogative powers' (powers once exercised by the sovereign monarch, now de facto exercised by the government). Judicial review of the exercise of prerogative powers by the executive is highly controversial. As the UK constitution is uncodified, the legal background

---

93 In *R v Broadcasting Standards Commission, ex parte British Broadcasting Corporation* [2001] QB 885, Lord Mustill rejected the notion that a body corporate could claim a right to privacy as a human right. Although the case is not conclusive on the issue (Lord Woolf takes the opposite view, and Hale LJ equivocates), Lord Mustill's reasoning on the point (at [48]–[49]) is the most developed.
94 [2019] UKSC 41, [2019] 3 WLR 589.
95 Prorogation is a period of suspension that marks the end of one parliamentary session and, when the prorogation ends, the commencement of a new session.

concerning the nature and extent of these powers is often rather opaque; their exercise is traditionally controlled by convention rather than legal rules as such, but these conventions rely upon governments' adhering voluntarily to established practice. In the tense political climate in which the UK found itself at that time, where successive governments had, through their behaviour, eroded the effect of constitutional conventions, Miller argued that the courts should step in and regulate the use of this prerogative power through the establishment of a novel legal rule.

Both the lower courts and the Supreme Court had to grapple with three constitutionally significant questions. The first was whether the application was barred by statute – namely Article IX of the Bill of Rights 1688, which provides that 'proceedings in Parliament ought not to be impeached or questioned in any Court.' The second question was whether, if the Bill of Rights did not bar the application, the issue of prorogation was justiciable. Third, if the issue was justiciable, the question became whether the prime minister had acted lawfully. Implicit in the third question was a sub-question concerning the standards that the court would apply in order to determine legality.

The English divisional court had rejected Miller's application at first instance, finding that the matter was non-justiciable. However, the Inner House of the Court of Session in Scotland (Scotland's highest appellate court) had allowed a similar application by another applicant, Joanna Cherry, declaring the prorogation of Parliament unlawful.[96] In the Supreme Court, appeals from both these cases were joined together.

The Supreme Court unanimously held that the Bill of Rights did not preclude the Court from considering the case, and that, as a matter of common law, the legality of prorogation was justiciable. Having done so, it further found that the prorogation was unlawful as no good reason – indeed, no reason at all – had been advanced by the government as justification for the exceptional length of the prorogation.[97] Key to the Court's ruling was its creation of a novel legal rule governing prorogation: where prorogation has the effect (whether intended or not) of stymieing parliamentary scrutiny of the executive, that prorogation will not, without justification, be lawful.

The judgment (separate sections of which were drafted by Lady Hale and Lord Reed) is, as one would expect, written eruditely and gives the impression of being an uncontroversial statement of clear legal principles on the matters at hand. It has been hailed, in some quarters, as vindicatory, representing the triumph of legality over politics. As the former Court of Appeal judge Sir Stephen Sedley has said: 'as much by its unanimity … as by its reasoning, [the judgment] has re-lit one of the lamps of the UK's constitution: that nobody, not even the Crown's ministers, is above the law.'[98] Thus Sedley suggests that the unitary-ness of the judgment is what lends it its authority.

---

96 *Cherry v Advocate General* [2019] CSIH 49.

97 *Miller* (n 94) [61].

98 S Sedley, 'In court: the prorogation debacle' (2019) 41(19) *London Review of Books* 16.

226 *Thomas D.C. Bennett and Olivia Reilly*

But, as with the other two example cases we have considered, all is not as it seems. *Miller* is an enormously controversial judgment. The main areas of controversy are pointed up expertly by Martin Loughlin.[99] Central to his critique of the judgment is his assertion that it represents a paradigmatic shift in the way that the Court conceives of the British constitution. '[The judgment] claims that, rather than consisting of a set of rules and practices, the British constitution rests on some overarching framework of constitutional principles of which the Court acts as guardian.'[100] This, in his view, begs the question: the triumph of the legal constitution over the political (or politico-legal) one assumes the existence of the legal constitution in the first place. Loughlin is adamant that the highly legalised vision of the constitution that the Court has invoked in *Miller* represents a paradigmatic shift away from the politico-legal understanding of the constitution that has prevailed (albeit with various less radical shifts in emphasis) for decades.

Thus Loughlin's analysis drives home the point that we are making in this chapter: the *appearance* of cogency that a unitary judgment creates is not necessarily reflective of *actual* cogency. Rather than grappling with the complexities of the constitution conceived as a politico-legal artefact, where lawyers must struggle with the essentially political nature of the value judgments they are making when interpreting the constitution, the Supreme Court reconceptualises the constitution as an essentially *legal* artefact. As a legal artefact, the constitution appears far less complex. The standards involved in interpreting it cease to appear political and instead appear legal; they become cold, lifeless standards, easily applied to the matter at hand. In this way, the Court holds, with remarkable swiftness and sureness of footing, that the prime minister has given no legally recognisable reason (let alone a good one) for the length of the prorogation that he sought. Moreover, the Court presents this reconceptualisation not as if it was a reconceptualisation, but instead as if it was the clear and obvious way to conceptualise the constitution. In other words, it performs law's 'amazing trick' once again. The Court pursues simultaneously the two narratives that Fish tells us are integral to this trick, which is central to formalist legal method.[101] These are, first, a tendentious narrative in which authority (precedent) is cited and (re)interpreted in such a way as to dispose of the case at hand in a novel fashion, in a way that fundamentally alters the shape of the law in this field. Second, a parallel narrative is pursued that disavows the radicalism inherent in the first narrative. In this way, the Court effects a paradigmatic shift (according to Loughlin) while simultaneously claiming not to.

Our aim here is not to take sides over an intensely politically controversial matter. Instead, we simply say that *Miller* purports to be clear and straightforward, but it is in fact neither. It is acutely controversial. *In extremis*, it may be said – as

---

99 M Loughlin, 'The case of prorogation' (Policy Exchange 2019) 6. <https://policyexchange.org.uk/wp-content/uploads/2019/10/The-Case-of-Prorogation.pdf> 15 December 2019.
100 Ibid.
101 Fish (n 85).

Loughlin insists – to have paradigmatically shifted our understanding of the nature of the British constitution. At the very least, there are major questions as to the nature of the constitution, upon which a range of different views can legitimately be held and defended, that go wholly unaddressed in the judgment. To the extent that constitutional matters are addressed, only one perspective on them is offered.

The judgment itself thus gives no real sense of the degree of controversy surrounding the issue that the Court has been tasked with deciding. But, before we leave the case, we should mention one further feature of note. The judgment deploys a highly visual metaphor in order to communicate the effect of its judgment to its addressees. The order that had led to the prorogation after it was introduced into Parliament is said to be 'null and of no effect,' 'as if the Commissioners had walked into Parliament with a blank piece of paper.'[102] The metaphor is significant because it is visuocentric in exactly the way we associate with the Fancy. It purports to encapsulate the key elements of the Court's reasoning in a single image. The simplicity offered is obviously attractive: everyone can comprehend that a blank sheet of paper contains no valid instruction. But it belies the reality – that there is another, competing conceptualisation of the constitution (as a politico-legal artefact), according to which the Commissioners did not walk into Parliament with something akin to a blank piece of paper but instead with an entirely valid Order in Council for prorogation. Thus, we see again, this time laid bare, that the clarity and certainty that the Court purports to give us are beguiling, but misleading. In truth, the constitutional terrain upon which this decision sits is highly controversial, inescapably political, and not amenable to the quick and easy treatment that the unitary judgment tries to impress upon us.

Clarity and certainty?

The unitary judgments in *R v R*, *Lee v Ashers*, and *Miller* purport to give us certainty and clarity. *R* tells us that a man can indeed be guilty of raping his wife. *Lee* tells us that a couple who identify as Christians cannot be required by law to produce a cake bearing a pro-same-sex-marriage message that they feel is contrary to their religious beliefs. *Miller* confirms that the prime minister cannot prorogue Parliament for so long that its function as a check on the executive is undermined.

R v R is a remarkably short judgment, running to just eight pages, in which no mention is made of the retrospective nature of what the court is doing, nor of any potential impact upon the rule of law. *Lee* is longer, running to 30 pages. This adds to the impression that it is a detailed, considered statement of the law, increasing the confidence with which many will treat it. But it, too, contains significant flaws. It leaves wholly unanswered – even unrecognised – issues of acute controversy, including one (the issue of whether companies can exercise human rights) that sits in tension with statements from the same court on the same issue (albeit in a slightly different context). *Miller*, meanwhile, deals with its acutely politically and legally controversial constitutional conundrum in a brisk 71 paragraphs, unfolding across

---

102 *Miller* (n 94) [69].

228 *Thomas D.C. Bennett and Olivia Reilly*

just 24 pages. (For comparison, an earlier *Miller* case, in which the applicant successfully challenged the government's asserted power to trigger the UK's departure from the European Union under Article 50 of the Treaty on the Functioning of the EU, led the Supreme Court to issue multiple judgments – including three dissents – to the tune of 283 paragraphs across 98 pages.) But, in its briskness, the real controversies underlying the constitutional question before the court are seriously downplayed. As such, the only clarity and certainty provided by these cases are of a limited, simplistic, reductionist type. It is more apparent than real; more fanciful than reflective of the real complexity of the matters at hand.

Someone sceptical of our argument might well ask, at this point, whether the three cases upon which we have dwelt are really representative of common flaws in unitary judgments, or whether they are just memorable outliers. To such an objection, two points may be made. First, we do not say that all unitary judgments are, or are likely to be, flawed in this way. But we do say that there is a greater likelihood of these sorts of flaws going uncorrected if only one, unitary judgment is produced. This first point leads to a second. Flaws in individual judgments are, of course, not ideal. But the real problem here is the more frequent adoption of a practice that is designed to give the appearance of a level of certainty that is simply not achievable. Although we can point out flaws in individual cases – and we could give examples *ad nauseam* – of far larger concern is the return to the systemic prominence of an approach to judging that, rather than acknowledging the difficulties in achieving genuine clarity and certainty, actively promulgates the misleading impression that they are eminently achievable. We develop this point in the next section, in which we link Coleridge's account of visuocentrism to the pursuit of certainty inherent in legal formalism.

Formalism and the Fancy

Those who express a preference for unitary judgments overwhelmingly do so by making the argument (or, perhaps more commonly, the bald claim) that this type of univocal judicial utterance provides greater clarity and certainty than judgments featuring multiple voices (whether in concurrence or dissent).[103] Baroness Hale (as she then was) expressed such sentiments in *OBG v Allen*, saying that, '[t]here should be no doubt, and no room for argument, about what has been decided and why.'[104] This was certainly the motivation behind Carnwath LJ's (as he then was) calls for the House of Lords and Supreme Court to produce more unitary judgments and fewer multiple ones.[105] The Court of Appeal itself has made use of unitary judgments as its default approach for a number of years, on the basis that the practice 'reduces the material that has to be read, avoids the opportunity for differences of opinion and provides greater clarity.'[106] The kind of clarity aimed at

103 See, e.g., Neuberger (n 61).
104 *OBG* (n 62).
105 n 63.
106 Lord Phillips (Master of the Rolls), *Review of the Legal Year* 2001–02. See also R Munday, '"All for one and one for all": the rise to prominence of the composite judgment within the Civil Division of the Court of Appeal' (2002) 61 *CLJ* 321.

in such formalist thinking is of a particular kind, one related to the definition of 'clear' as '[e]asy to understand, fully intelligible, free from obscurity of sense' and 'free from doubt.'[107] In other words, a reductionist, simplistic notion of clarity, prioritising a lack of ambiguity over the recognition of complexity. As such, it ignores an alternative sense of clarity as transparency – as the presentation of the totality of a phenomenon in all its messy complexity.

Pursuit of a simplistic, formalist type of clarity and certainty provides a link between the unitary judgment practice and one of the core aims of legal formalism. For formalism assumes that it is possible to lay down legal pronouncements with absolute clarity (of this 'fully intelligible, free from doubt' sort). (Upon this presumption, formalism further counsels that doing so is desirable.) But Coleridge warns us to suspect claims to stability or clarity as limited and illusory, concealing a more complex truth. As such, Coleridge's work aligns broadly with core themes in the school of legal thought that arose in opposition to formalism and that counsels attentiveness to law's context, impact, and particularity: (American) legal realism. This should not surprise: Coleridge's accounts of the Imagination and the Fancy are broadly realist in nature.[108]

Clarity as transparency – focusing on understanding the totality of a phenomenon – is something that Coleridge tells us can be achieved only with the Imagination. It is only by rigorous commitment to detail that knowledge can be achieved:

> In order to understand a thing we must know all its component parts, and to be certain that we understand it, we must be certain that all the parts that belong to the thing are present to our mind, and that no others are imagined to be there.[109]

Unitary judgments undermine clarity as transparency in their pursuit of clarity as elimination of doubt.

The unity that Coleridge tells us the Imagination achieves is committed in its pursuit of unity in multeity to clarity as transparency. As such, we can link the Imagination to the pursuit of this more realist, non-formal type of clarity. For the Imagination is, as we noted earlier, 'a faculty devoted at once to unifying *and yet* to particularising,' thereby achieving a unity that does not reduce plurality into a single uniformity but brings together plurality within an unstable, progressive interconnection.[110]

---

107 'clear, adj, adv, and n' (*OED Online*, OUP December 2019) <www.oed.com/view/Entry/34078> accessed 15 December 2019.

108 MJ Kooy points out that Coleridge can be seen to display an affinity with realist political thought in the work that he (Coleridge) undertook drafting legal provisions for Malta in 1805. Kooy finds this affinity in Coleridge's willingness to manipulate rule of law principles in order to draft controversial provisions for reasons of political expediency. See 'Coleridge and the rule of law' in B Hough and H Davis, *Coleridge's Laws: A Study of Coleridge in Malta* (OpenBook 2009) xvi, xxiv.

109 ST Coleridge, *Logic* (JR de J Jackson ed, Princeton University Press 1981) 215.

110 Perry (n 28) 34.

230 *Thomas D.C. Bennett and Olivia Reilly*

As John Beer observes, Coleridge's 'ultimate gift to human thinking' was a 'gift for double perception, for thinking at more than one level'[111] (a skill also cultivated by lawyers for whom the 'talent for being beforehand with' their 'critics in analysing' themselves is also desirable).[112] Coleridge aspired, as Seamus Perry observes, 'to the very greatest and most comprehensive kind of coherence,'[113] yet his commitment to a 'strenuous and self-scrutinising imaginative life'[114] leaves him 'principally divided between the rival attractions of unity and division themselves.'[115] This complexity extended to his political thought. As David Erdman observes, 'he is never single-sided or single-minded but always both Jacobin and anti-Jacobin, Radical and Tory, poet and moralist, intermingled.'[116] Coleridge demonstrates the limitations of aspiring to unity as uniformity as a means to achieve authority, providing instead a model of a committed intellectual rigour, not content to omit or minimise in order to achieve an appearance of clarity.

Bruns argues that the law 'can only emerge in a space that is logically anarchic ... a place of "open indeterminacy" where the thing is suddenly otherwise than we thought.'[117] As such, he compares it to *Hamlet* – 'whatever makes us think, or anyhow think twice.'[118] The Imagination is capable of capturing this disruptive quality in the law, not reflecting a fanciful, formalist appeal to the appearance of stability and authority, but expressing the instability inherent in the law itself, closer to the Imagination in its disruptive processes than to the reductive stability and fixity associated with the Fancy. As the recently retired president of the Supreme Court Lady Hale observes extrajudicially (somewhat ironically, given her own proclivity, as president, for producing unitary judgments), without a full impression of the diversity within the Court's decision (the multiple perspectives and means of reaching a judgment, and acknowledgment of the complex points of law addressed), 'something distinctive would be lost.'[119] The word 'distinctive' is suggestive; derived from the Latin *distinguére* to 'separate, divide,'[120] it deftly captures the need to acknowledge the separate opinions of individual judges. It facilitates a recognition that what makes the court itself 'distinctive,' what lies at the basis of its authority, is the ability of its expert judges to achieve consensus, while at the same time taking individual 'responsibility for his or her own decision'

111 J Beer, *Romantic Influences: Contemporary - Victorian – Modern* (Palgrave Macmillan 1993) 165.
112 Perry (n 28).
113 Ibid 2.
114 Ibid 1.
115 Ibid 4.
116 D Erdman, 'Introduction' in ST Coleridge, *Essays on his Times* (D Erdman ed, Princeton UP, 1978) vol 3, lxv.
117 Bruns (n 4) 65.
118 Ibid.
119 Baroness Hale, 'Judgment writing in the Supreme Court' (Supreme Court First Anniversary Seminar, 30 September 2010) < https://www.supremecourt.uk/docs/speech_100930.pdf> accessed 1 November 2019.
120 'distinct, adj and n' (*OED Online*, OUP September 2019) <www.oed.com/view/Entry/55670> accessed 2 November 2019.

A *Coleridgean dystopia*   231

according to the judicial oath.[121] In the Court, as in society at large, 'a living *whole*' can only be achieved if each individual unites 'with the whole' but 'shall yet obey himself only and remain as free as before.'[122]

Coleridge's division between Imagination and Fancy has implications for language itself, revealed as he demonstrates the formal workings of the Fancy by analogy with written language: 'Life may be *inferred*, even as intelligence is from black marks on white paper – but the black marks themselves *are truly "the dead letter"*.'[123] Only in coadunation with 'life' and 'spirit' can the written word be freed from its objectified death and released from a restricted 'space of possibles' into one more attuned to principles, to human feeling, and to context.[124] In contrast to the limited, tightly constrained normative space provided by the Fancy, the Imagination reveals that texts (both legal and literary) are open to interpretative possibilities always already available to the reader in practice.[125] Coleridge's thought thus leaves open the possibility of a transition from the reified formal written law to the organic, unfolding manifestation of the state, the *living* law. The state is comprised, Coleridge argues, of 'two antagonist powers or opposite interests [...] those of permanence and progression'; 'the interest of permanence is opposed to that of progressiveness; but so far from being contrary interests, they, like the magnetic forces, suppose and require each other.'[126] The permanence of principle and the formal law combines with the progressive exercise of the free will to create a harmony of continuity and improvement that preserves continuity while ensuring progress and improvement. At this point of interpretation, law is released from the words on the page, the formal shape given by the Fancy to the concepts of the Understanding.

121 Ibid.
122 *Friend* (n 38) vol 1, 192.
123 *CN* vol 3 (n 27) 4066; original emphasis.
124 The phrase, the '*dead letter*', invokes a longstanding theological debate around the terms of 2 Corinthians 3:6, 'the letter killeth but the spirit giveth life,' and suggests the influence of John Milton, who argued that the Reformation had been necessary because 'men came to scan the scriptures by the letter, and in the covenant of our redemption, magnified the external signs more than the quickening power of the Spirit.' Similarly, for Coleridge, the distinction between letter and spirit is not 'between a carnal letter and a spiritual mystery hidden in allegories' but 'Calvin's distinction between outward, formal knowledge and inward, living apprehension' (H MacCallum, 'Milton and the figurative interpretation of the Bible' in M Nyquist and FG Mohamed (eds), *Milton and Questions of History: Essays by Canadians Past and Present* (University of Toronto Press 2012) 64). See Milton's *Tetrachordon*: 'Men of most renowned vertu have sometimes by transgressing, most truly kept the law; and wisest Magistrates have permitted and dispenc't it; while they lookt not peevishly at the letter, but with a greater spirit at the good of mankinde, if alwayes not writt'n in the characters of law, yet engrav'n in the heart of man by a divine impression' (The John Milton Reading Room, Dartmouth University <https://www.dartmouth.edu/~milton/reading_room/tetrachordon/genesis/text.shtml> accessed 5 April 2019).
125 See Mullender (n 36).
126 ST Coleridge, *On the Constitution* 24.

232　*Thomas D.C. Bennett and Olivia Reilly*

Here we see Coleridge's realist leanings. Echoing his distinction between spirit and letter, he asserted in 1814 that principle is the 'Aim, Rule, and Guide' of the law, a 'spirit' that provides continuity between former ('our ancestors') and current interpreters of the law. It is not inherent in the formal law, and so the law in practice depends on its application: 'Principle on its application to Practice must be limited & modified by circumstance, our Reason by our Common Sense.'[127] More boldly, in *The Friend*, Coleridge asserted that, 'the wisdom of Legislation consists in the adaptation of Laws to circumstances,' meaning that circumstances may arise where 'the spirit of the statute interpreted by the intention of the Legislator would annul the letter of it.'[128] As Holmes put it: 'The life of the law has not been logic; it has been experience':[129]

> The language of judicial decision is mainly the language of logic … But certainty generally is an illusion … Behind the logical form lies a judgment as to the relative worth and importance of competing legislative grounds, often an inarticulate and unconscious judgment, it is true, and yet the very root and nerve of the whole proceeding.[130]

For Holmes, like Coleridge, the source of 'moral truth' lies 'in the creative and unconscious processes of the individual mind,'[131] as implied in his acknowledgement of the 'inarticulate and unconscious judgment' that occurs 'Behind the logical form.' This resonates with Coleridge's suggestion that what matters is the law in practice – the interaction between codified rules, their underlying principles, the specific circumstances of the case at hand, and feelings profoundly connected

---

127　*CL* (n 54) vol 3, 537–8.
128　*Friend* (n 38) 246.
129　OW Holmes, Jr, *The Common Law* (Little Brown 1881) 1. Anne Dailey notes that Wendell Holmes, Jr was a frequent reader of Romantic writers, 'notably, Wordsworth, Coleridge, Carlyle and Goethe' (AC Dailey, 'Holmes and the romantic mind' (1998) 48 (3) *Duke Law Journal* 429, 431 <https://www.jstor.org/stable/1373058> accessed 2 October 2019). Dailey suggests that Holmes's definition of law as 'The prophecies of what the courts will do in fact, and nothing more pretentious' (OW Holmes Jr, 'The path of the law' (1897) 10 (8) *Harv LR* 457, 461) is underpinned by 'a view of human nature strongly reminiscent of eighteenth-century Romantic literature and philosophy' (Dailey 431). She observes that Holmes 'asserted the existence of such fundamental and nonempirical psychological concepts as unconscious motivations, instinctual desires, inner conflict, irrationality, imagination and transcendent faith in "the infinite"' (431); 'For Holmes, heroic greatness inhered in the lawyer's ability to harness his imaginative powers in pursuit of transcendent insight' (434). In highly Coleridgean fashion, Holmes's thought is, Dailey argues, animated by a 'conflict in his thought,' a 'struggle to develop a satisfying empirical approach to law that also accounted for the depth and complexity of human nature' (437). He 'rebelled against what he called the "insufficiency of *facts*"' suggesting Coleridge's criticism of 'matter-of-factness' as an attachment to stability and objectification – the products of the Fancy.
130　W Holmes, Jr, 'The Path of the Law' ibid.
131　Dailey (n 129) 431.

A Coleridgean dystopia   233

to morality. It is in the practice of the law that its 'life' or 'spirit' is found. Yet unitary judgments, in pursuit of clarity as elimination of doubt, seek to obscure these inarticulate and unconscious judgments taking place behind the logical form, or at least to reduce them so that only one such behind-the-form judgment might be discerned. The law's life is removed by the (Fancy-driven) determination to fix it, death-like, within a simplified form.

Despite these sorts of objections to its fanciful claims and aims, formalism nonetheless persists and is, today, resurgent. Its resurgence is made possible in part because the certainty and stability that it appears to provide – clarity as elimination of doubt – are persuasive and beguiling. The Fancy is attractive in the simplified version of mind it supplies and the apparently secure, fixed version of meaning it provides.

Because of its reliance on printed words, law is inherently highly susceptible to the attractions of the Fancy. When those words are used in such a fashion as to give an impression – an appearance – of clarity and certainty, masking those issues that remain unclear and uncertain, formalism's idol looms into view. Legal form-alism arises, in no small part, out of the empiricism against which Coleridge firmly set his stall and that he saw as rooted in the 'magical' lure of the Fancy. The empirical bias of the Fancy drives a determination to taxonomize and to codify legal norms, treating 'law' as a body of authoritative rules that is essentially distinct from the broader socio-political context out of which it emerges. Law, in short, is thought – in the eyes of formalists – to exist in its own world: a world of legal norms. This enables – and requires – formalists to draw sharp distinctions between, for example, matters of law and matters of politics (as the Supreme Court explicitly purports to do in *Miller*).[132]

Unitary judgments from our highest court attempt to separate both law from politics and law from judges (by removing their individuality), positing the appearance and, therefore, the possibility of an objective, univocal, fixed authority in the law. This is a practical manifestation of the formalist Fancy. Moreover, it exerts considerable influence, as it emanates from a place of authority and results in judgments that will generally be regarded, regardless of their merits or content, as binding statements of law.[133] When the Court speaks with one voice, the image of clarity and certainty that this creates is one that onlookers are given every incentive to believe is an accurate one.

There is also a clear link between the Fancy's drive towards simplification – attempting to fix and reduce ideas within minimised states – and a correlative thrust in the unitary judgment practice. Unitary judgments are designed to reduce matters of controversy within them to univocal states by fixing the *range* of mat-ters deemed relevant. This can be achieved simply by not mentioning matters that, on a less minimised view, would indeed have relevance to the decision at hand. Consider: in *R v R*, the House of Lords fixed the issues at play as relating solely to existing precedent on the question as to whether the ancient common law

132 See, e.g., *Miller* (n 94) [1].
133 By mainstream legal positivists, at least.

234   *Thomas D.C. Bennett and Olivia Reilly*

exemption for husbands from rape charges was still effective. In so doing, it limited the scope by removing from consideration the rule of law concerns to which we have drawn attention. Similarly, in *Lee v Ashers*, the Supreme Court fixed the case as one concerning individuals and their rights, minimalising by not considering whether the company, separately to its owners, might be in breach of statutory provisions on discrimination. Something similar happens in respect of constitutional controversy in *Miller*. Attempts to limit the materials of the law are an expression of the '(formalist) hope' that words can be ordered 'in such a way as to constrain what interpreters can then do with them.'[134] Purporting to provide certainty by omission is really an admission that certainty can only be provided by leaving things out. This reveals such 'certainty' to be illusory. It asserts the necessity of clarity, not as elimination of doubt, but as transparency.

Coleridge's Imagination presents a challenge to resurgent formalist orthodoxy, for he reminds us – perhaps uncomfortably – that the appearance of clarity is just that: an image provided by the Fancy that can only be achieved by minimising or simply ignoring the full intellectual complexity at play. This challenge should spur us to ask penetrating questions of unitary judgments and – just perhaps – to reconsider the practice of issuing them itself.

Escaping the Coleridgean dystopia:the disruptive Imagination

The rise of the unitary judgment practice in the first decade of the UK Supreme Court's existence has links to a resurgent formalism that is profoundly resonant with a world-view dominated by the Fancy. Coleridge's promotion of the Imagination as a corrective to this may be particularly fruitful if we can link it to an alternative legal practice. The obvious practice in which to seek such links is the practice of issuing multiple judgments (including both concurring and dissenting judgments).

For Coleridge, the Imagination provides a corrective to the Fancy's emphasis on fixity and certainty. It 'unfixes' the objects of the Fancy – 'dissolves, diffuses, dissipates, in order to re-create.'[135] A part of the Imagination's creative nature is, thus, necessarily disruptive in character.

The presence of multiple judgments in a case makes plain points of disagreement between the judges. This promotes transparency and undermines the misleading, idolatrous image of certainty and clarity promoted by the unitary judgment practice. But, in highlighting points of disagreement at least as much as it does points of concurrence, the practice of issuing multiple judgments is disruptive. It is, of course, this disruptiveness to which legal formalists, committed as they are to the notion that all legal disputes have a single 'right' answer, are opposed. Yet Coleridge tells us fixed concepts are only ever simplified versions of concepts that can only truly be understood when disrupted by the Imagination, which releases them from certainty into an unstable process connected to context,

134 Fish (n 85) 147.
135 *BL* (n 11) vol 1, 304.

subjective feeling, and unwritten principles. The American legal realists of the 20th century were committed to the notion that the law should not be some abstract, detached set of rules but should connect, in a very real fashion, to the lives of its addressees and to the social, political, and cultural context of the day.[136] Assuming this is indeed desirable, a case can be made for returning the practice of issuing multiple judgments to prominence by drawing on the importance of the Imagination as a corrective to the profound limitations of the Fancy, as elaborated by Coleridge.

Only once the mind has become freed from the limitations of the Fancy can it achieve knowledge of things 'in their essential powers,' in relation 'to other powers,' and in their unity, 'distinct yet indivisible.'[137] This further suggests the possibility that such mental emancipation can allow the individual to experience their subjectivity in relation to others in a harmonious community. The Imagination melts the image that had become the idol of contemporary philosophy and transforms it into something fluid, released from its finite boundaries, to reveal a 'living' meaning: it is 'the fusing power, that fixing unfixes, & while it melts & bedims the Image, still leaves in the Soul its living meaning.'[138] Meaning as transformative and re-creative can only be realised, not in the black marks on white paper, the formal stability of language printed on the page, but in the productive oscillatory instability of the Imagination. It is revealed only when objective fixity melts and recedes.

Within what he conceived as an organic process of interpretation and precedent, Coleridge reinforces his belief that knowing must be a process: 'Thought formed not fixed – the molten Being never cooled into a Thing.'[139] In an 1817 letter to Lord Liverpool, he complained that, whereas the 'ancients' were concerned with 'the birth of things,' 'the self-subsistence, yet interdependence, the difference yet Identity of the forms' or '*acts* of the world,' materialist philosophy limited knowing to a static, fixed visualisation of phenomena as *already made*. Under the supremacy of the Fancy, 'all fixed principles, whether grounded on reason, religion, law or antiquity, were to be undermined' by applying to them the 'criterion of the mere understanding, disguising or concealing the fact, that the rules which alone they applied, were abstracted from the objects of the senses, and applicable exclusively to things of quantity and relation.'[140] That this 'habit of thinking' influences the whole 'mass of our principles' suggests the risk of producing an inactive, unreformed public ripe for exploitation and liable to be moved by populism, converting thinking individuals to a 'mass.'

Kuiken argues that the theory of Imagination that Coleridge provides in *Biographia* further reveals the political risks he conceived in empirical thinking. He argues that Coleridge's division of Imagination into Primary and Secondary

136 K Llewellyn, 'Some realism about realism' (1931) 44 *Harvard LR* 1222.
137 *LHP* (n 5) vol 1, 193.
138 *CN* vol 3 (n 27) 4066.
139 ST Coleridge, *The Notebooks of Samuel Taylor Coleridge* vol 2 (K Coburn ed, Routledge & Kegan Paul 1962) 3159.
140 *Friend* (n 38) vol 1, 439.

aspects represents an act of 'withdrawal,'[141] whereby the Imagination can be enacted and yet also withdrawn from the space of representation.[142] This, he asserts, is connected to Coleridge's concept of Reason as similarly characterised by withdrawal, so that it cannot be mistakenly identified with a specific sovereign (the people or the monarch), giving that sovereign absolute power as the embodiment of absolute reason.[143] Such a confusion in the collective Imagination emerges from the idolatry of the visual, mistaking the conditional embodiment of the unconditional for its absolute manifestation, the letter for the spirit of the law, and the representative of sovereignty for its absolute ground. Thus, Coleridge's critique of the Fancy in the phrase the 'despotism of the eye'[144] invokes not only its tyranny over the mind, but also the potential this power has to encourage political absolutism by attempting to posit the sovereign as the embodiment of Reason. Underlying such an assumption is the belief that the principles underlying the law and politics can be embodied, reflected in Coleridge's robust objection to a written constitution, which would break the link between permanence and progression and suggest that the complexity of the constitution can be defined, limited, fixed.[145] Coleridge argues in *The Friend* that the National Assembly had 'intoxicated' the people of France with 'high-sounding phrases' ('the *inalienable sovereignty* of the people') and led them on to the 'wild excesses and wilder expectations' of the Revolution and the Terror, which, disappointing their expectations, prepared the way for 'military despotism.'[146]

This is the emergent dystopia Coleridge could foresee. And there are indications that it is coming to pass today. Populism is on the rise across the globe. In the face of the troubled times in which we live, people demand certainty, even as they vote for policies destined to provide instability (of which the UK's referendum on EU membership in 2016 is a prime example). Short, sharp, inaccurate (and sometimes entirely meaningless) political slogans succeed in attracting votes where more detailed, albeit more accurate, statements fail to land. During troubled times such as these, support for policies likely to deliver instability is nevertheless related closely to a desire for certainty. The desire has its roots in a human tendency to seek out tighter social norms when faced with social instability.[147] The nationalism underpinning the pro-Brexit vote, for example, and the election of the overtly nationalist 45th president of the United States are manifestations of this desire.

141 Kuiken (n 16) 89.
142 Kuiken (n 16) 97.
143 Kuiken (n 16) 103–4.
144 *BL* (n 11) vol 1, 107.
145 Coleridge, *On the Constitution*.
146 Ibid, vol 1, 194. See Kuiken (n 16) 107–8.
147 MJ Gelfand et al, 'Differences between tight and loose cultures: A 33-nation study' (2011) 332 *Science* 1100; M Gelfand, *Rule Makers, Rule Breakers: How Culture Wires Our Minds, Shapes Our Nations and Drives Our Differences* (Robinson 2018), 69–72. Gelfand helpfully summarises her research in 'Here's the science behind the Brexit vote and Trump's rise' (*The Guardian*, 17 September 2018) <https://www.theguardian.com/commentisfree/2018/sep/17/science-behind-brexit-vote-trump> accessed 15 December 2019.

The Supreme Court came into being in 2009, in the immediate aftermath of a global financial crisis and with the UK embroiled in two major military conflicts (in Afghanistan and Iraq). Throughout its first decade in existence, major political turmoil has unfolded within the UK (two general elections failing to deliver a majority government and a referendum on EU membership with profound constitutional implications). Undoubtedly, the Court has been living, as has everyone in the UK, through troubled times. Against that background – that context – it is no surprise that the Court should adopt a practice with the aim of providing greater certainty. For, as the American realist jurist and scholar Benjamin Cardozo observed, judges are no more able to escape that instinctive 'stream of tendency' within each of us 'which gives coherence and direction to thought and action' than other mortals.[148] To seek out tighter social norms – providing greater certainty and stability – in troubled times has been shown to be a natural psychological reaction.[149] But the formal certainty – the clarity as elimination of doubt – that the unitary judgment practice achieves is seriously lacking in substance. It is a lifeless abstraction, a fixed image of certainty that seeks to rest the authority of the court on visual idols rather than a recognition that its power lies in its operation, in the collective expertise of its judges *as individuals* in practice.

Coleridge tells us that, exceeding the operation of the aggregative Fancy and the conceptualising Understanding, the mind must embrace the instability of the Imagination's mediation between subjective and objective – its capacity to move beyond the fixed and the known. Relying on the appearance of consensus, unitary judgments eliminate (or at least hide) this mediating process from the Court's output, leaving fixity in its place. The practice shifts attention away from the realities of dissent (and differing but concurring reasons) as part of the achievement of consensus, and of disunity as part of an imaginative approach to unity. In so doing, it obscures the very source of its authority in an attempt to secure its fixity and certainty.[150] The unitary judgment becomes a depersonalised, collective expression of a formal consensus, a stability that inheres only in those words on the page. Meanwhile, by omitting alternative lines of argument (both concurring and dissenting), the practice prevents the law's addressees from seeing – and consequently from understanding – the continuity of the law as organic progress. Coleridge argues in his *Lay Sermons* that the 'antidote' to the exaggeration of the powers of the Fancy 'must be sought for in the collation of the present with the past.'[151] We must be Janus-faced, capable of achieving progress alongside continuity. Without 'antecedent knowledge,' as he explains in *The Statesman's Manual*, 'Experience itself is but a cyclops walking backwards, under the fascination of the past.'[152]

---

148 BN Cardozo, *The Nature of the Judicial Process* (Yale University Press 1991) 12.
149 See Gelfand et al and Gelfand (n 147).
150 Lee (n 78) makes an argument in defence of concurring judgments that raises a similar point about the usefulness of concurring judgments in buttressing a majority conclusion.
151 *LS* (n 3) 10.
152 *LS* (n 3) 43.

Conclusion

We do not say that all unitary judgments are individually problematic. There are certainly instances in which, despite the fact that they cannot provide absolutely certainty or clarity, they are helpful in giving a relatively firm sense of direction to the law's addressees. Nor is it our intention to advocate disagreement for disagreement's sake; where judges are genuinely able to find consensus, they should express that consensus. Our concern with the unitary judgment practice is that the seductiveness of its false promises to secure clarity and certainty may see it rise, unchecked, to a position of dominance within the judicial landscape. For, although the impact of suppressed disagreement within a single case may not be widely felt, its impact across the body of cases affected by this resurgent practice is likely to be profound. Just as judges must be free to express consensus, so they must be free also to express not only strong dissent but also minor disagreement, even if only as to the route by which one reaches an agreed conclusion. The alternative is that the institutional pressure to produce unitary judgments insidiously stifles debate, which – as we have seen – can lead to important legal issues going not only unanswered, but wholly unrecognised. This does a disservice to all. But it will be most keenly felt by the law's addressees, who will have to live in the sort of visuocentric, formalist dystopia that Coleridge foresaw. Fortunately, he bequeathed to us an account of the tools needed to comprehend the need to escape it, and to prosecute that escape. It is up to the judiciary now to use them.

13 Against the failure of the legal imagination[1]

Literary narratives, Brexit, and the fate of the Anglo-British constitution

Matteo Nicolini

VERONA UNIVERSITY, ITALY AND NEWCASTLE UNIVERSITY, UK

In *Reimagining Britain*, the Archbishop of Canterbury Justin Welby reflects on how Brexit – that is, the United Kingdom's decision to withdraw from the EU – should be addressed. According to him, Britain is undergoing a 'rare' constitutional process of change, which gives us 'The opportunity, necessity and challenge to reimagine our society.' This process 'requires ... wide-leadership and imagination to grasp it,' which cannot be 'achieved by ample resources, but by a change of mood, a decision, or a historic change ... It cannot be forced but may be seized,' or, as the case may be, 'missed.'[2]

Legal scholars may consider it unusual to begin an essay on the post-Brexit British constitution by quoting Welby's book. Nevertheless, the book perfectly grasps what this constitutional moment means to Britain.[3] The Archbishop suggests we approach Brexit *by a change of mood*, which should assist us both in reconciling Britain's legal tradition with the current state of affairs and in infusing the politico-legal discourse with a new constitutional creativity.[4] The present situation demands powerful acts of imagination: 'decision' and 'historic change.'

---

1 This chapter has grown out of, and benefited from responses to, papers I gave at the Annual Conference of the Society of Legal Scholars in 2018 (Queen Mary University of London), in Newcastle Law School in 2019 (to the Eldon Society), and in City University's Law School (while participating in a symposium on Law in Troubled Times in 2019). I have also benefited from the responses to earlier drafts of this chapter made by Nicolas Besly, Francesco de Cecco, Ruth Houghton, Richard Mullender, and Ian Ward.

It pertains to the activities of the Research Team on 'Decision-making processes and sources of law,' which is part of the research excellence project Law, Changes and Technology,' Ministry of Education, and carried out by the Law School of the University of Verona.

2 J Welby, *Reimagining Britain: Foundations for Hope* (Bloomsbury 2018) 5.

3 On 'constitutional moments' see BA Ackerman, *We the People: Foundations* (Belknap Press of Harvard University Press 1991).

4 BA Ackerman, 'Constitutional politics/constitutional law' (1989) 99 *Yale LR*, 456–58, 503–07.

240 *Matteo Nicolini*

This chapter contributes to the conversation. First, it challenges the legal positivistic approach usually applied to Brexit. Second, it goes beyond the limits marked by legal studies and engages in cross-disciplinary investigations in order to ascertain how Brexit has an impact on the concepts that underpin the British constitution: the common-law legal tradition (the past), constitutional complexity (the present), and the legal imagination (the future).

This means that the essay has to reappraise the concept of 'complexity,' the transformative effects of which might support Britain's transition towards the post-Brexit discourse. Throughout British constitutional history, complexity has traditionally been managed by acts of imagination – which, in constitutional terms, count as *acts of legal imagination*. As this essay seeks to demonstrate, British constitutional creativity has accommodated complexity according to a two-level pattern: imagination-legislation or, as the case may be, invention-positivism.

My contribution will be that of a comparative legal scholar. When assessing how Brexit affects the Anglo-British Constitution,[5] I will employ the possibilities comparative law offers for cross-disciplinary research, the 'expansive view' of which leads to grasp 'the truest expression' of the 'essence and potentials' of Brexit.[6] To this end, any full understanding of Brexit must entail a full understanding of the underlying principles of the context in which it operates – that is, the common-law legal tradition.

Veering towards the extremes: Brexit between legalism and politics

Much has been written about Brexit. The subject has indeed attracted much debate among lawyers. The details need not detain us here;[7] suffice it to say that it has a huge impact on how scholars conceive of the British constitution, and that the debate has veered towards the extremes: *politics* and *legalism*.

The difficulties British constitutional agents had to confront account for such a polarisation. First, the UK Supreme Court ruled on how Article 50 Treaty on the European Union (TEU) should be triggered.[8] In replying to the preliminary ruling from the Court of Session in *Wightman*, the EUCJ allowed the UK to unilaterally revoke its intention to withdraw from the EU.[9] The EU apex court has thus added layers of complexity to Brexit. In a sort of 'compulsion to grand

---

5 I owe this term to I Ward, *The English Constitution. Myths and Realities* (Hart 2004) 2, 24, 125, 144.

6 R Weisberg, *Poetics: And Other Strategies of Law and Literature* (Columbia University Press 1992) 227. For more on the potentials of comparative law in cross-disciplinary research, see VG Curran, 'Dealing in difference: comparative law's potential for broadening legal perspectives' (1998) 46 *AJCL* 657.

7 See G Wilson, 'Making sense of Brexit: the legal, political and global context' (2019) 5 *Revista General de Derecho Público Comparado* 1–35.

8 See *R (Miller) v Secretary of State*, *R (Webster) v Secretary of State*, and *Wightman & Others v Secretary of State*, respectively [2017] UKSC 5; [2018] EWHC 1543 (Admin); [2018] CSOH 61. See D Campbell, '*Marbury v. Madison* in the U.K.: Brexit and the creation of judicial supremacy' (2018) 39 *Cardozo Law Review* 921.

9 Case C-621/18 *Andy Wightman v Secretary of State* [2018] ECLI:EU:C:2018:999.

Against the failure of the legal imagination   241

politics,' it intruded upon the dynamics of the British constitution and performed as one of its legal actors.[10]

Second, the notice of withdrawal from the EU and any revocation of that intertwine with the agenda of British representative institutions. This is apparent in the law-making process: it is sufficient to remember the enactments of both the European Union (Withdrawal) Act (EUWA) 2018 and the EUWA 2019, the tumultuous parliamentary proceedings on the Trade Bill 2017–2019, the multiple votes rejecting the Withdrawal Agreement, the approval of The European Union (Withdrawal) (No. 2) Act (EUWA 2) 2019, and the new Withdrawal Agreement signed in October 2019.[11]

There is also the advice given by the Privy Council to Her Majesty to prorogue Parliament. As it frustrated parliamentary scrutiny over ministerial responsibility in managing Brexit, the Supreme Court declared it 'unlawful' and 'void and of no effect,' thus adding fuel to the ongoing political debate.[12] As a consequence, Parliament authorised its own dissolution by passing the Early Parliamentary General Election Act (EPGE) 2019. The general election, which was held on 12 December 2019, then returned a landslide Conservative majority in the House of Commons. Under the aegis of PM Boris Johnson, Conservatives promised to 'Get Brexit Done' by passing the European Union (Withdrawal Agreement) Act 2020 (EUWA 2020).

The UK left the EU on January 31, 2020; but there is still room for constitutional speculation.

Focusing on parliamentary legislation, the EUWA 2018 confirms that the constitutional debate has veered towards *politics* and *legalism*. The Act will secure both continuity and discontinuity when 'exit day' becomes part of British constitutional reality. Continuity refers, for example, to the retention of EU law in force on 'exit day,'[13] whereas discontinuity points to several tenets of EU law: with a few minor exceptions, the principle of supremacy of EU law, the binding force of the EUCJ precedents, the Charter of Fundamental Rights, and the rule in *Francovich* will cease to be part of UK law after exit day.[14]

There is something intriguing in such predicaments. The EUWA 2018 retrospectively acknowledges the supremacy of EU law, in relation to which it codifies the doctrine of judicial precedent. Since *London Street Tramways* and the *Practice Statement*,[15] we have constantly been taught that announcements of common-law principles are 'narrative aspects of judicial opinions,' which ought not to be left in

---

10 R Mullender, 'The European constitution and "the compulsion to grand politics"' in NW Barber, M Cahill, and R Ekins (eds), *The Rise and Fall of the European Constitution* (Hart 2018), 208.

11 See Trade Bill HC Bill (2017–19) [122].

12 The advice given by the Prime Minister in his capacity as Privy Counsellor on 28 August 2019 was quashed in *R (on the application of Miller) (Appellant) v The Prime Minister (Respondent), Cherry and others (Respondents) v Advocate General for Scotland (Appellant) (Scotland)* [2019] UKSC 41 [69].

13 EUWA 2018, s 2(1) and s 6(1) for the interpretation of retained EU law.

14 EUWA 2018, s 5, s 6(4), sch 1(4).

15 *London Street Tramways Co Ltd v London County Council* [1898] AC 375; *Practice Statement* [1966] 1 W.L.R. 1234 (HL).

the hands of legislators.[16] On the one hand, the EUWA 2018 ties together common-law principles and the supremacy of EU law as already recognised in the 'Factortame saga.'[17] On the other, it styles the 'rule in *Francovich*' after the fashion of the common law before deliberately discontinuing the 'right in domestic law ... to damages in accordance with the [same] rule in Francovich.'[18]

The EUWA 2018 is more an exercise in futility than one in procedural constitutional creativity. By merely referring to parliamentary procedure, the Act is saturated with a profound lack of imagination.[19] The Act was passed before the Withdrawal Agreement was finalised. As it solely intended to withdraw the UK from the EU, to transfer most EU law into UK law, and to provide a process for amending any such transferred law, it was beyond its scope to make provision for new arrangements post-Brexit. Despite this, the Act makes provision for a withdrawal agreement;[20] legal changes to give effect to the Withdrawal Agreement were due to be included in a separate bill.

Anxiety is apparent when we consider how Brexit affects the British territorial constitution.[21] Not only is the EUWA 2018 vague on how the Irish border should be managed, but its backstop, which remains unsettled notwithstanding the new Withdrawal Agreement,[22] is also imbricated with major parliamentary dynamics. Furthermore, as the EU is a multilayered integration process, the withdrawal will also affect the subnational communities of Wales and Scotland. This explains why their devolved institutions have tried to secure legal continuity by enacting their legislation.[23] As the reference of the Scotland Bill to the Supreme Court has demonstrated, judicial and parliamentary constitutional creativity strongly disagrees with the territorial constitution. According to the Court's

---

16 Weisberg (n 6) 10.

17 See E Deards, 'The Factortame saga: the final chapter' (1999) 8 *Nottingham LJ* 101.

18 EUWA 2018, s 4; sch 1, s 5(1).

19 EUWA 2018, s 13 (parliamentary proceedings), s 17 (refugee protection), s 18 (customs arrangements) and s 19 (interaction with EU law and agencies). The EUWA 2019 exhibits the same lack of imagination.

20 s 13 EUWA 2018.

21 s 3 of the Northern Ireland (Executive Formation etc) Act 2019 was meant to preserve parliamentary scrutiny in case a no-deal Brexit was likely to be delivered on 31 October 2019. On the territorial constitution, see M Nicolini, 'Reforming the territorial constitution in Italy: some reflections on durability and change' in Gabriele Ables and Jan Battke (eds), *Regional Governance in the EU. Regions and the Future of Europe* (Edward Elgar 2019).

22 EUWA 2020. See also Sylvia de Mars and others, *Bordering Two Unions: Northern Ireland and Brexit* (Policy Press 2018).

23 SP Bill 28 UK Withdrawal from the European Union (Legal Continuity) (Scotland) Bill [as amended at Stage 2] Session 5 (2018); Law Derived from the European Union (Wales) Act 2018 (anaw 3) as repealed by The Law Derived from the European Union (Wales) Act 2018 (Repeal) Regulations 2018, SI 2018/1211, reg 2. See also M Keating, 'Brexit and the territorial constitution of the United Kingdom' (2018) 98 *Droit et société* 59–69.

positivist approach, 'reimagining Britain in the aftermath of Brexit' is a subject matter that falls within the legislative competences of the UK Parliament.[24]

Legalism and *politics* also affect the exit date, which is punctiliously established by the EUWA 2018.[25] The Act exhibits *relaxed political tactics*, as the definition can be amended by regulation.[26] The multiple rejections of the first withdrawal agreement and the delays in approving the 2019 agreement made these tactics go above and beyond the most lucrative political imagination. The exit day has been amended three times so far, and, under s. 2 EPGE 2019, a general election took place on 12 December 2019.[27] This prevented the UK from crashing out of the EU without an agreement but, at the same time, made the UK take part in the EU parliamentary elections, thus adding another layer of complexity to Brexit.

Organising communities: Brexit and the lack of political invention

Brexit has added fuel to the fire of the dispute on the nature of the British constitution.[28] I assume that the British context is 'politico-legal rather than purely legal';[29] consequently, it is impossible to assess Brexit within the realm of pure constitutional speculation.

Welby acutely grasps the point: Brexit will require changes

> in how Britain works in terms of its relationships with the rest of the world. The British vision for our diversity and for human flourishing needs establishing in the context of our past, the threats and difficulties of the present, and in faithfulness to our future.[30]

Brexit is *the* current 'organising theme' within the British community. Not only does this community display attentiveness to the organising theme, but it is also *à la recherche* of a renovated 'morally eligible foundation on which to organise [its] practical affairs.'[31] As noted in the introductory paragraph, Brexit will affect the

---

24 *The UK Withdrawal From The European Union (Legal Continuity) (Scotland) (rev 2)* [2018] UKSC 64.
25 EUWA 2018, s 20.
26 EUWA 2018, s 20(4).
27 The European Union (Withdrawal) Act 2018 (Exit Day) (Amendment) Regulations 2019, SI 2019/718, reg 2; The European Union (Withdrawal) Act 2018 (Exit Day) (Amendment) (No. 2) Regulations 2019, SI 2019/859, reg 2. The European Union (Withdrawal) Act 2018 (Exit Day) (Amendment) (No. 3) 2019, SI 1423/2019, reg. 2.
28 See R Mullender, 'Transmuting the politico-legal lump: Brexit and Britain's constitutional order' (2018) 39 *Cardozo Law Review* 1020; JE Kushal Murkens, 'Democracy as the legitimating condition in the UK constitution' (2018) LS 38 42. See also JAG Griffith, 'The political constitution' (1979) *MLR* 42 1.
29 R Mullender, 'The meaning of *Miller*: a meditation on the politics of the legal constitution' (2017) 22 *Revista General de Derecho Público Comparado* 3.
30 Welby (n 2) 10.
31 R Mullender, 'Context, contingency and the law of negligence (or from islands to islands of time)' (1997) *Bracton Law Journal* 29 25.

244   *Matteo Nicolini*

politico-legal concepts that lie at the heart of the British constitution. In particular, the 'idea of a political or legal imagination' will be central to the post-Brexit scenario. The same idea of law and 'the extent to which we accept it as valid … rests … in our collective and individual political imagination.'[32]

This reappraisal might also give rise to difficulties. The change in how politico-legal concepts interact has some bearing on the socio-economic context, which is experiencing challenges accentuated by the political vagueness and the legalistic solutions of the EUWA 2018. This encourages societal fragmentation and polarisation. Within this context, global mobilisation, labour migration movements, and economic freedom of movement of capital and goods generate even sharper cross-cutting cleavages in the intersections of law, governance, and societies.[33]

Finally, the debate discloses a *lack of political invention*. Again, the vagueness enshrined in the EUWA 2018 points to the inability of British representative institutions to manage the 2016 referendum result. This sits at odds 'with the Burkean view of representative democracy, which requires that while listening to representations of constituents, an elected representative must not surrender his judgment to theirs.'[34] The prorogation of Parliament in order to deliver a 'no deal Brexit' was deemed impracticable, as it was able to inflict a deep wound on responsible government.[35]

Brexit has raised difficulties that were unforeseen in the immediate aftermath of the 2016 referendum; such difficulties should be tackled with invention and pragmatism. There is indeed

> a link between our policies and expressed values and the deep magic is what enables us to embrace change without losing all continuity with the past or the ability to make sense of the facts before us.[36]

I will now address this 'deep magic' – that is, the British legal imagination – in order to reappraise Brexit and its legal consequences. In order not to lose 'all continuity with the past,' I will consider it within the context in which these consequences take place: that is, the common-law tradition.

---

32 I Ward, *Shakespeare and the Legal Imagination* (Butterworths 1999) 1.
33 On these concepts, see M Nicolini, 'The constitutional implications of democracy in governing complex societies' (2017) 21 *Revista General de Derecho Público Comparado* 5–16.
34 Wilson (n 6) 12. Nicolini, 'Implications' (n 33) 18, argues that such a departure from Burkean view is made possible because 'Pluralistic contemporary societies lack … homogeneity. The governance of societal complexity … is thus unattainable through representative government alone.'
35 S Fowles, 'Can the prime minister prorogue Parliament to deliver a no deal Brexit?' (10 June 2019) UK Const L Blog <https://ukconstitutionallaw.org/> accessed 12 July 2019.
36 Welby (n 2) 16.

'Reimagining will inevitably happen': challenging the failures of legal imagination

The lack of social and legal imagination in how Brexit has been managed so far is also triggered by the 'resurgent formalism' in legal studies. This has increased 'the focus on law as a form of rational, reasoned science,'[37] where legal concepts are 'value-neutral' and 'objective.'[38]

Legal imagination and complexity do not fit into this legalistic approach to the law. The resurgent formalism does not require acts of legal imagination, but *acts of simplification*, which reduce the inherent complexity of the world and, therefore, strip away 'whatever in the outside world' does not match the Cartesian mind or 'is tedious and beyond one's capacity to master.'[39]

Alan Watson terms these acts 'failures of the legal imagination.' They are also the failures of legal positivists, who remove 'elements from earlier theories' – the pragmatism inherent in English legal culture – 'without realizing that the fragment left' – that is, the piece of legislation that is the EUWA 2018 – 'cannot bear its own weight.'[40]

There is indeed a sense of 'disarticulation' in how British political agents have dealt with Brexit so far. This vagueness reminds me of the 'mental fog' that, in Oakeshott's opinion, prevents 'political activity' from understanding the world. It resembles 'A mind [that is] fixed and callous to all subtle distinctions.' Hence, 'emotional and intellectual habits become bogus from repetition and lack of examination, unreal loyalties, delusive aims, false significances are what political action involves.'[41]

This disarticulation also stems from the sectionalism that political parties display. If it turns out to be a type of 'societal fragmentation,' complexity becomes the cause of Brexit. Within this confused scenario, local actors – not to mention the forces of globalisation – seek to settle uncertainty, and leadership develops its own policies – even the most radical ones – in order to face the state of flux.[42] Not only does this undermine the constitution as *the* safe normative space, but it also boosts the 'creation of spaces of collective rebellion' in the midst of the current state of affairs.[43] In so doing, however, public leaders transform the cause of the problem into the same presupposition (the

---

37 E Jones, 'Transforming legal education through emotions' (2010) 38 *LS* 451–52. I owe the expression 'resurgent formalism' to Thomas Bennet.

38 See TA Smith, 'Neutrality isn't neutral: on the value-neutrality of the rule of law' (2011) 4 *Washington University Jurisprudence Review* 51; K Greenawalt, *Law and Objectivity* (OUP 1992).

39 DL Patey, 'Swift's satire on "science" and the structure of Gulliver's Travels' (1991) 58 *ELH* 816.

40 A Watson, *Failures of the Legal Imagination* (University of Pennsylvania Press 1988) 124–5.

41 M Oakeshott, 'The claims of politics' (1939–40) *Scrutiny* 8 148. See E Corey, 'Worlds of experience: aesthetics' in E Podoksik (ed), *The Cambridge Companion to Oakeshott* (CUP 2012) 101–2.

42 If considered as a confused scenario, complexity might also frustrate contractual obligations, as in *Canary Warf (Bp4) T1 Ltd. v European Medicines Agency* [2019] EWHC 335 (Ch). See W Day, 'Isn't Brexit frustrating? [2019] *CLJ* 270 (note).

43 See R Mullender, 'There is no such thing as a safe space' (2019) 82 *MLR* 549. On collective rebellion when confronting the state of flux, see D Silver, 'Everyday radicalism and the democratic imagination: dissensus, rebellion and utopia' (2018) 6

246 *Matteo Nicolini*

scenario) of the policies they might adopt. This means that, following Brexit, complexity will be so deeply imbricated both in the politico-legal constitution and in the social context that public leaders will have difficulty in finding a viable legal solution for it. This will add additional layers of complexity: Brexit

> requires a renewal of values, a reinvention and reshaping of national purpose that is deliberate and integrated with actions at every level, which is reflective of the technological, social, moral, and religious contexts.[44]

As Welby states, 'Reimagining will inevitably happen': without any positive acts of legal imagination, the alternative will be both social and legal disquietude. If Britain does not manage Brexit and its social, political, and legal consequences, the acts of imagination will 'occur thoughtlessly through the mere passage of time, in which case it is likely to be bad.'[45] The societal context requires these acts of legal imagination in order to frame renovated relations between state and society for the post-Brexit scenario.

A procedural state of mind: managing complexity by acts of legal imagination

Such acts of imagination are made possible because complexity, which is usually considered part of the problem, is inherent in British legal and constitutional history. Britain has always been able to manage complexity by acts of constitutional creativity, because she possesses what I term a 'procedural' state of mind, the origins of which are deeply rooted in her legal culture. This mind gives primacy to 'procedural creativity,' which means that not only do acts of imagination reveal a particular attentiveness to contingencies, but that they also cope with them. Procedural attentiveness, which has governed the complex evolution of the common law, is 'substantive law administered in a given form of action.'[46]

This chapter is not another legal historical essay on the evolution of the Anglo-British constitution. In contrast, my purpose is limited in scope: as a comparative legal scholar, I intend to complement my research by setting it in its socio-legal historical context. Maitland vividly upheld such a methodological approach: 'History involves comparison,' and the 'lawyer who knew nothing and cared nothing for any system but his own hardly came in sight of the idea of legal history.'[47]

As the legal historical approach upholds, the United Kingdom developed as a 'complex' constitutional system where legal diversity flourished. On the British

> *Politics and Governance* 161–68; Extinction Rebellion, *This Is Not A Drill. An Extinction Rebellion Handbook* (Penguin 2019).

44 Welby (n 2) 19.
45 Ibid.
46 FW Maitland, *The Forms of Action at Common Law* (AH Chaytor and WJ Whittaker eds, CUP 1936) 3.
47 FW Maitland, *Why the History of English Law Is Not Written: An Inaugural Lecture Delivered in the Art School at Cambridge on 13th October 1888* (CUP 1888) 11.

Against the failure of the legal imagination 247

Isles, the legal system of England and Wales coexisted alongside those of Scotland and Ireland; in the colonial era, the Westminster Parliament outlined a constitutional design whereby the most varied legal traditions of the world were accommodated under the guidance of imperial legislation.

The history of both the British Empire and the Commonwealth has been a history of reimagination. For example, the American Revolution put an end to both the 'Transatlantic Constitution' and the biggest trade market in the world[48]: 'exiting' the Empire implied 'exiting' the British customs union. Situated outside the British global market from 1783 onwards, the United States were put 'on the same footing as the ships of any European country in carrying to England the products of any other European country': 'Ignorance of this fact gave rise to one of [the] minor grievances against the British system.'[49] This did not prevent the United States, however, from reimagining their own future through a process that led to the Americanisation of the common law and its translation 'into some form of a written code, or digest, which would be concise and comprehensive enough' under the authored text of the US Constitution.[50]

The partition of the British Raj entailed negotiations and ratification of withdrawal agreements with India and Pakistan – that is, new, independent countries.[51] As with Brexit, there was not just a matter of British 'retained law'; independence also undermined the Empire's 'customs union' and 'the uniformity of the common commercial policy,' the pre-emptive effects of which were similar to those laid down in Article 207 TFEU.[52]

Unlike in the case of Brexit, the United States and the British Commonwealth were able to reconceptualise themselves by acts of legal imagination.

Imagination, reinvention, and the British 'manufacturing tradition'

Whereas history helps us to detect the non-legal variables that may affect the legal system, comparative law brings them to the fore. Non-legal variables are seldom value-neutral; on the contrary, they usually enforce specific agendas and trigger changes in the realm of the law. Owing to its critical approach,[53] the comparative

---

48 SM Bilder, *The Transatlantic Constitution. Colonial Legal Culture and the Empire* (MIT Press 2004).

49 Cf. DO McGoveny, 'The Navigation Acts as applied to European trade' (1904) 9 *The American Historical Review*, 725–730.

50 See WE Nelson, *Americanization of the Common Law: The. Impact of Legal Change on Massachusetts Society, 1760–1830* (Harvard UP 1975); P Schneck, *Rhetoric and Evidence. Legal Conflict and Literary Representation in U.S. American Culture* (de Gruyter 2011) 120.

51 See DK Coffey, '"The right to shoot himself": secession in the British Commonwealth of Nations' (2018) 39 *Journal of Legal History* 117.

52 On such pre-emptive effects see Case C-305/18 *FENS spol. s r.o. v Slovenská republika – Úrad pre reguláciu siet'ových odvetví* [2018] ECLI:EU:C:2018:986. See also BA Melo Araujo, 'UK post-Brexit trade agreements and devolution' (2019) 39 *LS* 555.

53 'Comparative law cannot remain purely descriptive. Comparative lawyers must criticise': FH Lawson, 'Comparative law as an instrument of legal culture' in *The Comparison, Selected Essays*, Vol II (North-Holland 1977) 78.

248 *Matteo Nicolini*

method is devoted to detecting paradigms for explaining such legal changes; furthermore, it unveils long-term trends that go beyond the social environment in which they originated.

It is a matter of applying the 'subversive potential of comparative legal thinking.'[54] However, the methodological problems are both procedural – that is, they consider how the acts of imagination occur in the penetration of the British constitution[55] – and substantive. As an act of legal imagination, comparative law is also an act of 'constitutional awareness.'[56] If the comparative method allows us to penetrate the surface of the British constitution, constitutional awareness reveals its complexity.

The acts of imagination are related to reinvention, which is a type of manufacturing tradition, typical in constitution-making processes. As Laurence Tribe highlighted,

> the very identity of 'the Constitution' – the body of textual and historical materials from which [fundamental constitutional] norms are to be extracted and by which their application is to be guided – is ... a matter that cannot be objectively deduced or passively discerned in a viewpoint-free way.[57]

It follows that the legal imagination consciously decides to use legal, literary, traditional, and social materials that have their roots in the past. This is the most relevant feature of British manufacturing tradition: paraphrasing James Boyd White, this has always had its 'major focus of interest, and the central value, [in] the life of the imagination working with inherited materials and against the inherited constraints.'[58]

By resorting to such a manufacturing tradition, the legal imagination engages in deliberate reengineering practices, which involve 'the addition, amendment, or replacement of (at least) one cardinal element of a constitutional idea' central in the process of identity construction.[59] To sum up, imagining a constitutional identity entails the appropriation of non-legal elements, as well as their subsequent modification and adaptation in order to match the new constitutional design. Like a poet, the legal imagination, sings 'for his contemporaries' and recalls 'to his hearers' minds well-known situations which could be conjured up by merely alluding to well-known events and personages.'[60]

---

54 GP Fetcher, 'Comparative law as a subversive discipline' (1998) 46 *AJCL* 684. See also HM Watt, 'Further terrains for subversive comparison: the field of global governance and the public/private divide', in PG Monateri (ed), *Methods of Comparative Law* (Edward Elgar 2012) 270–88.

55 See VG Curran, 'Cultural immersion, difference and categories in U.S. comparative law' (1998) 46 *AJCL* 64.

56 C Hill, *A Turbulent, Seditious and Factious People: John Bunyan and His Church* (Verso 2016) 8.

57 LH Tribe, 'A constitution we are amending: a self-defense of a restrained judicial role' (1983) 97 *Harvard LR* 440.

58 J Boyd White, *The Legal Imagination* (University of Chicago Press 1985) xii.

59 S Stephenson, 'Constitutional reengineering: dialogue's migration from Canada to Australia' (2013) 11 *International Journal of Constitutional Law* 872.

60 RA Williams, *The Finn Episode in Beowulf. An Essay on Interpretation* (CUP 1926) 4.

Against the failure of the legal imagination   249

The British procedural state of mind matches such processes of reinvention and manufacturing. First, the law has traditionally acted as a bridge linking 'reality to an imagined alternative.'[61] Second, within the British constitution, this type of manufacturing tradition has also accommodated complexity according to a two-level pattern: imagination and legislation – that is, invention and positivism. In Britain, there has usually been 'a mind that tells a story and a mind that gives reasons.'[62] Third, the common law requires judges to be inventive, and the judiciary has the 'function of developing the common law ... and discarding judge-made rules' if these 'have outlived their purpose and are contrary to contemporary concepts of justice.'[63] Finally, legislation has always been 'used to direct the society along particular economic religious or political lines.' This is the 'paradigmatic example of [British] historical particularism ... because it gives expression to the view that, as conceptions of justice change over time, so too should common law rules.'[64]

This pattern allows us to engage in intense cross-disciplinary research. This is the case for law and humanities, which provide us with new 'possibilities' and renovated 'perspectives.' Culture

> is a generously rich and complex system of thought and expression, of social definitions and practices, which can be learned and mastered, modified or preserved, by the individual mind.[65]

Needless to say, the Anglo-British legal tradition is 'part and parcel of [this] complex normative language and mythos,' where legal and literary 'narratives in which the corpus juris is located' are governed by those 'whose wills act' upon them.[66] Invention and legal imagination have thus constantly intermingled throughout British constitutional history, which has been 'shaped by poets and polemicists,' whereas jurists and parliamentary oligarchies have given retrospective readings of constitutional events.[67] For example, the changes in eighteenth-century English literature and society forged a totally new public opinion, which led to the formulation of an equation between the rise of the novel and legal imagination. The novel, which is part of the eighteenth-century context, may be considered 'an experimental inquiry into the ethical implications of contemporary social change.'[68] These changes resulted in an era of legal reforms whereby

---

61 Watson (n 40) 36.
62 Boyd White (n 58).
63 *Cassell & Co Ltd v Broome* [1972] AC 1027, 1127, *per* Lord Diplock.
64 Mullender, Context (n 31) 27.
65 Boyd White (n 58) xii.
66 RM Cover, 'The Supreme Court, 1982 term – foreword: nomos and narrative' (1983) 97 *Harvard LR* 3–68.
67 I Ward, *Law and the Brontës* (Palgrave Macmillan 2012) 98.
68 M McKeon, *The Origins of the English Novel, 1600–1740* (Johns Hopkins UP 2002), xxiii. On the equation between legal change and the rise of the novel in eighteenth-century England see M Nicolini, 'Writing for the "scholar and the gentleman". Language, society, and legal education in Blackstone's *Commentaries*' (2018) 24 *The Cardozo Electronic Law Bulletin* 1.

England reimagined herself: 'the law had therefore to consider all the complicated relationships which were being created through the machinery of credit and joint enterprise,' agriculture, finance, and society.[69]

Legal imagination is, thus, a crossroads that facilitates contact between legal narratives and the social, linguistic, and literary context. It requires us to go beyond the 'boundaries of a constitutional struggle'[70] and to engage in a multi-disciplinary assessment of complexity.

'Attentiveness to contingencies': how the British legal imagination works

According to Richard Mullender, Britain's constitutional order is a 'composite' of three elements: the legal, the political, and the dispositional. Legal imagination pertains to the third element. Not only does it find 'expression in the effort to identify contingencies (most obviously, internal and external threats) that may disrupt the order's operation,' but 'attentiveness to contingency' is well equipped when it comes to confronting complexity.[71] When managing it, the dispositional attitude takes a variety of forms. Milsom depicts the first of these:

> Largest changes have never been deliberate. ... The life of the common law has been in the abuse of its elementary ideas. If the rules of property give what now seems an unjust answer, try obligation ... if the rules of tort, say deceit, give what now seems an unjust answer, try another, try negligence. And so the legal world goes round.[72]

Such acts of imagination evolve slowly, as it takes years – if not centuries – to incorporate their by-products into the legal system.

The second form of legal imagination is directly linked to British constitutional history. Apart from the mainstream constitutional narrative,[73] the Anglo-British constitution is saturated with 'alternative' legal narratives. Originally set at the margins marked by constitutional law, they were not incorporated (or were incorporated to a limited extent) into the establishment constitution. These narratives are made up of

---

69 TFT Plucknett, *A Concise History of the Common Law* (5th edn, Butterworth 1956) 68.

70 W Bagehot, *The English Constitution* (CUP 2001) 183.

71 Mullender, 'Transmuting' (n 27) 1020–21.

72 SFC Milsom, *Historical Foundations of the Common Law* (2nd edn, OUP 1981) 6.

73 On the mainstream narrative, see C Hill, *The Century of Revolution 1603–1714* (Routledge 2000) 1: the 1603–1714 period was 'the most decisive in English history ... What happened in the seventeenth century is still sufficiently part of us today, of our ways of thinking, our prejudices, our hopes, to be worth trying to understand.' On the alternative legal narratives, see M Nicolini, 'Turning *Vanity Fair* into *The Celestial City*: England's legal narratives of the body politic from Bunyan to Thackeray' (2018) 12 *Pólemos* 128.

subsidiary episodes and ideas in the English revolution, the attempts of various groups of the common people to impose their own solutions to the problems of their time, in opposition to the wishes of their betters who had called them into political action.

Alternative legal narratives share several common features. First, they added complexity to the legal system. Second, they promoted change in the constitutional order: indeed, they turned the English world 'upside down'[74] in order to 'change some of the fundamental ordering principles of existing society.'[75] Third, these movements targeted the mainstream institutions and aimed to frame new representative institutions. These narratives challenged parliamentary sovereignty by affirming 'the dependence of parliament on the electorate and the subordination of the individual member to his constituents.' This, evidently, stretches back to the 'democratic tradition of the seventeenth-century Puritanism.'[76]

Edmund Burke vividly explains how the 'erratic course' of the 1640–60 constitutional events was incorporated into the body of the mainstream constitution:

> The people of England well know, that the idea of inheritance furnishes a sure principle of conservation, and a sure principle of transmission; without all excluding a principle of improvement. It leaves acquisition free; but it secures what it acquires ... By a constitutional policy, working after the pattern of nature, we receive, we hold, we transmit our government and our privileges, in the same manner in which we enjoy and transmit our property and our lives.[77]

The British procedural state of mind is apparent in how this kind of organic constitution works.[78] In Pocock's terms, this unceasing process of creation and recreation is the result of 'the accumulations and refinements of experience,' whereby the 'wisdom of generations' is distilled and 'each decision [is] based on the experience of those before and tested by the experience of those after.'[79] This accounts for why 'political memory' might be among the acts of legal imagination: it implies 'an act of selection and sheer repetition and makes its connections with a degree of temporal indifference.'[80] This assumption holds particularly true when it comes to outlining the English (and afterwards British) body politic, which had

---

74 Psalm 146:9; Acts 17:6. C Hill, *The World Turned Upside Down: Radical Ideas During the English Revolution* (Penguin 1975) 13.
75 R Foxley, *The Levellers: Radical Political Thought in the English Revolution* (Manchester UP 2013) 7.
76 Sir DL Keirr, *The Constitutional History of Modern Britain 1485–1951* (5th edn, Adam & Charles Black 1957) 349.
77 E Burke, *Reflections on the Revolution in France* (Penguin 1986) 119–20.
78 E Jones, *Edmund Burke and the Invention of Modern Conservatism, 1830–1914. An Intellectual History* (OUP 2017) 27–8.
79 JGA Pocock, *The Ancient Constitution and the Feudal Law. A Study of English historical Thought in the Seventeenth Century* (an issue with retrospect, CUP 1987) 35.
80 K Killeen, *The Political Bible in Early Modern England* (CUP 2017) 9.

252 *Matteo Nicolini*

been imagined as mainly English, Anglican, and conformist. Religious conformity had been considered essential for the preservation of the mainstream constitutional narrative. The acts of legal imagination that aimed at establishing the Protestant constitution[81] were duly executed through legal reforms.[82] But legal imagination also required congruence between the body politic and its representative institutions, and the Test Act 1673 prevented non-Anglicans from voting and being elected to the House of Commons.[83]

The governance of such a diverse human landscape required a good dose of pragmatism, which in turn was grounded in acts of imagination. As it was the law that set a 'clear divide between conformists and dissenters,' legalistic conformity would have probably triggered 'Schism by Law' and rendered 'derisory parliament's dignity.'[84] Consequently, the acts of legal imagination relied on pragmatism, which gave rise to a kind of relaxed conformity. First, the use of the royal prerogative loosened legal conformity; second, the two-level pattern whereby the British manufacturing tradition accommodated complexity turned such acts of legal imagination into pieces of legislation. The relaxed pragmatism culminated in the progressive emancipation of non-Anglicans.[85] These narratives were eventually incorporated when Parliament passed the first Reform Act of 1832, which allowed alternative legal narratives to be represented in Parliament. This put an end to the congruence between Anglicanism, the body politic, and its representative institutions.

There is a third device that has traditionally accommodated complexity within the British constitution. Legal fiction is usually used when a rapid adjustment is essential. Mansfield resorted to it to make commercial law evolve, as well as to assert the Privy Council's jurisdiction over overseas territories. But it also guides constitutional change, say, when it comes to *restoring* English constitutional identity. Restoration here has a limited connotation, pretending that 'Charles II had reigned from the moment of his father's death.' This means that Charles II

---

81 See GFA Best, 'The Protestant constitution and its supporters, 1800–1829' (1958) 8 *Transactions of the Royal Historical Society* 105.

82 See J Rose, *Godly Kingship in Restoration England. The Politics of the Royal Supremacy, 1660–1688* (CUP 2011) 9. See the Act of Supremacy 1534; the Act of Submission of the Clergy 1534; the Act of the Ten Articles 1536; the Act Abolishing Diversity in Opinions 1539; the Clarendon Code – i.e. the Corporation Act 1661; the Act of Uniformity 1662; the Conventicle Act 1664; the Five Mile Act 1665; the Occasional Conformity Act 1711; and the Schism Act 1714.

83 Test Act 1763. See Rose (n 82) 187.

84 Rose (n 82) 95. See also AC Dudley, 'Nonconformity under the "Clarendon Code"' (1912) 18 *The American Historical Review* 69.

85 See the Catholic Relief Act 1778 and 1788, the Catholic Emancipation Act 1829, the Test and Corporation Acts (1828), the Ecclesiastical Commission (Peel's Tory Government 1835). Legislation has also put an end to the imaginative disqualification of those professing the 'Popish Religion.' This part of the Act of Settlement 1701 was implicitly repealed by s 2(1) of the Succession to the Crown Act 2013: 'A person is not disqualified from succeeding to the Crown or from possessing it as a result of marrying a person of the Roman Catholic faith.'

began to reign on 30 January 1649. When he acceded to the throne on 29 May 1660, 'he had been reigning for eleven years and more.'[86]

Restoration contributed to the drawing of the boundaries of the constitution and avoided the incorporation of alternative narratives. Not only did '[t]he settlement of 1660 [mark] another attempt to answer [constitutional and political] questions,' it also marked an attempt to 'possibly ... avoid answering them.'[87] In Dryden's words,

> Some lazy ages lost in sleep and ease
> No action leave to busy chronicles,
> Such whose supine felicity but makes
> In story chasms, in epochs mistakes,
> O'er whom Time gently shakes his wings of down
> Till with his silent sickle they are mown.[88]

Dryden's enthusiastic eulogy, which hinted at Charles II's accession to the throne, reflected the fiction of the Restoration.[89] However, Charles II's constitutional policy was not able to prevent alternative narratives from populating the Anglo-British constitution. This had already surfaced in the aftermath of the 1641 constitutional crisis and prospered throughout the interregnum. When the Restoration began, a constitutional transformation had already taken place. The seventeenth-century revolution publicly advocated politico-constitutional reforms and secured a renewed lexicon. Lexical items such as sovereignty, democracy, franchise, and religious freedom became widely used in political discourse and infiltrated the constitutional framework.[90] England did not miss this constitutional moment – and she reimagine herself.

Reconciling legal change with the respect for forms: complexity, pragmatism, and the British constitution

The Anglo-British constitution has always tried to accommodate, *by acts of legal imagination*, complexity and variety within its politico-legal order. Milsom, however, objected to such a strategy:

> How could our ancestors be so perverse in doing so deviously what could be done directly? How could they descend to tricks to reach desirable results?

---

86 FW Maitland, *The Constitutional History of England* (HAL Fisher ed, CUP 1908), 283 and 282, respectively.
87 RM Bliss, *Restoration England 1660–1688* (Routledge 1985), 1.
88 J Dryden, 'Astræa Redux. a poem on the happy restoration and return of his sacred Majesty Charles the Second,' *Selected Poems* (Penguin 2001), vv. 105–110.
89 John West, *Dryden and Enthusiasm. Literature, Religion, and Politics in Restoration England* (Oxford UP 2018).
90 For more on these issues see Nicolini, 'Turning' (n 73) 128.

254   *Matteo Nicolini*

> Certainly, if we view the common law on the eve of reform as a piece of social engineering, we see [this] as ... extravagant.[91]

Milsom's statement raises new issues, which are directly related to how Britain was able to cope with complexity. Indeed, legal imagination and legislative action were conceived of as means for recovering public and shared values within British society. Not only does the law organise society, but it also secures predictability by reforms: it complements legal imagination by giving the latter a rational form.

The two-pattern system, according to which the British constitution has been functioning for at least four centuries, is able to turn social engineering and legal imagination into effective legal change. I term it *pragmatism*, as it reconciles legal change with respect for form. Lawyers

> recognize the duty to obey the law so long as it is law, while doing their best to have it changed, whether by seeking to have unfavourable precedents distinguished or overruled, or by promoting amending legislation, even an amendment to a constitution.[92]

In facing the Brexit scenario, British society seems to have lost such pragmatism. As already noted, the debate has progressively narrowed political discretion and legal imagination. This has inhibited the use of legislation as a means of public policy and severed the British politico-legal order from its inherent pragmatism. The legalistic and formalistic approach to Brexit upholds this assumption. Legal scholars, politicians, and the media have mainly focused on minute legal technicalities, thus losing sight of the most relevant features of socio-political reality. This reminds me of Watson's sharp critique of Austin's and Hart's positivism:

> Positivism as exemplified by John Austin ... and Herbert Hart ... is not concerned with the major issues of the nature of law ... how it comes about that scholars of that eminence can concentrate on relatively unimportant and formal issues?[93]

It is not my purpose to draw a psychological profile of formalistic scholars. There is probably a politico-legal policy behind such a lack of imagination. The language used in the EUWA 2018 demonstrates this, as in the case of the Charter of Fundamental Rights, which will not be part of domestic law after exit day.[94] However, a complex mechanical procedure operates: Brexit does not affect the retention in domestic law 'of any fundamental rights or principles': these exist 'irrespective of

---

91 Milsom (n 72) 6–7.
92 FH Lawson, 'Legal orthodoxy' in *Many Laws, Selected Essays*, Vol I (North-Holland 1977) 51.
93 Watson (n 40) 107.
94 EUWA 2018, s 5(4).

the Charter,' references to which 'in any case law are … to be read as if they were references to any corresponding retained fundamental rights or principles.'

It is true that law requires 'a technical language' with 'precise terms' for expressing 'precise ideas.'[95] But there is another characteristic of the law: like the organic constitution, its meaning is the outcome of a process of Pocock's 'accumulations' distilled by the 'wisdom of generations.' This 'indicates that while *our* meaning what we say may be based upon how we use that language, *its* meaning is already secured.'[96]

Confronting the failures of legal imagination: reimagination or isolation?

There are at least two, albeit opposing, scenarios when it comes to confronting such a lack of legal imagination for the post-Brexit scenario. The first exception stresses the necessity to redevelop 'counter-narratives' as 'essential components of the future of Britain.' Indeed, 'Ideological hegemony is always a threat when it is combined with … an intolerance of dissent.' To this extent, 'The dangers of monolithic understanding of right and wrong and of the purpose and worth of humans' have caused the 'marginalization of diverse views and, more often, oppression and tyranny.'[97]

The second exception, which points to isolation, was framed by the current Prime Minister, Boris Johnson. When resigning from his post on 9 July 2018, the then British Foreign Secretary affirmed that Britain was 'truly headed for the status of [EU] colony.'[98]

By addressing the complexity of Brexit in colonial terms, politicians disregard how the process of partition from the EU might have an impact not only on Northern Ireland, but also on the British overseas (i.e. colonial) territories in Europe, namely Gibraltar and the Sovereign Base Areas of Akrotiri and Dhekelia in Cyprus. Not only did the latter adopt the euro as their currency, but they are also included within the borders and the customs territory of the EU.[99]

The way in which the Sovereign Bases' borders have been handled so far reveals another failure of legal imagination. The topic has been addressed in legalistic

---

95 FW Maitland, 'Of the Anglo-French language in the early year books' in *Introduction to Year Books of Edward II* (Selden Society 1903), xxxiii–xxxiv.

96 TD Eisele, 'The legal imagination and language: a philosophical criticism' (1976) 47 *University of Colorado Law Review* 368; original emphasis.

97 Welby (n 2) 262–63.

98 See Boris Johnson's resignation letter <https://ig.ft.com/boris-johnson-brexit-letter/> accessed on 4 July 2019.

99 Protocols No 3 and No 10 on the Sovereign Base Areas of the United Kingdom of Great Britain and Northern Ireland in Cyprus annexed to the Act concerning the conditions of accession of the Czech Republic, the Republic of Estonia, the Republic of Cyprus, the Republic of Latvia, the Republic of Lithuania, the Republic of Hungary, the Republic of Malta, the Republic of Poland, the Republic of Slovenia, and the Slovak Republic to the European Union and in accordance with the terms of that Protocol [2003] OJ L 236/940 and 955.

256 Matteo Nicolini

terms, as if these British territories were in watertight compartments and their borders were lines and figures. This counter-colonial narrative is grounded in 'firm frontiers,' which are in turn bound up with the existence of 'assertive states.' It appears to me that, conversant in lines and figures, this imagined Britain did not exactly know where she could assert her 'demands for resources' and 'create [her] first line of defence.'[100]

The process of recovering public shared values should not be thought of in terms of divides, cleavages, and lines; on the contrary, it should consider the UK a space to be completely reimagined. Not only does this counter-colonial predicament demarcate the UK territory, it also unveils a 'particular cognitive mode of gaining control over the world, of synthesising cultural and geographical information.'[101] This usually makes the demarcated areas 'depopulated, often void of human traces, visually "empty".'[102] With the complicity of legal scholars, politicians fill the void: their cartography dispossesses 'the colonized,' whose 'cartographies [and] understanding of territory and boundaries' are thus neglected.[103]

If Britain were to be considered an empty box to be filled with new values,

> Values ... would be dictated by the powerful and rich, and imposed through self-interest. Economics would drive decision making. Vision would be tactical, not strategic. ... Long-term investment in social, spiritual and moral capital would be feeble to non-existent.[104]

Odd as it may seem, if it were to occur, there would be a *reverse colonisation*. Indeed, this policy would overturn the British colonial project. With an act of imagination, the UK had usually imagined the geographies of the colonised lands, and, in so doing, it filled the space by making them functional to its own interests and trading companies. If Great Britain were not able to reimagine itself, the new settlers (i.e. economic actors and investors) would reimagine Great Britain's public values according to their own 'commercial geography, ... capacity for classifying and constructing taxonomies of territories, climates and peoples,' which merely aim to match their 'understandings and needs of colonial expectations.'[105]

By contrast, Britain should assert her own *imaginative legal geography*[106] – that is, the spatial relationship between her communities and her territory. Maitland labelled this relation as 'belongs of public law,' as it entailed a close connection

---

100 J Black, *Maps and Politics* (University of Chicago Press 1988), 123.
101 Black (n 100) 18.
102 A Gordon and B Klein, 'Introduction' in A Gordon and B Klein (eds), *Literature, Mapping, and the Politics of Space in Early Modern Britain* (CUP 2001) 2.
103 Black (n 99) 19.
104 Welby (n 2) 16.
105 L Veracini, 'The imagined geographies of settler colonialism' in TB Mar and P Edmonds (eds), *Making Settler Colonial Space. Perspectives on Race, Place and Identity* (Springer 2010) 182. For more on Brexit and borders, see S Douglas-Scott, 'Brexit, boundaries and the power of images' (2019) 19 *Pólemos* 85 ff.
106 FW Maitland, *Township and Borough: The Ford Lectures 1897* (CUP 1964) 6–7.

between land and community.[107] Britain could then consider the performativity of the border as regards the EU. Boundaries, in general, convey a relational meaning and allow both the UK and the EU to define their territorial identity by mutually engaging in an intense dialogue on how to build (i.e. imagine) their mutual future relationships. Indeed,

> The great period of change and reform in the way we behave as a nation have come from a combination of huge events and overseas influences. We have never been just some island off the north-west coast of mainland Europe.[108]

Reimagining the territorial constitution

Although there is much that is shared between the legal geographies of Great Britain and Europe, there is still much to be done to reimagine Great Britain's relationships with its devolved governments. Again, such relations must not be governed by technicalities, as the EUWA 2018 fantasises. On the one hand, the Act aims to replace the three-layer system of EU multilevel governance by merely repealing any reference to EU law supremacy. On the other hand, it sets additional restrictions and constraints on the devolved legislatures, which now stem from the retained EU law – that is, from the recovered sovereignty of the British Parliament.[109]

It could certainly be argued that the concept of 'retained EU law' is a timely parliamentary legislative creation, an effective act of imagination capable of reconciling Great Britain's past with Great Britain's future. Yet, there is something that reflects the political vagueness of the Act and its lack of legal imagination. First, if 'the intended effect is continuity,' then

> the existing body of EU law is frozen ... and adopted as UK law. The content of EU law as it stands at [exit day] is therefore going to be a critical piece of legal history for the purpose of UK law for decades to come. The legal reality will not, however, be one entirely of continuity – far from it.[110]

Second, I contend that the solution embedded in the EUWA 2018 by no means represents the best of all parliamentary achievements. It is not just a problem related to the renovation of Scotland's constitutional identity after 1707, the recognition of which is the outcome of the 1998 devolution. Indeed, a plan for the Irish border still remains one of the most controversial issues, and the post-Brexit scenario is likely to trigger a re-articulation of the British territorial constitution. It is a matter of mobility of persons, of *constitutional imagination*, as well as of definition of common and shared values within the constitutional landscape.

107 Maitland, *Township* (n 106) 11 and 29.
108 Welby (n 1) 271.
109 EUWA 2018, sub-ss 12(1), 12(3), and 12(5). See T Mullen, 'Brexit and the territorial governance of the United Kingdom' (2019) 12 *Contemporary Social Science* 283–84.
110 J Segan, 'The European Union (Withdrawal) Act 2018: ten key implications for UK law and lawyers' (26 July 2018) UK Const L Blog <https://ukconstitutionallaw.org/> accessed 12 July 2019.

258 *Matteo Nicolini*

If, then, the territorial constitution is likened to that of 'legal geography,' this means that we must completely reimagine the legal spatial relationship between the British community and *its* territory. Northern Ireland will probably be a test: historically juxtaposed 'belongs of public law' have confronted each other there to assert their own connection between land, community, and law.

Hence, the constitutional framework, within which devolution is to be rearticulated, might be firmly rearranged around values shared by the four British communities.

Governing Brexit: pragmatism, opportunism, and the role of comparative law

Finally, *governance of complexity* is topical. The lack of legal imagination can cause a shift from pragmatism to opportunism. Whereas the former denotes developments that 'occur through the unexpected use or misuse of existing institutions or by unusual uses or legal argument or by curious borrowings,' the latter points to how jurists 'can go a considerable way at times toward alleviating defects in official lawmaking.'[111] It might also be 'A particular failure of the legal imagination: that of state authorities to create the law that was wanted.' Indeed, 'such successful opportunism shows a readiness on the part of the state authorities to allow others' – namely, the private international investors not democratically accountable – to 'make a considerable part of the law' in the post-Brexit scenario: 'Successful juristic opportunism can only proceed out of such failure.'[112]

As externally imposed values, these might completely disregard the needs and the interests of the British community. This triggers a change in the process of legal imagination and in the paradigm for recovering public values. The global legal imagination probably promises 'a kind of impending radiant future for humanity,'[113] but hides a *narrative of superiority* covering the 'asymmetrical relationship' between the actors of globalisation, where the dominant group endeavours 'to impose its cultural order to the subordinate' groups.[114] Opportunism as a surrender to the law-makers of globalisation conceals an even more treacherous policy. Whereas comparative law presupposes complexity and variety, globalisation requires efficient markets and homogeneous politico-legal constitutions throughout the world: only common legal devices ensure improved economic performance. This means that opportunism promotes homogeneity, which, in an economically oriented environment, aims to simplify legal complexity. If it were the case, homogeneity would saturate the British politico-legal constitution. This

---

111 Watson (n 40) 87 and 96.
112 Ibid.
113 M Xifaras, 'The *Global Turn* in legal theory' (2016) 29 *Canadian Journal of Law & Jurisprudence* 216. See also G Gong, *The Standard of 'Civilization' in International Society* (Clarendon Press 1984); M Koskenniemi, *The Gentle Civilizer of Nations: The Rise and Fall of International Law 1870–1960* (CUP 2001) 132.
114 SE Merry, 'Law and colonialism' (1991) 25 *Law & Society Review* 890, 894.

also means that, in a globalised economic world, the British constitution would act as mere recipient of the values proposed by the policies of globalisation.[115]

The national government would become accountable as far as global economic governance is concerned. Financial dominance would cause a shift from the political to the economic sphere, where the Westminster government would rely on a new form of confidence between the political power and the sovereign financial market, where the 'distressed sovereign debt can be sold on private equity markets and the debtor [is] subjected to the harsh economics of private law.'[116]

Against this background, additional efforts in the practice of the potential, subversive comparison are required. Scholars should, whenever possible, oppose the vagueness of political choices and, at the same time, support the process of recovering public and shared values in the aftermath of Brexit. This process brings complexity back to the fore and engages in the two-level intense dialogue with imagination and legislation, invention and pragmatism.

In a globalised world, the struggle of contemporary comparative law aims to allow society to gain control of its legal imagination when it comes to forging its own values and securing its own future. It is the struggle we must engage in if we want to preserve complexity as the main composite of the Anglo-British legal tradition.

While reimagining Britain, we might also learn from Britain's past legal narratives. These 'were not perfect' – Justin Welby acutely upholds – but were able to provoke 'people to reimagine the future.' The UK indeed grew from these acts of legal imagination; the 'hope is that in the future [she] rediscovers the power of the narrative that has shaped it for so long and set its values so deeply.'[117]

---

115 BA Simmons and Zachary Elkins, 'The globalization of liberalization: policy diffusion in the international political economy' (2004) 98 *American Political Science Review* 171–89.

116 Watt (n 24) 276.

117 Welby (n 2) 283.

Index

abortion 115–16
academic degrees 24, 27, 29–31, 33
academics 4, 216
accuracy goals 118–19; *see also* directional
   goals
Ackerman, BA 201n29, 204–5, 239n3
Act Abolishing Diversity in Opinions 1539
   252n82
Act of Settlement 1701 252n85
Act of Submission of the Clergy 1534
   252n82
Act of Supremacy 1534 and 1559 252n82
Act of the Ten Articles 1536 252n82
Act of Uniformity 1662 252n82
Acts of Parliament 36; *Act Abolishing*
   Diversity in Opinions 1539 252n82; *Act*
   of Settlement 1701 252n85; *Act of*
   Submission of the Clergy 1534 252n82;
   Act of Supremacy 1534 and 1559
   252n82; *Act of the Ten Articles 1536*
   252n82; *Act of Uniformity 1662*
   252n82; *Bipartisan Campaign Reform*
   Act 2002 95; *Conventicle Act 1664* 252;
   Corporation Act 1661 252; *The Five Mile*
   Act 1665 252; *Human Rights Act 1998*
   220, 223; *Occasional Conformity Act*
   1711 252n82; *Reform Act 1832* 70, 252;
   The Schism Act 1714 252n82; *Test Act*
   1673 252
Ad Fletam Dissertatio 34n1
adjudication 79, 81, 92–3, 111, 119;
   constitutive 90; legal 111; legitimate 76,
   90; pathological 91; practice of 79, 81
Admissions and Guarantee Clauses (United
   States Constitution) 204, 204n40
advocacy 32, 115–16, 121
agenda 11, 140, 241, 247; European
   integration 9; Fleta's expression of
   sovereign authority served Hobbes's 51;

new legislative 224; revolutionary 151;
   socio-political 126
Åklagaren v Hans Åkerberg Fransson 84,
   84n59
Alito, Justice Samuel 95, 98
All Souls College, Oxford 26
American frontier 12, 195–205
American government 201
American Revolution 247
American Supreme Court *see* Supreme
   Court of the United States
amicus briefs 10, 114–17, 129
Amos, Andrew 8, 27–8
analysis 10, 115, 155, 195; cognitive 121;
   general 112; historical 115; legalistic
   220; policy 127; precedential 102;
   scientific 140; textual 9
Ancien Régime 134–5, 137–8, 145–9, 155
Anglo-British constitution 6, 12, 239–40,
   246, 250, 253; *see also* British
   constitution
anthropology 2, 6, 11, 76, 134, 152,
   152n125, 152–4, 156; literary 152;
   political 2, 6, 11, 134, 152–4, 156
anti-Laudian tracts 60
The Apotheosis of James I 53
appellant's actions 220–1
appellate courts 80, 206, 225
apprentices 18–19, 23, 182, 187, 190
Arendt, Hannah 77, 163n32
Areopagitica 60
arguments 19, 23, 31–2, 59, 61, 111, 113,
   115, 119–22, 126–7, 162, 187–8, 190,
   221, 228; ancient order of 182, 188;
   emotional 127; evaluating political 123;
   invoking 82; legal historical 51, 128;
   long-running 188, 220; merit-based
   119, 123–4; moral 172; oral 112; on
   policy 125; rational 110

Index 261

Aristotle 170
armies 58, 61, 64, 69–70, 200
Artefacts of Legal Inquiry 3
attitudes 92, 104–5, 111, 120–1, 123–4,
    139, 170, 196; judicial 111, 116–17,
    119, 124, 130; justice's 123; personal
    121; procedural 44
attorneys 18, 22, 25, 118, 128
Austin, John 27, 95, 254
authority 31, 37–9, 42–3, 51, 57–9,
    79–80, 83, 88, 102–3, 187–8, 206–7,
    223, 225–6, 230, 237; ascribing 137;
    central governmental 45; establishing
    79; existing 79–80; judicial 38; sovereign
    37, 51; statements of constituent 91;
    supreme 147; systems of 79, 81

Badiou, Alain 140, 140n48, 141, 150, 156
Bagehot, Walter 69, 250n70n70
Baker, Sir John Hamilton 8, 18n4, 22n25,
    36, 186n52, 186n53, 187n56, 187n56
Barnes v Glen Theatre 106–7
barristers 20, 24, 26, 29, 32, 160;
    Chancery 25; educating 24; practising
    25, 27; senior 25
Bastille 135, 138–9
beliefs 6–7, 79, 81–2, 88, 90, 93, 95,
    97–9, 101, 103–7, 118, 123–4, 128,
    164, 235–6; inherent 93; political
    221–2; preexisting 96; public's 75, 91;
    religious 221–2, 227; systems of 93,
    105, 107–8, 122
bench (Common Bench) 18–20, 23–4,
    47–8, 113–14, 124, 127, 158–9, 163,
    172, 189–90
benchers 24, 26
Bennett, Thomas 3, 12, 133, 157n1
Bentham, Jeremy 139
Berlin, Isaiah 136n18, 147n98
biases 104, 111, 116–19, 122–4, 233;
    empirical 233; judicial 111; personal
    118, 122; pre-existing cognitive 116–17;
    pre-existing negative 119
Bill of Rights 1688 225, 242
Biographia Literaria 209n11, 210,
    212–13, 235
Bipartisan Campaign Reform Act 2002 95
bishops 20, 49, 57–8
Black Books of Lincoln's Inn
    (administrative records) 22
Blackstone, William 8, 26–8
body politic 5–6, 94, 250–2
bondmen 34, 40–1
borders 42, 140, 197, 200, 202–3, 255–7

Bottiroli, Giovanni 184
boundaries 81–2, 91, 111–12, 175, 250,
    253, 256–7; constitutional 113; finite
    235; legal 7, 109
Bourdieu, Pierre 135, 140–1, 150, 156;
    historical writing *On the State* 141;
    regards the French Revolution as a
    'watershed' 141; traces the history of the
    modern state's emergence as an impartial
    institution 141
Brexit 6–7, 12, 224, 239–40, 242–7,
    254–9; 'no deal' 242, 244; and the
    *European Union (Withdrawal) (No. 2)
    Act 2019* 241–3, 247; and the *European
    Union (Withdrawal) Act 2018* 241,
    241n13, 241n14, 242, 242n18,
    242n19, 242, 242n20, 243–5, 254,
    254n94, 257, 257n109; 'exit day' 241,
    243, 254, 257; and the 'layers of
    complexity' 240, 243; ministerial
    responsibility for managing 241;
    and President Donald Trump 7;
    reappraising 244
Breyer, Justice Stephen 112, 116
Brissot, Jacques Pierre 139–41, 149, 151, 153
Britain 7, 13, 239, 243, 246, 249–50,
    254–7
British Commonwealth 247
British constitution 226–7, 239–41, 243–4,
    248–9, 252–4, 259
British territorial constitution 242, 257
Britton 34, 47–9
Bucklew v Precythe 112, 112n18, 112n19,
    113–14
Burke, Edmund 144, 251

Cacioppo, JT. 119–22, 124
Cambridge University 8, 17–18, 20n15,
    21, 28–32, 59, 80, 246; academic
    qualifications 18; and the Blackstone
    lectures 27; combines lectures,
    discussions, and exercises 28; and the
    Downing professors 27
Camus, Albert 11, 157–8, 163–4
canon law 17, 46–7
Carlyle, Thomas 138, 148
cases 23–5, 31–2, 35–6, 40–1, 83–4, 88–9,
    93–4, 99–101, 111, 113–17, 127,
    216–20, 223, 225–6, 228; criminal 39;
    exemplar 93; flag-burning 107;
    individual 115, 128, 188, 207, 228;
    labor-law 129; non-unitary 216, 218;
    politically charged 115, 117; privacy
    161; real 8, 23, 31, 93

262 *Index*

Chancery clerks 20–1
Charles, Prince 57
Cherry v Advocate General for Scotland 92, 225, 241
Church courts 17–18
Church of England 17, 54, 62–3, 70
Churchill, Winston 70
civil law 17, 26, 198
Civil War (American) 196, 198–201, 204
Civil War (English) 8, 61
CJEU *see* Court of Justice of the European Union
clerks 25, 40, 43, 47–8; articled 25, 28, 32; Chancery 20–1; king's 187; law 129
coexistence 78, 197, 199; and hybridisation of different cultures 197; of a private, loosely regulated initiative 199
Coke, Lord Edward 23, 50, 182, 184, 186, 189
Coleridge, Samuel Taylor 56, 206–11, 211n25, 211–15, 229–31, 231n124, 232–7; and *Biographia Literaria* 209n11, 210, 212–13, 235; commitment to the plurality and diversity of community 214; and the concept of 'Fancy' as a faculty of mind 12, 81, 92, 177, 206–11, 213–15, 227–37; concept of the mind's structure 209; division between Imagination and Fancy 231, 235; dystopia 206–38
common law 4, 7–8, 22–5, 31, 35–6, 183, 186, 188–91, 220–1, 225, 232–3, 242, 246–7, 249–50, 254; rights 223–4; rules 249; tradition 189–90
comparative law 99, 178–9, 181, 183, 198, 240, 247–8, 258
'concurring' a priori (judicial pronouncement) 96, 103, 109, 186, 206, 208, 217–18, 228, 237, 255
conscience 26, 60, 68, 161, 222–3; Christian 62; good 221; person's 158
constitutional boundaries 113
constitutional change 196, 202, 214, 252
constitutional creativity 13, 239, 242, 246
constitutional crises 5, 82, 85, 87–8, 90, 92, 253
constitutional debates 241
constitutional design 247–8
constitutional development 196, 198
constitutional events 249, 251
constitutional history 246
constitutional identity 196, 248, 252, 257
constitutional imagination 6, 76, 87, 90, 257

constitutional interpretation 94, 99n50, 103, 105, 107
constitutional law 80, 248, 250
constitutional monarchy 135–7, 145, 147, 149
constitutional programmes 201
constitutional transformations 204–5, 253
The Constitutions of Melfi 39
constitutive ambiguity 180
controversy 56, 128, 155, 196, 207, 218, 226–7, 233; acute 219, 227; constitutional 234; generated intense theoretical 10; political 138
Conventicle Act 1664 252
convictions 99, 101, 112
Cooper, James Fenimore 199
Corporation Act 1661 252
corporations 95–6, 103
Costantini, Cristina 11
County Court judges 223
County Courts 222
Lower Courts 220, 222, 225
Court of Admiralty 17
Court of Justice of the European Union 5, 9, 76, 83–92
courtrooms 1, 18, 25, 130
courts 7–9, 18–27, 29–30, 32, 45–6, 79–80, 83–90, 92–7, 99–109, 111–18, 126–30, 186–8, 216–20, 224–8, 230–3; in action 19, 23; central 25; domestic 84–5; EU apex 240; interpretational approach 94–5; King's 18–19, 21, 47; legitimacy and protection of individual reputations 130; lesser manorial 18; national 84–5, 87
Cover, Robert 174, 176
credibility gap, exposing the 79, 81–2, 88
crimes 37, 39, 41, 43–5, 49, 171, 202
criminal liability 220
criminality 37, 41, 43, 45
crises 1, 190, 201, 204; constitutional 5, 82, 85, 87–8, 90, 92, 253; economic 210; fiscal 6; perceived contemporary 82
critics 136, 202–4, 230
Critique of Pure Reason 77
cross-disciplinary research 240
Crown 26, 34, 37–8, 41–2; appointments 26, 34; judicial authority 38; sovereignty 37
culture 78, 94, 98, 144, 197, 202, 249; American 195, 247; classical 202; Eastern 12, 197; frontier 202; legal 47, 180, 185, 246

Dailey, Anne 232n129
dal Mar, Maximilian 3
damages 7, 35, 223, 242
Danton, George-Jacques 134–41, 146–9, 151; and the enigmatic character of his approach to politics 149n113; has the appearance of a committed parliamentarian 149; and his programmatic imagination 153; powers of apprehension 147; republican ardour of 137, 146; and the sociological imagination in the life of 146–7; tries to bring a long-lived process of development to a culmination 141
de Bracton, Henry 8, 34, 47, 51
de Glanvill, Ranulf 8, 38, 51
De Legibus 47
de Ranulf, Glanvill 38, 51
de Tocqueville, Alexis 69, 70n72, 126n144
death 39, 55, 58, 63, 112, 136, 138, 146–7, 199–200
death penalty 43–5
debates 3–4, 91, 93, 112, 115, 123–5, 127, 174, 178–9, 199, 205, 221, 238, 240–1, 244; constitutional 241; legal 112; political 241; retrospective criminalisation 221; theological 231n124n124
debts 26, 223, 259
decisions 75–6, 83, 85, 87–92, 94–6, 104–5, 107, 115–16, 168, 171–2, 186–8, 219–24, 227, 230, 239; belief-oriented 96; constitutional 126; constitutive 90; fateful 65; king's 136–7; legitimate 75, 91; pathological 90; rational 127; tragic 82; unanimous 83
Declaration of Right 1689 69–70
Deleuze, G. 175
Delgado, R. 126n145, 128
Delledonne, G. 6n28, 12
democracy 6, 70, 114, 126, 137, 142, 156, 195, 205, 243–4, 253; constitutional 5; Jacksonian 202; liberal 5, 82; representative 244
Desmoulins, Camille 133–7, 139–41, 146–9
devices 10, 62, 111, 173, 176, 188, 190, 252; common legal 258; heuristic 114; inventive 174; literary 185; popular 129; storytelling 111, 129; substantive 190; systemological 183
devolution 257–8
Dickens, Charles 133, 156n143, 177n19
Dickson, B. 216n64, 217n66
directional goals 119

disagreements 108, 148, 151, 207, 218–19, 234, 238; institutional 149; minor 238; politico-legal 156; suppressed 238
discourse 10, 26, 34, 78–9, 111, 124, 131, 203; common 34, 48, 51; legal 11–12, 181–2; politico-legal 239, 253
discrimination 221–2, 234
disputations 8, 18, 23–4
disputes 59, 79, 83, 85, 88, 103, 136, 234, 243
'dissenting' a priori (judicial pronouncement) 96, 103, 109, 186, 206, 208, 217–18, 228, 237, 255; *see also* 'concurring' a priori (judicial announcement)
District of Columbia v. Heller 95–6
diversity 4, 198, 212, 214, 230, 243, 246
domestic law 242, 254
drafters of the Constitution 96, 97n24
Drogheda massacre 64, 64n58, 65
drugs 112, 148, 169
Dworkin, Ronald 143, 152, 156, 160, 162, 168, 172

Early Parliamentary General Election Act 2019 241, 243
ECHR *see* European Convention on Human Rights
economy 182, 259; international political 259n115; of learning 187
education 7, 17–18, 20, 25–6, 32, 38, 101, 163, 239; formal 8, 25; lawyer's 30; responsibilities 30
Edwards, L.H. 119, 121–2, 124, 126–7, 129
egalitarian 136–7, 146, 153–6; basis 149–50; commitments 135
Eikon Alethine 60
Eikon Basilike: The Portraiture of His Sacred Majesty in His Solitudes and Sufferings 55–9, 61, 63
Eikonoclastes 55, 60–3, 65
Elgar, Edward 175
emotions 3, 124; capacity to control the 152; evoking 127; judging 164; a judicial reputation based on 111; subjective 214
Emperor Frederick II 38–9
England 17–19, 21, 23, 25–9, 31, 34–6, 51, 59–60, 64–5, 67–71, 186, 219–20, 247, 250–1, 253; and the common law 34, 36, 42, 47, 52, 182, 185–6; historical development of legal education in 8; late thirteenth-century 47; legal world of

264 *Index*

the late thirteenth-century 47, 49; and
progress of legal education in 17, 30n42,
31n47, 33; and the relevance and
authority of Roman law in 51;
transition from an absolute monarchy to
a republic 9

English Law 8, 17, 26–7, 41, 45, 49,
184–5, 187–9, 191, 246

English law books 27

English lawyers 18–19, 22, 185

English legal education 17, 28, 32

English legal traditions 183, 185

English Reformation 62–3

English Revolution 69, 251

EPGE see *Early Parliamentary General
Election Act 2019*

essays 2–4, 11, 32, 56, 60–2, 70, 92,
133–4, 142, 152, 155, 195, 239–40,
248; collected 13, 142, 174;
controversial 104; critical 174; early
70, 172; historiographical 195; legal
historical 246

European Convention on Human Rights
85, 220, 222–3

European judiciary 87

European Union 7, 83, 88, 198, 224,
228, 240–3, 255, 257; and the
distribution of power 9; member states
5, 83–6, 89, 91

*European Union (Withdrawal Agreement)
Act 2020* 241 242n22

*European Union (Withdrawal) (No. 2) Act
2019* 241–3, 247

European Union (Withdrawal) Act 2018
241, 241n13, 241n14, 242, 242n18,
242n19, 242, 242n20, 242–5, 247,
254, 254n94, 257, 257n109

European Union Charter of Fundamental
Rights 76, 84, 241, 254–5

European Union Legal Order 86, 92, 145,
175, 197

EUWA 2019 see *European Union
(Withdrawal) (No. 2) Act 2019*

EUWA 2018 see *European Union
(Withdrawal) Act 2018*

Eversole, Deborah Tully 105

evidence 21, 35, 45, 59, 83, 102, 104,
107, 116, 123, 125, 127–8, 151, 184,
215; anecdotal 128; direct 102;
empirical 123; 'the judge heard all the'
172; limited 111; new 58, 123;
scrutinising 119; symptomatic 190

examinations 8, 24, 32, 41, 49, 94, 99,
201, 206, 208, 221, 245; Law Society's

31n45; and lectures combined with
classes 8; voluntary 28; written 24

exceptions 11, 36, 40n34, 42–3, 46,
88n80, 89, 158, 169; *see also* warranties

executions 9, 55–6, 58n22, 59, 112; of
King Charles I 54, 60, 71; and the role
of Oliver Cromwell 71; 'a sacrifice
demanded by history' 70–1

exemptions 220–1, 234

exercises 1–2, 7, 10, 19, 21–4, 28, 75, 79,
90–1, 140–1, 144, 147–9, 152, 224–5,
227; academic 2, 23; constitutive 87, 90,
92; formal 32; impartial truth-finding
119; neutral fact-finding 115;
pathological 82, 87

'exit day' (Brexit) 241, 243, 254, 257

'expressive conduct' 100–2, 106

factions 58, 148

'Factortame saga' 242, 242n17

failure 3–4, 6, 107, 212, 214, 239, 241,
243, 245, 247, 249, 251, 253, 255,
257–9; human 174; of legal imagination
245, 255, 258

Failures of the Legal Imagination 3,
245n40

Fairfax, Lord General Sir Thomas 63–4,
66, 68, 68n69

The Fall 157

'Fancy' 12, 81, 92, 177, 206–11, 213–15,
227–37

Feltham, Owen 58

Ferne, Sir John 174

Fet Asaver 47–8, 51

fidelity 65, 140–1, 160, 162

First Amendment *see* United States First
Amendment

Fish, Stanley 9, 94n9, 104–5, 105n95,
107, 220n85, 221n86, 221, 226

The Five Mile Act 1665 252

flags 38, 99–103, 105

Flaubert, Gustave 82

Fleta 8, 34–8, 40–2, 45–52; author of 35,
37, 39–40, 45, 48–9, 51; author's imagining of legality 47; cited by Hobbes in
*A Dialogue Between a Philosopher and a
Student, of the Common Laws of England*
51; expression of sovereign authority
served Hobbes's agenda 51; and John
Selden's *Ad Fletam Dissertatio* 34n1;
legal imagining shared imaginings with
other related thirteenth-century
common-law treatises 51; organised into
six books comprising multiple chapters

36; and *Prologue* 38–9; treatment of the inalienable rights and privileges of the king 50

force 40, 44, 54, 124, 128, 176, 178, 182, 184, 191, 196, 204, 213, 241, 245; authoritative 188; legitimating 176; political 134; state police 200

formalism 4, 12, 206–8, 207n1, 215, 228–9, 233; legal 4, 207, 212, 214–15, 228–9, 233; and the optics of judgement 206–38; resurgent 12, 234, 245

formalists 109, 213, 220–1, 226, 233–4

Forster, E.M. 173–4, 176

Fraley, Scott 9–10

framers 94, 97–9

France 68, 133–8, 140–1, 144, 146–8, 152–3, 236, 251; 'absolutist' 147; and the eighteenth-century Enlightenment as a political force 134; and the French Revolution 2, 10–11, 69, 133–56; most prestigious school (the Lycée Louis-le-Grand) 135; politico-legal life shifts in a democratic direction 138; pre-revolutionary 133; revolutionary 147, 151; society 137, 139; and a *Tale of Two Cities* 133

Francovich, rule in 241–2

'fraternity' 137, 142, 150, 156

Frederick II, Emperor 38–9

free expression 100–2, 106

freedom 3, 40, 88, 99–101, 116, 124, 136, 154, 222–3; economic 244; religious 253; of speech 99, 101

freemen 34, 40–1

French Revolution 2, 10–11, 69, 133–56

frontier 6, 195–202, 204–5; anxiety 195, 201; end of the 196, 199; experience 195–6, 198, 203; force 200; life 197–8, 203–5; myths 195; north-western 200; project 196; violence 203

Frontier Battalion of Texas Rangers 200

gaols 42–3

gardens 64, 68

Gauden, John 56, 56n8, 58, 71

GDL *see* Graduate Diploma in Law

Ginsburg, Justice Ruth Bader 109

Girondins 140, 148–9, 151, 153

globalisation 5, 198, 245, 258–9

goals 90, 104, 170–1, 215; accuracy 118–19; directional 118–19; final 183; political 80; ultimate 130

God 37, 39, 61–2, 65–6, 94, 145, 166, 174, 185

Gonville Hall 20n15

governance 37, 198, 244, 246, 252, 257–8; authoritarian 82; global 6, 248, 259; multilevel 257; territorial 198

government 67–8, 96, 100, 102, 105–6, 137, 141, 147, 151, 200, 204, 224–5, 228, 251; ancient 69; devolving 257; egalitarian philosophy of 141, 148; federal 95, 204; ministers 143; national 198, 259; representative 244; republican form of 204–5

Graduate Diploma in Law 31

graduates 18, 24, 30

graduation 24, 32, 116, 189

grief 169–70

groups 25, 31–2, 45, 117, 134, 149, 151–2, 155, 176, 183, 189, 251, 258; activist 111; lobbying 127; particular 127, 172; social 128, 134, 176

guillotine 138, 147, 149, 153

guilt 41, 43, 45, 219, 227

habits 185–6; common 187; intellectual 245; pleasure-seeking 28; retaining old 200

Hale, Sir Matthew 25–6

Hallam, Henry 70, 140, 187

Hart, HLA 153, 156

The Harvard Law School 21

heirs 35, 41, 45

Hemingway, Ernest 172

Hengham, Justice Ralph 36, 47

Hengham Magna 47–8, 51

heuristics 120–1, 130

historians 35, 46, 55, 70, 140, 183, 187, 195

historical particularism 249

history 13, 36, 52, 62, 67–70, 83, 97–8, 141, 148, 188, 199, 201, 231, 247; constitutional 246; human 176n16; legal 29–30, 35, 46–7, 52, 246–7, 257; of reimagination 13, 247; study of 52

History of England 69

History of English Law 187n57

Hobbes, Thomas 50–2, 67, 152–3, 156; cites Fleta in *A Dialogue Between a Philosopher and a Student of the Common Laws of England* 51; disputatious 154; and the *The Elements of Law* 50; explicit about engaging the works of Edward Coke and John Selden 50; ignores Selden's analysis of Fleta 51; and the

266   *Index*

Leviathan 50, 67; withholding information about his sources in *Leviathan* 50
Holmes, Oliver Wendell 52, 232, 232n130
homicide 34, 37, 41–2, 49
House of Lords 206, 215–20, 233; abolishment of 54; cases 217n72; and the Supreme Court replacing the 206, 217, 228
human brain 144–6
human rights 135, 212, 223, 227
Human Rights Act 1998 220, 223
humanities 3, 5, 30, 141, 145, 172, 213, 249, 258
Hungary 83, 255; adopts controversial constitutional and institutional reforms 85; and democratic backsliding in 86
husbands 44, 219–20; conformist 82; and rape charges 234; and the undertakings not to molest wives 220n83; and wives who are partners in crime 44
hypotheticals 111, 113–14, 127, 130; judicial 112–14, 126, 128–30; use of 111–12, 114

ideology 6, 76, 78–9, 81, 87, 179, 181–2, 214; empiricist 211; established 81; healthy 81, 87; political 103, 117; repetitive 81; and utopia 78–80, 82, 87
imagination 2, 133–4, 149–51, 153; acts of 239–40, 246, 248, 250, 252, 256; collective 236; constitutional 6, 76, 87, 90, 257; cultural 76, 79; democratic 245; dialectic 110; disciplined use of 7; geopolitical 179; judicial 112, 114, 129; literary 180–1, 204; moral 144–6; pathological 9, 76, 81–2, 87, 90, 92; productive 2, 7, 75–81; reproductive 75–6, 78; social 78, 80; sociological 143, 145–6; stylistic 3, 11, 173, 190; utopian 87
imagining 34, 40–2, 45, 47, 52, 208, 248; author's 48; of English common law 52; legal 34–7, 49, 51; of royal authority 37
implications 47, 160–1, 169, 197, 206, 231, 244; constitutional 237, 244; ethical 249; political 115; strategic 182
imprisonment 35, 42–3, 135; *see also* prisons
inflexibility 139, 144–5, 150, 155; and 'hubris' 144, 150, 155, 169; and intolerance 139
information 50, 115, 118–19, 123, 128, 142, 187, 223; decision-makers

processing 119; factual 117, 123–4; newsworthy 223; processing 118, 256
Inner Temple 20, 25
Inns of Chancery 18n4, 21, 21n18, 22n24, 25
Inns of Court 8, 18, 21–2, 24–6, 29–30, 32, 188
Inns of Court School of Law 30n43, 31n45
institutions 12, 25, 29, 86, 88–9, 91, 126, 137, 140–1, 143–4, 146, 150, 197, 202; formal 175; impartial 141; political 133, 152–3, 157
integration, multilayered 242
integrity 129, 158–64, 166–7; accounts of 11, 157; conditions of 158, 167; institutional 160; of law 159–61; personal 158; professional 159–60
interests 3–4, 6, 27, 87–9, 100–1, 103, 106, 115, 117, 119, 219, 222–3, 231, 256, 258; alleged 103; asserted 102; claimed 102; esoteric 30; human 223; national 70, 106
'internal coherence' (achieving) 11, 157–8, 160, 162, 167–8, 172
internal narratives 110, 117–19, 124, 126
interpretation 9–10, 51, 92–6, 98, 102–5, 107, 109, 112, 114, 159, 162, 164, 231, 235, 241; defensible 148; judicial 7, 93; official 110; precedential 99, 103; responsive 99, 103–4; theories of 93, 107; unbiased 104
interpretational theory 96, 105
interpretive paradigms 195, 197
inventions 4, 71, 243–4, 249, 251, 259
Ireland 157, 242, 247; and the (Brexit) plan for the border of 242, 257; and the 'apprentices of the Bench' 19; and Oliver Crowell's campaign in 55, 64

Jacobins 140, 148–9, 151, 153, 230
James I, King 53, 55, 69
Jefferson, Thomas 196
Jesus Christ 58, 60, 63
Johnson, Boris 241, 255
judges 9–11, 31–2, 75–6, 90, 104, 107, 109–11, 113–14, 116–30, 157–63, 166–72, 186–7, 205–7, 217–18, 237–8; appellate 162; domestic 84; escaping the pathological tendency for self-deception 76; expert 230; individual 12, 104, 124, 159–60, 167, 206, 230; lacking integrity 171; retirement age 82; retraining of 171; selecting of 172; senior 206

judgment, clear 92
judgments 116–17, 124, 128, 162–4, 169, 172, 182–3, 186, 206–8, 216, 219, 221–3, 225–8, 230, 232–3; controversial 226; dissenting 88, 217–18, 234; exercising 99; individual 12, 207, 228; legal 118, 213; single 216–17, 219; subjective 109; unconscious 232–3; written 110
judicial appointment process 82
judicial hypotheticals 112–14, 126, 128–30
judicial imagination 112, 114, 129
judicial impartiality 122–3, 127
judicial integrity 6, 157, 159–61, 163, 165, 167, 169, 171; and internal coherence 157–72
judicial legitimacy 109, 111, 125–7, 130
judicial partisanship 124
judicial precedent 125, 183, 241
judiciary 82, 99, 125–7, 216, 238, 249; biased 124; European 87
jurisdictions 13, 18, 83–5, 175, 198
jurisprudence 4, 12, 27, 29–30, 69, 76, 89, 119, 212, 258; contemporary 2; context-restrictive 109–10; theoretical 4; universal 17
justices 9–11, 42, 45, 47–9, 51, 83–5, 88, 91, 93, 96, 98, 113, 158–64, 175, 222; appellate 104; chief 19, 47; dissenting 103; federal 104
Juxon (King's chaplain) 54–5

Kagan, Justice Elena 109
Kant, Immanuel 75–7, 79, 81, 175, 181, 208, 210
Kantorowicz, Ernst 38–9
Keith, Lord 219–21
Kennedy, Justice Anthony 95
King Charles I 53, 53n1, 54–5, 57, 57n13, 58, 58n23, 59–63, 65, 67, 69–71
King Charles II 54, 252–3
King Edward I 34–6, 38
King James I 53, 55, 69
King's Bench 47
The King's Book 55–7, 60–3
King's courts at Westminster 18–19, 21
knowledge 1, 19, 26, 28, 41, 62, 77, 121, 126, 178–9, 181, 208, 215, 229, 235; formal 231; legal 190; metaphysical 209; political 208; prior 121–2
Kuiken, Kir 210, 235–6
Kuklinski, J. 120, 127
Kunda, Z. 118, 123–5

land 35, 45–6, 94, 173, 236, 257–8
land law 18–19, 21–2
language 34, 78–9, 97, 99, 110, 112, 116–17, 138, 142, 144, 184, 186, 213, 231–2, 254–5; contemporary 175; federal 198; placeholding 156; under determinate 156; written 231
law 1–259; canon 17, 46–7; civil 17, 26, 198; constitutional 80, 248, 250; degrees 27, 29–31; domestic 242, 254; faculties 17, 30; and literature 4, 179; and politics 10, 75, 82, 236; procedural 39; reports 19, 31, 185–6; schools 17–18, 29, 31, 116, 169, 239; statutory 35; students 18, 21, 26–7, 29–30, 32, 52; teachers 24, 30
lawyers 1–3, 5, 11–13, 20, 24–6, 33, 129, 142–3, 160–1, 164, 173–4, 176–7, 180–1, 187–8, 190; aid 34; canon 20; constitutional 198; ex-trial 163; secular 17
lectures 8, 18–19, 21–8, 31, 135, 208–9; combined with classes, and examinations 8, 28; earliest datable 22; elementary 19, 21; inaugural 26–8, 246; interactive 31; introductory 27; private 26; special 30
lectureships 22, 24, 29
Lee v Ashers Baking Company Ltd 221–2, 223n2
legal arguments 10, 23, 32, 111, 113, 117, 258
legal authority 37, 39, 45, 188
legal boundaries 7, 109
legal change 4, 6, 115, 195, 247, 249, 253–4
legal culture 47, 180, 185, 246–7
legal debates 112
legal diversity 246
legal education 2, 4–5, 7–8, 17–19, 21, 23, 25–9, 31, 33, 113, 135, 245, 249; historical development of 8; modern 28; opening up opportunities for interdisciplinary study 4; progress of 8; vocational 30
legal formalism 4, 207, 212, 214–15, 228–9, 233
legal formalists 109, 213, 220–1, 226, 233–4
legal history 29–30, 35, 46–7, 52, 246–7, 257
legal humanism 3, 173, 175, 177, 179, 181, 183, 185, 187, 189, 191
'legal imagination': acts of 240, 245–8, 251–3, 259; British 186, 244, 250; and

268   *Index*

complexity 245; failures of 245, 255, 258; global 258; and invention 249; lack of 12, 255, 257–8; linked to improvisation 3, 243; patterns of 8; and the 'power of productive apostasy' 143; in troubled times 1–13
legal imagining 34–7, 49, 51
legal language 34, 180–1
legal literature 44, 47, 178, 185
legal narratives 250–2, 259
legal principles 32, 111, 113, 116, 221
legal reasoning 3, 111, 180, 182, 184
legal scholars 1, 3–4, 7, 93, 129, 133, 183, 196, 239, 254, 256
legal style 183–4
legal systemology 1, 6, 47, 110–11, 127, 130, 143, 159–60, 178–9, 247, 250–1
legal theory 4–5, 10, 27, 81, 109, 175, 258
legal traditions 11, 173, 180, 182, 184, 207, 239–40, 247
legislation 31, 34–5, 81, 220, 232, 242, 245, 249, 252, 254, 259; amending 254; imperial 247; parliamentary 241; reforming 34–6
legislators 75, 232, 242
letters 12, 59, 173, 179–80, 190, 231–2, 235–6
Leviathan 50–1, 67, 153
LGBTQ+ community 222
liability 44, 220, 223
Liber Augustalis (also known as *The Constitutions of Melfi*) 39
liberty 60, 125, 136–7, 142, 150, 156, 196
'license of crimes' 39
Lincoln's Inn 20, 22, 30
'literary anthropology' 152
literary critics 104
literature, and law 4, 179
litigation 18–19, 110, 114
lobbyists 115
logic 18, 87, 90, 144, 177, 185–6, 209, 229, 232–3
London University 8, 27, 29, 31
Lonesome Dove 197–9, 201–5
Loughlin, Martin 133, 226–7
Louisiana Purchase 198
Lund, Nelson 98
Luther v Borden 204n39, 204

Macaulay, Thomas Babington 68–70
Madame Bovary 82
Magna Carta (Latin for Great Charter of Freedoms) 22, 36, 70
Maitland, F.W. 191, 246, 256–7

majority government 237
majority opinion 95–6
'manifest theft' 43
Mantel, Hilary 2n6, 2, 10–11, 133–42, 145–55; *Ancien Régime* 134–5, 137–8, 145–9, 155; and the French Revolution 2, 10–11, 69, 133–56; and her account of Antoine Saint-Just 136, 139, 149; identifies the eighteenth-century Enlightenment as a political force 134; and Jacques Pierre Brissot 139–41, 149, 151, 153; on law, politics and misery 133–56; and the 'law-school boys' 134–6, 138, 146, 148, 150, 153, 155–6; *A Place of Greater Safety* 2, 133
manuscript moot-books 23
Marat, Jean-Paul 141, 141n51
marriage 68, 94, 219
Marston Moor massacre 65
Marvell, Andrew 55, 64–8, 71
Mary Queen of Scots 55
McFall, Lynne 11, 157–60, 167
McGilchrist, I. 142n59, 144, 144n72, 145–7, 155, 170n83, 170
McMurtry, Larry 6, 12, 195, 197–9, 202–4
McSweeney, Thomas 47–8
'meditations' (of the king) 57, 61, 63, 243
merit arguments 116, 119, 122–3, 130
Middle Temple 20, 22
Mills, Charles Wright 143, 147
Milsom, SFC 253–4
Milton, John 60, 231n124; and *Areopagitica* 60; and King Charles 61; *Tetrachordon* 231
Modern Social Imaginaries 10–11
modes 9, 11, 80, 179, 183–5, 188, 211; constitutional 85; decision-making 100; particular cognitive 256
modesty 142, 150, 170
moot-books 23
moots 8, 18–25, 32; effective 24; late-medieval 23; modern 23; and readings 18, 22–5
morals 8, 81, 104, 106
motivations 121, 162, 165, 167, 172, 228; in cognition 118; and the coherence between principle and 11, 157–8, 160, 162; to deliver the optimal outcome 122; personal 118; for the reasoning of judges 118
Mullender, R. 11, 241n10, 243n28, 243n29, 243n31, 245n43
multilayered integration 242
murders 34, 37, 41–2, 49

Mustill, Lord 224n93
myths 155, 175, 240

narratives 110, 118, 127, 129–30, 175, 226, 249–52; alternative 253; cultural 110; extra-legal 111; informal 111, 116; internal 110, 117–19, 124, 126
Naseby massacre 65
National Judiciary Council, Poland 83
'national razor' *see* guillotine
negligence 46, 243, 250
Neuberger, Lord 216
Nicholas, Sir Edward 57
Nicolini, Matteo 1, 12
Nietzsche 163, 169
Nikulin, D. 76n10
Northern District Court of Illinois 106
Northern Ireland 221–2, 242, 255, 258; *see also* Ireland
novel disseisin (land dispossession) 34–5, 45–6, 48
Nun Appleton Priory 63–4, 68
Nyhan, B. 123

Oath of Engagement 64, 67–8
O'Callaghan, Patrick 6, 11, 133
Occasional Conformity Act 1711 252n82
O'Connor, Justice Sandra Day 103
operations 9, 31, 77, 79, 84, 88, 122, 138, 143, 147, 150, 153, 211, 215, 237; brain's 144–6; law's 6; mental 141; 'presencing' 145, 147
opinion 83, 91, 95, 98, 100, 103, 105–6, 127, 176, 186, 228; contemporary 25; contestable 82; political 61
originalism 97–9; conscientious 98; interpretation 96; living 98
Ormrod Committee on Legal Education, 1971 29
ownership 45–6; claims of 35; person's 40; Roman 47
Oxford University 26

paintings 9, 57n13, 166–7
Palladian style (architecture) 53
'Pamela prayer' (Milton) 58n23
panegyric oration 39
panegyric oration (eulogy) 39
Parliament of England 20, 36, 51, 55, 57, 59–60, 64–5, 92, 219–20, 224–5, 227, 241, 244, 251–2
parties 10, 21, 35, 48, 83, 88, 110, 113–15, 117–19, 121, 123–4, 126–9,

162, 187–8, 219; extremist 6; new political 201; Tory party 70, 230
partisanship 111, 124
pathological tendencies 76
pathology 81
Peel, Robert MP 252
penalties 35, 41, 43–4
peripheral-route processing 120–1
Perry, Seamus 211, 214, 229–30
personal liability 223
pessimism 2, 134, 152–4, 156, 163
philosophers 30, 51, 152, 163, 171, 214
philosophy 92, 109, 142, 158, 163, 206–8, 210, 232, 235
A Place of Greater Safety 2, 133
plagiarism 58
plaintiffs 35, 46, 161
Plato 151, 155, 163
plea rolls 186–7
pleadings 19, 22–5, 61, 126, 176, 186–7
pluralism 5, 184, 214
plurality 86, 207–8, 212, 214, 229
poems 55, 64, 67, 179, 253
poets 12, 55, 68, 71, 181, 206, 230, 248
Poland 5, 9, 76, 85–90, 255; and the *Commission v Poland* case concerning the undermining of the national judiciary 85; constitutional crisis in 82–3; determination to honour its distinctive form of life 9; infringement proceedings against 83, 85; and the judiciary 84; and Polish judges 85; and Polish reforms 86; and the rule of law in 9, 76, 82; Supreme Court ruling on the validity of elections 83
police power 106
policies 63, 109, 113, 130, 187, 236, 244–6, 256, 259; commercial 247; constitutional 251, 253; nuclear 99, 103; politico-legal 254; protest 104; public 254
political actions 245, 251
political anthropology 2, 6, 11, 134, 152–4, 156
political campaigns 222
political coexistence 78
political commentators 82
political debates 241
political imagination 210, 243–4
political philosophers 152
political philosophy 52, 136, 142
political protests 100, 107
political spending 95
political structures 86, 201

270 *Index*

political vision 79–80, 82
politicians 86, 254–6
politico-legal: artefacts 226–7; concepts 244; structure 137; understanding 226
politics 2, 4–5, 8, 10, 58–9, 68, 70, 75, 124, 149, 210, 233, 240–1, 243, 252–3; judicial 115; papistical 62; playing 124
Pulitzer, H. 169
post-Brexit scenarios 6, 239–40, 242, 244, 246, 255, 257–8
power 37, 39, 50–1, 75–6, 78–80, 83, 86–9, 91–2, 134–6, 148–50, 175, 179–80, 210–11, 213–14, 236–7; absolute 236; hierarchies 126; image-forming 214; living 210–11; mental 209; prerogative 224–5; structures 203
practical actions 155–6
precedent 8, 21, 24, 94, 97–8, 102–3, 105–6, 116–17, 121, 124–6, 130, 189, 191, 226, 235; binding 188; copying 25; decisive 161; existing 80, 233; judicial 125, 183, 241; legal 189; unfavourable 254
primary imagination 210–11
principles 35–6, 86, 91–2, 109–10, 157–62, 167–8, 172, 175, 210, 213, 231–2, 235–6, 240–1, 251, 254–5; absolute 209; common-law 241–2; constitutional 226; formalist 109; of land law 19, 22; mandated 160; and motivation 11, 157, 160, 162, 167, 172; political 198; refining normative 110
prisoners 116, 150, 166
prisons 35, 42–3, 135
Privy Council 92, 241
problems 5, 10, 13, 23, 32, 95–7, 102, 129, 134, 144, 150–1, 155, 245–6, 251, 257; legal 206; methodological 248; persistent crime 43; personal 143; practical 134, 149, 155
procedural law 39
procedure 1, 17–19, 37, 41, 44–6, 48–9, 52, 86, 89, 114, 128–9, 179, 186, 188, 242; complex mechanical 254; decision-making 129; and jurors 37; legal 49, 188; parliamentary 242
proceedings 10, 83, 88–9, 93, 114–15, 128–9; appellate 128; civil 34; formal 55; legal 112, 120; parliamentary 241–2
process 79–80, 118–19, 141, 149, 160, 163, 171–2, 184, 186, 196–8, 210–12, 214, 247–9, 255–6, 258–9; adjudicative 111, 221; constitutional 239, 248;

decision-making 90, 109; democratic 130; election 95; federalising 198; judicial 212, 216, 237; law-making 241; legal 136; mediating 237; political 96, 110; psychological 158; systematic 111
productive imagination 2, 7, 75–81
professions 18, 29–31, 157, 164; judicial 157; legal 20, 31–2, 35, 52, 136, 160, 190, 200
programmes 148, 151, 156, 201
projects 76, 87, 180–1, 196
Prologue 37–9
protections 45, 85, 161, 219, 223–4; judicial 85; legal 84; privacy 161; refugee 242
Protestant constitution 252
Protestant historiography 67–8
protests 10, 83, 100, 103, 105, 107, 171
provisions 2, 46, 83–4, 89, 98, 207, 242; controversial 229; existing 83; legal 88, 97, 229; legislative 222; statutory 213, 234
public values 256, 258
punishments 39, 41, 43–5, 112, 164
pupillage 25, 27–8, 32
pupils 25, 32, 136

Quaestiones de statutis 22–3
quaestiones disputatae 17
qualifications 18, 20, 24, 43, 216
Queen Mary University, London 4, 133, 239

R (Miller) v The Prime Minister 92n92, 224–7, 233–4, 241n12, 243n29
'rainbow bridge' 173–4, 178, 190–1
rape 49, 220, 234
raping 219–20, 227
ratifiers of the Constitution 96
Raz, Joseph 207, 207n1, 220
real cases 8, 23, 31, 93
realists 109, 220–1, 229
reappraisal 182, 244
reasoning 79, 113–14, 118, 146, 216, 223, 225; consensus-based 218; exploratory 113; issue-related 118; legal 3, 111, 180, 182, 184; motivated 118; prioritised narrative 110; rule-based 110; valid interpretational 96
rebuttals 60, 63, 87
Reform Act 1832 70, 252
Reformation 58, 60–2, 67, 169, 231
reforms 13, 29, 35, 82–3, 85, 144, 254, 257; controversial 85; institutional 85;

legal 249, 252; politico-constitutional 253; significant 35
regicide 60, 63, 208
Rehnquist, Justice William 97, 103, 106
Reifler, J. 122–4
reimagination, history of 13, 247
Reith Lectures 75
relationships 2, 4, 9, 35, 47–8, 76, 85, 87, 91, 143, 178, 210, 243, 257; asymmetrical 258; dialectic 81; established 87; mutable 179; public's 123
religion 59, 68, 101, 210, 222–3, 235, 253; adherents 222; conformity 252; 'counterfeit' 61; primitive 214
religious beliefs 221–2, 227
reports 21, 116, 182, 185–90; contemporary 66; psychological 171; social scientific 116
republic 9, 54, 57, 65, 67, 71, 135, 137–9, 142, 146–8, 151, 199; established American 202; famed 53; new 60, 65
Republic of Hungary see Hungary
Republican Party (United States) 196
republicanism 135, 137, 145
reputation 122, 166, 189; of Danton as a gifted advocate in the dying days of the *Ancien Régime* 147; gaining a 136; high 179; judicial 111, 128
research 2–4, 117–18, 183, 236, 246; capabilities 33; comparative 195; contemporary 117; cross-disciplinary 240; doctoral 30; historiographic 197; interdisciplinary 3–4; mechanism 104; new 123
retirement age 82
retrospective criminalisation debate 221
revolutions 54, 68–70, 133–41, 144, 146–8, 152, 155–6, 236, 250–1; see also French Revolution
rhetorical 4, 9, 18, 39, 56, 148, 162, 164, 167, 181–2, 221, 247; appeals 127; listening 124, 126; modes 19; powers 148; questions 37
Richardson, HG 36n16, 37n18
Ricoeur, Paul 9, 76, 78, 91; analysis of ideology and utopia 79–80; draws a line between legitimate and illegitimate judicial decision making 80; findings of 90
rights 31–2, 35, 44, 46, 50, 66, 95, 114, 116, 135, 150, 164, 196, 222–5, 234; abortion 121; ancient 67; constitutional 96; electioneering 95; equal marriage

116; fundamental 76, 84, 241, 254–5; inalienable 50–1; legal 222; sovereign monarch's 50; statutory 223; writ of 23, 48–9
robberies 34–5, 42, 44–5
Roberts, Justice John Glover 94–5
Robespierre, Maximilien 11, 133–7, 139–41, 145–7, 149, 151, 153–4; aims for the use of the constitution for the benefit of the people 154; devotion to the framework he seeks to make a social reality 146; and the legal imagination displayed in his thinking 145; secures a place as a deputy in the Third Estate 136, 138; sends Danton and Desmoulins to the guillotine 149; tries to bring a long-lived process of development to a culmination 141
Roman civil law and traditions 17, 46–7, 51
Roman curia 17
Roman jurists 46
Rousseau, Jean-Jacques 146, 152
royal authority 8, 37–8
royal collection 53, 57n13
Royal Commission 1854 (to investigate the study of law in the Inns of Court) 29
royal courts 23, 40, 47–8
royalists 55, 59, 63–4; England 57; moderate Anglican 56; Owen Feltham 58; propagandists 55
Royston, Richard 56, 59
Rubens, Peter Paul 53, 68–9
rule 9, 52, 76–8, 82–9, 91–2, 109–14, 118, 123–5, 158–62, 171, 220–1, 226–7, 234–5, 241–2, 249–50; authoritative 233; codified 232; jurisdictional 45; legal 110–11, 124, 225; neutral 110; procedural 111; textualising 186
rule of law 89, 110, 229n108

Saint-Just, Antoine 136, 139, 149
salaries 32, 83
scaffold speeches 53–5, 66
Scalia, Justice Antonin 9, 93–9, 129
Scheuerman, WE 2n4, 152n128
The Schism Act 1714 252n82
Schmitt, Carl 1–2, 152–3, 156
scholars 4, 26, 49, 105, 130, 240, 254, 259; academic 3; formalistic 254; originalist 97; single formalist 207
scholarship 4, 27, 30, 117, 121; context-restrictive 130; context-rich 109–10; legal 2, 7, 10

272 *Index*

science 28, 236, 245; arcane 25; cognitive 118; reasoned 245; social 125
Scotland 68, 225, 241–3, 247, 257
Scottish subjects 54–5
scriptural canonisation 185
scriptural disputation 59
scriptures 61, 63, 186, 231
scrutiny: close 119; public 171; strict 101, 107
Second Amendment *see* United States Second Amendment
'secret theft' 43
sectionalism 5–6, 245
Sedley, Justice Sir Stephen 225
Selden, John 34, 50–1
self-empowerment 91
sentences 23, 43, 109, 112, 171
sentencing 170–1
settlers 202, 205, 256; new 256; plain 201; protecting 199
sexual orientation 221–2
Shakespeare, William 3, 22, 62, 75, 244
Sidney, Sir Philip 58
The Significance of the Frontier in American History (essay) 195
slave traders 171
slogans 99, 150, 236
social and economic crises 210
social capital 151, 155–6
social imaginaries 10–11, 134, 146, 153–4, 156
social improvement 134, 141, 151, 154–5
social justice 154, 176
social media 1
social practices 8, 78, 81–2, 181
society 2–3, 20, 95, 99–100, 102, 133, 142–3, 145, 148, 150, 153–4, 156, 244, 246, 249–50; changing 104; complex 244; divided 204; feudal 136; medieval 34; multicultural 203; pluralist 130; political 4
solicitors 25, 28, 32, 160
Solum, Lawrence 97
Sontag, Susan 183
sovereign powers 50
sovereign rights 50
sovereignty 37, 50–1, 140, 150, 190, 236, 253; inalienable 236; monarchical 51; parliamentary 92, 251; recovered 257
'sovereignty of purpose' 104
speech 54, 100–2, 135, 137, 164, 182, 220; constituted expressive 100; a defence of concurring 219; free 105;

political 95, 107; protected 101; symbolic 94, 101, 103
Spence v Washington 100–1
Spoon, Jake 202–3
State of Texas 94n4, 99–106, 199
Statute of Wales 1284 49
Statute of Westminster 1275 and 1285 35n5
statutes 10, 19, 21–3, 31, 34–5, 43–4, 46, 48–9, 95, 97–8, 100, 103, 106, 225, 232; collections of 34, 49; compendium of 36, 51; earliest 17; legal 41
statutory law 35
Stevens, Justice Paul 96
stolen property 43–4
Stone, Geoffrey 64, 98
Stourzh, G. 164n42, 164, 166n62, 167, 169, 169n80, 169, 171n90
Strange's Inn *see* Lincoln's Inn
Stuart, Charles 9, 54, 58, 60–3, 65–6, 70
students 1, 4, 8, 17, 19–29, 31–3, 51; counsel 32; enabled 19; fellow 32; potential 28
subjects 8–10, 18, 23, 28, 31, 33, 37–8, 58, 61, 116, 118–21, 128, 175, 180, 213–14
substantive rebuttals 60, 63, 87
Sumption, Jonathan 75, 75n4, 75
suppression of expression 100, 102–4, 187, 191
Supreme Court of the United Kingdom 54, 206, 215–20, 233
Supreme Court of the United States 7, 10, 109, 112, 114–15, 126, 128–9, 204, 206–7, 215–18, 221–6, 228, 230, 233–4, 241–2; application of various methods of constitutional interpretation 94; *Barnes v Glen Theatre* 106–7; *Bucklew v Precythe* 112, 112n18, 112n19, 113–14; Justice Antonin Scalia 9, 93–9, 129; Justice Byron Raymond White 103; Justice Clarence Thomas 99; Justice Elena Kagan 109; Justice John Glover Roberts 94–5; Justice Paul Stevens 96; Justice Ruth Bader Ginsburg 109; Justice Samuel Alito 95, 98; Justice Sandra Day O'Connor 103; Justice Stephen Breyer 112, 116; Justice William Rehnquist 97, 103, 106; prorogation judgment 92

A Tale of Two Cities 133
Tamanaha, B. 124n127, 124, 125n133
Taylor, Charles 146n94, 153, 153n134, 154

Taylor, Jeremy 56, 56n9, 78n26
tensions 5–6, 79, 149, 173, 176, 185, 190, 219, 221–2, 227
territories 198, 203–5, 252, 255–6, 258
Test Act 1673 252
TEU *see* Treaty on the European Union 9, 83
Texas *see* State of Texas
Texas Court of Criminal Appeals 99, 101
Texas Rangers 199–200
Texas v Johnson 94n4, 95, 99, 101–7
theft 34, 37, 42–5
theological debates 231n124n124
Third Estate 136, 138
Thomas, Justice Clarence 99
Tory government 252
Tory party 70, 230
tourists 166–7
traditions 3, 8, 24, 90, 99, 126, 178, 182, 184, 186, 188–9, 191; common-law 244; constitutional 195, 198; democratic 126, 251; legal 11, 173, 180, 182, 184, 207, 239–40, 247; manufacturing 247–9
transformations 99, 201, 204, 211–12; new radical 185; unexpected 87
transition 9, 12, 197, 213, 231, 240; into a new legal reality 12; to a new order 9; from the reified formal written law to the organic 231
transparency 12, 174, 183, 215–16, 219, 229, 234
treason 41
treatises 19, 34, 47–9, 51; common-law 51; late thirteenth-century 48; legal 49; significant 51; statutory 48
Treaty on the European Union 9, 76, 86, 89, 240
trials 10, 19, 55, 58–9, 63–5, 70, 75, 136, 139, 147, 186–7
tribunals 84–5, 88, 92, 223
trust 11, 30, 42, 59, 65, 69, 157–8; of judges 157; mutual 86; of politicians 157; public 126
truth 10, 42, 54, 61–2, 67, 86, 98, 107, 115, 140, 157, 168, 227; anterior 162; complex 229; eternal 82; and falsehood 60, 178; moral 232; semi-subjective 111; single all-encompassing 128
Turner, Frederick Jackson 195
tutorials 28, 31–2

The Union of Crowns 53
unitary judgments 12, 206–8, 215–19, 221–2, 226–30, 233–4, 237–8

United Kingdom 4, 109, 133, 153, 206, 215–16, 220–1, 224–5, 237, 240, 242–3, 256–7, 259; changes in legal education opening up opportunities for interdisciplinary study among undergraduates 4; and the complex constitutional system 13; and the *European Union (Withdrawal) (No. 2) Act 2019* 241–3, 247; and the *European Union (Withdrawal) Act 2018* 31n47, 241, 241n13, 241n14, 242, 242n18, 242n19, 242, 242n20, 243–5, 254, 254n94, 257, 257n109; laws of the 241–2, 257; and the opinion polls showing the high trust ratings of the judicial profession 157n2; post-Brexit trade agreements 6, 247n52; and society's pragmatism as a form of constitutional imagination 6; and the Supreme Court (formerly the House of Lords) 54, 206, 215–20, 233
United Kingdom Court of Appeal 216, 222, 228
United Kingdom Supreme Court *see* Supreme Court of the United Kingdom
United States 33, 100–1, 129, 195, 201–3, 247; and the American Revolution 247; constitutional change and shaping the constitutional identity of the 196; diversity and inclusiveness of frontier life 198; and the election of a nationalist 45th president of the 236; and the emergence of a quasi-authoritarian system of territorial governance 198; and the influence of the federalising process un EU law 198n15; and the intrinsic diversity of frontier life 198; in the late nineteenth century 198; and the Louisiana Purchase 198
United States Congress 100, 104–5, 130, 204
United States Constitution 94–9, 103–5, 107, 112, 204, 247
United States Court of Criminal Appeals 88, 94, 96, 101, 230
United States Declaration of Independence 105
United States First Amendment 94–5, 99–103, 106
United States Second Amendment 96
unity 82, 102, 125, 211–13, 215, 229–30, 235, 237; imaginative 4, 212; national 100–3; spirit of 213
universities 17–18, 20, 22, 24, 26, 29–30, 32

274 *Index*

Upon Appleton House 64, 68n66
US *see* United States

victims 41, 148, 220, 222
Viner, Charles 26n33, 27n37
Virtue, Emotion and Imagination in Law and Legal Reasoning 3
voices briefs 10, 111, 114–19, 121–30
voluntary examinations 28
von Bogdandy, Armin 197, 197n13

warranties 40n34, 88n80
Watson, Alan 3, 75, 245, 249, 254, 258
Wawrzyszczuk, Aleksandra 109–30
Welby, Archbishop J. 243
Westminster courts 18–21, 25, 27n37, 35–6

Westminster I (Statute) 1275 35
Westminster II (Statute)1285 35
Wexford massacre 64, 64n58, 65
Wheeler, ES 56n7, 57n15, 60n27
Whig histories 69–70
White, James Boyd 2–3, 7, 248–9
White, Justice Byron Raymond 103
wisdom 29, 99, 144, 169–70
The Wise Rule of James I 53
'withdrawal' (Coleridge's concept of Reason) 236
Withdrawal Act see *European Union (Withdrawal) Act 2018*
Wood, T. 123–4
writs 21–2, 24, 35, 46, 48, 57
written examinations *see* examinations

Printed in the United States
By Bookmasters